THE HISTORY
OF THE
NINTH
(SCOTTISH)
DIVISION

1914 – 1919

By
JOHN EWING, MC

INTRODUCTION BY
FIELD-MARSHALL LORD PLUMER
G.C.B, G.C.M.G, G.C.V.O.

PUBLISHED BY
THE NAVAL & MILITARY PRESS

THE MENIN GATE. YPRES

Frontispiece

THE HISTORY OF THE 9TH (SCOTTISH) DIVISION
1914-1919

By JOHN EWING, M.C.

BREVET-MAJOR, LATE 6TH K.O.S.B.

INTRODUCTION BY
FIELD-MARSHAL LORD PLUMER
G.C.B., G.C.M.G., G.C.V.O.

WITH COLOURED AND OTHER ILLUSTRATIONS
AND MAPS

LONDON
JOHN MURRAY, ALBEMARLE STREET, W.
1921

Printed and bound in Great Britain by
ANTONY ROWE LTD, EASTBOURNE

INTRODUCTION

By FIELD-MARSHAL LORD PLUMER,

G.C.B., G.C.M.G., G.C.V.O.

I HAVE been asked, as Commander of the Second Army, to write a short introduction to the history of the work of the Ninth (Scottish) Division during the Great War.

The Division served in other armies and under other Army Commanders, and they could, and I know would, bear testimony similar to mine as to the value of the services of the Division; but it happened that for a considerable period in the early days of the Campaign and in the glorious final advance it was in the Second Army, and presumably on that account the invitation was made to me.

First of the new formations organised by Lord Kitchener in 1914, the Division was one of the earliest to proceed to France in 1915, and from that time till the conclusion of operations in 1918 there was hardly a phase of the war or an important action in which they did not take a prominent part.

Composed as they were of troops drawn from the land which has from time immemorial been famous for its fighting men, they were later in the campaign supplemented and strengthened by soldiers from South Africa, and the combination proved, as it was bound to be, irresistible.

Fortunate in their Divisional Generals, their subordinate leaders and their staffs, the Division was always one which could be relied on to carry out successfully any duties entrusted to them if it was humanly possible to do so, and any Corps or Army Commander to whom they might be allotted considered himself fortunate in having them under his command.

I hope this history will be widely read.

It is a record of a wonderful development of fighting efficiency steadily maintained throughout four very strenuous years.

It is a fine illustration of the determination and dogged pertinacity which we are all proud to know were the characteristics of the troops of the British Empire throughout, and which undoubtedly won the war.

It points the moral of what can be accomplished by a body of men who never recognised defeat, and to whom any temporary failure was merely an incentive to further effort.

Those who served in the Division can feel that they are handing down to their descendants as a legacy of imperishable fame a record of achievements worthy of the glorious traditions of their forefathers and of the regiment whose name they bore.

With troops such as fought in the Ninth Division, however prolonged the struggle may be, there never can be any doubt of the ultimate issue.

PLUMER, *F.-M.*,
Late Commander, Second Army, B.E.F.

MALTA, 17*th October* 1920.

PREFACE

THIS story has been compiled from Battalion, Brigade, and Divisional diaries, supplemented by the narratives of individual officers, and, it is hoped, will prove a record of interest to all who served or were connected with the Ninth Division.

To the numerous officers of the Division who have assisted me by their suggestions and criticisms and by the loan of documents, I take this opportunity of expressing my deep sense of gratitude. My sincere thanks are due also to the Staff of the Historical Section of the Committee of Imperial Defence for the ready courtesy with which they placed at my disposal every facility for consulting documents and maps.

To the following officers for constant and ungrudging help I am particularly indebted,

> Captain W. Y. Darling,
> Lieut.-Colonel P. A. V. Stewart,
> Lieut.-Colonel T. C. Mudie,
> Major W. Lumsden,

and to my wife for most valuable assistance both in the compilation of the narrative and in the correction of proofs.

J. EWING.

EDINBURGH,
    October 1920.

Note.—The titles of infantry battalions are given in full in the Order of Battle, Appendix I., but to save space in the narrative the word "battalion" has been omitted, *eg.*, the 11th Bn. The Royal Scots is referred to as the 11th Royal Scots.

With the exception of Loos all battles are described from right to left.

ix

CONTENTS

CHAPTER I

ARMS AND THE MAN

August 1914 to May 1915

CHAPTER II

FIRST EXPERIENCES IN FRANCE

May 1915 to September 1915

CHAPTER III

BATTLE OF LOOS

25th to 28th September 1915

CONTENTS

CHAPTER IV

THE SALIENT AND "PLUG STREET"

OCTOBER 1915 TO MAY 1916

CHAPTER V

THE CAPTURE OF BERNAFAY WOOD, AND THE BATTLES FOR TRONES WOOD

JULY 1916

CHAPTER VI

LONGUEVAL AND DELVILLE WOOD

JULY 1916

CHAPTER VII

THE BUTTE DE WARLENCOURT

OCTOBER 1916

CHAPTER VIII

ARRAS

NOVEMBER 1916 TO APRIL 1917

CHAPTER IX

THE BATTLES OF ARRAS

THE ACTIONS OF 9TH APRIL, 12TH APRIL, 3RD MAY, 5TH JUNE 1917

CHAPTER X

PASSCHENDAELE, 1917

ACTIONS OF THE 20TH SEPTEMBER AND THE 12TH OCTOBER

CHAPTER XI

PREPARATIONS FOR DEFENCE

OCTOBER 1917 TO 21ST MARCH 1918

CHAPTER XII

GERMANY'S SUPREME EFFORT

21ST TO 29TH MARCH 1918

CHAPTER XIII

THE GERMAN OFFENSIVE IN FLANDERS

APRIL 1918

CHAPTER XIV

METEREN AND HOEGENACKER RIDGE

MAY TO SEPTEMBER 1918

CHAPTER XV

FROM YPRES TO LEDEGHEM

28TH SEPTEMBER TO 14TH OCTOBER 1918

CONTENTS

CHAPTER XVI

FROM LEDEGHEM TO THE SCHELDT

14TH OCTOBER TO 27TH OCTOBER 1918

CHAPTER XVII

CONCLUSION

28TH OCTOBER 1918 TO 15TH MARCH 1919

APPENDICES

LIST OF ILLUSTRATIONS

LANDSCAPES

From Water-colour Sketches by Captain F. E. Hodge, late R.F.A.

PORTRAITS

B

MAPS

At End of Book

HISTORY OF THE NINTH (SCOTTISH) DIVISION

CHAPTER I

ARMS AND THE MAN

AUGUST 1914 TO MAY 1915

THE great European War that broke out in 1914 was the inevitable result of the conditions that moulded the nineteenth century. In many respects the history of the century had disappointed the high hopes with which the period opened. The overthrow of Napoleon's hegemony in 1814 imposed on his conquerors the task of effecting the settlement of Europe, and it was expected that the chief Powers would grasp the opportunity to settle all questions that had been a source of friction, and especially to satisfy those nationalist aspirations which had been the most potent factor in contributing to the defeat of Napoleon. It was even hoped that an attempt would be made to realise the brotherhood of man in some sort of federation.

In all these respects the work accomplished by the Congress, which met at Vienna in 1814, fell short of expectations. The chief statesmen of the Powers had been the foremost opponents of the French Revolution, and they had little sympathy with the nationalist sentiment that found its most vigorous expression in Germany, Italy, and Poland. Moreover, the political

1

ambitions and interests of the allies required the most delicate handling, if Europe was to be saved from another war. Thus the Eastern Question, the cause of considerable uneasiness throughout the century, never came within the consideration of the Congress. No attempt was made to express the unity of Europe in any form of federation, unless the Holy Alliance be accepted as an effort to achieve that end. Above all, the necessity of satisfying the political interests of the various members of the alliance, in many cases already arranged by treaties, caused nationalist aspirations to be neglected, and in some cases flagrantly disregarded, as in the arrangements affecting Belgium, Italy, and Norway. Thus Nationalism could only be developed in opposition to the Vienna Settlement and only by war could its aims be realised. In consequence the development of nationalities, which is the notable fact of the century, was accompanied by the assertion of military force, and the freedom of nations went hand in hand with militarism. What had been won by the sword was maintained by the same means, and towards the close of the nineteenth century Europe formed an armed camp, each nation supporting a huge armament, which drained its resources but which it dared not diminish lest it should fall a prey to a more powerful neighbour.

With Europe thus constituted every question that revealed rivalries and differences was a peril, and there was no influence so baneful as that exercised by the Eastern Question. On more than one occasion it caused the gravest anxiety to the Chancelleries of Europe, and war was averted mainly by reason of the comparative equality of the opposing groups formed by the chief states. In the last quarter of the century the predominance of Germany was the governing factor in the situation. She built up an alliance of the Central European states and her influence displaced that of Russia in Constantinople. The full scope of her ambitions was not realised in this country, but it was vaguely felt that they were not compatible with the interests of the British Empire. Certain definite events showed that German policy, though not actively hostile, was unfriendly to us. She seized the oppor-‘ tunity created by the Jameson Raid to fling the first open challenge to British power, and one of the principal results of the Boer War was the creation of the German Fleet, which could only have been intended as a weapon against Britain. In other directions the claims and threats of Germany constituted a constant danger to the peace of the world. She picked quarrels with France over Morocco in 1904 and 1911, and openly made preparations to support Austria against Russia in 1907. Her increasing truculence in foreign affairs ultimately forced Britain, France, and Russia into a close agreement in order to safeguard their interests.

The occasion of war was the assassination of the Austrian Archduke Francis Ferdinand in the streets of Serajevo on the 28th June 1914. But the emotions aroused by this despicable crime would never have led to war had it not been for the determination of Germany to bring matters to a crisis. Her designs in the Balkans and Asia Minor largely depended upon the cordial co-operation of Austria, of which she could be certain only while the Emperor Francis Joseph was alive. In 1914 he was already over eighty years of age, and it was advisable to turn to account the quarrel between Serbia and Austria caused by the Serajevo murder.

The nature of her ties with France and Russia as well as the invasion of Belgium by German forces compelled Britain to take arms against Germany. No other course was possible. The significant and gratifying feature of our intervention was the unanimity with which general opinion supported the Government, and very few protested against the obligations that honour required the nation to undertake.

The war formed by far the most exacting test to which the democracy of Britain had yet been subjected. The last great European War had been waged by Britain under an aristocracy, which, despite many mistakes, had ultimately achieved victory by steadfast and unquenchable courage. There were many, especially those of the type who, like Thucydides, doubted the ability of a democracy to govern an Empire, who feared that the resolute spirit of Pitt and Castlereagh had vanished, and that the country would take refuge in ignoble neutrality. But all fears and doubts were dissolved by the manner in which the nation as a whole took up the gage that the Kaiser had thrown, and the course of the struggle showed that the Empire possessed in full measure the more robust qualities it had shown under royal and aristocratic rule, though before victory was achieved it had surrendered all power to a small oligarchy, and allowed itself to be subjected to a degree of compulsion and restraint that had not been contemplated when hostilities began.

It was fortunate that the name and services of Lord Kitchener were at the disposal of his country, for no other man enjoyed to such an unusual degree the trust and esteem of his compatriots. He was universally recognised as the man pre-eminently fitted to lead the nation in its hour of peril, and his perspicacity and sanity of judgment inspired general confidence. It is difficult to overestimate the sobering and steadying influence that his personality exercised throughout the land. Perhaps more quickly than any other man he grasped the gravity of the situation, and his first speech as Secretary of State for War warned the people of Britain that the conflict would not be the short, sharp affair many expected it to be.

All available resources for war were immediately employed. The small but extremely efficient Regular Army, at once transported to France, played no inconsiderable part in checking the first onrush of the German armies, while the Navy swept the seas and bottled up the hostile fleet in its harbours. But our Regular land forces, amounting to little more than 150,000 men, were a scanty and inadequate contribution to the titanic contest that was raging in Europe, and Lord Kitchener asked the civilian population to furnish fresh armies. His appeal was answered with magnificent alacrity; recruiting offices, which were opened in every large town in the United Kingdom, were besieged by volunteers and the staff had to work day and night to cope with the rush.

The pick of the nation offered itself for service. Youth, which had hitherto satisfied in sport and athletics its craving for adventure, was attracted rather than repelled by the novelty and danger of war, and young men in thousands left workshops, offices, and universities to join the Colours. Others, not so numerous, were drawn from the class of casual labourers, and they cheerfully submitted themselves to a routine more irksome though more wholesome than any to which they had been accustomed. There was a minority of more mature men who, having envisaged the situation, bravely sacrificed their prospects on the altar of duty. The standard of physique was exceptionally high, and many who afterwards passed the tests with ease were rejected in the early months of the war. After selection the "First Hundred Thousand," the salt of their race, were sent to the various battalion depots, and then on to the training camps near Salisbury Plain.

One of the first divisions formed from the New Armies was the Ninth (Scottish) Division, and its composition was as follows :—

G.O.C.—Major-General C. J. MACKENZIE, C.B.

G.S.O.I.—Lieut.-Colonel C. H. DE ROUGEMONT, M.V.O.

A.A. & Q.M.G.—Colonel A. V. PAYNE.

26TH (HIGHLAND) BRIGADE.

Brig.-General—H. R. Kelham, C.B.

B.M.—Capt. H. W. B. Thorp.

8th Bn. The Black Watch (Royal Highlanders)	Commanded by Lieut.-Col. Lord Sempill.
7th Bn. Seaforth Highlanders (Ross-shire Buffs, The Duke of Albany's)	Lieut.-Col. W. T. Gaisford.
8th Bn. The Gordon Highlanders .	Lieut.-Col. G. Staunton.
5th Bn. The Queen's Own Cameron Highlanders . . .	Lieut.-Col. D. W. Cameron of Lochiel.

27TH INFANTRY BRIGADE.

Brig.-General—W. Scott Moncrieff.

B.M.—Capt. A. I. R. Glasfurd.

11th Bn. The Royal Scots . .	Lieut.-Col. H. H. B. Dyson.
12th Bn. The Royal Scots . .	Lieut.-Col. G. G. Loch.
6th Bn. The Royal Scots Fusiliers .	Lieut.-Col. H. H. Northey.
10th Bn. Princess Louise's (Argyll & Sutherland Highlanders) . .	Lieut.-Col. A. F. Mackenzie, M.V.O.

28TH INFANTRY BRIGADE.

Brig.-General—S. W. Scrase-Dickins.

B.M.—Captain C. J. B. Hay.

6th Bn. The King's Own Scottish Borderers	Lieut.-Col. H. D. N. Maclean, D.S.O.
9th Bn. The Scottish Rifles (Cameronians)	Lieut.-Col. A. C. Northey.
10th Bn. The Highland Light Infantry	Lieut.-Col. J. C. Grahame, D.S.O.
11th Bn. The Highland Light Infantry	Lieut.-Col. H. C. Fergusson.

ROYAL FIELD ARTILLERY.

C.R.A.—Brig.-General E. H. Armitage, C.B.

B.M.—Captain K. P. Ferguson.

Commanded by

50th Brigade, R.F.A.   .   .   .   Lieut.-Col. A. C. Bailward.

51st Brigade, R.F.A.   .   .   .   Lieut.-Col. A. H. Carter.

52nd Brigade, R.F.A.   .   .   .   Lieut.-Col. F. W. Boteler.

53rd Brigade, R.F.A.   .   .   .   Lieut.-Col. C. N. Simpson.

The first three brigades had four 18-pounder guns and the 53rd Brigade four 4·5 howitzers, and each brigade had a B.A.C.

THE ROYAL ENGINEERS.

C.R.E.—Lieut.-Colonel H. A. A. Livingstone, C.M.G.

63rd Field Company   .   .   .   Capt. C. Doucet.

64th Field Company   .   .   .   Capt. W. E. Francis.

90th Field Company   .   .   .   Major C. S. Montefiore.

PIONEERS.

The 9th Bn. Seaforth Highlanders (Ross-shire Buffs, The Duke of Albany's)—Lieut.-Col. T. Fetherstonhaugh.

THE ROYAL ARMY MEDICAL CORPS.

A.D.M.S.—Colonel C. Cree.

27th Field Ambulance .   .   .   Lieut.-Col. O. W. A. Elsner.

28th Field Ambulance .   .   .   Lieut.-Col. W. E. Hardy.

29th Field Ambulance .   .   .   Lieut.-Col. F. R. Buswell.

ARMY SERVICE CORPS.[1]

9th Divisional Train—Major R. P. Crawley, M.V.O.

9th Divisional Supply Column, Motor
Transport .   .   .   .   Major Dugmore.

104th Company   .   .   .   Major H. MacDougal.

105th Company   .   .   .   Capt. J. R. King.

106th Company   .   .   .   Capt. F. K. Norman.

107th Company   .   .   .   Capt. C. de M. Hutcheson.

[1] An A.S.C. Company was attached to each brigade : the 104th to the divisional troops, the 105th to the 26th, the 106th to the 27th, and the 107th to the 28th Brigade.

The divisional train was responsible for arranging matters of supply between the Division and the Corps concerned. The task of the supply column was to work between the railhead and the divisional A.S.C. and it

In addition to these units the Division was equipped with Ordnance and Veterinary Sections, D.A.D.O.S. being Major J. S. Brogden, and the A.D.V.S. Major W. H. Nicol. There were also a battery of R.G.A., a company of Cyclists, and a squadron of the Glasgow Yeomanry.

During the period of training several changes in command occurred. General Mackenzie went to France in October 1914 and was succeeded by Major-General Sir C. Fergusson, who had commanded the Fifth Division in the original Expeditionary Force. In March 1915 Sir C. Fergusson crossed to France to take over the II. Corps and his successor was Major-General H. J. S. Landon. In the 26th Brigade Brig.-General E. St G. Grogan, C.B., succeeded Brig.-General Kelham on the 16th November, while Lieut.-Colonel Harry Wright, D.S.O., a veteran of the famous Kandahar march, took over the command of the Gordons in February 1915; in the 27th Brigade, Brig.-General C. D. Bruce succeeded Brig.-General Scott Moncrieff in January, and Lieut.-Col. R. C. Dundas was appointed to the command of the 11th Royal Scots in October. Changes occurred also amongst the Gunners and the Sappers, and by the time the Ninth was ready to cross the Channel the 50th Brigade was commanded by Lieut.-Col. C. C. van Straubenzee, the 52nd by Lieut.-Col. A. M. Perreau, and the 53rd by Lieut.-Col. K. K. Knapp, while the 63rd Field Company was commanded by Major L. W. S. Oldham, and the 64th by Major G. R. Hearn.

After the various units were organised, training [1] was

formed part of the Division until 1917 when supply columns became Corps troops. The Battalion Quartermaster drew the supplies for his unit from the company attached to his brigade.

[1] The best account of life and training in the Division is contained in the well-known volume, *The First Hundred Thousand*, by Ian Hay, who was an officer in the 10th Argyll & Sutherland Highlanders.

carried on with the utmost vigour. An average of eight hours a day was spent in fitting the men for the grim business of war; it was a heavy strain but their keenness and excellent physique enabled them to undergo the hardships without a murmur. The difficulties at this early stage were enormous owing to scarcity of instructors and lack of stores, clothing, and arms, but there was a sprinkling of Regular officers and N.C.Os., and with their skilled assistance the several units soon reached a very creditable state of efficiency.

The problems regarding stores and clothing were solved comparatively quickly, but at first the men in their civilian clothes with various types of headgear presented an appearance more ludicrous than martial. The training was on lines identical with those of the old army and a similar syllabus was carried out with satisfactory results. The hardest lot fell to the young recently commissioned officers; they went through exactly the same routine as the men but they were also obliged to spend their spare time learning their particular duties as officers. The parsimonious scrutiny to which in peace times all army estimates had been subjected now showed its crippling effects. The manual dealing with tactics and strategy, *Field Service Regulations*, was excellent in its statement of general principles but it did not give a young officer, unfamiliar with military terms, much assistance in such a matter as the handling of a platoon. In this respect the German Army was much better equipped than ours and possessed numerous pamphlets for the guidance of junior and non-commissioned officers in their profession. The war revealed the need of similar assistance for the British Army and a spate of unofficial publications flooded the book-shops, but none were as good or as

useful as the official pamphlets, notably S.S. 143 and
S.S. 135, which unfortunately did not appear until
the war had been long in progress. The lack of such
guidance in 1914 was almost as serious as the scarcity
of munitions and added enormously to the difficulties of
training.

The course of training was naturally affected by
experience of the war and lectures by officers from
France were followed with the closest attention. The
siting of trenches gave rise to a keen controversy which
raged for a considerable time; some held that they
should be dug on the forward slopes of a hill, others
that they should be on the reverse slope. But the
experience of France showed that such niceties and
distinctions were really unimportant and could be
disregarded, since men dug in only where the enemy
allowed them to do so. The infantry devoted much
time to musketry and digging, and as a fair proportion
of the men were miners the Division became very
proficient in the rapid excavation of trenches.

As the weeks passed the troops were gradually
taken through the various stages necessary for efficiency,
and training by units was followed by field manœuvres
in which the whole Division took part. Reviews and
route marches were always welcome as a change from
the ordinary routine and the divisional field days in
March and April were an agreeable as well as a useful
exercise. *Esprit de corps* had taken firm root in the
several formations, and each unit, after the fashion of
all British soldiers, considered itself the salt of the
army. The divisional *esprit de corps* had not yet
attained the fierce intensity that was afterwards to
distinguish the Ninth; that resulted later from the
ordeal of battle, but a good start in the right direction
had been made.

After eight months of incessant and strenuous training the men were fit and eager for active service and instructions for a move to France were daily expected. But in 1915 spring had passed into early summer before the orders were received. With them came a rousing exhortation from H.M. King George V. on the 10th May :—

" Officers, Non-Commissioned Officers, and Men of
the Ninth (Scottish) Division,

"You are about to join your comrades at the Front in bringing to a successful end this relentless war of more than nine months' duration. Your prompt patriotic answer to the Nation's call to arms will never be forgotten. The keen exertions of all ranks during the period of training have brought you to a state of efficiency not unworthy of my Regular Army. I am confident that in the field you will nobly uphold the traditions of the fine regiments whose names you bear. Ever since your enrolment I have closely watched the growth and steady progress of all units. I shall continue to follow with interest the fortunes of your Division. In bidding you farewell I pray God may bless you in all your undertakings."

CHAPTER II

FIRST EXPERIENCES IN FRANCE

MAY 1915 TO SEPTEMBER 1915

ALL units had practised entraining, and the move
to France was accomplished without a hitch. The
artillery were the first to go, the advance parties leaving Bordon on 8th May; the infantry brigades left in
order of priority, beginning with the 26th on the 10th
May. Vehicles, animals, and transport crossed from
Southampton to Havre, and the infantry from Folke-
stone to Boulogne. By the 15th May the whole Division
was concentrated around the pleasant and important
little town of St Omer. It had the distinction of being
the first division of the New Armies to reach France.

After spending two days near St Omer, the Division
marched to billets south of Bailleul, the average
march for each unit being 15 miles. G.H.Q. were
established at the Chateau le Nieppe; the 26th Brigade
was at Bailleul; the 27th at Noote Boom; and the 28th
at Outtersteene. Arrangements were quickly made to
train the various branches in trench warfare. All the
field artillery brigades, except half of the 51st R.F.A.,
were attached to the Sixth Division for instruction.
The 9th Heavy Battery went over to the III. Corps,
and from this moment ceased to be a corporate part of
the Division. Similarly the infantry received their first
experiences of trench duties under the Sixth Division,

and spent a spell in the line near Armentières by brigades at a time. The 27th Brigade moved into the front line on the evening of the 20th May; it was relieved on the 22nd by the 28th, and it in turn on the 24th by the 26th Brigade, which remained in the line till the 26th. Sappers were employed by the III. Corps in improving the second line defences near Armentières, and the infantry soon realised that they were expected to be as useful with the shovel as they were with the rifle. On the 27th May the 26th Brigade proceeded to Nieppe and Armentières "under the tactical orders of the Sixth Division"; this fine phrase simply meant that the men had to work on trenches and strong points.

Meantime the Division received constant instruction in bombing. When the opposing trenches lay near each other, it was dangerous for a man to show himself above the surface, and a method had to be discovered by which hostile positions could be attacked without the aggressors having to expose themselves to rifle or machine-gun fire. The only weapon that could fulfil this purpose was the bomb. In the hands of determined men it was a useful and valuable weapon, and against a vigilant and stubborn enemy it was sometimes the only means by which progress could be made. In 1915 and the early part of 1916 there were few men on either side who were not pugnacious, but the trouble was that when troops became stale with months of underground warfare, the bomb fight tended to result in a stationary conflict, no serious effort being made to gain any ground. In 1915, however, there was no staleness, the chief difficulties being the large variety of bombs and the multiplicity of names that each bomb possessed. Most of them were worked by a time fuse, but the stick hand-grenade exploded on percussion and was a weapon probably more dangerous to the thrower and his comrades than to the enemy. The Mills No. 5 Bomb, which afterwards became the standard one used by the British Army, was exploded by a time fuse of five seconds; but more common at that time was the Bethune Bomb, which was the one chiefly used by the Division at Loos. With all these varieties the average man could throw between 20 and 30 yards. For a longer distance, rifle-grenades, that is bombs fired from rifles, had a range up to about 200 yards. Heavier bombs could be thrown by trench mortars, of which there were at first numerous types, and several kinds of catapults were used. An imposing-looking engine was the West Spring Gun. It could hurl a bomb about 400 yards, but required eight men to work it, and needed an enormous emplacement, which a hostile aeroplane would have had little trouble in spotting. It threw up the bomb a tremendous height into the air; if a cricket ball were substituted for the bomb, that gun would form an excellent contrivance for giving cricketers practice in catching. The trench mortars in use at the time had all the same defect: they were cumbersome, and could not be quickly brought into action.

Many hours were devoted to the training of the men in the art of bomb-throwing, and factories for making bombs were started by the Sappers. Unfortunately on the 27th May a deplorable accident caused considerable loss of life. A factory at Nieppe Station was blown up, and Lieut.-Col. Uniacke, the A.A. and Q.M.G., who was riding past at the time, was killed. Six officers and 4 men were wounded, and 7 men killed. Every reasonable precaution had been taken by the Sappers in charge, and the explosion was probably due to the instability of the explosive.

While the Division was still near Bailleul, it was visited by Sir John French who inspected the 27th and 28th Brigades on the 29th May. Near the end of the month the 26th Brigade received a new Commander, Brig.-General Grogan[1] returning to England and his place being taken by Brig.-General A. B. Ritchie, C.M.G., on 30th May. By the 2nd June all detachments had received some slight experience of the trenches. On the 6th, the Division marched by night to training grounds near Busnes where D.H.Q. were installed, and till the 25th, training was carried on vigorously, particular attention being paid to bombing. On the 16th, speculations on the possibility of the Ninth taking part in a battle were aroused by it being placed under readiness to move at two hours' notice. This order was due to an unsuccessful engagement carried out by the British Army near Festubert, but the Division was not required and training continued without interruption.

On the 26th June orders were received to relieve the Seventh Division in the line near Festubert, and accordingly the 26th and the 27th Brigades took over the front line on the nights of the 1st and 2nd July. The 28th was in reserve. This was the first occasion on which the Division was responsible for a section of the front line, which it held east of Festubert until 18th August, and during this period all ranks became acquainted with the trials of trench warfare.

The advantage of ground was with the enemy. Occupying the ridge east of Festubert the Germans were able to control their artillery fire by direct observation. The weakest point in our line was

[1] This was the result of an order issued by G.H.Q. fixing an age limit for Brigadiers.

C

"The Orchard," a sharp salient, which was held at
tremendous cost and risk; and it was here that the
Division had most of its casualties, as the enemy
kept it constantly under fire from artillery and
trench mortars. Our artillery could do little at that
time to help the infantry. For every shell that we
had the Germans had ten, and each attempt to
retaliate resulted in a fiercer and heavier bombardment. Until our gunners were supplied with enough
material to enable them to compete with the enemy,
the best policy was to refrain from annoying him.
The infantry particularly disliked the feeble efforts
at retaliation by our artillery because they alone felt
the consequences. For a similar reason all trench
mortar officers[1] were unpopular. When a mortar was
fired that particular section of trench was drenched by
the enemy with "Minnies."[2] It was therefore natural
for the garrison to treat trench mortars and their
teams with disapproval if not hostility, and it was
usually only by stealth that the T.M. officer was
able to fire at all.

Another part of our line to which the enemy paid
considerable attention was an old trench lying between
the front and support trenches, known as the "Old
German Line." We did not occupy it on account of
its stench and filth, but the Germans believed that
we did, and persistently shelled it. They were
encouraged in their error. A few men were sent to
light fires in this trench, and after they had performed
their task they withdrew in haste; for as soon as
the enemy observed the smoke rising, he commenced
to shell vigorously. No one was known voluntarily

[1] See *The First Hundred Thousand*, p. 280.
[2] "Minnie," the popular name for German Trench Mortars, from
Minenwerfer.

FESTUBERT

to enter this trench except the Prince of Wales, who used to prowl round it in search of souvenirs. He paid a number of visits[1] to the line while we held it, and his natural daring must often have caused his escort the keenest anxiety. It was not safe to go up to the forward saps in daylight, but His Royal Highness insisted on doing so, and he also took a photograph of a wounded man who was being carried down from one of them.

In spite of the immense preponderance that the enemy enjoyed in artillery, the men found in the life more of interest than of peril. Patrolling was a new form of enterprise that appealed to the bolder spirits. 2nd Lieut. Bellamy of the 11th Royal Scots took over a patrol of three men in broad daylight on the 5th June, and on reconnoitring found that the enemy had constructed a new trench. On the 13th June, 2nd Lieut. Murray of the 12th Royal Scots stalked a German patrol and shot one man; and on the same night Corporal Morrison of the 6th Royal Scots Fusiliers frightened away a working-party and brought back a *chevaux de frise*. Even the commonplaces of trench life had at this time the spice of novelty, but an incident that happened to Sergeant J. M'Hardy, of the machine-gun section of the 8th Black Watch, was certainly unusual as well as whimsical. This N.C.O. had just hung up his kilt in the trenches to dry when the back blast of a shell blew it over the parapet towards the enemy's lines. The unfortunate man had to go kiltless until dusk, when he hopped over and recovered his garment. On the 8th July, the Divisional area was visited by

---

[1] On one occasion no horse was provided to take the Prince up to the trenches. He, therefore, borrowed one belonging to the machine-gun officer of the 27th Brigade, and it was afterwards known as "Prince."

Lord Kitchener, who inspected the 26th Brigade, at that time in reserve, and detachments of the Ninth between Locon and Hinges.

On the 18th August the Division was relieved by the Seventh, and moved to the training area near Busnes, where D.H.Q. were established. On the next day it was again visited by Lord Kitchener, who inspected it in a big field, and he expressed himself as highly pleased. From this date till the end of the month training was carried on continuously, and the men were frequently practised in issuing rapidly from their own trenches and attacking another line. These manœuvres raised hopes that they would soon be tested in an important battle.

The whole Division was anxious for a fight. It had now been more than three months in France, and had become thoroughly acquainted with the ordinary routine of trench warfare. Life had turned out to be much less trying than most of the men had imagined, for casualties had been comparatively few, and there had been no thrills. It was always unpleasant, of course, when the trenches were pounded, but these periods were only occasional and seldom of long duration. It was not the danger, but the drabness of trench life that worried the men, who found that the outstanding features of this kind of warfare were hard work and discomfort. The latter however they were compelled to get rid of as soon as possible, and most of them quickly became skilled in constructing habitable and cosy dugouts. The trivial round was one of constant toil, and cleanliness was insisted on more as a necessity than as a virtue. The chief strain was due to the interruption of sleep; for the exigencies of trench duties made it impossible for anyone to sleep for more than a few hours at a time.

Above all, the men felt that the reputation of the Ninth could not be solidly established without a battle. They yielded to none in their admiration of the magnificent feats accomplished by the grand regiments of the line, which had borne the first shock of the German hordes; but they were anxious to show that they were both fit and ready to take their place with the regulars. The fierce test of action was needed to reveal the worth of the Division, and every man hoped that it would not be long delayed.

It soon came. When on the 2nd September the Ninth took over from the First Division the trenches east of Vermelles, the men had reached the scene of their first battle.

The plan of a large operation had been adumbrated at the beginning of August, but had it depended on the situation on the Western Front it is doubtful if any important enterprise would have been attempted. The costly failure of the joint British and French offensive in May proved that the Western Allies had not yet accumulated the preponderance in artillery necessary to secure the superiority of fire that was essential for success. Both in numbers and in quality the allied infantry surpassed that of the enemy, but the German defences were skilfully selected, strongly fortified, and powerfully supported by artillery.

Events on the Eastern Front, however, rendered it imperative to create a diversion. The summer was a period of disaster for the Russian Armies; they had been out-generalled and were retiring rapidly before the vast German and Austrian forces, which, focussing on Warsaw, had made those gigantic outflanking movements that had ended in the capture of that city. It was feared that the fate of Petrograd hung in the balance. The Western Allies therefore decided to help the hard-pressed Russians by an attack on a large scale, which might bring some tangible gains, and would at least compel Germany to transfer forces to the West and thus weaken her offensive in the East.

The general scheme drawn up by the High Commands of the Allied Forces reflected their hopes rather than their expectations. The French Tenth Army and the I. and IV. Corps of the British Army were to advance due east in the direction of Valenciennes; at the same time the French main attack was to be made from Champagne on Maubeuge. If these enterprises were successful, the victorious forces would join hands about Valenciennes and Maubeuge, thus cutting off all the enemy within the salient, Rheims–Royon and Arras.

The plan was too ambitious. The reluctance of the British leaders to undertake a premature operation was perfectly justified, and when they committed themselves to an attack, they ought to have limited themselves to a scheme proportionate to their resources. It is therefore impossible to condone the reckless optimism that shaped the plans for the Battle of Loos. They revealed a disposition to underrate the adversary. The lessons of the German failures at Ypres, of the battles at Hill 60, and of the Allied offensive in May were ignored. If an attack had to be made, it should have been confined to the capture of tactical points within a limited objective. A break - through was then impossible. The experience of the war and the resources at the disposal of Sir John French did not justify the attempt in 1915, and the presumptions of the Higher Command were shattered by the facts of the battle.

The task of the First Army was to pierce the first and second lines of the German defences from Haisnes in the north to Hulluch in the south; then, after capturing Meurchin and Pont à Vendin, to move rapidly on Carvin, and so protect the left flank of the French Army. The northern part of the operation was to be carried out by the I. Corps, the southern part by the IV. Corps. In order to give this enterprise every chance of success, subsidiary attacks were to be made on other parts of the British front to prevent the enemy from reinforcing the main point of attack.

Conscious of its weakness in artillery material, the British Command hoped to compass the demoralisation of the foe by a discharge of gas along the front of the principal onslaught. This was the first occasion on which the British Army used gas,[1] and it was hoped that its effect would so paralyse the defenders that the assaulting troops would be able to secure with little resistance the German second line in spite of the wire that was too far distant for the artillery to cut.

The task of forming the northern defensive flank[2] of this attack was entrusted to the Ninth Division, which, after carrying the line Railway Work–Fosse No. 8–Haisnes, was to push on to Douvrin. Similarly, the southern division of the IV. Corps was to form a defensive flank facing south near Loos. If these flanks were secured and consolidated, it was expected that the intermediate divisions of the I. and IV.

---

[1] So completely was the chance of success considered to depend upon the use of gas that the attack was to be cancelled if the wind was unfavourable; instead, a minor operation was to be carried out by the 7th Seaforths against the HOHENZOLLERN REDOUBT.

[2] On the left of the Ninth the Second Division had to carry out two operations: first, to capture the Givenchy salient, and second, and more important, to attack the German front line trenches and then move on Auchy. Should the latter attack succeed, the Second Division was to form the defensive flank of the Army as far as Haisnes, from which point it was to be carried on by the Ninth Division.

Corps, supported by the XI., would be able to force their way between these flanks as far as the Deule Canal, and even farther if the resistance of the enemy was negligible.

There was a gap between the right of the British forces and the left of the Tenth French Army. In this area lay the colliery district of Lens, consisting of masses of miners' cottages, pits, and slag heaps, admirably adapted for an obstinate and protracted defence. During the French offensive north of Arras in May and June advance had been slow and losses heavy, owing to the stubborn opposition of the Germans posted in the villages of Carency, Givenchy, and Souchez. The Lens area afforded even greater advantages to the defenders, and it was decided that the French and British forces should work round the south and north of the town and join hands to the east of it.

An operation of importance involves an enormous amount of hard work and anxiety for all branches of the Staff, from G.H.Q. down to brigades. The Staff[1] is the brain of the Army, and its function is to supply everything—from bombs to operation orders. It consists of two distinct branches: the A. and Q. branch, which is responsible for discipline, procuring supplies, and making arrangements for the comfort of the troops in such matters as billets and baths; and the G. branch,

[1] It is common knowledge that at military concert parties the Staff shared with the Sergeant-Major and the Quartermaster the distinction of being the chief butt of the witticisms of the troupe. This is due partly to the British soldier's inveterate love of "chaff," and partly to the fact that the duties of the Staff officer, particularly in the higher formations, secured him comparative immunity from danger. The average infantryman was too much occupied with the ordinary details of his daily task ever to give any thought to the harassing and important duties that the Staff had to perform. Occasionally, of course, the latter made a bad slip. During the Battle of Arras, for example, a battalion in the 27th Brigade received a message to the effect that sacks for bayonet training were available ! Such blunders were naturally cherished by the Regimental officer.

which is concerned with training and operations. For success, the best devised plan depends greatly upon the care with which details are worked out. The actual attack is made by the infantry. Upon the dash and gallantry of the soldiers and the initiative and resource of the subordinate commanders, the Higher Command has to rely for the consummation of its hopes ; but the arduous task of the infantry is considerably eased if the preliminary preparations are the best possible from the resources at the disposal of the Staff. Good Staff work consists in eliminating chance and hazard and in strengthening assurance of success.

The frontage on which the Ninth Division was to assault was 1600 yards. On the 16th August, the G.O.C., Major-General Landon, held a conference, when the proposed operations were discussed. It was decided to assault with two brigades, each with two battalions in the front line, the 26th on the right and the 28th on the left, with the 27th in reserve.

The objectives of the 26th Brigade were, first, the Hohenzollern Redoubt, Fosse Trench and Dump Trench ; and second, a line on the east side of Fosse 8 through the Three Cabarets to the Corons de Pekin (first objective). Should this task be accomplished, the brigade was to go on to the neighbourhood of Pekin Trench (second objective). If at this stage the line was prolonged to the north by the 28th Brigade and the Second Division, the 26th and 28th were to advance east on Douvrin. Should, however, the Second Division fail, these brigades were to attack Haisnes and form a defensive flank facing north-east.

On the left, the 28th Brigade had first to secure the Railway line from the Corons de Marons to the junction of Les Briques and Train Alley (first objective), and then advance to its second objective in the neighbourhood

of Pekin Trench.   The further action of the brigade
depended upon the progress of the Second Division.

The 27th Brigade was to be in reserve some 2000
and 2800 yards in rear of the front line.   Its rôle
was either to support the attempt on Fosse 8, or if
that was successful, to move on to Haisnes and
Douvrin.   Battalion commanders were given a free
hand as to the formations to be adopted, subject to
the proviso that each unit was to be in three lines.

The date of battle, after several postponements, was
eventually fixed for the 25th September.

The task of the Division in its first important
engagement was not an easy one.   In the excitement
of battle even the best of soldiers are liable to go astray
if they are required to change direction at any time
during the advance.   For this reason it is desirable
that objectives should be allotted so that it is possible
for the assailing troops to advance at right angles to
their position of assembly.   In the present case the
advance in a north-easterly direction up to the line
of the Fosse fulfilled these conditions, but from this
point the Ninth was required to swing east and con-
verge on a narrower front.   Fortunately the difficulties
of this operation were diminished by the presence of
such conspicuous landmarks as the villages of Haisnes,
Cité St Elie and Douvrin, but it was nevertheless an
extremely complicated one for an untried division to
undertake.

The Ninth took over the line east of Vermelles on
the 2nd September, and arrangements had to be made
at once so that all preparations would be completed
before the battle.   The front trenches, as taken over
from the First Division, were too far from the German
line to be suitable for the forward assembly trenches.
The First Division had projected an attack on the

Hohenzollern Redoubt, and for that purpose had pushed forward a number of blind saps. Our first intention was to join up the blinded sap-heads by a parallel, and open them up just before the onset; but as gas was to be used, the saps were opened up at once and then joined by new fire trenches. This was accomplished in one night, each battalion digging 350 yards, thus bringing our front trenches within 150 yards of the German line. In addition, a support line was made in the rear, with numerous short communication trenches running back to the old front line, with the result that it was possible to accommodate the whole Division in the trench system.

As it was imperative to regulate the traffic with a view to preventing congestion on the day of attack, special communication trenches were prepared for the wounded. For each of the attacking brigades two communication trenches were allotted, one to be used for "up" traffic, the other for "down," and to diminish the chance of confusion, each was labelled and marked. On the capture of the enemy front line, these communication trenches were to be connected with it; and, to save time and labour, blinded saps were run forward 50 yards and more. In all, about 12,000 yards of trenches were dug before the battle.

The chances of success largely depended upon the ability of the artillery to demolish the enemy's defences. Until the moment of the assault the artillery were under the orders of the Corps. Unfortunately the heavy guns at the disposal of the Corps were few in number, there being only twenty 6-inch Howitzers and twelve of higher calibre.

The infantry attack was to be preceded by a four days' bombardment. The 18-pounders had to cut the wire along the enemy's front. Known and suspected strong points were to be shelled; and during night, paths, roads, communication trenches, houses, and all places where the enemy was likely to collect, were to be kept under fire. In the work of sweeping approaches, machine-guns were to co-operate with the artillery. The preliminary bombardment was arranged for the 21st September, its object being to pulverise the German fortifications and to demoralise the defenders. Only in this way could the neutralisation of the hostile rifle and machine-gun fire necessary for an attack by infantry be secured. In order to keep the Germans uncertain of the exact time of the assault, two feint attacks were arranged. At noon on the 21st September, the 26th Brigade was to induce the garrison of the Hohenzollern Redoubt to man its parapets by preparations that seemed to indicate an immediate attack; thereupon the German trenches were to be shelled with shrapnel. A similar operation against Madagascar Trench was to be undertaken by the 28th Brigade on the third day of the bombardment.

The orders for the artillery were issued on the 20th September. On the morning of the battle, first the enemy front line system, then Pekin Trench, and the Three Cabarets were to be shelled for ten minutes. In the following ten minutes the artillery fire was to be brought back to the front line for five minutes; it was then to move east and remain for thirty minutes in the vicinity of Pekin Trench between Haisnes and Cité St Elie. The great proportion of shell used was shrapnel; H.E. was limited and was used chiefly by the heavy artillery.

The control of its own artillery reverted to the Division at the moment of the assault. In order that no opportunity might be lost in the event of a rapid success, two batteries were earmarked to follow up the infantry. These were to be taken out of their emplacements on the night of the 24th, and kept limbered-up ready to advance at a moment's notice. Forward positions for these guns and observation posts were reconnoitred from a study of the map and of the country from Annequin Fosse; and three roads were prepared and bridged where they crossed the trenches. Other bridges were to be carried by the batteries to enable them to cross captured trenches. One brigade of artillery was affiliated to each of the assaulting infantry brigades and the remainder was kept under the immediate control of Brig.-General Armitage.

The effect of machine-guns and trench mortars depends chiefly on the resource of the team commanders. Each of the infantry battalions had four machine-guns, while fourteen were distributed in rear of the front line to co-operate with the artillery. Five minutes after the commencement of the bombardment, these guns were to open intensive fire on hostile communication trenches for thirty minutes. During night they were to play on enemy communication trenches, and on the wire to prevent the Germans repairing the gaps cut by the artillery fire. On the day of the attack they were to open intensive fire five minutes after the beginning of the bombardment for fifteen minutes; they were then to fire deliberately for ten minutes, thereafter resuming intensive fire for other ten.

On the right of the Division an important rôle was assigned to the trench mortars. Between the Ninth and the Seventh Divisions was an interval of 200 yards; and to cover this gap 2-inch trench mortars and 2-inch Stokes mortars were to fire smoke-bombs to prevent the enemy in Big Willie from enfilading the left of the Seventh. It was realised that the most formidable

task had been allotted to the 26th Brigade and arrangements were made for one 2-inch mortar, one battery
of 1½-inch mortars, and one Stokes gun to go forward
with it.

The discharge of gas formed an essential part of
the scheme of the British Army ; and its effects were
expected to make up for deficiency in artillery material.[1]
The Germans were known to have safeguards against
gas, but it was hoped that they would be taken by
surprise, and that the fumes would be rolling over their
lines before they had time to don their helmets.   At
the worst, it was expected that the discomfort of
wearing the helmets would impair the efficiency of
their troops and partly demoralise them.

The gas was to be discharged from cylinders, each
weighing from 130 to 160 lbs., and emplacements were
made to accommodate twelve at intervals of 25 yards
along the front of the Division.   The work of carrying
up and fixing the cylinders in position was a heavy
business.   They were brought by train to a siding east
of Bethune, where the road ran alongside the railway,
and at night they were transferred to lorries, each of
which carried about thirty.   The lorries were then
driven to Cambrai and Vermelles, where they were met
by carrying parties, which conveyed the cylinders to the
front line.

These parties were organised in groups of thirty-
six men for every twelve cylinders, and each group was

----

[1] The effect of the German gas attack in May had produced a powerful
impression upon both the army and the public. Since that time the
energies and experiments of British scientists and doctors had provided the
army with an efficient protection consisting of a chemicalised canvas bag
with two gas-proof openings for the eyes. In the event of an attack this
bag was pulled over the head, its loose ends being tucked in round the
neck and covered up by the tunic so that the gas found no aperture to
evade the chemical barrier.

commanded by an officer.   The work was unpopular as
well as arduous, for the men had little liking for gas
and none cared to handle anything connected with it.
The cylinders had to be carried for more than 2000
yards up long and winding communication trenches,
and when the weather was wet the heavy burden
of the men was aggravated by the difficulty of maintaining their balance on the slippery duck-boards.
Occasionally shelled areas had to be traversed, an
anxious period for any party with cylinders.   To ease
the work as far as possible, the communication trenches
up which the men had to travel were marked by white
arrows, and kept clear of unnecessary traffic.   Fortunately the weather was favourable.   If it had been other-
wise, this weight could scarcely have been managed by
three men.   Altogether 4000 men were employed in
the transference of 1200 cylinders.   When these were
fixed in their emplacements the infantry had no further
responsibility concerning them, for they were then
under the care of the Special Gas Company, R.E., which
was to discharge the gas on the day of the assault.

In addition to the cylinders, each emplacement had
four triple and eight single smoke-candles.   These were
to be lit by the infantry, and used alternatively with the
gas, so that the period of discharge for smoke and gas
would extend to forty minutes, as it was known that
the enemy had, as a protection against gas, oxygen
cylinders which lasted for only thirty minutes.   Two
minutes before the infantry left the front line, all gas
was to be turned off and the smoke thickened by
means of triple candles to form a screen behind which
the infantry could form up and advance.

One Field Company, R.E., and one company of the
9th Seaforths (Pioneers) were attached to each brigade
for the rapid consolidation of captured positions, and

the digging of new communication trenches. Thus, the 90th Field Company, R.E. and "B" Company, 9th Seaforth Highlanders, were attached to the 26th Brigade, the 63rd R.E. and "D" Company, 9th Seaforth Highlanders, to the 28th, and the 64th R.E. and "C" Company, 9th Seaforth Highlanders, to the 27th. Supplies of ammunition, stores, and tools were placed at intervals along the whole front and, as far as possible, these dumps were made at the junction of the "up traffic" communication trenches, and the support line. As the bomb was to be the principal weapon of the infantry after the first stages of the attack, numbers of special bomb depots were formed. In addition to S.A.A., picks and shovels, water, medical stores, and rations were placed in the forward dumps.

Medical Aid Posts were arranged at convenient points. In order to effect the evacuation of the wounded from the forward areas with the utmost speed, each brigade dug one communication trench for wounded only. These trenches were wider than the usual communication trench, the corners being rounded off, so that stretchers could be carried with comparatively little inconvenience. A loop was made leading off them, about 2000 yards in rear, and in each loop was a dressing station in a dug-out about the size of an ordinary room. Serious cases were to be brought round the loop, dressed, and then passed out at the farther end into the communication trench. Walking cases were expected to go straight on without passing through the loop.

The maintenance of communication was a most important matter, and every conceivable means, ranging from the pigeon to the human being, was to be used. The ordinary connection by telephone was to be established as far as possible, and visual stations, from which messages could be transmitted by flag or lamp, were to be set up as well as pigeon stations. Between the battalion commander and his company commanders the medium was the runner, the most reliable of all means of communication. The Division had one wireless set, which was worked by four men, and this was attached to the 26th Brigade H.Q.

The question of the men's equipment for battle was important. A heavy weight would retard progress and exhaust their strength, yet it was necessary to supply them with sufficient material to consolidate their gains and to enable them to beat off enemy counter-attacks. Accordingly packs were dumped, the men going into action with haversacks only, and each one carrying two empty sand-bags, and all, except bombers, signallers, and runners, were to be supplied with 200 rounds of ammunition. Owing to the use of gas, the men on the morning of the attack were to wear their gas helmets like a cap.

All these preparations were satisfactorily accomplished by the evening of the 24th September. During this period of strain, the health of Major-General Landon broke down, and on the 8th September he returned to England and was succeeded by Major-General G. H. Thesiger, C.B., C.M.G. The G.S.O.I. was Lieut.-Col. S. E. Hollond, who joined the Division at the beginning of September, and the A.A. and Q.M.G. was Lieut.-Col. A. A. M'Hardy.

CHAPTER III

BATTLE OF LOOS [1]

25TH TO 28TH SEPTEMBER 1915

THE terrain, which was the scene of the Division's first battle, included the feature of greatest tactical importance on the front of the British attack. The general advantage of ground and observation was held by the enemy. East of Vermelles a railway, which ran northeast to join up with the railway connecting Bethune and La Bassée, screened the country west of it from German observation, except from their highest posts at Fosse 8 and the Tower Bridge at Loos, which overlooked the British lines except right down in the Vermelles valley. East of the railway the country was very open and the only trees were those that fringed the Hulluch road; the whole country bore a close resemblance to Salisbury Plain or the moors of Linlithgow, with mine-heads and slag-heaps dotted about. East of Vermelles, the country ran nearly flat to a slight but important crest, then falling to a shallow dip where the trenches faced each other, rose again through the German trenches to another crest about 700 yards west of Cité St Elie. This crest concealed the second line of the enemy from ground observation.

The main front lines of the British and the enemy

[1] See Map.

LOOS

p. 32

were about 500 yards apart and between them jutted out in a south-west direction from the northern part of the German front line the maze of trenches and fortifications known as the Hohenzollern Redoubt. Direct communication between the Redoubt and the main line, which was here known as Dump Trench and Fosse Trench, was secured by two communication trenches, named North Face and South Face, running from north-east to south-west. Two trenches, Big Willie and Little Willie, running respectively east and north, protected the flanks of the Redoubt. But the chief features of the enemy's defences were Fosse 8 and the Dump—an accumulation of débris, which is a familiar sight in all mining areas—and from these points the enemy could look right up the valley that was the scene of the British attack. Of equal importance was the Double Crassier on the extreme right which, with the Fosse and the Dump, formed the key of the whole tactical position, and until they were captured and held, guns could not be brought up to give close support to the infantry in any advance beyond the first system of trenches. If nothing more was secured, the operation would amply justify itself.

On the 21st September the preliminary bombardment commenced at 7 A.M., and in reply the German artillery fired little beyond their usual. At noon on the same day, the first of the feint attacks was made, when the 26th Brigade opposite the Hohenzollern Redoubt opened two minutes' rapid fire with rifles and machine-guns on Big and Little Willie. In addition, the men did all that was possible to make the foe believe that an attack on the Redoubt was imminent; bayonets were shown over the parapet, dummies were moved about, the men shouted, and pipes and bugles sounded

the charge.   This demonstration caused the Germans[1]
to man their parapet, and as our artillery deluged their
front trenches with shrapnel five minutes after noon,
it was believed[2] that heavy losses had been inflicted
on the garrison.   During the third and fourth days
of the bombardment, the reply of the German artillery
became more rapid and intense.   When on the 23rd
an operation, similar to that carried out by the 26th
Brigade two days previously, was made by the 28th
Brigade against Little Willie and Madagascar Trench,
it was noticed that the enemy heavily shelled our
reserve trenches.   At night infantry patrols were sent
out to ascertain the effect of our artillery fire on
the German wire, and their reports showed that
numerous gaps had been made, but unfortunately on
the front of the 28th Brigade patrols failed to examine
the enemy's wire.[3]   This was largely due to the desire
to save the men from being exposed to our own
artillery fire; but the omission had lamentable consequences.   Not till the small hours of the 25th was
the hour of zero communicated to the battalions.   As
the wind was favourable, the main operation was to
be undertaken.   Zero was fixed for 5.50 A.M., and
forty minutes after zero the infantry were to leave
the trenches.

At 5.50 A.M. our artillery opened, and gas and
smoke were discharged along the whole front.   The

[1] Those opposite the Ninth Division belonged to the One hundred and
seventeenth Division.

[2] Under the circumstances there could be nothing stronger than
"belief"; it was impossible to go to the German lines to find out how
many had been killed or wounded.

[3] The wire was fairly well cut by the 18-pounders wherever it was
possible to observe it, but the stretch opposite the front of the 28th
Brigade was invisible from any point on our side.   It was, therefore, the
more essential that the result of the artillery fire in this part should have
been ascertained by patrols.

scene had a terrible grandeur, and the combination
of gun-fire, gas, and smoke produced a wonderful
effect of mingled whites, greys, yellows, and browns.

On the left of the Division, Brig.-General Scrase-
Dickins arranged to attack with the 6th K.O.S.B. on
the right and the 10th H.L.I. on the left. These were
supported respectively by the 11th H.L.I. and the 9th
Scottish Rifles, and they held the front line till the
evening before the 25th, when their places were taken
by the attacking battalions; the 63rd Field Coy. R.E.
and "D" Coy. 9th Seaforths also took up their assembly
positions that night. Unfortunately the arrangements
of the brigade were upset at the last moment by the
Second Division taking over a portion of its line, the
28th Brigade being left with only one communication
trench for the passage of troops and for "up" and
"down" traffic. Ten minutes after the crash of our
guns had announced the hour of zero, the German
counter-bombardment fell on the front and communication trenches; the supporting companies and battalions, which were moving up from the rear trenches
to the front, suffered serious losses, which included
Lieut.-Colonel H. D. N. Maclean, D.S.O., and his
adjutant, Captain Keith of the 6th K.O.S.B.

At 6.30 A.M. the 6th K.O.S.B. and 10th H.L.I.
left our front line and advanced in three lines against
the German trenches. On the right, the leading companies of the K.O.S.B., now commanded by Major
Hosley, pressed forward, at first without suffering
very severely. Major Hosley was wounded on the
parapet but refused to go back, and insisted on leading his battalion forward. The wind unfortunately
was fitful and was not strong enough to carry on the
gas, so the leading companies lay down until it had
moved on. As soon as the two supporting companies

crossed our front parapet, they came under a withering rifle and machine-gun fire, but in spite of many casualties they continued to push on and became mingled with the leading companies. More conspicuous now than the crash of the guns was the menacing and ominous "rat-tat" of the enemy machine-guns, and when the K.O.S.B. resumed their advance, officers and men were mown down by a terrible fire, to which they could not reply. Nevertheless the survivors pressed on with magnificent determination, but the German wire was found to be virtually intact. In front of the enemy's line was a covered trench crammed with stakes and barbed wire and as soon as the foremost men stepped on the top covering, they fell through and became entangled amongst the wire. The air teemed with bullets, and the survivors, impotent to advance but too stubborn to retreat, had very heavy losses. The battalion was now leaderless. Of the 19 officers who went into action, 12 were killed and 7 wounded, and as a consequence the brigade received no news from the battalion during the morning. It is believed that a few men, favoured by incredible luck, forced their way into the German front trench, but being unsupported they eventually fell back and reached our original front line during the night.

The 10th H.L.I. on the left of the brigade had no better fortune. As the wind was too weak to carry the gas forward from our trenches, many of the men were suffering from the effects of it when they left the front line. At the very start the ranks of the battalion were thinned by a storm of shell, rifle and machine-gun fire, a considerable number being killed and wounded on the parapet. With fine courage the men pushed on but were unable to penetrate the enemy's wire, which had been scarcely damaged. Before vicious machine-

gun fire from Madagascar Trench, Railway Work, and
Mad Point, the attack melted away, and most of the
survivors struggled back to the trenches from which
they had set out, none having broken through the
German wire.   The losses in officers and men were
exceptionally severe; Lieut.-Colonel Grahame was
gassed and his adjutant killed.   As the whole signalling staff of Battalion H.Q. had been knocked out by
a shell, Brigade H.Q. were without definite news of the
disaster until noon, when Major H. C. Stuart reported
in person.

In war, no news invariably means bad news, and
consequently during the early hours of the attack
suspense and anxiety reigned at Brigade H.Q.   The
gloomy forebodings with which the absence of information had filled the minds of Brig.-General Scrase-
Dickins and his staff were deepened by a message,
received from the 9th Scottish Rifles at 8.15 A.M., that
the 10th H.L.I. were asking for reinforcements.   As
it was also known at 7.50 A.M. that the attack of the
Second Division on the left had failed, there was no
longer any reason to doubt that the brigade had experienced a serious check.   Anxiety about the situation on
the front of the 28th Brigade had an unsettling effect
on the plans of the Division.   The 26th on the right
had in the meantime made good progress, but General
Thesiger hesitated to support it with the full strength
of the 27th until he had definite information concerning
his left brigade.   At 9.10 A.M., however, the Division
learned from a telephone message that the attack of the
28th Brigade had been repulsed.

Since this check exposed the 26th Brigade to the
chance of a counter-attack from the north, the left
brigade was ordered to launch another attack, and
after a thirty minutes' artillery bombardment the 11th

H.L.I. on the right and the 9th Scottish Rifles on the
left advanced against the enemy's lines at 12.15 P.M.
But the bombardment was not sufficiently heavy to
demolish the German strong points, and the only
effect of the hopeless gallantry of the "Rifles" and
the H.L.I. was greatly to increase the enormous losses
of the brigade. The attack was swept away by the
enemy's rifle and machine-gun fire. As the result of
these two attacks the 28th Brigade had lost about two-
thirds of its effective strength and the great majority
of its officers had been killed or wounded. It was
now unfit for further action and was withdrawn to its
original line, which it was barely strong enough to hold
effectively.

The primary cause of the repulse was the failure of
the artillery to cut the enemy's wire. During the
preliminary bombardment that wire ought to have been
examined nightly by patrols, and the neglect to do so
was a cardinal blunder for which the brigade had to
pay a heavy price. The extravagant hopes entertained
of the power of gas to demoralise the enemy had been
rudely shattered; it was a hindrance and not a help,
and its baneful effects were confined to our own men.
In face of uncut wire and the enemy's intact defences
the attack could be no more than a forlorn hope,
although with well-nigh incredible courage the men
did all that men could do to achieve the impossible.
It was a failure, but one that shed lustre on the men
that failed.

The second attack was an offence against a well-
understood military principle that was too often
neglected in the warfare in France. When men have
failed in an attack, it is generally futile to send other
men to make another attack in the same way; it
encourages the defenders and doubles the losses of

the assailants. The hope of smashing, by an artillery bombardment of thirty minutes, defences that had remained intact after four days' bombardment, betrayed an almost unbelievable optimism. The most feasible way was to send a part of the 27th Brigade to follow behind the 26th, and attack the enemy in Madagascar Trench from the south. But if no units of the 27th Brigade were available, it would have been wiser to send round some of the 11th H.L.I. and 9th Scottish Rifles to the Dump, from which point they could have assaulted the German positions from flank and rear. Persistence in a frontal attack showed a serious lack of flexibility in the Higher Command in making use of the resources of the Division.

On the front of the right brigade, Brig.-General Ritchie decided to attack with the 7th Seaforths on the right and the 5th Camerons on the left; these were supported respectively by the 8th Gordons and 8th Black Watch. The task of the leading battalions was to secure the first objective, which included the Hohenzollern Redoubt, the German main trench beyond it, and Fosse 8 with the Three Cabarets and the Corons de Pekin. When this was accomplished the Gordons and the Black Watch were to pass through, and, swinging in a south-easterly direction, capture the second objective. The assembly of the brigade and the units attached, the 90th R.E., "B" Coy. 9th Seaforths, and the trench mortar batteries, was completed on the evening of the 24th without a hitch, the two assaulting battalions being in position in the front and support trenches, and the support battalions in the reserve trenches.

The period prior to an attack is always a trying time, and the men welcomed the crash of guns that announced the hour of zero. At the same moment the gas and smoke were discharged, and the 2-inch trench mortars smothered Big Willie and the South Face of the Hohenzollern Redoubt with phosphorous smoke-balls.

At 6.29 A.M. the assaulting battalions jumped out of their trenches, and were marshalled for the assault in front of our own wire, screened by the smoke from the candles. This had the effect of steadying the men and allowed the advance to be made without confusion or disorder.

Between Fosse 8 and the Redoubt there was a hog-back ridge; the Seaforths and the Camerons advanced south and north of it respectively. At the very beginning the former lost touch with the latter, who were delayed for ten minutes by gas hanging in the front trenches. The Seaforths made straight for the Hohenzollern Redoubt, suffering consider-able losses from rifle and machine-gun fire from the right flank, and captured the southern portion of it after a brisk fight, in which a good many officers were killed or wounded. Then the battalion bombed its way up the communication trenches to the German main trench, and without waiting for the Camerons, pushed forward past Fosse 8, clearing all the miners' cottages and seizing the Three Cabarets. At this point the battalion, after being reorganised, lined the Corons Trench immediately east of Fosse 8 about 7.30 A.M. A few of the men slightly lost direction and wandered up the trench that led from the Corons to the ridge in front of Cité St Elie and Haisnes. The battalion had accomplished its job in very fine style and in good time.

On their left the Camerons had a ghastly experience. When, after a ten minutes' wait to allow the gas to pass on, the men began to advance, they were shot down by a galling fire from the left, the first two lines of the battalion being almost annihilated. To cross that fatal field was a task that even the stoutest

of men might have shirked without shame. But the
Camerons were inspired by a compelling sense of
duty, and undeterred by the fear or spectacle of
death, they made of danger the spring-board of a
leaping hardihood. With superb heroism they pressed
doggedly through the fatal zone, where lay the
greater part of the battalion. Nothing but death
could stop such men. After capturing the Redoubt
they moved on to Fosse 8 and, having made their way
through the miners' cottages, halted at the north
edge of the Corons de Pekin about 7.45 A.M. The
Camerons had reached their objective, but at a
terrible cost; of the 800 men and 20 officers who
crossed our line, only 2 officers and 70 men were
left. It was a thrilling feat of arms, which men
of the 5th Camerons will ever remember, and the
very story of which served to inspire future drafts
with the courage of the glorious dead.

Thus by 8 A.M. the Seaforths and Camerons had
established themselves on the east of Fosse 8, and
the men began to consolidate their positions. But
there was a gap between the battalions, and the
troops were heavily shelled from the Cemetery that
lay south of Auchy.

Meantime the supporting battalions were advancing
rapidly. At 6.30 A.M. the Gordons and Black Watch
moved up from their positions in the reserve line to
the front trenches. They crossed our parapet at 7 A.M.,
and with praiseworthy steadiness pressed through the
hostile barrage, which was falling on our front line.
The Black Watch lost greatly through heavy machine-
gun fire from the north, their gallant C.O., Lieut.-
Colonel Lord Sempill, being badly wounded. The
Gordons, on reaching the Redoubt, took prisoner a
number of Germans who had concealed themselves

in shelter when the Seaforths passed over. At
Dump Trench the Black Watch had a sharp fight
with some of the enemy, who had been overlooked
by the Camerons, and captured a number of prisoners.
On their right a party of the Gordons bombed down
to the Window in the German main trench, in order
to clear the front for the Seventh Division.

After passing the main trench the bulk of the
Black Watch, instead of swinging to the south-east,
pushed on through the Corons and came into line
between the Seaforths and Camerons beyond the
miners' cottages. The remainder of the battalion,
roughly about a company, went on with the Gordons,
who at 7.40 A.M. moved down Fosse Trench and then
diverted their attack in an easterly direction on Cité
St Elie and Haisnes. They carried and went over
Fosse Alley and reached Pekin Trench a few hundred
yards short of Haisnes soon after 8 A.M., but they
had lost many of their number and could go no
farther. The enemy's resistance was far from being
broken and the advance had been made under continuous shell and machine-gun fire. Haisnes was
at that time lightly held and would have fallen to
fresh troops, but by the time the leading ranks of the
27th Brigade arrived the village had been strongly
reinforced.

Farther west and to the left rear of the Gordons,
the Black Watch and the Seaforths made an attempt
to advance towards Pekin Alley, but a German
battery, situated about 1000 yards east of the Cabarets,
and flanked by machine-guns, inflicted considerable
casualties and pinned the men down to their trenches.
This ill-starred effort cost the Seaforths their leader,
Lieut.-Colonel Gaisford being killed. The situation of
the 26th Brigade was not a happy one. It was clear,

as the ordeal of the Camerons and Black Watch had foreboded, that the attack of the 28th Brigade had failed. It was necessary to consolidate the line in front of Fosse 8, and to safeguard the left flank; but under the continuous and accurate shell fire of the enemy, it was practically impossible to accomplish any work. The trenches were in an appalling mess, having been terribly smashed by our artillery; Corons Alley was particularly bad, since the enemy had flooded it before retiring. About 9.30 A.M. the brigade received some welcome artillery support, when the battery commanded by Major C. W. W. McLean moved into position south-west of the Fosse and opened fire on the Cemetery, Cemetery Alley, and Lone Farm in turn.

At 9 A.M. the position of the 26th Brigade was as follows : the Seaforths, Black Watch, and Camerons held the trenches east of Fosse 8 from Fosse Alley to the north end of the Corons de Pekin, and to guard the left flank, a small party was posted at the Railway crossing. Additional protection was afforded by the machine-guns of the Camerons, which were posted at Little Willie, and commanded the ground on the left of the brigade. The enemy was in strength in Pekin Alley, Cemetery Alley, Lone Farm, and Madagascar Trench. About 600 yards to the right front, the remnants of the Gordons and some Black Watch were established in Pekin Trench, not far from Haisnes. Unsupported on either flank, and exposed to a murderous fire, the position of this garrison was most precarious, and could only be maintained with the help of the 27th Brigade.

On the evening of the 24th September, the battalions of the 27th Brigade were assembled in reserve trenches. From this position to the front line there were two routes, by the communication trenches termed Railway

Alley and Fountain Alley. Previous reconnaissance
had shown that the time required to reach the front
line by these routes was 1 and 1½ hours respectively,
and the move of the brigade was arranged to enable it
to reach the front trenches as soon as they were
vacated by the 26th Brigade. But all the previous plans
made for the regulation of traffic in the communication
trenches broke down during the action, and the men
of the 27th found their advance checked by carrying
parties, stragglers, and returning wounded. The average
progress seemed to be about 30 yards every 20 minutes,
and there were many long halts. Not only were the
men exhausted by this tedious and tiring passage, but
they suffered heavily from the enemy's shell-fire. It
would have kept the men fresher, and would probably
have saved casualties, if the battalions had moved out
of the trenches and advanced across the open.

The first battalion to cross the front line was
the 12th Royal Scots. It should have been followed
by the 11th Royal Scots, but this battalion was
seriously delayed in the trenches, and the 10th Argylls
were the second battalion to pass the line. The
order of battalions, however, as arranged by the
brigade, was restored during the advance, the Argylls
halting to allow the 11th Royal Scots to get into
their proper position. Under orders from General
Thesiger, the 6th Royal Scots Fusiliers were kept back
in the front trenches owing to the failure of the 28th
Brigade. On entering "No Man's Land," the 27th
Brigade came under intense rifle and machine-gun fire
from Cité St Elie, and from north-east of the Fosse.
About 11 A.M. the 11th and 12th Royal Scots passed
through the Gordons and advanced on Haisnes, but
they were scourged by terrific rifle and machine-gun
fire, and could make progress only by short, sharp

rushes. A few men penetrated into the outskirts of the village, but they could not maintain their position, and were forced to withdraw. Till the evening, the survivors of the Royal Scots lay out in the open about 300 yards east of Pekin Trench, and in the afternoon the situation of the Royal Scots and men of the Seventh Division on their right became intolerable. They were numbed by cold and rain and suffered grievously from the enfilade fire which the enemy directed on them from Haisnes, so at 4 P.M. the men were withdrawn to the line of Pekin Trench on the right of the Gordons.

The Argylls, who followed close behind the Royal Scots, established themselves in Fosse Alley. Observing that the left flank of the men in Pekin Trench was exposed, they sent forward a company to protect it, but it was held up by unbroken barbed wire, and, after the company commander had been shot down while trying to cut it, the remainder fell back on Fosse Alley. Haisnes was now strongly held by the enemy, and there was little chance of taking it without strong artillery support. Brig.-General Bruce received orders at 3.30 P.M. to secure the village, and, leaving instructions for the 6th Royal Scots Fusiliers to follow on, he left Central Boyau and went forward to Fosse Alley to reconnoitre the position. As both Haisnes and Cité St Elie were strongly garrisoned by the enemy, and as his brigade had been very heavily punished, he considered that an attack[1] on Haisnes was out of the question. The decision was sound. Even if the village had been captured, the strength of the Division would have been too dissipated to offer any chance of effective defence against a resolute attack.

[1] Brig.-General Bruce sent back by the machine-gun officer of his brigade an important account of the situation to Brig.-General Ritchie.

The presence of Brig.-General Bruce steadied the garrison of Pekin Trench, and under his direction two companies of the Royal Scots Fusiliers were sent forward to support the Royal Scots by occupying the trench on their left. The position at Pekin Trench, however, needed more reinforcements than Brig.-General Bruce had at his command in order to make it secure, and the small garrison had a very bad time. The men were exposed to a continuous and merciless fire, and the trenches were full of dead, dying, and wounded. To add to their misery rain fell heavily, the rifles became clogged with mud and could not be fired, and the fuse-lighters of the Bethune bombs were so damp that it was impossible to ignite them.

The initiative now rested with the enemy,[1] whose numbers were being hourly augmented, and numerous bombing attacks were made on the garrison. Against the most desperate odds a brilliant defence was made. "C" Company of the Gordons, under Captain J. E. Adamson, beat off three powerful and determined attacks from the railway and the village; but with diminishing numbers and want of food, water, ammunition and bombs, it was not possible for it to hold on indefinitely. The great majority of the officers were dead or wounded, and most of the bombers had become casualties. The men could do no more, and during the late afternoon and evening the Gordons retired to Fosse Alley, but here their right flank was attacked by German bombers from Cité St Elie, and they were compelled to fall back on our front line.

The position of the Royal Scots in Pekin Trench became untenable when the Gordons were forced back,

---

[1] In the course of the battle the Germans brought up the 2nd Guards Reserve Division, the 10th Bavarian Regiment, and a battalion of the 123rd Division.

and the longer they held on the more dangerous became the situation; for both flanks were exposed, and the enemy was becoming more confident and aggressive. The Germans with abundance of bombs made numerous attacks against the Royal Scots, so to avoid being surrounded, the garrison fell back to Fosse Alley in the evening. After organising the remnants of his brigade along Fosse Alley and satisfying himself that it was in touch with the Seventh Division on the right, Brig.-General Bruce established his H.Q. in the Quarries. This was an unfortunate choice, for though he was now in close touch with the Seventh Division he was too far away for General Thesiger to get quickly into communication with him.

Meantime the main body of the 26th Brigade maintained its position. In spite of rain and a deluge of shells, the sappers of the 90th Coy. R.E., assisted by infantry and pioneers, rapidly improved the trenches and made them stronger for defence. The behaviour of the men was beyond all praise; their dogged endurance and marvellous cheerfulness raised them above the misery of their surroundings. The sappers were always ready to lend a hand to the infantry whenever the enemy counter-attacked, and when the shelling became too severe for any work to be done, they gave invaluable aid by manning the trenches on the flanks of the infantry. More effective artillery support was now available for the harassed brigade. At 10.30 A.M. No. 7 Mountain Battery R.G.A. came into action near Fosse 8 and engaged targets near the Railway and Les Briques; while the whole of the 52nd Brigade R.F.A. and one Howitzer battery under the command of Lieut.-Colonel Perreaux, were in action south-west of the Dump by 4.30 P.M.

When darkness fell on the field of battle, the

E

situation of the Division was as follows: Though the 28th Brigade had been bloodily repulsed, the 26th had captured and was holding the Dump and Fosse 8. The bulk of the brigade held a line east of the Fosse, and this line was extended to the south by the 27th Brigade, which held Fosse Alley and was in touch with the Seventh Division on the right. The task now before the Division was to convert the captured trenches into strong defensive positions and to link them up with our original front line. But the enemy was bent on preventing any work being done, and the difficulties were enormous, owing partly to scarcity of tools and material, and partly to the downpour of shells. In spite of these drawbacks and the constant counter-attacks that frequently interrupted digging, the trenches were considerably strengthened and were protected by wire placed 50 yards in front of them by the sappers and the infantry. Equally emulous in toil and heroism were the pioneers of "B" Coy. 9th Seaforth Highlanders, who laboured hard to complete the two communication trenches from the front line to the Hohenzollern Redoubt. This task was not finished until the forenoon of the 26th, for the men had frequently to drop their tools and drive back bombing parties of Germans who were working up Little Willie. The achievement of the 9th Seaforths was a shining example of pluck and endurance, and they were as notable for their fighting as for the value and quality of their work.

Counter-attack is the soul of defence, and it was clear that the Germans were preparing to make a big effort to regain Fosse 8 and the Dump. The issue of the battle hung on the fate of these two places, and all that could be done was done to strengthen our hold on them. But the enemy knew the whole ground

thoroughly and having no longer fear of attack farther
north, could draw largely on his reserves to make a
strong thrust.   The defenders were weary and
exhausted, and the Corps decided to relieve the 26th
Brigade by fresh troops from the 73rd Brigade of the
Twenty-fourth Division.

Accordingly in the evening of the 25th the leading
troops of the 73rd Brigade, under their own brigadier
who received his orders from General Thesiger, arrived
in the neighbourhood of the Fosse.   The relief was
carried out like any ordinary one, and the defence of
the Fosse was taken over by three battalions.   The
Sussex Regiment held from the junction of Slag and
Fosse Alleys to the north end of the Fosse, and this
line was continued by the Royal Fusiliers, who held
from the left of the Sussex Regiment through the
Corons.   The Northamptons, whose task it was to
protect the left flank, held a line from the north end
of the Fosse along Corons Alley and thence down the
North Face of the Redoubt.   The relief was a lengthy
business, owing partly to the guides being uncertain of
their position in the dark, and partly to the fact that
this was the first acquaintance of the 73rd Brigade with
trenches, and it was not till the early hours of the
26th that the last men of the Highland Brigade
were relieved.   Just after the Sussex Regiment had
taken over the trenches from the Seaforths and Black
Watch, the enemy made a strong counter-attack and
gained a footing in the line, but on learning what had
happened, the Highlanders at once turned back and
delivering a resolute bayonet charge drove the enemy
out.   After being relieved, the remnants of the 26th
Brigade returned to our original front line trenches,
where they were reorganised.   The six batteries of
R.F.A., which, under Lieut.-Colonel Perreaux had

rendered invaluable support to the 26th Brigade, were
withdrawn during the night, as their exposed position,
when daylight came, would have meant annihilation.

The difficulty of defending the Fosse was
increased by the withdrawal of the 27th Brigade
during the evening. It is fairly certain that the
brigade could not have been in close touch[1] with
the Seventh Division, for the Germans, making good
use of their knowledge of the ground, penetrated
during the night between the Ninth and Seventh
Divisions and attacked and captured the Quarries
from the rear. To the Seventh Division this attack
came as a complete surprise, and amongst the prisoners
was Brig.-General Bruce, while Captain Buchan, his
brigade major, was killed. This untoward event
exposed the right flank of the garrison in Fosse Alley,
and enemy bombers, forcing their way up the trench
from the south, compelled the 27th Brigade, now
commanded by Lieut.-Colonel Loch, to withdraw to
its original front line trenches.

The task entrusted to the 73rd Brigade was one
of great responsibility. For seasoned troops, the holding of the Fosse was not a very difficult matter. It
commanded a field of fire for at least 500 yards, and
there were not many trenches to block against enemy
bombers. But the 73rd was composed of raw troops—
they had recently arrived from England, and, moreover,
they were exhausted by their long march from near
St Omer. The enemy's pressure was maintained
chiefly by means of bombing attacks, but none of

---

[1] There is a good deal of obscurity as to what actually happened, but
as the front of the Quarries had been wired by the sappers of the Seventh
Division, and as troops of the Seventh Division were still holding out in
the east of the Quarries when the western portions were in the hands of
the enemy, it is certain that the Germans could have effected a lodgment
only from the rear.

the men of the 73rd Brigade had ever thrown a bomb; few knew how to use one, and all felt an exaggerated respect for a weapon about which they knew so little. Moreover, they carried only 120 rounds of ammunition per man, and they were short of food, water, and tools. These deficiencies could not readily be repaired, for it was hazardous and difficult to carry up supplies to those in the front line through the shell-swept zone between the Hohenzollern Redoubt and the Fosse. The most urgent task of the brigade was to protect the right flank of the Fosse, and two companies of the Middlesex Regiment were sent to hold Big Willie and Slag Alley.

At 6 o'clock on the morning of the 26th all three brigades of the Division were in our original front line trenches, and Fosse 8 and the Hohenzollern Redoubt were garrisoned by the 73rd Brigade. During the night our artillery maintained a constant fire on Madagascar and Les Briques Trenches, and on Cemetery Alley and Pekin Alley, and efforts were made to strengthen the defences of Fosse 8, and open up communications. The 63rd R.E. with great difficulty dug a trench from the front of the left brigade to the corner of Little Willie; it was completed by the 27th, and was held by bombers of the H.L.I.

The chief cause of anxiety to General Thesiger was the gap between the 73rd Brigade and the Seventh Division. At 9.45 A.M., therefore, he ordered the 27th Brigade to reoccupy and hold Dump Trench, and this was done in the afternoon of the 26th. As our command of the right flank, however, was threatened by the Germans occupying the Quarries, it was decided to drive them out. The Seventh Division was to assault the Quarries, and the 6th Royal Scots Fusiliers, who were placed

under the orders of the 73rd Brigade for the purpose,
were to co-operate by bombing down Fosse Alley.
This operation was eventually arranged for 4.30 P.M.
Meantime, the 73rd had been severely punished, but
though it became slightly unsteady under the cease-
less shell-fire, it clung to its position during the whole
of the 26th.

Our attack on the Quarries was repulsed, the
Seventh Division gaining only a foothold in the
south-east corner.   The 6th Royal Scots Fusiliers
made their way along Fosse Alley without opposition,
but it was too risky to press on until the Seventh
Division had captured the Quarries.   Another attack
was ordered by the Corps, when the Ninth Division
was to secure Fosse Alley and join up with the Seventh
Division at the Quarries.   The operation, which was
carried out at 2.30 A.M. on the 27th, was unsuccessful,
for although the Royal Scots Fusiliers, supported by
the Argylls in Fosse Alley, reached Point 45, the
Seventh Division failed to overcome the resistance of
the Germans in the Quarries.

The unsteadiness of the 73rd Brigade on the
afternoon of the 26th was a source of great uneasiness
to General Thesiger and his staff, and at 5.30 A.M. he
moved up to the Fosse to ascertain the exact state of
affairs.   Early in the morning some of the defenders
of the Fosse began to retire, and a telephone message
from the 26th Brigade, received at 6.15 A.M., stated that
a few men of the 73rd were leaving their positions, and
that support was urgently required.   The ordeal had
been too severe for untried troops.   During the 26th
they had held the Fosse against many attacks, but the
constant storm of shot and shell to which they were
exposed, and the general misery of their surroundings,
aggravated by the thick drizzle of a grey September

MAJOR-GENERAL G. H. THESIGER, C.B., C.M.G.

[Face page 52.

dawn, weakened their power of defence.[1] Before the German attacks they gave way, and for a time it seemed that the Hohenzollern Redoubt would be lost as well as the Fosse. It was here that the gallant General Thesiger, who had gone forward to reconnoitre the position in person, was killed. He belonged to a well-known military family, and, though his career with the Ninth had been brief, he had proved himself a sterling and able commander, and his death at the crisis of the battle was a serious calamity.

The situation was saved by men of the 26th Brigade; 70 of the Black Watch and 30 Camerons were sent up to the Redoubt about 10 A.M. This party rallied the remaining defenders, and checked the German advance after stubborn and prolonged bombing fights. The enemy made strenuous efforts to reach the Redoubt from Little Willie, and heavy bombing went on there all day. For his heroic bravery in one of these encounters, Corporal James Dalgleish Pollock of the Camerons was awarded the V.C. When the enemy bombers in superior numbers were storming a way into the Redoubt from Little Willie, Corporal Pollock jumped out of the trench, and, bombing the Germans from above, forced them to retreat. For an hour he maintained his position though exposed to a hail of bullets, and did not retire until he had been severely wounded.

Reserves were at once sent up to meet the danger, and the divisional mounted troops were placed under Brig.-General Ritchie. At the same time, the artillery shelled Madagascar Trench, Mad Point, Cemetery Alley, and Lone Farm. A brigade of the Twenty-

---

[1] The gallant record of the Twenty-fourth Division in the war after the Battle of Loos is a sufficient proof, if any were needed, that the failure of the 73rd Brigade at Loos was entirely due to inexperience.

eighth Division was ordered by the Corps to relieve the
73rd Brigade, which the Corps still believed to be in
possession of the Fosse.   Small parties of the 73rd
held their positions in the Fosse up to noon ; but, long
before that hour, the enemy had penetrated the
defences, and was even attacking the Redoubt.

On the right of the Division the 27th Brigade
maintained its position in Fosse Alley for a considerable
time, and at 5 A.M. an attempt of the enemy to rush
the trench was easily repulsed by rifle and machine-gun
fire.   The weak point of the line was on the extreme
right, where it was exposed to a flank attack by the
Germans from the Quarries and Cité St Elie.   From
9 A.M. the Royal Scots Fusiliers were engaged in a
continuous and furious bomb fight, and supplies of
bombs were passed to them as quickly as they could
be brought from the dumps.   On the left the Argylls
sent up a machine-gun[1] to support the Sussex Regiment
of the 73rd Brigade.   When the 73rd withdrew from
the Fosse, the position of the garrison in Fosse Alley
became hopeless.   The Argylls and the Fusiliers were
now attacked not only from the flanks but from the
rear, and it was imperative for them to withdraw before
they were surrounded.   It was a model retirement.
The men never wavered or showed any inclination
to retreat until ordered to do so, and their well-directed
rapid fire inflicted numerous casualties on the enemy.
Under a devastating hail of bullets they faced about to
stem the hostile advances on the word of command.
Closely followed by the Germans, the Argylls and the
Scots Fusiliers withdrew to Dump Trench, which their
pursuers did not venture to attack.   The operation
reflected the greatest credit on all concerned.   After

---

[1] The machine-gun team never yielded a yard ; the gun was destroyed
by shell-fire, and all the members of the team were killed or wounded.

Dump Trench was reached, many of the men went back to bring in their comrades who had been wounded. Lieut.-Colonel Mackenzie of the Argylls was hit during the retreat, and Private M'Fadyen with great gallantry went out and brought him in, though previously several men had been wounded in the same attempt.

When the Corps was informed of the loss of Fosse 8, it ordered the 85th Brigade (Twenty-eighth Division) to advance immediately and counter-attack across the open. But this brigade was delayed while coming up, and at 3 P.M. the 26th was ordered to counter-attack the Fosse at once. All the troops of the brigade had been continuously engaged, and most of the men were leg-weary and tired out by the exertions of the last two days. Its total strength now mustered less than 600 bayonets, and there were few officers left. Nevertheless a very gallant charge was made over ground pitted by bullets and shrapnel; the men reached the West Face of the Hohenzollern Redoubt, but beyond this they could make no further progress. From Mad Point and Madagascar Trench the approaches to Fosse 8 were swept by rifle and machine-gun fire under which no man could move and live; and the enemy's artillery, posted near Auchy, drenched the Redoubt with shrapnel. But although the Highlanders failed to capture Fosse 8, their arrival saved the Hohenzollern, and put new spirit into the officers and men of the 73rd Brigade. The onslaughts of the enemy against the Redoubt were definitely checked, and he was driven back to Fosse 8.

By 8 P.M. the 85th Brigade had arrived. One battalion was in Big Willie, two companies held the West Face of Hohenzollern, one battalion was moving up Central Boyau on Little Willie, and one was still at Vermelles. The remnants of the 26th Brigade and

some of the 27th were holding Hohenzollern with part
of the 73rd. Portions of the 27th were also in Dump
Trench and our original front line. The enemy's bombardment was still intense, and to avoid casualties it
was decided to withdraw the 73rd Brigade and the
26th and 27th Brigades of the Ninth Division. At
midnight, therefore, the 26th went back to the old
reserve trenches, and the 27th to its old assembly
positions; on the 28th both brigades were drawn back
to the neighbourhood of Bethune. The 28th Brigade,
which ever since the 25th September had been engaged
in clearing trenches and burying the dead, was not
relieved until the 29th, on which date it joined the
rest of the Division at Bethune. The artillery, which
remained in the line covering the Twenty-eighth Division
until its own artillery arrived, were relieved on the 1st
October. Brig.-General Armitage received a letter
from Major - General Bulfin thanking him for the
efficient support of his batteries.

The active part of the Division in the battle ended
on the 27th September. No battle of the war has
excited so much controversy as Loos; it has been
claimed as a victory and deplored as a defeat. Defeat
means not merely the loss of or the failure to secure
definite tactical and strategical gains, but also, and
chiefly, the decline of the men's moral. This was
emphatically not the case with the men of the Ninth
Division. Even the bald narratives of the action as
described in the battalion diaries reveal a note of
triumph. The moral of the troops of the 28th Brigade,
even after disaster, remained unshaken, and many men
of the H.L.I. joined in with the Camerons at the Fosse.
The capture of the Dump and Fosse 8 by the Highland
Brigade will rank as one of the finest feats of arms ever
performed by the Division, and the glorious counter-

attack on the 27th September was the best evidence that up to the end of the battle the Highlanders never lost heart.   If the work of the 27th Brigade was less conspicuous, its several battalions had fought with great courage and tenacity, and the defence of Fosse Alley by the Argylls and the Scots Fusiliers, besides taking heavy toll of the enemy, prevented him from using his full strength in an attack on the Redoubt.   When the Division was withdrawn from the conflict it had solidly established its reputation as a first-rate fighting division. From the men's point of view the main thing achieved was that they had measured themselves against the Germans at their best and had proved themselves the better men, and this was perhaps the chief result of the battle for the New Armies.   In future actions, the men always entered into the fray with the consciousness of superiority that is the fundamental basis of moral. At the same time, it would be idle to deny that the resistance of the enemy had shown both gallantry and resource, and the small number of prisoners [1] taken was a sufficient indication that the foe's courage had not been shaken by the preliminary bombardment.   The losses of the Germans on the first day were probably less than ours, as their front defences were held chiefly by machine-guns, and most of their field-guns [2] had been withdrawn in time.   Their counter-attack was admirably organised and was carried out with skill and determination, though it was during this phase of the battle that they suffered their most serious losses.

The general feeling of the Division, however, was that if there had been more artillery to support it, and

---

[1] Five officers and 168 other ranks were captured by the Division.

[2] Two German guns were left near the cottages at the Fosse. After dark on the 26th B/50 Battery took two limbers up to the cottages and brought back one of the guns ; the other could not be found.

better arrangements to reinforce it or relieve it with
fresh troops, a heavy disaster would have been inflicted
on the enemy. Under the circumstances, it had accomplished as much as was possible. When the Second
Division, which could not have been expected to get
forward without the aid of gas, was paralysed by the
failure of the gas, the attainment of all the Ninth's
objectives became impossible. Auchy on the left
bristled with machine-guns, housed numerous batteries,
and was a position of such commanding strength that
any attempt to advance far beyond the Fosse became
a forlorn hope. How formidable the obstacles were
may best be judged by the inability later of such
divisions as the Twenty-eighth, Guards, and Forty-sixth
to make any impression on the hostile defences.

It was the first action of the Division and it was
inevitable that mistakes should be made, but most of
them were venial. Not enough consideration had
been given to the necessity of guarding the rifles
against bad weather, and the Bethune bomb was useless in damp. It also proved a misfortune to allot
a complete company of the R.E. to each brigade;
owing to the failure of the attack on the left, the
63rd Field Coy. R.E. had no definite task to carry
through, and it was impossible to withdraw it, as
it had become involved in the fighting. The trench
mortar teams attached to the 26th Brigade had a sorry
time. The team of the 2-inch mortars were all knocked
out, and though two 1½-inch mortars reached Fosse 8
they could find no targets, and the two officers in
command were killed. These mortars were too unwieldy to carry forward, and as matters turned out,
it would have been better if they had been used
on the left to mask the fire from the Railway Work
with smoke-bombs. It is possible that if this had

been done, the assault of the 28th Brigade would have succeeded.

Perhaps the most deplorable feature of the battle was the comparative breakdown of the medical arrangements for the evacuation of the wounded from the forward areas. Many of them lay out not for hours but for days, and not a few shocking and pathetic sights were to be seen between Hohenzollern and Pekin Trench. This was entirely due to lack of staff. Doctors and regimental stretcher-bearers worked with the greatest heroism to bring in the wounded, but they were too few, and many of them were shot down. In a big engagement, especially in trench warfare, the staff of stretcher-bearers should be enormously increased if the wounded are to be expeditiously and satisfactorily evacuated. The importance of this cannot be over-estimated, because nothing so depresses a man as the fear that if injured he will be left out to die. The memory of such scenes as were too common at Loos lingered with the survivors, and remained after other impressions had become faint.

Most of the battle arrangements were beyond the control of the Division. The use of gas on its front did more harm than good, and there is no evidence to show that it affected the enemy in the least. One of the results of Loos was to give "smoke" a bad name, since in several cases it had caused a serious loss of direction. This, however, was not the case with the Ninth Division. The only complaint of the 26th Brigade was that the wind was hardly strong enough to carry the smoke ahead It formed an effective screen for the infantry, and, in the opinion of the Seaforths, it saved them many casualties.

Strategically and tactically the results of the battle were disappointing. The Germans received a severe fright, but their system of defence, based on mutually supporting strong points garrisoned mainly by machine-gun crews, answered its purpose by delaying our advance sufficiently long to enable them to bring up reserves with which they counter-attacked our troops weary and spent through the strain of battle. These counter-attacks did not deprive us of all our gains, but the vexatious effects of our failure to keep Fosse 8 and the Dump soon became manifest; for the Loos salient, which had been won in the south, could not be held easily or economically, since from these points the enemy commanded the only valley where we could establish satisfactory artillery positions to support the front line. The employment of new divisions that had not been given an opportunity of completing their training by a spell of trench warfare was unfair to the men, and indicated unsound judgment on the part of the Higher Command. But, indeed, the operation was on a scale too big for the resources at the disposal of the British Field-Marshal.

The battle, however, takes rank as one of the most important of the war. The lessons deduced from it laid down the lines upon which British tactics and strategy were based until the end of 1917. Unbalanced optimism gave place to calculated—perhaps exaggerated—caution; an immediate break through was given up as impracticable, and the British forces sought to wear down the enemy and to achieve victory largely by weight of numbers and artillery.

CHAPTER IV

THE SALIENT AND "PLUG STREET"

OCTOBER 1915 TO MAY 1916

IT was a sadly battered Division that concentrated near Bethune.   Caked in mud, unshaven, and unkempt, with tunics tattered and filthy after three days of continuous exposure, the men showed none of the "spick and span" appearance that it is the pride and custom of the British soldier to present.   But they were in high spirits and full of confidence, and their exploits were rewarded with a flattering message [1] from General Gough, the Commander of the I. Corps.   The losses [2] of the Division had been exception- ally heavy, and most serious were the casualties amongst the senior officers.   The divisional commander had been killed, and out of the 12 infantry C.Os. only 4 remained ; grave losses also occurred amongst majors

[1] "On leaving the I. Corps, the G.O.C. wishes to tell the Ninth Division that he thinks their conduct in the assault on the German lines was beyond all praise, and no words can express the value of their gallantry and self-sacrifice to our country.

"They showed during the heavy fighting not only great dash and courage, but endurance and discipline, and the highest qualities of a soldier.

"He can only wish them the best of all fortune in their future efforts, and he is sure that they will maintain the high standard as soldiers and men that they have already reached."—(Order from I. Corps, dated 30th September 1915.)

[2] See Appendix IV.

61

and captains.[1] There is no factor more useful in the difficult task of reorganisation than the experienced control of senior officers ; but this work in most of the battalions had to be undertaken by second lieutenants with little experience, and no automatic knowledge of how things should be done.

The Division was most fortunate in its new Commander. Major-General W. T. Furse, C.B., D.S.O., was an officer of proved ability, energy, and imagination. Under his vigorous direction reorganisation was rapidly completed, and deficiencies in stores and equipment were made up. He thoroughly understood that a division was a unit and not a mere congeries of battalions, batteries, and field companies, and he realised that the battle from which the Ninth had recently emerged offered a grand opportunity for fostering and stimulating *esprit de corps.* " The Ninth (Scottish) Division " soon became a name in which every soldier in it took an intense and jealous pride ; each man believed that he belonged to the best unit in the best division in the best army in the world. Such a spirit is not to be despised ; it inspires a corporate heroism that is greater than the bravery of any individual, and even the meanest is roused to triumph over his natural timidity rather than allow the glory of his division to be tarnished. No man took a more conspicuous part in building up and encouraging this spirit than General Furse.

For most of the battalions new leaders had to be

---

[1]   *Killed and Wounded* (exclusive of subalterns).

6th K.O.S.B.	. . . lost 9	9th Scottish Rifles	.	. lost 6
8th Black Watch	. „ 8	11th Royal Scots	.	. „ 4
7th Seaforth Highlanders .	„ 8	10th H.L.I. . .	.	. „ 4
8th Gordon Highlanders .	„ 8	11th „ . .	.	. „ 4
6th Royal Scots Fusiliers .	„ 8	12th Royal Scots	.	. „ 3
5th Cameron Highlanders .	„ 7	10th A. & S. H. .	.	. „ 3

LIEUT.-GENERAL SIR W. T. FURSE, K.C.B., D.S.O.

[*Face page 62.*

found. The only C.Os. who remained with the Division were Lieut.-Colonel Cameron of Lochiel of the Camerons, Lieut.-Colonel Loch of the 12th Royal Scots, Lieut.-Colonel Northey of the 9th Scottish Rifles, and Lieut.-Colonel Fergusson of the 11th H.L.I. During the next few months the following Commanders were appointed—

26TH BRIGADE.

8th Black Watch—

Lieut.-Colonel G. B. Duff of the Camerons, from the end of December 1915 to March 1916.

Major Sir George Abercromby, from March 1916 to April 1916.

Lieut.-Colonel G. W. E. Gordon, from 9th April to 20th September 1916.

7th Seaforth Highlanders—

Major C. P. M. Burn, from 5th October to 16th December 1915.

Lieut.-Colonel F. J. Marshall, from 16th December 1915 to 15th April 1916.

Lieut.-Colonel J. Kennedy, D.S.O., from 2nd May to 5th August 1916.

8th Gordon Highlanders—

Lieut.-Colonel A. D. Greenhill-Gardyne, from 27th October 1915 to March 1916.

27TH BRIGADE.

Brig.-General W. H. Walshe, to 17th March 1916.

Brig.-General G. F. Trotter, C.M.G., D.S.O., M.V.O., to May 1916.

11th Royal Scots—

Lieut.-Colonel W. D. Croft, from 4th December 1915.

6th Royal Scots Fusiliers—

Major J. H. Dutton, D.S.O., to 8th January 1916.

Lieut.-Colonel The Right Hon. Winston Churchill, to May 1916.

10th Argyll and Sutherland Highlanders—

Lieut.-Colonel H. Pelham Burn, D.S.O., from 10th December 1915 to April 1916.

F

28TH BRIGADE.

6th King's Own Scottish Borderers—
  Lieut.-Colonel J. C. W. Connell, D.S.O., from 4th December 1915.

10th Highland Light Infantry—
  Lieut.-Colonel H. C. Stuart, D.S.O., to 6th January 1916.
  Lieut.-Colonel Grahame, D.S.O., from 6th January 1916.

11th Highland Light Infantry—
  Lieut.-Colonel R. F. Forbes, January to May 1916.

In the Sappers, Lieut.-Colonel Livingstone had been wounded, and the new C.R.E. was Lieut.-Colonel Carpenter.

The Division had barely time to scrape off the mud before it was ordered on the 29th September to proceed north to join the V. Corps in the Salient.[1] The move was carried through partly by route march and partly by rail. On the 3rd October, D.H.Q. were established at Hooggraaf, about two miles south of Poperinghe, and on the morning of the 5th the 26th and 27th Brigades relieved the Seventeenth Division in the trenches near Hill 60. The line taken over by the Ninth lay south of Zillebeke, and extended from north of Hill 60 to a point south of the Ypres–Comines Canal near Oosthoek. The enemy's line ran along the higher ground, and the distance between the British and the German trenches varied from 25 to 400 yards. The salient feature on our front was The Bluff, which rose steeply from the ground on the north side of the Canal and completely dominated the sector.

During the three months that the Division remained in the salient it passed a time of almost unmitigated

[1] There were many salients in the British line, but "The Salient" was Ypres.

gloom and discomfort.   As the days shortened and
winter came on, hardly a day passed without rain, and
mud was lord and sovereign over all.   It seemed to
suck away a man's vitality and enthusiasm, and even
a short march involved an expenditure of physical
energy out of all proportion to the distance traversed.
The whole of Flanders, engulfed in mud, had the
aspect of an enormous swamp; and the leaden skies,
in a sombre rain - grey monotint, were in harmony
with the drab-coloured earth.   Even the roads were
ankle-deep in glutinous mud, and the constant traffic
was often checked by stoppages caused by particularly
bad parts.   Thus the passage of the infantry to and
from the trenches was like a feverish nightmare; for
the men had to march about ten miles through clinging
mire along roads choked with transport, and often
shelled.   The rest huts at Dickebusch and Canada Huts
were dismal and repellent shelters; they were swept
by draughts, and through their leaky roofs the rain
dripped down on the disconsolate inmates.   The area
round them was one vast sea of mud, where it was
impossible for a unit to carry out any training worth the
name.   Without constant training there is a tendency
for discipline to be relaxed, and a man who is allowed
to loll about as he pleases is apt to lose all smartness
in himself and pride in his unit.   As far as possible,
everything was done to maintain strict discipline, and
the A. & Q. department worked its hardest to secure
baths for the men and clean changes of clothing, but
in spite of this the rest huts were more demoralising
than the front line, where the strictest trench discipline was upheld and where there was constant work
to do.

This period was notable as the reign of the second
lieutenant.   For over a month every company in the

26th Brigade was commanded by one; and this was the case with most of the other battalions. At first this undoubtedly rendered the task of General Furse more difficult, since youth and gallantry do not form a complete substitute for knowledge and experience; but the apprenticeship and training in responsibility, which these months brought to the young officers, supplied him with a large body of keen, confident, and efficient leaders who were later to demonstrate their value at the Battle of the Somme.

The divisional commander was quick to make the most of his opportunities, and he resolved to fortify youth and keenness with knowledge and practice. On the 7th November he opened the Ninth Division School at Poperinghe, which served a double purpose in promoting training and in encouraging *esprit de corps*. By this means not only did the officers gain a real knowledge of their manifold duties, which it was impossible for them to acquire amongst the swamps at Dickebusch and Canada Huts, but also the company officers of one unit were brought into contact with those of other units, and thus mutual understanding and sympathy were created. The first commandant of the school was Lieut.-Colonel Loch who was assisted by Captain Drew, the adjutant of the 5th Camerons, and the instruction was both theoretical and practical. It is impossible to over-estimate the value of this school in increasing the efficiency of the Division.

Certainly the safest and in many ways the most desirable place during these winter months was the front line system. A battalion spent four days in the front line trenches, four days in support, and four in rest at Dickebusch or Canada Huts. The support positions had most of the discomfort without any of the safety [1] of the front line; they had little protection and were frequently shelled, many casualties being suffered. The most perilous spot on the route to the front line was Ypres. No man of British blood could walk through it without feeling a deep thrill of awe and reverence as he gazed on the ruins of the beautiful town, the name of which will ever be associated with the most heroic and imperishable feat of British valour and endurance. But it was no place to linger in; it formed a nexus of roads, and virtually the whole of the traffic between the trenches and the back areas had to pass through it. Hence it was constantly shelled by the enemy, and any body of men that succeeded in passing through it without loss was extremely fortunate. After the toilsome march, the trenches seemed a veritable haven of refuge. They were in fact partly trenches and partly breastworks; for it was impossible to dig to any depth, since water was quickly reached, and the parapets had to be raised high above the level of the ground to protect the men from enemy bullets. The high parapets made the line unpleasantly conspicuous, for they formed an easy mark for the enemy's trench mortars and artillery, which had numerous posts for observation.

Between October and December the Division was gradually shifted from the south to the east of Zillebeke. The line taken over from the Seventeenth Division was held until the night of the 15th October, when the 27th Brigade on the right was relieved by the 72nd Brigade of the Twenty-fourth Division. On the day preceding the relief the Argylls had a tragic mishap. At 4 A.M. on the 15th the Germans exploded a mine

---

[1] When the front trenches lay near each other, the artillery, in order to avoid hitting their own people, fired generally on the enemy's support and rear trenches

about 25 yards in front of a trench not far from The
Bluff.   The explosion was very violent, and although
the front trenches had been cleared in view of the
known existence of hostile mines on this part of the
line, heavy casualties were suffered in the support
and communication trenches, 15 being killed and 50
wounded.   On the same morning at 1.30 A.M. the
enemy blew a small mine just outside the trenches
held by the Camerons, who had 5 killed and wounded.
During the night of the 16th/17th October the 28th
Brigade took over the part of the line held by the
7th Brigade on the left of the 26th; this brought the
northern limit of the Division to a point just east of
Armagh Wood.   A further rearrangement took place
on the nights of the 8th/9th and 9th/10th November
when the 27th Brigade took over the front line trenches
east of Sanctuary Wood, which at that time still presented the appearance of a wood and was full of thick
undergrowth.

These alterations brought changes in position
without any in conditions, for all along the front the
trenches were in a very bad state and could be maintained in tolerable order only by constant labour.   After
a shower of rain (and it always seemed to rain in
the salient), there was the common story of dug-outs
collapsed and parapets fallen in.   At the best of times
the trenches were ankle-deep in water; pumps were
used, but they effected only a temporary improvement,
because there was no place to which the water could be
drained.   Long thigh gum-boots were issued to the
men, and these helped to keep their feet dry, though
they could not make them warm.   In spite of whale-oil
and anti-frostbite grease, it is not surprising that many
were evacuated to hospital suffering from trench feet.
Want of sleep, perpetual cold, filth, and wet were the

ordinary features of life ; notwithstanding the coats of goatskin that were issued it was impossible for the men to keep warm.   During a man's short spell of sleep his feet became numb, and he was forced to get out of his shelter and stamp in order to restore circulation ; and when he was awake he had to squelch about continually in mud, which plastered everything up to his head.

The sappers and pioneers did their utmost to improve matters, but as regards getting rid of the water their efforts were as the labours of Sisyphus. They revetted the trenches, made dug-outs, improved and kept in repair a light railway, which was used for bringing up rations and engineering materials, but more could have been done if the infantry had co-operated whole-heartedly with the sappers.   The latter were a comparatively small body of skilled men, and they were supplied with working parties from the infantry. The infantryman, however, believed that he was doing not his own job but the sapper's, and he did as little as possible unless there was someone standing over him.   This was the attitude not merely of N.C.Os. and privates, but of many officers, and in this respect there was a striking contrast to the German Army, where the private was taught to realise that in working under a sapper he was working for himself.   It would have been well if the British soldier had been taught the same lesson from the beginning of his training.   As it was, the work accomplished by an infantry party depended largely upon the infantry officer who was in charge of it, and too often he considered it the proper thing to let his men do as little as possible.

The position held by the Division from near The Bluff north of the Canal to Sanctuary Wood was about 5000 yards in length, which was a long line for a

weak[1] division to hold. Most of the units were
still far below strength, and when parties left the
front line to bring up rations, the trenches appeared
deserted. The line was commanded by the enemy
along the entire front, and, lying in a salient, it was
shelled from all sides. Any movement east of Ypres
was impossible except after dark, and one dared not
show a head in Zillebeke during the day. At some
points the lines were so close that they could not
be safely shelled except by trench mortars. At one
part on the front of the 27th Brigade, where the
trenches were only about 20 yards apart, the enemy
occupied a position known as the "Birdcage." It
was a wooden framework with wire netting and a
trap-door in the top. Whenever he was peevish, he
opened the trap-door and heaved out a bomb, shutting
the door after him. This contrivance was hit by a
trench mortar on the 23rd November, but the Germans
at once repaired it; however, it was blown to atoms
five days later by a mine. The enemy had more guns
and more ammunition, but a resolute effort was made
by General Furse to dispute his artillery superiority
by means of a "Retaliation Tariff."[2] Whenever the
enemy bombarded a part of our lines he was subjected
to a bombardment of greater severity; this encouraged
the infantry and stimulated the gunners, but failed to
silence the Germans. Occasional bombardments also
took place at such times as the enemy was suspected
to be involved in a relief.

Even more than the shelling the men disliked the
constant mining that was being carried on along the

[1] That is, in numbers.
[2] For each trench mortar bomb . . 1 salvo of 18-pounder H.E.
    „ enemy torpedo . . . 2 salvos „ „
        and 2 4·5-inch howitzers.
    „ enemy 5·9 shell . . . 1 8-inch shell.

front. In this, as in artillery, the Germans were the masters, though our tunnellers, with a view to cheering the infantry, declared that they controlled the situation. Except for the Argylls no serious casualties were suffered from mining, but the men in the front system of trenches lived in a constant state of suspense. This was reflected in the reports of sentries, and never a day passed without some one saying that he heard "subterranean noises, probably enemy mining."[1] Undoubtedly our miners had an anxious and harassing time. On the night of the 30th November, having heard noises, they sent out a listening post, which came upon some mine cases and broke into a hostile gallery. The tunnelling subaltern and one of his corporals entered it, and though they met some Germans succeeded in firing a charge and destroying the gallery.

Under the most dismal and depressing conditions the work of the A.S.C. and transport was beyond all praise. This was probably the most trying period in the whole war for them, yet in spite of casualties and delays caused by mud and bad roads, they never failed to deliver the rations. Every night they had to run the gauntlet through Ypres, fully conscious that a torrent of shells might descend upon them at any moment. The wear and tear on wagons and limbers was enormous, and numerous losses were suffered both in personnel and horses. Throughout the winter the excellence and regularity of the rations did more than anything to keep the men in good heart.

[1] Noises, alleged to be German mining on the Corps' front, were actually traced to (a) revetting, (b) sentries stamping their feet, (c) rats burrowing on the parapet, (d) a loose beam or branch blown by the wind, (e) running water, (f) the beat of a man's own heart, (g) a half-dead fly buzzing at the bottom of a hole (this was taken for a machine drill), and (h) actual mining.

Before the Division was relieved from the salient an important change was made throughout the whole Army as regards machine-guns. Prior to the war the importance of machine-gun fire had not been realised by our Army, and consequently we neither had enough of them nor knew how to make the best tactical use of those we had. The type employed was the Vickers, of which two, and later four, were issued to each battalion, but the gun was a heavy weapon for infantry to handle, and required a high standard of special training. Since 1915 a new and lighter machine-gun, the Lewis, was being introduced; it was more easily carried, and it was possible for an average man to master it after a fortnight's instruction. Moreover, it was cooled by air and could be fired from a very light mounting; indeed an expert could fire it without any mounting at all. It was an admirable weapon for infantry, and when issued there was no need for battalions to have their own Vickers Guns. In fact the advantage of using the latter under brigade control had been apparent even before the Battle of Loos, and all brigades in the Division had appointed brigade machine-gun officers. At Loos, all the infantry battalions had at least two Lewis Guns and some had four, but on the 30th November the establishment was fixed at four per battalion, that is, one per company. On the same date the Vickers Gun detachments were formed into machine-gun companies, one company being attached to each brigade, and each company consisted of four sections, with two machine-guns per section.[1]

On the 7th December, the welcome news was received that the Ninth was to be relieved by the

---

[1] The machine-gun was reckoned to be equivalent to thirty rifles.

Fiftieth Division before the end of the month. The
tidings were greeted with unfeigned joy. Though
the men had borne the mud and discomfort with
wonderful stoicism, they loathed the salient and were
glad to leave it.[1] It was undoubtedly the worst and
most disagreeable spell of trench life that the Division
experienced during the war. Even after the troops had
been heavily punished in the Battle of the Somme,
many of the men declared that they would rather go
through another such battle than return to the salient
under the conditions that prevailed in the winter of
1915.

The first to leave were the divisional mounted
troops, who departed for the II. Corps' area on
the 12th December. But before the last battalions
were relieved on the 20th, they experienced a new
alarm. Ever since we had entered the salient there
were rumours that the enemy intended to make a gas
attack, and on the 14th December information was
received from the Corps that the Germans were preparing one on the front of the Second Army. Next
day, therefore, the artillery proceeded to pound their
front parapets in case they should have installed
cylinders. During the small hours of the 19th our
whole front was subjected to an exceptionally heavy
bombardment, and it was clear that the long threatened
gas attack was at last being delivered. Clouds of gas
drifted as far back as D.H.Q., but the enemy did not
follow up with an infantry attack, for the artillery
were ready and proceeded to shell the adversary's
trenches without delay. The main enemy effort was

[1] Even under the most damping circumstances the men maintained a
sense of humour. A platoon commander of the 12th Royal Scots on
asking a man, standing in a water-logged trench, how he liked his
surroundings, received the unexpected reply—" Weel, sir, this is no like
Sauchiehall Street."

made to the north of the Division, but in no case did he find the defenders unprepared. As if disappointed at the frustration of his designs, he shelled the whole divisional area with vindictive violence throughout the 19th and the 20th, and several casualties were caused among the outgoing and incoming battalions. On the 20th the whole of the Division was relieved except the artillery, the last of which departed on the 22nd.

From the 20th December 1915 till the 26th January 1916, the Division enjoyed a welcome and needed respite from trench warfare, and General Furse made the most of the time to bring it up to concert-pitch. After a long term in the line, when there are few opportunities for training, a man is inclined to become slack; further, trench life is bad for the feet, and several route marches are necessary to bring the men into good condition. The Division, except the artillery, was now in billets round Merris, where D.H.Q. were established. The land was pleasant and undulating, and was covered with numerous cosy and cheery farms, a striking contrast to the mud flats of Flanders. The artillery were stationed at the Artillery Training Camp at Watten, where they underwent a vigorous course.

Cleanliness was the first essential; excellent baths were available and also clean clothing. Then followed smartening-up drill, and each brigade was inspected in turn by the Corps Commander in route marching. It was now that the Ninth began to reap the fruits of the Divisional School that had been established at Poperinghe. General Furse held frequent conferences with his brigadiers and battalion commanders, in order to ensure that the training should be carried out on useful and uniform lines. A high average standard was aimed at in bombing and in rifle shooting and when the men returned to the line their bearing, efficiency, and moral left little to be desired. Yet the time was not all spent in work, the average amount of training being about five hours per day. Football matches were played daily, and the Divisional Band and the Concert Party—"The Thistles"—provided a welcome entertainment during the evenings. The type of football played was, of course, Association. There was one thrilling Rugby match between the officers of the 28th Brigade and those of the 26th, and a stirring game ended in a draw. It was during this period of rest and training that the Right Hon. Winston Churchill arrived to take over the Command of the 6th Royal Scots Fusiliers at the beginning of January 1916.

On its next visit to the trenches, the Division experienced one of its most enjoyable times in France. On the 24th January 1916, it commenced the relief of the Twenty-fifth Division in the Ploegsteert area, and this was completed by the 31st. D.H.Q were established at Nieppe, but were transferred on the 13th February to Steenwerck on account of shelling. The front trenches lay east of Ploegsteert Wood; they were in comparatively good condition and reliefs could be carried out in daylight. There were excellent billets for the battalions and brigades in reserve, where a considerable amount of training could be carried on. In order that battalions should always occupy the same trenches, and so learn everything about them, the 28th Brigade held always one part of the line, while the 27th and 26th relieved each other in the same trenches. Six days "in" and six days "out" was the rule for each unit.

From the end of January till the end of May 1916, the Ninth held the same line, which was one of the most pleasant areas along the British front. There was constant work to be done, but the results of labour were soon apparent. The trenches were firmly revetted, numerous fire-steps were built, and the communication trenches were kept in good order. In addition, many dug-outs were made and several concrete emplacements for machine-guns constructed, and on leaving the area both sappers and infantry could claim that they had handed over model trenches.

The advent of spring and the peaceful aspect of the cultivated country combined to render everyone cheerful. In this sector the astonishing hardihood of the old French farmers was seen at its best. They used to plough fields almost up to the front line. When shelled, they unharnessed the horses and went back to their farms without accelerating their pace in the slightest, but as soon as the firing ceased, they calmly resumed ploughing as if nothing out of the way had occurred. Ploegsteert Wood itself was a charming spot. As the days lengthened and spring advanced, the wood presented an arcadian appearance. April was a halcyon month. The very huts nestling among the trees, bourgeoning into a beautiful foliage, seemed to fit in with the brightness of their surroundings, and the songs of thousands of birds made one feel at times that the war had ceased to be.

Life was not altogether a picnic, however. The wood itself was intermittently shelled by the enemy, and the trenches were occasionally subjected to heavy bombardments. The worst experience fell to the 11th Royal Scots. Near their trenches the German position protruded in a salient, which was known to our men as the "Birdcage," on account of the tangle of wire with which it was protected. Mining operations were undertaken against this salient, and the infantry

"LAWRENCE FARM"

(From a sketch by the Rt. Hon. Winston S. Churchill of his Battalion Head-quarters)

supplied large working parties for the purpose. But the enemy must have discovered that there was a mine, and he determined to destroy it. On the evening of the 13th May the position held by the Royal Scots was violently shelled and trench mortared, and shortly after, the Germans came over in three parties of 20 each. Some of them succeeded in entering our trenches, but the Royal Scots, though dazed by the severity of the bombardment, put up a splendid resistance. Captain Henry with a small party made an immediate counter-attack, and after a lively scuffle expelled the enemy. The Royal Scots losses, due mainly to the hostile barrage, were 16 killed, 61 wounded, and 8 missing. The Germans, who were the 104th Saxons, left 10 corpses in our trenches, and had failed in their attempt to destroy the mine-shaft.

General Furse strove to foster the offensive spirit throughout the Division, so sections were known as "fighting" sections, to impress upon each man that his principal duty was to fight. He exhorted all the battalions to make "No Man's Land" "Ninth Division Land," and the men did their utmost to carry out his instructions. Every night the area in front of the battalions in the line was actively and persistently patrolled. But this was not enough for the G.O.C.; he wanted the men to secure prisoners; "Corpses are more important than acres" was his constant injunction. Though the raids engineered in this sector were not successful, the experience gained helped later to make it one of the finest raiding divisions in the Army; it was learning to walk, and was learning rapidly. All ranks realised and never forgot that on taking over trenches it was not their job to sit still and wait for things to happen, but to devise enterprises to worry the enemy as much as possible. The Ninth was never happy until it felt that it had established ascendency over the enemy opposite it.

With this intention, a minor operation was undertaken by the "Rifles" on the 1st March. The scheme was carried out at 11 P.M. A small party went out with Bangalore torpedoes,[1] which they placed in the enemy's wire and exploded. Then dummies, which had been fixed in "No Man's Land," were worked by string from the front trenches so as to present the appearance of troops moving forward. At the same time, the enemy's lines were raked by rifle and machine-gun fire, trench mortars and rifle grenades, and by shells from the artillery. Only two casualties were suffered by the "Rifles," and as it was probable that the Germans manned their parapets on hearing the explosion and seeing the dummies moving, it is likely that their losses were much heavier. A more ambitious raiding scheme was attempted by the Argylls on the night of the 25th/26th March. At 1.52 A.M. two Bangalore torpedoes were placed under the enemy's wire, and a party of 2 officers and 30 men left the trenches ready to enter the German line after the explosion had cleared a gap. The torpedoes were fired at 2 A.M., but the raiding party slightly lost direction and missed the gap. The failure was really due to inexperience and insufficient preparations.

If the Division was disappointed with the result of its raids, it had every reason to be pleased with its success in sniping. When it first took over the line, the German snipers held the upper hand. But the sniping officers in each battalion vied with one another

---

[1] The Bangalore torpedo presented the appearance of a drain pipe. It was filled with ammonal and fired with a fuse. It was most effective in clearing a gap in wire, and could be made any size by joining several sections together.

in ingenious devices to gain the advantage over the enemy, and before the Division left the sector our snipers were distinctly on top. In every intelligence report from the front line battalions several hits were claimed by the snipers. It was while in this area that the machine-gun companies commenced the practice of indirect fire.[1] This was carried out nightly, in order to sweep the roads and places which the Germans were likely to use at night. Here, too, air fights came to be of frequent occurrence, and excited the greatest interest among the men. One day a hostile plane received a direct hit through the engine and crashed down in our lines; there cannot have been many occasions during the war when an anti-aircraft gun was so conspicuously successful.

The favourite amusement of the artillery was firing at German observation posts. At Les Ecluses a tall factory chimney that overlooked our lines was the chief target, but for a long time defied our gunners, and the German observers had become so confident that they were seen one morning shaking dust out of a carpet or something of that nature over the top of the stalk. This was very exasperating, but our gunners had the best of it when the observation post was knocked out by the third round of a 12-inch Howitzer, which landed at the base of the chimney.

Hitherto the headgear worn by the men was the Balmoral. It had a touch of the picturesque, but it offered no protection against shrapnel. The steel helmet now made its appearance; it was much heavier, and at first required some knack to balance it properly. For a time the men wore it only on compulsion and preferred to use it as a washing basin

[1] Targets were selected from the map, the guns being sited according to the estimated distance.

G

or a soup bowl, but it became more popular when its manifold advantages in protecting the head, not only from shell splinters but from knocks against overhead traverses and the woodwork of dug-outs, were realised. In the course of a few months a man came to regard the steel helmet as one of his best friends.

A few changes in command took place during this period. Lieut.-Colonel Pelham Burn was transferred to the Gordons, and his place in the Argylls was taken by Lieut.-Colonel W. J. B. Tweedie. Lieut.-Colonel Loch, C.M.G., was promoted to a brigade in the Fifty-sixth Division, and he was succeeded by Lieut.-Colonel H. L. Budge. Lieut.-Colonel Cameron of Lochiel, whose health had broken down, had to give up the command of the Camerons to Lieut.-Colonel Duff. The most important change was in the artillery. On 1st February 1916 Brig.-General H. H. Tudor, C.M.G., succeeded Brig.-General E. H. Armitage, C.B., in the command of the Divisional Artillery. He was destined to influence profoundly the work of the Division by his use of the guns.

In April 1916 three batteries, D/50, D/51, and D/52, were taken away from their own brigades and formed into the 53rd Brigade R.F.A., which was composed entirely of 18-pounders. Thus, in the spring of 1916, the Ninth Divisional Artillery consisted of the 50th, 51st, and 52nd Brigades, each with three 18-pounder batteries and one Howitzer battery, and the 53rd with three 18-pounder batteries. All batteries were on a four-gun basis. About May the Brigade Ammunition Columns of the 50th, 51st, and 52nd Brigades were broken up or absorbed into the Divisional Ammunition Column, so that the reorganised D.A.C. consisted of No. 1, No. 2, and No. 3 sections, and "B" echelon. In addition, the organisation of trench mortars was placed on a more satisfactory basis. The weapon to be used by the infantry was the Stokes Mortar, a mobile and easily managed gun with an ingenious, quick-firing device, which enabled it to fire 30 shells a minute. The shell was a particularly deadly one, and made a most menacing and terrifying sound on explosion. In each brigade, Stokes Mortar Batteries were organised from personnel drawn from each battalion with the purpose—thoroughly attained—of encouraging the entity and *esprit* of the brigade. Heavier mortars than the Stokes were to be worked by the artillery, and on the 8th March 1916 the 9th T.M. Brigade, of three batteries, was formed. Before this date there had been one T.M. Battery, called the 41st T.M.B., manned by men from the R.G.A. and from the Seaforth Pioneers. At first the brigade had three types of mortar, the 1½-inch, 2-inch, and 3.7-inch, but, after a few months, only the 2-inch mortar was used. In April 1916 a heavy mortar, the 9.45-inch, popularly known as " The Flying Pig," was introduced, and the V/9 Heavy Trench Mortar Battery was formed to work it.

The period of rest and training, the comparatively pleasant interlude of trench life, and the resourceful and vigorous control of General Furse all combined to make the whole Division a happy family. Each man in it swore by " The Ninth "; and this was the finest tribute to the efficiency of the G.O.C.'s leadership. It was, therefore, with consternation that the news was received on the 16th March that the brigades were to be reorganised. The inherent clannishness of the Scot revolted at the idea of friends being taken away and of strangers coming in. But the reorganisation was made necessary, not by the malicious indifference of G.H.Q., but by the dearth of recruits. Scotland

had raised more service battalions than it was possible
to find drafts for under the voluntary system, and
it was necessary to amalgamate several of them.
The battalions marked out by G.H.Q. to leave the
Division by the 6th May were the 8th Gordons, the 6th
Royal Scots Fusiliers, and the 10th and 11th H.L.I.
The arrangement also meant the break-up of the
28th Brigade. This was intensely disliked, but it was
recognised as inevitable. The knowledge that these
old friends were leaving to join the famous Fifteenth
Scottish Division helped to reconcile the Ninth to the
change. On the 4th May it was announced that the
mounted troops were also to be withdrawn. To take
the place of the Gordons in the 26th Brigade, the
Argylls were transferred from the 27th; the 6th
K.O.S.B. and the 9th Scottish Rifles replaced the Royal
Scots Fusiliers, and the Argylls in the 27th Brigade.
The South African Brigade had its own Field Ambulance, and the 29th Field Ambulance consequently left
the Division. Brig.-General Scrase-Dickins was retained
by an accident, which deprived the 27th Brigade of
Brig.-General G. F. Trotter who fell from his horse
and broke his arm.

The place of the 28th was filled by the South
African Brigade, most of whose members had already
seen service in Egypt. Nothing much was known
about them in the Division except that they were the
pick of South Africa, and that was saying a great deal.
The brigade was commanded by Brig.-General H. T.
Lukin, C.M.G., D.S.O., and consisted of the 1st, 2nd,
3rd, and 4th South African battalions; the last-named,
being the South African Scottish, wore the kilt of the
Atholl tartan. They were commanded respectively by
Lieut.-Colonel F. G. Dawson, C.M.G., Lieut.-Colonel
W. E. C. Tanner, C.M.G., Lieut.-Colonel E. F.

PLOEGSTEERT WOOD

Thackeray, C.M.G., and Lieut.-Colonel F. A. Jones, C.M.G., D.S.O. Brig.-General Lukin reported at D.H.Q. on the 22nd April, and on the following day the 2nd and 3rd battalions joined the Division. On the 29th the whole brigade was inspected by Sir Douglas Haig, near Steenwerck. Its appearance was very impressive, and even the most fastidious critic was bound to admit that the South Africans were an exceptionally fine body of men. From the 6th May they took over the trenches lately occupied by the 28th Brigade, and the men rapidly became acquainted with the conditions of warfare on the Western Front. From the first it was apparent that their standard of discipline was very high, and their critical Scottish comrades realised that the Division had been greatly honoured in having such a doughty brigade attached to it.

The stay of the Division near Ploegsteert soon drew to a close. On the 20th May instructions were received from the Corps that it was to be relieved by the Forty-first Division before the 1st June. The relief was commenced on the 27th May, and completed on the 30th. Thus ended a most agreeable experience of trench duty, and all who have survived since that date will ever cherish happy recollections of Ploegsteert Wood.

CHAPTER V

THE CAPTURE OF BERNAFAY WOOD, AND THE BATTLES FOR TRONES WOOD

JULY 1916

AFTER leaving the Ploegsteert area the Division was concentrated in billets near Bomy, where D.H.Q. were established. The men were in the best of spirits, and training and recreation were carried on with vigour and keenness, while the glory of the summer and the genial weather raised the usual hopes that the year would see the end of the war. The Division had recaptured all the enthusiasm that had animated it on landing in France, and in addition it had behind it a year's experience of warfare. The sojourn near Bomy was shorter than had been expected, and the design of the G.O.C. to hold a horse show on the 13th and a Divisional Field Day on the 14th June had to be abandoned. This cancellation of the horse show was a huge disappointment; every unit had taken extensive trouble to prove that it had the best turned out transport in the Division, but the men were able at least to console themselves with the knowledge that their transport and horses were in first-rate condition.

Orders were received by the Division on the 11th that it was to join the XIII. Corps,[1] commanded

[1] The XIII. Corps was under the Fourth Army, commanded by General Sir H. Rawlinson, K.C.B.

by Lieut.-General Sir W. H. Congreve, V.C., and that the move was to take place by rail on the 16th. These, however, were followed by instructions commanding the Division to move on the 13th, and on that date the entrainment of units was commenced. Two days later the Division was concentrated near Vaux-en-Amienois where D.H.Q. were established.

It was obvious to the dullest man that the Division was intended to take part in some business more enterprising than the mere holding of a section of trenches. The whole hinterland behind the trenches was a hive of industry and traffic. Swarms of troops from every part of the kingdom were to be seen in every village; at night the roads groaned with the passage of guns of all sizes and of transport carrying every conceivable variety of material, and the whole countryside was covered with dumps containing R.E. material, bombs, shells, and stores of all kinds. Hospitals and aerodromes formed additional villages in the district. The back areas of the Somme in the summer of 1916 were the busiest centres of activity in the whole world. It was a wonderful exhibition of the resources of the British Empire, and a visible proof of the diligence with which workers at home had applied themselves to the manufacture of munitions of war. It was not a feverish bustle that one witnessed, but a steady and systematic application of labour; every movement was directed by an organisation that was not surpassed by any other nation in the war. The whole of the work performed by Britain in its administrative arrangements has probably never been appreciated at its full value. It had a most heartening effect on all who saw it, and gave the men an inspiring confidence in the determination and ability of the Allies to achieve a complete victory.

All this industry and all these preparations were the obvious prelude to a great battle, and on the 15th June the Division received from the Corps instructions for the attack that was to be made. The XIII. Corps was on the right flank of the British army, and its plan was to assault with two divisions, the Thirtieth on the right and the Eighteenth on the left, with the Ninth Division in reserve.

A feeling of optimism buoyed up both civilians and soldiers, though the events of 1915 had completely shattered the sanguine expectations aroused by the victory of the Marne. The Russians had been driven from Poland and had suffered a smashing defeat, from which they never fully recovered, though a censored press had represented the rout rather as a Russian triumph than as a German victory. That disaster, which was falsely believed in this country to harden the purpose of the great Slav Power, caused Russians to interpret the comparative inactivity of the Western Powers as a selfish neglect of her interests, and to detest the Government that had callously thrown into the slaughter men without arms or equipment. The brutal incompetence of the Russian bureaucracy was revealed in all its nakedness, and inspired the loathing and contempt that led eventually to its downfall. The tale of disaster did not end here; for Von Mackensen, assisted by the crafty and calculating treachery of Bulgaria, drove the Serbs from their country and all but secured Greece in the Teutonic net. The Salonica expedition, though it failed to render any service to Serbia, prevented Greece from joining the enemy. In the East, British prestige suffered two damaging shocks; the Dardanelles project ended in failure, and the Mesopotamian expedition, after a promising beginning, resulted in the surrender of a British force at Kut in April 1916.

The only offset against these misfortunes was the entry of Italy into the war in May 1915, but from the first her armies were employed solely on exclusively Italian interests. The offensive against Trieste, even if successful, could not have exerted a decisive influence on the course of the war, nor did it prevent Austria from using the larger portion of her forces in the East against Russia. Nevertheless a general feeling prevailed that our misfortunes had been due more to bad luck than to bad management, and on the principle that the dawn succeeds the darkest hour, 1916 was expected to prove as glorious as 1915 had been disappointing. More men were now in the field, and the supply of high explosives, which some thought to be more important than generalship, had been greatly increased. The poster of the most blatant of British weeklies, with the glaring inscription, "1916. Thank God!" accurately reflected the mind of the average man.

Thus the time seemed ripe for an action by the British forces on a big scale. The great German offensive against Verdun in April had been watched with feverish interest both in this country and in France. The first five days of that assault brought the enemy within measurable distance of his objective. It was feared that the famous fortress would fall into his hands, and hasty critics denounced the supine inactivity of the British armies. But at that time the preparations of Sir Douglas Haig were not completed, and a premature counter-attack would only have served the interests of the enemy. As it turned out, the defenders of Verdun, under the masterly generalship of Pétain, worked out their own salvation. The German thrust was stopped, but even at· the end of June large forces still menaced the fortress, and it was necessary that the British forces, stronger and better prepared than they had ever been, should do something to take the strain off their gallant ally.

Events in other theatres of war seemed also to call for immediate action. The attack by the Austrians in the Trentino in May threatened such serious consequences for Italy, that Russia, which appeared to have recovered from her defeat, was compelled to launch her offensive in the month of June. The brilliant successes of General Brussilov brought immediate relief to the armies of Italy, though they did not lessen the German pressure on Verdun. It was, therefore, sound policy to strike at the enemy, not merely to relieve Verdun, but also to assist our Allies in the other theatres of war by preventing the enemy from transferring troops from the West to other fronts.

The other object of the British Commander-in-Chief[1] was to wear down the strength of the enemy by a steady offensive. The choice of the battlefield was governed by the fact that the British armies were not sufficiently numerous to take the offensive on a large scale without the co-operation of the French, and the district selected was therefore in Picardy, where the two armies joined.

Picardy was one of the most delightful spots in France. Here there were none of the grimy coal-pits and slag-heaps that had figured so prominently in the Battle of Loos. This was the agricultural part of France, with wide open and rolling country, in which there was hardly a fence to be seen. The

[1] Sir Douglas Haig succeeded Sir John French as Commander-in-Chief in December 1915.

numerous small villages that broke the fields seldom contained more than a few hundred inhabitants. On the battle front the prominent feature was the extensive ridge running from Thiepval to Combles, with alternate spurs and valleys thrown out to the south-west. This ridge, which afforded the enemy magnificent observation over the British trenches and hinterland, was the main watershed of the high ground that stretched from the valley of the Somme in a north-easterly direction to the low-lying ground between Lens and Cambrai. Beyond this were the plains of Douai. On the western side the slopes, steep and rugged, were a formidable obstacle, but towards the north-east, the ridge fell in a gradual slope, rising again to a gentle ridge on the farther side of Bapaume. Beyond this second ridge, which was about a hundred feet lower than the main one, the country, broad and undulating, offered no great difficulty to an army that had won its way to it. But stiff fighting would be necessary to reach this, because these ridges formed the buttress that shielded the great railway centres of Cambrai and Douai. A feature of the terrain, especially in the south, was the large number of woods thick with summer foliage and carpeted with a dense undergrowth that made progress, except by means of the small paths running through them, all but impossible. These woods played an important part in the battle.

The main object of Sir Douglas Haig is indicated by his description of the Somme campaign as the "wearing-out battle." It is more commonly referred to as the policy of attrition, and under that name has been subjected to a good deal of criticism. But there is no question that the policy was based upon sound military principles that could not be neglected. The basis of good generalship is to wear down the enemy, force him to absorb his reserves and then smash him with fresh troops, and the Somme was intended to carry out this programme as far as possible.

The method adopted by Sir Douglas Haig to achieve his object was the result of the experience of Loos. On that occasion the Allies had grasped at more than they were able to hold, so it was now decided to carry on the advance by limited stages in order that the infantry, without being unduly exhausted and still within the supporting range of their artillery, would be able without great difficulty to parry the hostile counter-stroke. It was expected that a methodical advance on these lines, always adequately supported by powerful and efficient artillery, would eat into the enemy's strength and at the same time be carried out at a light cost.

"What we have, we hold" might be said to be the keynote of the limited objective method. It was solid and substantial rather than brilliant and inspiring, and it had certain defects which became clear in the course of the battle. It encouraged the infantry to depend so completely upon the artillery, that the tendency of the former was to lack confidence when unassisted by the latter. This led to a decline of initiative, which was further emphasised by the very fact that the objective was limited. Though the troops were exhorted to lose no opportunities of exploiting success, it was only natural for them to consider that they had done all that was wanted when they had accomplished the definite task assigned to them. Undoubtedly many opportunities were lost, as the Germans noted with thankfulness, and places, which we could have had for the mere trouble of walking up to them, fell into our hands later only after desperate and sanguinary fighting.

Moreover, after the first shock, the element of surprise was lost, as the terrain once selected was fixed, and the enemy was able to fathom our plans and arrange his defence accordingly. The periods between the stages of our advance gave him valuable time in which to reorganise his forces and strengthen his fortifications. With the enemy's moral high and his forces well trained and disciplined, the cost of progress was bound in any case to be heavy; but with the limited objective system, it was probably heavier than it would have been under a more flexible and elastic one. It is possible, too, that the method of proceeding by slow stages caused us to miss the chance of dealing a paralysing blow.

Prudence is a virtue in military matters as in other things, but excess of prudence is not without danger, especially in the case of coalitions. The exaggerated caution of Marshal Daun in the Seven Years' War is both an example and a warning. If at that time the continuance of the Austrian coalition could have been guaranteed, Daun's tactics would have led to the humiliation and probable dismemberment of Prussia; but before they had time to work their effect the defection of Russia ruined all the hopes of Austria. The general tendency is for coalitions to be weakened rather than strengthened by time, and this should be taken into consideration even in military affairs.

It can easily be seen that the task of Sir Douglas Haig was not a light one, and two substantial reasons weighed him strongly to the side of caution; he was conscious that his margin of numerical superiority[1] was small, and he had a suspicion[2] that his armies had not

---

[1] In July 1916 the strength of the British Army in France was 660,000. Despatches, p. 19.

[2] Despatches, p. 19, para. 2, line 5.

yet developed the efficiency essential for the carrying out of a campaign with far distant objectives.

On the eve of the battle the attitude of the Germans was one of assured confidence. From the high ground they occupied to the south of Arras they could not fail to detect the signs of an imminent offensive, and though the preliminary bombardment, which commenced on the 25th June, was supplemented by artillery demonstrations at Ypres and Arras, they had realised that the great attack would take place in the Somme, and in this district their defences were the strongest on the whole battle front. For eighteen months there had been no operation of any magnitude in the sector, and the enemy was given time to make his defences as perfect as they could be made. The front line trenches were protected with broad belts of wire entanglements, which had to be swept away before the attackers could come to grips with the defenders, and numerous and elaborate dug-outs had been constructed to protect the garrison during a bombardment. Most of these shelters went down into the earth for at least thirty feet, and some were so strong that even the most powerful shell could not penetrate them. While such shelters are excellent for protection, they have special dangers of their own. To one in a deep dug-out the noise of a bombardment overhead has a peculiarly sinister and terrifying sound; even a shell that bursts a hundred yards away seems to fall at his door. In such a case a man who thinks more of his own skin than of his duty is loth to leave his refuge, and there were many instances during the battle of enemy garrisons being trapped in their dug-outs before they had time to man their parapets. The Germans had also erected skilfully concealed machine-gun posts, strengthened by concrete, and they had several similarly protected posts for snipers. It was therefore with good reason that the Germans believed their positions to be impregnable.

As the time for battle drew near, the Division was moved closer to the front line, and on the 23rd it was concentrated near Corbie, where D.H.Q. were established. All the sappers and pioneers were busy on roads and dumps. Numerous conferences in connection with the battle were held by the G.O.C. On the next day the Ninth moved to Etinehem, and on the 27th to Grovetown, a city of dumps.

The Division was not to take part in the first day of battle, but it was instructed to be ready to do so when called upon. The A. & Q. Staff worked continuously to supply the men with all that was necessary for the fight. Two hundred rounds of S.A.A. per man were carried, except in the case of signallers, orderlies, and Lewis Gunners. The establishment of Lewis Guns per battalion had been doubled, each company having two and for the carriage of these weapons hand-carts had been issued, but they were of little use except in fine weather and on good roads. It was decided by G.H.Q. that each battalion should have a nucleus of officers for reorganisation; 20 were to go into the battle, and the remainder, including the second in command, was to be left at the First Line Transport. To simplify reorganisation during the engagement, each company wore shoulder bands of a distinctive colour.[1] For the carriage of stores, such as Stokes shells, machine-gun ammunition, R.E. Stores, and tools, parties were formed in each brigade from its several units.

The most scrupulous care was given to the question

---

[1] A Company wore red; B Company, yellow; C Company, blue; D Company, green.

of communications. These form the nerve system of
the military body, and if they do not work properly the
whole machine is thrown out of gear, and delay in the
transmission of messages may lead to the chance of
a victory being missed. Communications had not been
good at Loos, but the development and extension of
the functions of the aeroplane opened up a new and
more rapid means of communication. Men were to
carry flares, which when lit on the objective would
indicate to an observer from the air the general line
reached by the troops, and special machines, known as
contact aeroplanes and distinguished by streamers, were
allotted the task of maintaining communication with
the infantry. Should it be impossible to light the flares
on account of damp or other causes, the men were to
indicate their position by flashing mirrors. In addition,
a code of signals was arranged between a battalion
H.Q. and the aeroplanes, the messages from the
battalion being signalled by means of ground signalling
sheets. Further, to allow observers in the rear to
distinguish our men from the enemy, each man wore
on his back a square of yellow cloth or metal disc,
which was attached to the flap of the haversack.

An enormous advantage possessed by the British on
the eve of the offensive was the command of the air.
At no time during the war were the signs of our air
superiority so obvious to the infantry as in the summer
of 1916. The passage of an enemy plane over our lines
was then an event. The Germans were virtually
confined to the observation they secured from their
possession of the higher ground, and even the extra
observation they got by means of their balloons was
denied them. On the first day of the preliminary
bombardment our planes crossed the German lines
and swooped down on their balloons, which dis-

appeared in wisps of flame as they were hit. The enemy was practically blinded.

The assault was to be made on the 29th June. To prevent the date being conveyed to the enemy this was known and spoken of as " Z " day, and the days prior to the battle were designated by the corresponding letters of the alphabet. Thus the 25th June, on which date the preliminary bombardment commenced, was " V " day. During the last week of June the weather was bad, and zero was wisely postponed until the 1st July. Thick ribbons of mist floated over the landscape and rendered the work of the Flying Corps exceptionally difficult. Until the 27th June there were frequent and heavy showers of rain, and Grovetown became a sea of mud, but on the following day the sun shone from a cloudless sky, and a typical French summer day ushered in the greatest battle fought in history up to that time.

The bombardment that fell on the German lines was of an intensity far exceeding that at Loos, and to the distant observer their positions seemed to be shot into the air. The bursts of our shells resembled the smoke from an endless row of factory chimneys, stretching north and south, and through the fountains of smoke one could see sods of earth and fragments of timber leaping upwards. For six days the ground throbbed under the unceasing cannonade, and the nights, gleaming with the flashes of thousands of guns, were almost as bright as the days. In this bombardment the guns of the Ninth Division contributed their share, for they were in action with the artillery of the Eighteenth and Thirtieth Divisions. During all this period the enemy's artillery was extraordinarily quiet, as if reserving itself for the final attack.

On the 30th June the dispositions of the XIII.

Corps were as follows : North of the Peronne road lay the infantry of the Thirtieth and Eighteenth Divisions assembled ready for the attack next morning. The battle H.Q. of the Ninth Division were at Grovetown, in which were also concentrated two companies of the 9th Seaforths and the South African Brigade, which had attached to it the 64th Field Coy. R.E., and the 28th Machine-Gun Company. The 27th Brigade, supplemented by the 90th R.E. and "C" Company of the 9th Seaforths was in Billon Valley, Copse Valley, and Trigger Wood Valley. The 26th Brigade, with the 63rd R.E. and "A" Company of the 9th Seaforths, was in Grovetown and Celestins Wood. The Corps Cavalry Regiment, the 19th Motor Machine-Gun Battery, and a Corps Cyclist Battalion were also under the orders of the Division, the first being at Grovetown and the latter two at Vaux.

On the morning of the 1st July the frenzied intensity of the bombardment heralded the moment of attack, and at 7.30 A.M. the British troops left their trenches and advanced on the German lines. For the Ninth, lying in reserve, the day was one of feverish suspense. Messages received showed that matters were going well on the front of the XIII. Corps, but it was rumoured that a serious check had been experienced farther north. By nightfall the position was fairly definitely known. In front of Thiepval, Beaumont Hamel, and Serre, our advance had been completely checked, but farther south the attack had met with a success that exceeded expectations. The objectives of the Thirtieth and Eighteenth Divisions, Montauban and the spur on which it stood, had been captured without much difficulty and with slight loss.

On the evening of the 1st July the 27th Brigade placed two battalions, the 12th Royal Scots and the

6th K.O.S.B., at the disposal of the Eighteenth Division for working and digging. The enemy's artillery, now active, heavily shelled the garrisons of the captured positions, and on the 2nd July the Ninth Division was instructed to relieve the 90th Brigade (Thirtieth Division), which was holding Montauban. This task was entrusted to the 27th Brigade, and the South African Brigade was ordered to occupy the positions held by the former as soon as they were vacated. The relief began at 10 P.M., but owing to the congestion of the trenches and the unfamiliarity of the guides with the captured positions, it was not completed until 3 A.M. on the 3rd July. The 11th Royal Scots held the east and the 9th Scottish Rifles the west of Montauban, with the 6th K.O.S.B. and the 12th Royal Scots in support and reserve; their task was to consolidate and strengthen the defences of the village. The 90th Brigade had reported that the Germans were occupying Montauban Alley from the point where it was cut by the road from the village to Bazentin-le-Grand. This was too near for safety, and at 5 A.M. bombing parties from the 11th Royal Scots and 9th Scottish Rifles worked their way along the trench as far as Triangle Post, which they garrisoned. During the day this position was consolidated, new trenches were sited and commenced, and dumps were formed. All day the village and trenches held by the brigade were incessantly shelled.

At 3 P.M. on the same afternoon the brigade was ordered by the Thirtieth Division to capture and consolidate Bernafay Wood, about 500 yards east and north-east of Montauban. Between the British positions and the German second line system at Longueval and Delville Wood lay the two densely-foliaged woods known as Bernafay and Trones. These had to be cleared before the attack could be resumed, and, but for the check imposed by the limited objective, would in all probability have fallen to our troops on the first day. Brig.-General Scrase-Dickins arranged for the operation to be carried out by the 6th K.O.S.B. on the right, and the 12th Royal Scots on the left. The attacking battalions formed up, each on a company front, in Chimney Trench and the falling ground to the south-west of it. "B" Company of the 12th Royal Scots was to clear Montauban Alley from Triangle Post to the north-west corner of the wood. After a ten-minutes' bombardment the battalions attacked at 9 P.M., and the whole wood, as well as the trench between it and Triangle Post, was captured after a feeble resistance. Four field-guns and one machine-gun were taken by the 12th Royal Scots, and one machine-gun by the 6th K.O.S.B., while about 12 of the enemy were killed and 7 taken prisoners. The assailants had the greatest difficulty in maintaining direction owing to the darkness and the dense under-growth of the wood, consequently, when its eastern margin was reached, there was some confusion of units, and the consolidation of positions previously selected was delayed. After the capture of Bernafay, the K.O.S.B. held the southern and eastern sides of the perimeter, and the 12th Royal Scots the remaining post.

The wood had been an easy place to take ; it proved a costly one to hold. At 6 A.M. on the 4th July a violent hostile bombardment opened, and continued for six hours. The shelling was particularly severe in the portion of the wood lying south of the railway line, and the majority of the K.O.S.B. in this area had to be withdrawn farther within the wood. The work of consolidation was totally interrupted, and

casualties were heavy, the K.O.S.B. losing over 150
killed and wounded. By noon, however, all our
original positions were reoccupied, and the work of
consolidation was carried on with vigour. "D" Company
of the 12th Royal Scots, under Lieut. H. Crowden,
constructed a keep in the centre of the wood, a highly
creditable piece of work, because it was no light task
to dig in a soil through which tentacles of undergrowth
ran in all directions. Every day Bernafay Wood and
Montauban were plastered with shells from the enemy's
artillery. The ploughed-up village became a heap of
brick-dust and rubble, and the wood, which before its
capture had been so thick that the rays of the sun
could not penetrate it, became so thinned-out that one
could see through it from end to end. During one of
these bombardments the battalion H.Q. of the K.O.S.B.
were hit ; the Adjutant, Lieutenant Wright, was killed,
and Lieut.-Colonel Connell had a very narrow escape.
On the 5th July the garrison was reduced by the
withdrawal of a company of the K.O.S.B. to Oxford
Copse, and a company of the "Rifles" was also
moved back from Montauban Alley to the same place.
The lines between brigade and battalions were often
broken by shell-fire, and the work of the linesmen in
repairing and maintaining them deserved the highest
praise.

On the night of the 4th/5th July the remainder of
the Thirtieth Division was relieved by the Ninth. The
South Africans took over from the 89th Brigade in the
Glatz sector, and the Highland Brigade moved up to the
positions vacated by the South Africans. The Ninth
was now the right flank division of the British Army.
The 1st and 4th Regiments of the South Africans
held the line from the junction with the French to
Briqueterie Trench on the east of Montauban, with

the 3rd and 2nd Regiments in support and reserve respectively. It was still necessary for the British to clear the pear-shaped wood of Trones. The first attack was carried out on the 8th July by the Thirtieth Division, and from that date till the 14th the wood was the scene of a bitter conflict, in which it changed hands repeatedly. Trones was a particularly difficult place to take, as it was commanded from Longueval and from the Maltz Horn Ridge. Every possible assistance was rendered by the Ninth Division. On the night of the 6th/7th, the 27th Brigade sent out a patrol, which established a post in Longueval Alley only 300 yards from Trones Wood, while on the morning of the attack the artillery pounded the southern fringe of Longueval and the neighbouring trenches, and the 12th Royal Scots from Bernafay Wood covered the left flank of the Thirtieth Division with machine-gun fire. During this operation a plucky exploit was performed by Private J. Stevenson of the 12th Royal Scots. Having located a German sniper, he engaged him with his Lewis Gun ; he advanced across the open, and having fired off all his ammunition sat down and cleaned his rifle until more could be obtained. He was wounded in both arms, but nevertheless when one of his comrades was hit, he went about 600 yards to bring up a stretcher for him. The Thirtieth Division took Trones Wood, but by the end of the day had lost it all to a hostile counter-attack, except the south-west corner and Maltz Horn Trench.

On the night of the 8th July the 27th Brigade was relieved, and moved down to its old position in Billon Valley. The Third Division on the left took over the portion of Montauban Alley lying to the west of the Montauban – Longueval road ; the Highland Brigade occupied the trenches in front of Montauban, and the South Africans Bernafay Wood with their 4th Regiment. The 6th K.O.S.B., who had held the worst shelled portion of the wood, lost in five days 16 officers and 300 other ranks.

The attack on Trones was resumed at 3 A.M. next morning, but at the end of the day the position was exactly as it had been on the 8th. The 90th Brigade, which made the assault, was sadly battered, and a company of the 4th Regiment of the South Africans moved up at 9 P.M. to the south-west corner of the wood to its support. In addition a platoon from the same battalion reinforced the garrison of the Briqueterie, and the 3rd Regiment was ordered to be ready to support the 90th Brigade at ten minutes' notice. The attack was continued on the 10th without any gain, the Germans recapturing what they had lost by a well-timed counter-attack. On the same date the advanced post held by the Ninth in Longueval Alley was supported by the establishment of several intermediate posts. The sanguinary assaults on Trones Wood had no better fortune on the 11th, an attempt of a South African detachment to aid the Thirtieth Division by bombing up Longueval Alley to the apex of the wood being checked by machine-gun fire. During the counter-barrage of the enemy Lieut.-Colonel Jones of the 4th Regiment South Africans was killed, and the command of the battalion was taken over by Major D. M. MacLeod.

The unsatisfactory result of the fighting in Trones Wood affected disastrously the plans of the Corps for an attack on the enemy's second system of defences. Every day gained by the enemy added to his strength. On the 7th July the Division had received instructions for operations to be undertaken against Longueval and Delville Wood on the 10th, but the original scheme presupposed the capture of Trones Wood, consequently the date had to be postponed and the arrangements modified. The task of the XIII. Corps was probably the toughest on the whole front. It was to secure the ridge running from Waterlot Farm to Bazentin-le-Grand, and the key of this ridge, Longueval and Delville Wood, fell to the lot of the Ninth. The flanks of its attack were to be protected on the left by the Third Division and on the right by the Eighteenth, which was to clear Trones Wood. The great difficulty lay in the fact that the position of the XIII. Corps was already a salient, and that success would intensify it. The ground, moreover, was vital to the enemy, and he held it with seasoned troops.[1] The operation was of first-rate importance, since the possession of the high ground near Longueval was the pivot of Sir Douglas Haig's immediate plans ; it facilitated an attack on High Wood in the north, and it was an essential preliminary to an advance on Ginchy and Guillemont.

General Furse had foreseen the task that he would be called upon to perform. From Bernafay Wood the ground rose up to the height on which stood Longueval. The southern position of the village stood open to the view, but the northern part, intersected by numerous orchards, baffled scrutiny by disappearing into the shelter of Delville Wood.

Longueval lay along three roads whose junctions formed the centre or main square of the village. From this point one road ran north to meet the path midway between High Wood and Flers ; the second [2] ran south-west, skirting the western margin of Bernafay Wood ; and the third led in a south-easterly direction into

---

[1] These were the 16th Bavarian Regiment and the 6th Bavarian Reserve Regiment of the Tenth Bavarian Division.

[2] Where it entered the village, this road was known as Pall Mall.

Guillemont.   The northern road was marked on our maps as North Street.   From the square a street branched off westwards towards Bazentin - le - Grand, which was known as Clarges Street; on the eastern side where it ran into a grassy ride, practically bisecting Delville Wood, it was named Princes Street.   Parallel to Clarges Street, and about 300 yards north of it, lay Duke Street.   These, bounded on the west by Pont Street and on the east by Piccadilly, formed a rectangle. Between Piccadilly and North Street clustered the orchards of Longueval.   The enemy's front trenches ran along the south of the village, and then turned off towards the south-east, past Waterlot Farm along the western outskirts of Guillemont.   His rear defences lay in the hamlet and beyond the northern perimeter of the wood.

Ever since the Ninth Division had been in the line, the whole area in front of the German trenches had been constantly patrolled.   The brigadiers had been warned of what was to take place, and the whole Division was ready for the battle, so that when the final instructions were issued by the Corps on the 12th July only details required attention.

At 3.30 P.M. on the same afternoon the G.O.C. met his brigadiers and explained his plans.   The attack was to be carried out by the 26th Brigade on the right, and the 27th on the left, and for each there were three objectives.   The first for both was the capture of the enemy's front and support trenches near Longueval. The second task of the Highlanders was to secure the village south of the line Clarges Street–Princes Street, and the western edge of Delville Wood south of Princes Street; that of the 27th Brigade to take the greater part of Longueval lying north of Clarges Street.   Then the 26th, in order to safeguard the right flank, was to

secure the German system of defences between the
village and Waterlot Farm inclusive, while the 27th
was to clear the northern outskirts of Longueval and
the western margin of Delville Wood adjoining that
portion of the village. If these objectives were taken
easily, both brigades were to go on and occupy the
whole of the wood.

It was realised that the Germans were expecting
an attack. To keep them in uncertainty as to the
exact time of the onslaught, their lines were heavily
shelled every morning by the artillery, and to gain the
full advantage of surprise, what was virtually a night
attack was planned. The British Army might be un-
imaginative and unenterprising in strategy, but it was
bold and audacious in the use of tactical expedients.
A night attack demands the most careful arrangements
by the Staff and a high standard of discipline on the
part of the troops engaged. Zero was 3.25 A.M. on
the morning of the 14th July. This early hour made
the question of assembly one of more than ordinary
difficulty, but the G.O.C. had his scheme prepared.
The ground in front of our lines had been thoroughly
reconnoitred by patrols, and during the night a strong
line of scouts was to go up the crest of the rise in
front of the enemy's trenches. These men were to
be supported by Lewis Gun detachments, and the
exposed right wing was to be protected against an
attack from Trones Wood by a chain of posts, which
the Highland Brigade was to establish in 9·2-inch
shell holes, previously made for this purpose by the
artillery along the crest line of the spur running
from Longueval to Bernafay Wood. Under cover of
this force the attacking brigades were to form up
their leading battalions in their waves of attack on
the south-west slopes of the plateau. The whole

assembly was to be completed half an hour before zero.

On receipt of their instructions Brig.-General Ritchie and Brig.-General Scrase-Dickins arranged their dispositions. The former decided to attack with the Black Watch and Argylls in front, the Seaforths in support, and three companies of the Camerons in reserve. The Black Watch and the Argylls were to be on a two company front, each company being in open column of platoons with 70 yards between platoons. Thus each battalion was to be in eight waves. The supporting battalion had the same formation, and the fourth company of the Camerons was to carry [1] for the brigade. Two sections of the 26th Machine-Gun Company were to follow the 7th Seaforths, the rest of the company being in brigade reserve. One section of the L.T.M.B. was to follow the two attacking battalions, the remainder being under the control of the brigade. The Black Watch and the Argylls were to secure the first and second objectives, and the Seaforths the third.

Brig.-General Scrase-Dickins had the 11th Royal Scots and the 9th Scottish Rifles in front, and the 12th Royal Scots in support. The 6th K.O.S.B. carried for the brigade. Both attacking battalions had four companies in the front line, each company being in column of platoons with the requisite 70 yards' distance between platoons; thus each battalion was in four waves. The supporting battalion was in the same formation. Two Vickers machine-guns were to accompany each of the leading battalions, one

---

[1] During an engagement it was necessary to keep the infantry adequately supplied with ammunition, bombs, engineering material, rations, and water, so parties were always detailed to carry up these stores.

section followed the 12th Royal Scots, and two
sections were in brigade reserve. The first objective
was to be taken by the leading battalions, the second
by the 12th and 11th Royal Scots, and the third by
the 12th Royal Scots.

The reliefs necessitated by these arrangements were
carried out on the night of the 12th/13th. The 55th
Brigade of the Eighteenth Division relieved the South
African Brigade in the portion of Bernafay Wood lying
south of the Carnoy–Guillemont railway. The 27th
relieved the 76th Brigade of the Third Division in
Montauban Alley from the Montauban–Longueval road
to the Montauban–Bazentin-le-Grand road (exclusive).
On the right of the Ninth the Thirtieth Division was
relieved by the Eighteenth.

The artillery arrangements employed for the attack
on Longueval had exceptional interest; for they were
destined to give the Ninth a distinctive place among
the divisions of the British Army. Brig.-General
Tudor's main problem was created by Delville Wood.
As our experience of Bernafay had already demonstrated, shrapnel shells, by hitting the branches and
trunks of trees burst prematurely, and were as
dangerous to our own infantry as to the enemy. The
C.R.A. now resolved to carry out a plan that he
had long borne in mind. The artillery bombardment
preparatory for the attack was to commence five
minutes before zero; the customary shrapnel was
used, but after three minutes H.E. shell only. This
was a notable change from the ordinary method. The
H.E. had delay action, so that even if a tree was
hit by it the shell would complete its trajectory
before bursting.

In another respect, the Ninth resolved to adopt a
method commonly used by the French and already

employed by several British divisions, on the 1st July. Up to this battle all the attacks of the British Army had been preceded by a violent preliminary bombardment, and before the infantry advanced the artillery lifted well behind the enemy's trenches. The device known as the "creeping barrage"[1] was a logical development in the work of the artillery, since successive lines of defence had to be accounted for. The gunners were to support the infantry throughout the advance by shelling each successive portion of the enemy's line just in front of the oncoming troops. This would give the Germans less time to have their machine-guns ready and would enable the attackers to get to grips with them before their guns could be brought into action. For the attack on the 14th July, the rate of the barrage was to be 50 yards every one and a half minutes, and sheltered by this advancing wall of fire the infantry were to carry on the assault.

The full artillery programme consisted of eight separate barrages.[2] The first five continued from

[1] The "creeping barrage" does not creep—it really jumps. At Longueval the line of the barrage moved forward 50 yards at a bound. To a distant observer, however, the barrage did seem to creep forward, hence the name.

During this Somme Battle the use of the creeping barrage became universal by the British Army in all its attacks. Shrapnel was generally used, but the Ninth Division, having taken to H.E. and having found it successful, stuck to it. Which was the better of the two was controversial to the end of the war. In the Ninth the opinion was that the H.E. barrage had greater moral effect, was easier to follow, and did not throw such a strain on the artillery that the setting of fuses for a shrapnel barrage necessitated.

[2]

1st Barrage	.	.	.	5 minutes till Zero.
2nd ,,	.	..	.	Zero ,, Z. - 5 minutes.
3rd ,,	.	.	.	Z. - 5 mins. ,, Z. - 45 ,,
4th ,,	.	.	.	Z. - 45 ,, ,, Z. - 1·30.
5th ,,	.	.	.	Z. - 1.30. ,, Z. - 2.
6th ,,	.	.	.	Z. - 2. ,, Z. - 2·30.
7th ,,	.	.	.	Z. - 2.30. ,, Z. - 3·9.
8th ,,	.	.	.	Z. - 3·9 ... ...

five minutes before zero until two hours after it, by which time the whole of Longueval was expected to be in our hands. All this time the defences round Waterlot Farm were to be kept under fire, and the attack on the farm was to be made under cover of the sixth barrage, which was to open two hours after zero. The remaining barrages were intended to cover the assault on Delville Wood.

CHAPTER VI

LONGUEVAL AND DELVILLE WOOD

JULY 1916

NOT the least anxious part of the forthcoming battle was the assembly of the troops during the night of the 13th/14th July, for it was an audacious enterprise to form up in the darkness a large body of men within easy distance of the German lines, since the least suspicion of the manœuvre by the enemy was bound to lead to a dreadful catastrophe. The deepest silence was essential, and the operation was partly cloaked by the artillery, which throughout the night bombarded the village and the wood. The assembly was a great triumph of organisation for the Staff of the two brigades, and a proof of the high discipline of the men. The arrangements of the brigades differed slightly, but were equally successful in their results.

The 26th Brigade assembled on the northern slopes of Caterpillar Valley, with its left resting on the path leading from Montauban to Longueval. After the covering party, consisting of four platoons with two Lewis Guns, had taken post on the crest of the plateau, the brigade major, Major Drew, with the adjutants of the Black Watch and Argylls and forty markers, went out to mark off the ground. The plan was to work from the left of each battalion. The left markers of the Black Watch moved up the Bernafay–Longueval road, and the left of the Argylls up the

Montauban–Longueval path. Sixteen markers of the former, commencing from the rear, were posted in pairs at 70 yards' distance along the first of these roads. When this was accomplished, the front couple had reached a point about 500 yards from the enemy's front line. As each pair was posted, one man moved off at right angles with a tape about 150 yards long, and thus fixed the right of his wave or platoon. In the same fashion those of the Argylls were placed in position. Then at 12.25 A.M. the battalions, by companies in single file, moved out to line up on the markers, and as each platoon reached its left marker it wheeled to the right and fixed bayonets. The assembly of the brigade was effected without sound or hitch by 3 A.M. While the markers were being posted there was considerable shelling of the assembly area, but fortunately it died down before the arrival of the battalions. Owing to shelling, however, and sniping from Trones Wood it was found necessary slightly to contract the right of the Black Watch.

The assembly area of the 27th Brigade was on the immediate left of that of the 26th. About 10 P.M. the platoon that formed the covering party pushed forward to the northern slopes of Caterpillar Valley, and an hour later Major Teacher, the brigade major, with one officer and two N.C.Os. of the 90th Field Coy. R.E. moved out to place the tapes for the battalions. In this case the plan was to work from the centre. On a compass bearing, previously taken by Major Teacher, the first tape, 50 yards long, was laid, and others were placed in prolongation of the first. When completed the centre tape extended to a distance of 1000 yards, the work having taken forty-five minutes. Then the front tape was laid off at right angles, the flanks of each battalion being thus fixed. This was

DELVILLE WOOD

checked by an officer from each of the attacking battalions, who paced for 1000 yards along the roads that marked the flanks of the brigade. When the tapes were in position, the right and left markers for each unit were posted.

The battalions assembled in the southern portion of the valley at 12.30 A.M., each being in mass, in single rank, on a front of 225 yards. At 1.45 A.M. the 11th Royal Scots moved along the centre tape to their final position, and were followed by the 9th Scottish Rifles and the 12th Royal Scots. Though there was intermittent shelling, there were only five casualties, but these included Lieut.-Colonel H. L. Budge of the 12th Royal Scots, who was killed by a shell fragment as his battalion was passing through the west side of Montauban; the command of the battalion was then taken over by Captain J. E. MacPherson. The assembly was completed at 2.45 A.M.

The Division, by the satisfactory conclusion of this difficult operation deserved all the high praise [1] that it received from the G.O.C. and General Congreve.

[1] "Ninth Division Special Order of the Day, dated 15/7/16.

"1. The Corps Commander has asked me to tell the members of my staff, the brigadiers and their staffs, and all regimental officers, N.C.Os. and men, that in his opinion the Ninth Division carried out a very difficult feat of arms yesterday finely, that the assembly by night of a Corps within assaulting distance of the entrenched lines of an active enemy, could only be effected by divisions in which the staff work and the discipline were alike perfect, and that he is grateful to all. This is indeed high praise from such a soldier, and I need not say how proud I am to be allowed to convey such praise to the Ninth Division.

"2. For myself, I can only say with the deepest gratitude that you have once more proved to me what a glorious Division I have the great honour to command. However good the staff work and however good the leading, it would be impossible to win success against such an enemy unless every officer, N.C.O. and man was ready at all times to do more than his duty. On this I can always rely in the Ninth Division.—W. T. Furse."

I

At 3.20 A.M., when the light was just sufficient for one to distinguish friend from foe, the first barrage opened, and the leading waves moved as close to it as they could safely go. Five minutes later, on the hour of zero, the whole line moved forward to the attack.

On the right, Brig.-General Ritchie's men made on the whole very satisfactory progress. Most trouble was experienced by the Black Watch, whose right company encountered a stubborn resistance from a machine-gun nest on the south-east corner of Longueval. This post was covered by the fire of two field-guns in the south-west corner of Delville Wood, which were later withdrawn, and owing to the confined space in which they had to manœuvre the Black Watch were unable to get to grips with the garrison of the post, which held out until late in the afternoon. With this exception the objectives allotted to the battalion were taken by 10 A.M. At one time the leading men took up a position along Buchanan Street, a ride branching off Princes Street at right angles to the south of the wood, but this line could not be maintained as the left flank was in the air. At noon the line held by the battalion ran from the main square of the village north of the church and then south-east to within 100 yards of the west corner of South Street, the path skirting the southern edge of Delville Wood. Patrols were immediately pushed forward, but during the afternoon stiff resistance was experienced, and the patrols became standing picquets on the edge of the wood.

The Argylls, on the left of the Black Watch, met with complete success. The leading companies kept close to the barrage, leaving the supporting companies to clear the enemy's front trenches. The 11th Royal Scots on the left being delayed by uncut wire, "C" Company of the Argylls in left support came to their assistance by bombing to the north. This company killed at least 100 of the foe, and drove others along the front of the 27th Brigade. In this lively action a machine-gun was captured, a well-aimed bomb accounting for the whole team. The other companies of the Argylls in their impetuous eagerness ran into our barrage and suffered some casualties. Then until the barrage lifted the men lay down in shell-holes, while a piper played the regimental march. When the advance was resumed Clarges Street was reached without much resistance, and the battalion, having cleared the houses on the west side of the main street, commenced to consolidate.

Waterlot Farm and its defences had still to be taken before the job of the brigade was accomplished.

The left brigade was equally successful in securing its first objective. The first task, the capture of the enemy's front defences, was straightforward. Unfortunately on the front of the 11th Royal Scots delay was caused by wire, and gaps were cut by hand with very great difficulty, owing to machine-gun fire; but the battalion's Lewis Guns rendered great service by keeping down the enemy's fire, while a platoon of "A" Company, finding a gap in the right flank, went through and bombed down the opposite trenches. Lieut.-Colonel Croft's men rapidly effected the capture of this objective, though they had much stern fighting, and a party of 63 Germans was rounded up and taken prisoner by 2nd Lieuts. Turner and Fleming after a combined bombing attack, in which the battalion Lewis Guns, skilfully handled by Lieut. Winchester, played a noteworthy part.

Lieut.-Colonel Fulton[1] with the "Rifles" had an

[1] Lieut.-Colonel Fulton took over the command of the 9th Scottish Rifles in March 1916.

easier passage. The proffered resistance was rapidly overcome, and a company of the battalion, by bombing along the German trenches to the north, assisted the progress of the right battalion of the Third Division, which had been stopped by uncut wire. Many of the enemy were killed, and 80 were captured.

Thus by 4.15 A.M. the brigade had gained the whole of the first objective, but the second phase was more complicated. The 11th Royal Scots, which had been the right battalion, at this point became the left, and were to take Duke Street from its junction with Piccadilly to its junction with Pont Street. The 12th Royal Scots passed through the 11th on the first objective, and, wheeling to the east, advanced against the village. The death of Lieut.-Colonel Budge proved a great misfortune; for the task of the battalion, to secure Longueval from the corner of Duke Street and Piccadilly to a point on Princes Street on the fringe of Delville Wood, was one of extraordinary difficulty. The left battalion made good progress, and dug in on a line south of Duke Street; but the right battalion, coming under very heavy machine-gun fire and accurate sniping from a post in the orchards and from Piccadilly, was compelled to dig in on a line facing east, with its right flank on Clarges Street in touch with the Argylls, and its left in touch with the right of the 11th Royal Scots.

Thus the advance of the 27th Brigade was brought to a standstill before the second objective had been reached.

At first the working of the communications between D.H.Q. and the leading infantry was all that could be desired. In spite of the incessant shelling, messages came in quickly, and General Furse was able to keep in close touch with his attacking brigades. Thus, on learning that the 11th Royal Scots and the right

battalion of the Third Division had been checked by
undamaged wire, he sent out directions for the 26th
Brigade to assist the 27th, which in turn was to help
the Third Division.   As a consequence, the advance
was maintained practically without a halt.   At 5.5 A.M.
the G.O.C. learned that Brig.-General Ritchie's brigade
had secured its first two objectives, and an hour later
that the left brigade had captured everything except
the north of Longueval.   When at 6.29 A.M. he was
informed that the whole of the village was held by the
27th Brigade, he had every reason to be jubilant.

Unfortunately the information was inaccurate, as
a message at 7.20 A.M. made clear.   General Furse
knew that the check to the 12th Royal Scots was a
most serious matter.   The possession of the Longueval
plateau was the key to the operations against High
Wood in the north, and if the village was not taken,
the plans of Sir Douglas Haig would be thrown out
of gear.   Moreover, it was from Longueval that the
attack on Delville Wood was to be launched; without
it the operation would be more intricate.   The crisis
demanded decisive action, and the G.O.C. placed
the 1st South African Regiment under the orders of
Brig.-General Scrase-Dickins, who was instructed to
make every effort to clear the village.   General Furse
was also keenly concerned about Waterlot Farm, which
had yet to be taken by the Highland Brigade, since
its capture was the necessary preliminary to an attack
on Guillemont.   Realising that the 26th and 27th
Brigades had been heavily punished, he warned Brig.-
General Lukin that his brigade would be required to
take Delville Wood.

When the advance of the 12th Royal Scots was
checked, 2nd Lieut. A. Noble, now the most senior
officer on the spot, held a conference of the surviving

officers. It was decided to make another attempt with
two companies, and they moved forward at 7 A.M., but
did not get beyond Piccadilly. At 8.30 A.M. another
effort was made by the battalion from the line of
Clarges Street. Three sections with a Lewis Gun tried
to force their way up North Street by rushing from
house to house, but, after progressing fifty yards,
they were brought to a halt by machine-gun fire and
withdrew to the shelter of a barricade, which had
been erected at the junction of North Street and Clarges
Street.

At 8.48 A.M. Brig.-General Scrase-Dickins received
orders from General Furse. These were that the
village was to be bombarded, and that the brigade
was to make another attack at 10.30 A.M. But the
communications in front were not so satisfactory, and,
owing to the delay in the transmission of instructions,
the attack was not launched until 11 A.M. To supplement the artillery, Stokes Guns bombarded the orchard
area, concentrating on suspected machine-gun posts, but
the assault from the line of Clarges Street was again
defeated.

It was clear that the northern part of Longueval
could not be cleared by a casual or haphazard attack.
The enclosed nature of the oblong of orchards made
it difficult to locate the enemy's posts with certainty,
and the artillery were handicapped by the want of
a post from which to observe the fire. The problem
was in fact more intricate than was realised at the
time. The battering that the village had received from
our guns had only been sufficient to convert it into
a stronghold of immense strength. Amidst the jagged
and tumbled masonry the defenders had numerous
well-protected corners from which they could fire
without being detected, and the oblong was full

of shelters where the garrison could take refuge
from the fire of field-guns. The whole area needed
to be pulverised by heavy shells, as General Furse
soon realised. Against infantry alone the place was
virtually impregnable, since the scope for manœuvring
was limited and all approaches were swept by the
fire of the defenders. Such was the task that Brig.-
General Scrase-Dickins was asked to accomplish.

The 1st South African Infantry bore the brunt of
the next attack. Lieut.-Colonel Dawson's men had
moved up to the line of Clarges Street through heavy
shell-fire without a casualty. From noon till 2 P.M. the
northern part of the village was bombarded, but, as
it was believed that isolated parties of the 12th Royal
Scots were in the village, the shelling was directed
chiefly on the wood to the east of it. Then followed
a great deal of confused fighting in which, by the
nature of the ground, the South Africans were split
into a number of detached groups. Such reports
as reached Brigade H.Q. were so vague that it was
impossible to act upon them, and it was not till
10.44 P.M. that the position of the South Africans
was known. At that time one company was in
Piccadilly, immediately south of Duke Street; another
was trying to work round from Piccadilly to North
Street; a third was in reserve at the south-east corner
of the village; and nothing certain was known of the
remaining company, which was believed to be on the
east side of North Street. That night at 10.50 P.M.
Brig.-General Scrase - Dickins urged Lieut.-Colonel
Dawson not to relax his efforts and to endeavour to
clear the whole of the village before dawn, in order
that the attack on Delville Wood might be delivered
from it.

While the left brigade was engaged in sanguinary

conflicts among the orchards of Longueval, the Highland Brigade was endeavouring to capture Waterlot
Farm. This work had been allotted to the 7th
Seaforths, who were in Montauban Alley when the
battle commenced. As Lieut.-Colonel Kennedy
expected the enemy's counter-barrage to fall on
Montauban Alley, he arranged that his men should
follow as close as possible behind the Black Watch in
order to escape it, and thus the whole battalion
avoided the shelling except one platoon, which suffered
severely. Advancing on the heels of the Black Watch
the leading company entered the German front line
and passed along behind the wire in a north-easterly
direction. The next two companies consolidated the
enemy's front line and a support line, while the fourth
followed in support of the leading company. The
Seaforths, finding the Black Watch held up by the
machine-gun post at the south-east corner of
Longueval, attempted to outflank it by working along
Dover Street and Down Street on the south of the
village, but they were stopped by hostile fire from
Waterlot Farm. In spite of repeated efforts the
post held out, for the ground was all in favour of the
defenders.

At 2 P.M. Brig.-General Ritchie ordered the
Camerons to move up from Montauban. They were
to assist in clearing the village, co-operate in the
assault on the post that was holding up the Black
Watch and Seaforths, and push on to Waterlot Farm.
Under drenching shell-fire the Camerons marched up
by companies to the village, the outskirts of which
they reached at 4 P.M. Before dark one company
cleared the houses just north of Clarges Street and a
building immediately north of Princes Street, known
as the Hospice; another company, in co-operation

with the Black Watch and Seaforths, at last accounted
for the post on the south-east of the village, which fell
to a converging attack, the garrison being bayoneted
and three machine - guns being captured.　A third
company and a company of Seaforths then pressed on
towards Waterlot Farm, and in spite of severe machine-
gun fire and accurate sniping a good deal of progress
was made.　The main body took up a position just west
of the farm, while a party of the Seaforths advanced
down Longueval Alley until they came in touch
with the Eighteenth Division, which had done great
work that day by capturing the whole of Trones
Wood.

After a day of strenuous fighting, in which many
losses had been sustained, the Division had just failed
to win complete success.　The enemy still held the
north of Longueval and Waterlot Farm, and Delville
Wood still remained to be taken.　At midnight the
position was as follows: The Argylls held all the
south and south-west of Longueval, with lines
established in Clarges Street, Sloane Street, and the
old German front line from the Windmill to Pall
Mall; the Black Watch were in a semicircle round
the north - east corner of the central square, and
occupied also a line 300 yards long, parallel to and
50 yards south of Princes Street; three companies
of the Seaforths held the old German front line on
the right of the Argylls; the remaining company and
three companies of the Camerons were in Longueval
Alley as far as Trones Wood, just west of Waterlot
Farm.　On the left the 12th Royal Scots were consolidating along the line of Piccadilly, the 11th Royal
Scots occupied Duke Street up to Pont Street, and
the 9th Scottish Rifles were in the old German support
line on the left of the 11th Royal Scots.　The 6th

K.O.S.B. had not been involved in the fighting, but their work in carrying up stores of all kinds under continuous shell-fire had been of the greatest value.

That evening the G.O.C. met his brigadiers in Montauban, and discussed with them the operations to be carried out on the following day. The 27th Brigade was to continue its attack on Longueval, and the 26th on Waterlot Farm. Delville Wood was to be assaulted by the South African Brigade under cover of a creeping H.E. barrage. This attack was arranged for 5 A.M., and, should the 27th fail to secure the village during the night, was to be delivered from the south-west.

Delville Wood, in the shape of a rough pentagonal, overshadowed the village of Longueval. It was divided into a northern and southern portion by the grassy ride known as Princes Street. From this ride towards the north, and at right angles to it, ran auxiliary paths named Strand, Regent Street, and Bond Street; in the opposite direction similar pathways, Buchanan Street, Campbell Street, and King Street, led to the southern margin. About 200 yards south of Princes Street and parallel to it was the ride called Rotten Row.

The execution of the attack was entrusted by Brig.-General Lukin to Lieut.-Colonel Tanner. The forces available were the 2nd and 3rd and two companies of the 4th South African Infantry. Of the remainder of the brigade the 1st Regiment was involved in the fighting in Longueval, and two companies of the 4th were to assist the 26th Brigade against Waterlot Farm.

The assailants moved up from Montauban before dawn. Patrols having reported the enemy to be still in possession of the village, the South Africans assembled in a trench on the south-west corner of

Delville.   All the wood south of Princes Street
was cleared in two hours, the only strong resistance
coming from isolated snipers.   In the eastern portion
138 prisoners, including 3 officers, and one machine-gun
were captured, but the most difficult part remained to
be accomplished.   Owing to the situation in Longueval,
Lieut.-Colonel Tanner decided to clear the northern
portion from the east as far as the Strand, and this
work was entrusted to three companies of the 2nd
South African Infantry.   The resistance was surprisingly weak, the garrison having been thinned out
on account of the shelling to which the wood was
persistently subjected.   The chief obstacle was the
wood itself.   The profligate undergrowth and the
tangle of trees and branches brought down by our
artillery-fire rendered the laborious work of penetrating
it most exhausting.   When at length the perspiring and
breathless South Africans reached the margin, the
enemy's artillery opened a fierce bombardment on the
whole place, and rifle and machine-gun fire prevented
progress beyond the perimeter.

Shortly after 2 P.M. that afternoon Lieut.-Colonel
Tanner was able to report that he had taken the whole
of Delville Wood except the north-west corner.   The
problem now was how to hold our gains.   In ordinary
circumstances small posts with machine-guns would
have been the least costly and the most effective
method; for Bernafay had shown that for large bodies
of men a wood is only a death-trap.   But it was
impossible to do this.   The wood was 159 acres in
extent, and part of it was held by the enemy.   Moreover, the Germans were exceptionally well situated for
a counter-attack.   They were able to direct an accurate
fire on the wood from their batteries in the north, east,
and south-east; their trenches lay round its perimeter

and commanded all its approaches; and the possession
of Longueval ensured them a covered approach whenever they chose to deliver their stroke.   Under these
circumstances a strong garrison and constant vigilance
were essential.

After the posts were established along the perimeter, the most urgent matter was the provision of
shelter for the troops.   A plentiful supply of tools
had been carried up by the South Africans, and it was
impressed upon the men that notwithstanding their
weariness there could be no rest until trenches had
been dug.   But they had grasped the situation; it
was only too obvious that their lives depended upon
the speed with which they could dig themselves in.
But the spendthrift undergrowth and tangled roots
that crawled profusely in the soil of Delville Wood
were hard to cut, and while the men toiled they were
harried unceasingly by shell and machine-gun fire.   An
attempt to wire the edge of the wood was frustrated
by a counter-attack, which men of the 10th Bavarian
Division delivered against the north-east corner about
3 P.M.   This attack was easily repulsed by rifle-fire,
but the situation was critical, and between 12.45 P.M.
and 1.15 P.M. reports from the 26th Brigade and the
52nd Brigade R.F.A. having stated that the Germans
were massing on the north-west of the wood, the
artillery put a protective barrage round it.   In spite
of this the foe made persistent attempts to drive the
South Africans from the perimeter, but all attacks were
defeated with loss by the 2nd South African Infantry,
and by 4.40 P.M. the enemy drew off.   The heavy
casualty list of the South Africans was due mainly to
shell-fire.

General Furse gave instructions that the utmost
efforts should be made to strengthen the defences

during the night, and a company of the Seaforths
(Pioneers) was sent up to wire the wood. In a remarkably short time numerous trenches were dug by the
garrison, for a man works with a will when his life is
at stake. Arrangements were also made to send up
large supplies of stores and ammunition. Six and a half
companies were posted round the perimeter with three
in support. The western portion of Princes Street was
held by a half company of the 2nd South African
Infantry, and two companies of the 1st formed a
defensive flank on the side of the village. The H.Q.
of Lieut.-Colonel Tanner were at the junction of Princes
Street and Buchanan Street.

Meanwhile Longueval defied all assaults. Throughout
the night of the 14th/15th the 1st South African Infantry
had been engaged in a grim house-to-house combat
without making headway, and the 12th Royal Scots
were called on to make another attack. After a
preliminary bombardment of the oblong by the artillery
and the Stokes mortars, they moved forward at 8 A.M.,
when a desperate and plucky effort was made to clear
the village. For a time progress was made, and
word reached D.H.Q. that the whole of the village
was in our hands. The report was wrong. Two
sections of the Royal Scots worked up North Street,
moving from house to house, each of which was secured
only after a stern bombing fight. Small garrisons were
left in three houses, and the party reached more than
midway to Duke Street. At the same time another
section tried to penetrate the orchards from the west,
but failed to get beyond Piccadilly. The first party
on venturing into the open was subjected to heavy fire
from concealed machine-guns and compelled to retire
to the shelter of the houses; even the posts that had
been established in the houses could not be maintained,

for the garrisons were shelled out and forced to withdraw. If doggedness and grit could have won Longueval, the 12th Royal Scots would have had it. Undaunted by their previous reverses, they made another attack in the evening at 7.30. Three sections advanced from Clarges Street, but could not get beyond 50 yards; two other sections pressing on up North Street found the enemy alert and strongly reinforced, and were forced back to the point from which they had started, after inflicting severe losses by Lewis Gun fire. The men, utterly exhausted, could do no more.

On the 15th encouraging progress was made by the 26th Brigade, though it failed to secure Waterlot Farm. As soon as day broke, parties of the Seaforths and Camerons dashed forward and succeeded in establishing themselves in enemy trenches to the east of the farm; but, before they were able to consolidate these positions, they were compelled to withdraw to the northern end of Longueval Alley, owing to intense shelling from both our own and the enemy's artillery. As the brigade had suffered many casualties and was holding a widely extended line, reinforcements consisting of two companies of the 4th South African Infantry were sent to its assistance. With the support of these two companies, two platoons of the Camerons again attacked the farm and reached the trenches to the east of it before noon. The captured trenches were then taken over by the South Africans, who commenced to consolidate, but were driven out by the concentrated artillery-fire of the enemy. As we could not occupy the farm, we determined to prevent the Germans gaining access to it, and machine-guns were posted by the 26th Brigade and by the South Africans in Delville Wood so as to command all its approaches.

Thus at the close of the 15th the task of the Division had not been completed. Continuous fighting, involving serious losses, had resulted in the capture of all Delville Wood except the north-west corner. The men not actually engaged in fighting were busy consolidating positions and erecting strong points and keeps in the southern portion of Longueval, and all work had to be done under accurate and galling artillery-fire. The position occupied by the Division was peculiarly exposed to the enemy's artillery; it formed an elbow beyond the British line and was open to fire from the north, south, and east. On the night of the 15th there was a marked increase in the enemy's shelling; a hurricane of fire swept Delville Wood, and a fierce bombardment was concentrated on the southern and south-western portions of Longueval. In addition, hostile artillery searched the whole region from our front line to the back areas, causing trouble to our batteries and seriously interrupting the work of the transport and of carrying parties.

Each moment as it passed increased the difficulty of the task still to be accomplished by the Division. It was now very weak, not only on account of its casualties, but through exhaustion, strain, and exposure. General Furse had not a fresh battalion under his command. On the other hand, the foe was gaining in strength, and he was known to be bringing up other troops. But an attitude of passive defence was impossible; there was no security in our position until the Germans had been driven out of every part of Longueval and Delville Wood. These two places formed part and parcel of the same problem; with the clearing of the village, the enemy could not maintain his position in the north-west corner of the wood, and as soon as the whole of Delville was in our hands,

the garrison of northern Longueval would be exposed
to an attack from three sides.

But neither operation was easy of accomplishment.
What the G.O.C. wanted—time—he could not have.
The fighting of the last two days had clearly shown
that the northern defences of the village could not be
rushed.   The surest and most economical method of
clearing Longueval was to bombard it with heavy
artillery before the infantry advanced, and this had
been suggested on the 15th.   The heavy artillery,
however, was not under the control of the G.O.C.,
and the insistence of the Corps and Army Commanders
on the need for securing the hamlet without delay
prevented the suggestion being carried into effect.
Consequently, General Furse resolved to make use of
the ground that he had gained in Delville Wood, and
he ordered a combined attack on the village and north-
west corner of the wood to be made by the 27th and
South African Brigades.   The latter, after completing
the capture of the northern perimeter was to press
westwards to North Street, where it should join hands
with the former, which was to advance north and east.
This attack was to take place at 10 A.M. on the 16th,
after a preliminary bombardment by the 2-inch trench
mortars, which had been sent up to Longueval on
the night of the 14th/15th.

The assaulting forces consisted of two companies
of the 1st South African Infantry and two of the
11th Royal Scots.   The assault was made from the
line of Princes Street–Clarges Street, and was wholly
repulsed.   It was notable, nevertheless, for several acts
of outstanding gallantry.   During the South African
attack, a bombing party attempted to rush an enemy
post about 40 yards from our trenches.   The assailants
were beaten back, and the officer in command fell

wounded between the two lines. Then Private W. F. Faulds with two comrades, ignoring the hail of bullets from the enemy's machine-guns, left our trench and rescued the officer. Almost by a miracle the party got back unscathed, except one man who was severely wounded. Faulds, who received a V.C., performed a similar feat two days later, when he went out for a wounded man, picked him up, and carried him to a dressing-station under a fire so intense that it was believed to be impossible to bring in the wounded. Equally shining as an example of heroism was the work of 2nd Lieut. Turner and C.S.M. Allwright of the 11th Royal Scots. Both crept out to some wounded men, dressed them under a withering fire, and crawled in with the wounded on their backs. Though desultory fighting went on in the village all day, its only effect was to add to the length of our casualty list.

On the 16th July the 26th Brigade was occupied chiefly in consolidating and strengthening its defences and in establishing posts on the west of Waterlot Farm. Bombers and snipers crept close up to the farm and kept the garrison continually on the alert. Though it was held by their own snipers, the Germans persistently shelled it throughout the day. During the night the Seaforths were relieved in Longueval Alley by the Eighteenth Division.

The South Africans in Delville Wood had been woefully reduced by the furious bombardment to which they had been subjected, and in consequence the work of consolidation could not be carried on as far as safety demanded. During the 16th the firing on the wood continued, and considerable trouble was experienced from bold enemy snipers who had remained concealed amongst the shrubbery and undergrowth, but these were accounted for later in the day. The

K

most worrying feature of the situation was the extent of the gaps between the posts round the perimeter, and the task of a runner in carrying messages along the line was nerve-racking and perilous. The garrison was reinforced by a company of the 4th Regiment, which was sent to the east and north-east of the wood. All the officers and men showed very obvious traces of strain and fatigue, and Brig.-General Lukin asked the G.O.C. if his men could be relieved. There were no troops in the Division who were not exhausted, but General Furse promised that when the whole of the village and the wood had been captured, the South Africans in the southern portion of Delville Wood would be relieved by the 26th Brigade.

With regard to Longueval, he decided that it must be pounded into dust before another attack was made, so he asked the Corps to arrange for the fire of heavy guns, controlled by observation, to be concentrated on the northern part of the village. The original intention was to commence the bombardment at 4 A.M. on the 17th July.

But this scheme was frustrated by peremptory orders from General Rawlinson, directing that the village had to be cleared at all costs before dawn. Urgent orders were sent to Brig.-General Scrase-Dickins on the night of the 16th for the 6th K.O.S.B. and two companies of the 11th Royal Scots, supported by two companies of the 1st South African Infantry, to attack Longueval at 2 A.M. He was also instructed to withdraw his men from the front trenches to allow the oblong to be shelled by the heavy guns. This bombardment was to begin at 11 P.M. on the 16th, but had to be postponed until 12.30 A.M. on the 17th, owing to the difficulty and delay in withdrawing our infantry to a safe distance. In spite of the greatest gallantry, the attack was beaten off. The whole virtue of the project was lost when the heavy bombardment lasted only for an hour and was unobserved. This was the last effort of the 27th Brigade to capture Longueval. During the night, the 6th K.O.S.B. and 11th Royal Scots were withdrawn to Talus Boise, the "Rifles," who had been relieved on the night of the 15th by the 8th Brigade (Third Division), taking over the trenches of the latter.

At 9 A.M. on the 17th, Waterlot Farm was at length captured by the 26th Brigade. After a preliminary bombardment by artillery, the Camerons, supported by two companies of the 4th South African Infantry, rushed the farm, slaughtered the garrison, and proceeded to consolidate the buildings.

At the end of the day the whole Division was completely worn out. The nights were even more trying than the days on account of the intensity of the German shelling, and the strain on the South Africans, who were certain to receive the first shock of a counter-attack, was particularly severe. During the evening of the 17th July, Lieut.-Colonel Tanner was wounded, and the command of the garrison passed to Lieut.-Colonel Thackeray. That night General Furse decided to relieve the South Africans in the northern part of Delville, but both brigades requested the relief to be postponed on hearing of the operation against Longueval, which was to be carried out by the 76th Brigade of the Third Division on the morning of the 18th. During the hours of darkness, in addition to their usual artillery-fire, the Germans poured thousands of gas shells into the battery positions and back areas. A determined counter-stroke was delivered against Delville Wood from the north-west, and the enemy penetrated as far as Buchanan Street and Princes Street before he was driven back with heavy loss. Other assaults were made on the perimeter, but all were repulsed.

Longueval was attacked at 3.45 A.M. on 18th July by the 76th Brigade. At first, rapid progress was made, and shortly after 8 A.M. a report was received from the Third Division stating that it had captured all its objectives. A company of the Seaforths and a company of the Camerons co-operated with the Third Division in clearing houses in the north of the village. The enemy however still clung tenaciously to some of his posts; when parties of the 26th and 27th Brigades moved up to consolidate strong points in Longueval, they were stopped by machine-gun fire from German pockets.

The day was destined to be the most critical of the battle. At 8 A.M. the enemy opened a tremendous bombardment on Delville Wood and the village with guns of all calibres, and until 7 P.M. there was no diminution of the cannonade, which was probably the heaviest that the Division ever experienced. The whole earth vibrated and trembled from the impact of thousands of "crumps." All communications were broken down, and for a long time General Furse was ignorant of what was happening. Officers of his staff, particularly Major MacNamara, took great risks in going up to Longueval to ascertain the situation, but no definite information as to the fate of the South Africans could be gathered. About 2 P.M. the shelling increased in fury. Our front trenches were obliterated, whole sections of their occupants were annihilated, and the Germans launched a terrific attack. For this supreme effort they had brought up picked troops, consisting of the 7th and 8th Divisions of the famous Magdeburg Corps,[1] commanded by Sixt von Armin.

[1] This was the Corps which the old Army fought at Le Cateau in 1914.

After 2 P.M. the S.O.S. signal was seen in the wood and the village, and some of our men were noticed dribbling back from these places. Practically all the South Africans on the perimeter had perished, and the few survivors, stupefied by the ferocity of the shelling, fell back on Lieut.-Colonel Thackeray's H.Q. in Princes Street. At 3 P.M. waves of Germans poured through the wood and the northern part of Longueval, but now seizing their opportunity our machine-gunners took heavy toll of the men in field-grey. Lieut.-Colonel Thackeray's troops performed prodigies of valour, and in a sustained and delirious struggle the heroic defenders baffled every effort of the foe to break their ranks. In this grisly combat the Germans lost much valuable time, and when they pressed on, the gallant South Africans were still holding out.

General Furse was at Montauban when he heard of the counter-attack. It was not a time for hesitation, and he ordered the Argylls to advance at once and reoccupy all the ground north and west of Regent Street that had been evacuated. But the enemy's barrage along the line of Clarges Street was so thick that it was impossible to take the men through it.

Later, at 3.30 in the afternoon, Lieut.-Colonel Dawson received orders to collect all available men of the 1st and 4th South African Infantry, and take them up to the Strand and northern boundary of the wood. With about 160 men he set off on his desperate errand shortly after 4 P.M. On the way he met some officers, who reported that the whole of the garrison had been virtually annihilated. Accordingly he left his men in the old German trenches south-west of Longueval, and went off to find out how matters stood. Disorganised parties of men, their nerves sorely jangled by the bombardment, were streaming southwards through the village. When Lieut.-Colonel Dawson discovered that some of the South Africans were still holding out near Buchanan Street, he took his men into the village, and put them in trenches just north of Dover Street on the right of the 26th Brigade.

The crisis occurred about 6 P.M. By that time all Longueval north of Clarges Street was lost except for a few keeps garrisoned by Highlanders, but the gallant resistance of these posts proved of the greatest possible value. The enemy held all the wood outside the area occupied by Lieut.-Colonel Thackeray and his men, and the line of Buchanan Street which was held by the Camerons. All day the majority of the troops of the 26th Brigade had sheltered in the trenches south of Clarges Street from the fiendish shelling. During the worst spells, when nothing could be heard above the hideous din of the screaming and crashing shells, the men cowered into the sides of their trenches; but though wearied and exhausted they were full of fight, and when a short lull came they peered eagerly over the parapet hoping for a glimpse of the enemy on whom they might wreak vengeance for the horror of the bombardment. If any man stood out from his fellows that day, it was Lieut.-Colonel Gordon of the Black Watch. By the sheer force of his masterful personality he controlled the situation. After a brief consultation he and Lieut.-Colonel Kennedy of the Seaforths decided that the time was ripe for a counter-attack. A new line had been thrown forward along the railway that ran from Guillemont into Longueval. Shortly before 6 P.M. this line was reinforced by every available man from the Highland Brigade, and the whole pressed forward towards Delville Wood; at the same time, led by Lieut.-Colonel Duff, the Camerons swept westwards from Buchanan Street.   On clearing the main square, the Highlanders saw the field-grey ranks of the enemy emerging from the south-west corner of the wood.   For all who took part in that attack this was the most thrilling moment of the war.   For the space of a single second both sides hesitated, so dramatic was the meeting, and then from the left of the 26th line came the rousing command, " Forward, boys ! " and the Highlanders surged on like an irresistible wave. The Germans wavered, fired a few shots, and bolted into the shelter of Delville, refusing to face a force that was less than a fourth of their own strength. Carried away by the impetuosity of this magnificent charge, many of the Highlanders heedlessly followed the enemy far into the thicket, where many a brave man, marked on the casualty lists as " missing," met his fate in a lonely scuffle with the Germans.

It was then that the quality of control and discipline was most needed.   The whole value of the counter-attack would have been lost if the small force had pressed on into the wood ; it would have been surrounded and cut off by the overwhelming numbers of the foe.   Between them, Lieut.-Colonels Gordon and Kennedy rallied and re-formed the men.   Already they were in danger of being outflanked and a machine-gun, which had been missed during the rush, was taking heavy toll of their numbers from the rear.   The Camerons, whose C.O., Lieut.-Colonel Duff, had been severely wounded during the *mêlée*, fell back on Buchanan Street, and the remainder was brought back to the line of Clarges Street and a trench to the immediate north of the Church. This position was firmly held, and a supporting line on the railway was formed.   The attack so carefully planned by the enemy had been broken, and though the Highlanders had been

too few to recapture Delville Wood, their timely charge
had certainly maintained our grasp on the village.

All this time the South Africans had maintained
their position against prodigious odds at the corner of
Princes Street and Buchanan Street. Lieut.-Colonel
Dawson did all that was possible to assist them ; he
sent up reinforcements, ammunition, rations, and stores,
and towards midnight he went up to Lieut.-Colonel
Thackeray's H.Q. Every yard of the mangled wood
bore plain traces of the desperate fighting that it had
witnessed. "Devil's Wood" it was called by our men,
and that was the correct name. The South African H.Q.
were full of wounded, and there were no men available
to take them away. During the evening the remnants
of the South Africans took over Buchanan Street from
the Camerons, who were required to reinforce the
Clarges Street line. That night was a trying and anxious
time for Lieut.-Colonel Thackeray ; his forces were
small in number and were utterly spent. Three times
the Germans came on in force, but were repulsed with
heavy losses.

Our hold on southern Longueval was strengthened
during the night by battalions of the 27th Brigade.
After the relief was complete, the Clarges Street
line on the left was held by the 9th Scottish Rifles,
a company of the 18th H.L.I., and a company of the
6th K.O.S.B. ; three companies of the Borderers
formed a flank along Pall Mall, and the 12th Royal
Scots occupied the old German front line from Pall
Mall to the west.

By the evening of the 18th July, General Furse
had drawn up his plans for a counter-attack. The
force to be employed consisted of the 53rd Brigade,
which had been placed under his command. After
7.30 P.M., as it was clear that the Germans occupied

all the wood east of Buchanan Street and north of
Princes Street, a barrage was placed on it east and
north of these rides. The 19th Durham Light Infantry
were placed under the orders of Brig.-General Ritchie,
and were instructed to secure the southern portion
of the wood at 12.30 A.M. on the 19th July, but owing
to the shelling, the darkness, and the unfamiliarity
of the D.L.I. with the main features of the village,
this operation was postponed until 6.15 in the morning,
when the attack was delivered by the 53rd Brigade
under a H.E. barrage. Owing to delays, the infantry
did not begin to advance until 7.30 A.M., but they
succeeded in clearing the wood south of Princes
Street. In this operation the 53rd was effectively
assisted by Lieut.-Colonel Thackeray's men, who kept
up a destructive fire on the Germans. For some
unknown reason the 53rd Brigade failed to relieve the
South Africans, though it was asked to do so by the
26th Brigade.

This was the last operation directed by General
Furse against Delville Wood, and on the night of
the 19th July the relief of the Division commenced.
The remnants of the 26th on relief by the 8th Brigade
(Third Division) withdrew to Carnoy, and next day
marched farther back to the sand-pits near Meaulte.
The 27th was relieved by the 95th Brigade (Fifth
Division), and moved first to Talus Boise and then
to the Citadel. On the night of the 18th all the
South Africans, except those under Lieut.-Colonel
Thackeray's command, were withdrawn to Happy
Valley. Not until the evening of the 20th was this
valiant little detachment relieved, when Lieut.-Colonel
Thackeray with two wounded officers and 140 men
moved out to Talus Boise, rejoining next day the
fragments of the brigade at Happy Valley. With

the exception of the artillery,[1] the whole of the Division was relieved on the morning of the 20th July, on which date General Furse handed over the command of the sector to the G.O.C., Third Division.

The work of all the R.A.M.C. personnel and the regimental stretcher-bearers during the battle was worthy of the highest commendation. The conditions, especially from the 14th, were appalling, perpetual and ghastly shell-fire, an unceasing stream of wounded, and atrocious roads. In spite of all these difficulties the casualties were evacuated with wonderful rapidity, while the heroism and endurance of doctors and stretcher-bearers were almost beyond belief. Instances of the former squatting in shell-holes and dressing their patients under a murderous fire were innumerable. But, indeed, in the work of all men wearing the Red Cross the spirit of self-sacrifice shone at its brightest. The succouring of the wounded is an instinct with the British soldier, and there is no case known in the whole Army of a stretcher-bearer ever shirking his duty. More than once in the course of the cruel struggle, the shelling was so intense that it seemed impossible to rescue the wounded, but men were always ready to risk their lives (and in many cases they lost them) to bring their comrades in. When all were most exhausted, the work became most severe. From the 18th July, the arduous labour of dressing and evacuating the cases was a continuous strain, everyone working at the highest tension. The wounded who were left behind, when the Division moved out, it was beyond the power of anyone to reach;

[1] The artillery remained in the line until the 27th July, during which period it effectively supported the attacks of the Third and Second Divisions on Longueval and Delville Wood, Brig.-General Tudor acting as C.R.A. to both these divisions.

they lay in the area recaptured by the enemy in his counter-blow.

Throughout the action the work of the Sappers and Pioneers reached its usual standard; no higher praise than this could be desired. Apart from assisting the infantry to consolidate the captured positions and construct strong points, they had to keep roads in repair. Even in the summer of 1916 the roadways in the Somme area could scarcely cope with the enormous traffic that passed over them. For instance, the Maricourt–Montauban road, which was constantly used, was only fit for horse transport, though twenty tons of road metal were put on it daily by the Division. In the forward areas, the imperturbable manner in which Sappers and Pioneers worked under the heaviest fire aroused the sincere admiration of the infantry; they seemed to be men without nerves. Their losses were extremely heavy, a serious matter, as skilled men were not too numerous. The C.R.E., Lieut.-Colonel Barnardiston, was wounded on the 17th July and his place was taken by Major G. R. Hearn of the 64th Field Company.

The ordinary duties of the A.S.C. and the transport were attended with considerable risk, as the few roads were continually searched by artillery-fire. Not a night passed without its story of narrow escapes or of losses suffered. From the moment that the First Line Transport left its lines with stores and rations, the men knew that for several hours they had to run the gauntlet. The rugged, weird beauty of the shell-torn country, lit up fantastically by the gleam of the belching guns, escaped the eyes of men guiding their limbers round the edge of shell-holes and listening uneasily for the first signs of a hostile "strafe." In spite of the greatest skill in timing a dash through the worst areas, the transport of most of the battalions suffered grievously, especially on the nights of the 17th and 18th. The Argylls were particularly unlucky, for on the latter date their Quartermaster, Lieut. W. R. Weller, and their Transport Officer, 2nd Lieut. K. D. Thomson, were killed. Throughout the whole period, however, no battalion failed to receive its rations and stores—a very creditable fact, considering the severity of the fighting.

The attack on Longueval and Delville Wood will rank as one of the greatest examples of the fine fighting qualities of the Division. The operation was undertaken against a brave and alert foe, and had for its object positions that formed the pivot of the enemy's defensive system. The element of surprise, that made the capture of Montauban a comparatively easy matter, was lacking on the 14th July; the Germans expected an onset and were prepared for it. When all these things are considered, the marvel is that the Division was able to accomplish as much as it did. And the full magnitude of the achievement was probably not realised for some time; for not till more than a month later were the Germans driven from their last defences in Longueval and Delville Wood. Where failure was recorded, as in the case of the attacks on the northern part of the village, the melancholy roll of the killed and wounded was the monument of the devotion with which the men had attempted to do more than men could do. Out of a total of barely 3000, the 27th Brigade lost 81 officers and 2033 men, and the great majority of the killed and missing, 569 in all, left their bones in the blood-soaked undergrowth of the orchards of Longueval.

But even more remarkable than the dour resolution, with which the battle was carried on, was the extra-

ordinary capacity for endurance displayed by the men in
holding on to their gains. In France, the most difficult
part of an attack was not the winning of an objective
but the keeping of it after it was gained. The Germans
knew all about the art of war. Their counter-stroke on
the 18th July was admirably planned and skilfully carried
out, and it was made when the Division was at its
weakest. Never did the Ninth rise to greater heights.
Here and there under a hellish bombardment a few
dazed men straggled back, but the great majority of
them stood their ground. The defence of Delville Wood
by Lieut.-Colonel Thackeray's small band rightly takes
its place as one of the classic feats of the war. But
though less well known, the charge of the Highlanders
that saved Longueval when a serious disaster seemed
inevitable, is an achievement that ought to secure a
lasting place in our military annals. Not merely does
it illustrate the unflinching courage of the Highlanders
of the 26th Brigade, but it is a brilliant example of the
value of a prompt counter-attack boldly carried out by
even a few men against a resolute and numerous enemy.

Throughout the battle the unflagging support of the
artillery had been of the greatest assistance. The ideas
of Brig.-General Tudor had been triumphantly vindi-
cated by the events of the action, and the enthusiasm
of the infantry for the H.E. barrage was the best
justification of his methods.

In the three weeks' fighting the Division lost 314
officers and 7303 other ranks. The figures represent
about 50 per cent. of its strength and considerably
more than that of the infantry. But it had not fought
in vain ; it had retained nearly all that it had captured,
and when it was withdrawn from the battle, it had
established its name as one of the hardest fighting
divisions in France.

For its work it was generously commended by General Sir H. Rawlinson.[1] But most of all the men cherished the tribute of their own leader, General Furse, on 21st July:—"The Ninth Division is being withdrawn from the battle line. It has played a conspicuous and honourable part in one of the greatest battles in the world's history. We may all of us with justice be proud of having served in the Division during the past three weeks.

"From the bottom of my heart I want to thank you all—officers, N.C.Os. and men, for all you have done during these weeks of strenuous fighting.

"The demands made on all branches of the Division have been great, and right well have they been answered.

"The infantry, Highlanders, Lowlanders, and South Africans, have as usual had to bear the most continuous strain. To sustain appalling and continuous shell-fire, to try to dig for themselves trenches amongst the fallen

---

[1] "As it will be impossible for me to speak personally to the Ninth Division, I desire to convey to every officer, N.C.O. and man, my thanks and congratulations for the splendid work the Division has done during the Battle of the Somme.

"The attack and capture of the hostile second line system of defence, and the village of Longueval on the 14th July, was a feat of arms which will rank high amongst the best military attainments of the British Army, whilst in the capture of Delville Wood, the gallantry, perseverance, and determination of the South African Brigade deserves the highest commendation.

"Not only has the fighting spirit of the infantry of the Division been admirable, but the manner in which the divisional artillery has helped and supported the infantry shows that a high degree of training has been attained, and it is with regret that I am informed that the Division is to be transferred to another army. I trust that at some future time I may again have the honour of finding them under my command."

H. RAWLINSON,
General Commanding Fourth Army.

H.Q., FOURTH ARMY,
25th *July* 1916.

trees and through the roots of Bernafay and Delville Woods, to suffer heavy casualties amongst their comrades and friends, to go on day and night for a week or more without any relief and with only snatches of disturbed sleep, to bear all the time the stern responsibility of being the guardians of the very pivot of the Commander-in-Chief's manœuvre, and to maintain throughout, as they have done, an uncomplaining resolution, a cheerful bearing—for all this, we who have had other work to do offer the infantry our whole-hearted admiration and thanks.

"And the infantry, I am sure, will be the first to recognise the continuous assistance they have received from the artillery, who have been working at the highest pressure day and night since the 24th June, and are still in the line, as also from the Engineers and from the Pioneers, whose skilful help has always been at hand.

"Equally deserving our gratitude are the Surgeons and their untiring assistants, including the Chaplains, for the care they have given to the wounded without thought for their own safety; and none of us will easily forget all the difficulties overcome by the Supply and Transport Services.

"Lastly, I would thank the brigadiers and their staffs—and the various members of my own staff—for their zealous and efficient work, which has had so much to say to the successes we have gained. Nor do I forget the Signal Service—that invaluable and hard-worked channel of orders and reports.

"We shall miss with lasting regret the many comrades and friends we have lost, but they with you, thank God, have won fresh honours for the Ninth Division and success for our arms."

When the Division left the battle line it was only

the skeleton of what it had been on the 1st July, but as the enemy had employed no fewer than three first-rate divisions against it, one may assume[1] that his losses had been more numerous. This seemed to indicate that the intentions of Sir Douglas Haig were being fulfilled. Episodes such as the costly fighting in Longueval were inevitable in a battle of this magnitude, but in this case more might have been achieved with a greater economy of lives had it not been for the anxiety of the Fourth Army to prevent the programme of the British Commander-in-Chief being affected by delay. Its insistence on the necessity of securing Longueval at once did not allow General Furse a free hand to deal with the situation, and as it turned out, the attempt to rush matters was a spendthrift policy, and actually resulted in losing instead of saving time.

With the opening of the Battle of the Somme there was a noticeable change in the attitude of the men. They now realised the full seriousness and gravity of the business that they had undertaken, and they no longer entered into battle with the exuberant optimism that had filled the men at Loos with the belief that they could sweep away the defences of Germany at one blow. Their confidence was unshaken and their belief in ultimate victory assured, but if the Somme became for the enemy a Gehenna, it was also a supreme trial and test for the soldiers of the British Empire.

[1] There can be nothing stronger than assumption. The Germans used their divisions in battle for shorter spells than we did, and it is highly probable that we persistently overrated their casualties.

CHAPTER VII

THE BUTTE DE WARLENCOURT

October 1916

AFTER being withdrawn from the battle, the Division was allowed a reasonable interval in which to heal its wounds. The last few days in the Somme area brought a much-appreciated rest. All Picardy glowed under a mellow sun, and in the glorious summer weather it was no hardship to sleep in bivouacs. The forenoons were given over to training and the replacement of kit; the "Q" Branches and the Ordnance Staffs were kept busy making good the losses in equipment and material. In the broad lagoons of the Somme near Bray were magnificent bathing-places, to which the men were taken every day, and here there was an element of danger, for the current was strong, and a swimmer usually emerged from the river about a hundred yards from the spot at which he had entered.

Small drafts began to arrive to fill up gaps; all battalions were very weak in officers, and a company that had more than two was decidedly well off. Fortunately most of the commanding officers had escaped. In the 26th Brigade there were several changes; Lieut.-Colonel Tweedie of the Argylls had been wounded, and, though he remained at duty for

L

some time, he was obliged finally to enter hospital, and he was succeeded by Lieut.-Colonel Kennedy of the Seaforths on the 3rd August. Lieut.-Colonel R. Horn was appointed C.O. of the Seaforths, and Lieut.-Colonel H. R. Brown of the Camerons. In the 27th Brigade the command of the 12th Royal Scots passed to Lieut.-Colonel H. N. S. Fargus on the 23rd July. Most of the changes occurred in the South African Brigade. The 2nd South African Infantry had lost all its senior officers, and Major Heal of the 1st assumed command until he was relieved at the end of August 1916 by Lieut.-Colonel Christian from England. Major D. M. MacLeod of the South African Scottish was wounded on the 17th July, and his place was taken by Major D. R. Hunt. Lieut.-Colonel Thackeray had been wounded, but happily not seriously enough to cause his removal to hospital.

On the 23rd July the Division left the Somme district, and moved to the IX. Corps area, with D.H.Q. at Pont Remy. Most of this long journey was performed on foot under a broiling sun and over dusty roads, so that the march was extremely fatiguing. Two days later the Ninth was transferred to the IV. Corps[1] of the First Army,[2] and this move brought it into the centre of industrial France. For a few days units were concentrated in the large mining town of Bruay, where an enjoyable time was spent. The men had luxurious hot-spray baths at the mines, and changes of clothing; there were also numerous first-rate concerts and other entertainments, where leisure could be passed easily and agreeably. In a short time, however, units were sent out to country billets in the neighbourhood, where greater facilities for training

[1] Commanded by Lieut.-General Sir H. Wilson.
[2] Commanded by General Sir C. Monro.

were available. The 27th Brigade was particularly fortunate, for its area included a deep quarry full of water near Beugin, where all could indulge in bathing and swimming.

The Division, though no unit was yet up to strength, had almost recovered from its severe handling, when the 26th Brigade took over the trenches on the Vimy Ridge from the Thirty-seventh Division on the evening of the 12th August. Two nights later, the 27th Brigade occupied the line on the left of the 26th. D.H.Q. were established at Camblain L'Abbé, where they remained during the period the Ninth was at Vimy Ridge. The entire country in the divisional area was hilly and undulating, the most prominent feature being the Vimy Ridge, running north and south. It had been the scene of ghastly fighting in the early summer of 1915, and though the German lines lay along the crest of the ridge, our men gleaned some idea of the splendid fighting qualities that had carried their brave ally through the demolished villages of Carency and Souchez, and far up the western slopes. The best blood of France had watered the whole area, and it was with great reluctance that the French handed over the sector to the British. One of the communication trenches had been named after a famous regiment that had then played a proud and honourable part in the attack, and, when rumours were afloat that the Germans had retaken the ridge, some men of that regiment visited the area to ascertain the position. They were undeniably cheered and relieved to learn that the rumours were false, and that their British comrades kept a firm hold on all that had been entrusted to them.

The line taken over was divided into the Berthonval sector on the right, and the Carency sector on the left.

In the former, the opposing trenches lay far apart—at no point being closer than 70 yards—except for saps; in the latter, those on the far left were almost touching each other, and a man could throw a bomb into the enemy's trench without difficulty. The whole front was fringed with craters, which on the left were so numerous that they practically merged into one another. Where the line cut them were the most critical posts; here were the gates for an enterprising foe eager to secure prisoners. The trenches were not too salubrious, since many of the French dead had been buried in their walls or floor, and the usual work had to be done nightly and daily by infantry, sappers, and pioneers to make them substantial. In one part the sand-bags, full of rough pieces of chalk, had been thrown up in such haphazard fashion that the parapets appeared likely to collapse if a man sneezed. However, after a few weeks' hard toil there was a marked improvement. From our position a magnificent view extended towards the north, and it was significant of the tendency of the British Army at this time to work in water-tight compartments, that the division on the left never sent observers to our lines, and yet from there the best observation could be had.

Though all seemed to live on the edge of acute suspense because of the constant mining carried on by both sides, the stay at the Vimy was singularly uneventful. The approaches to the line were in very good order, and reliefs were carried out in daylight. A communication trench, cut right through the valley, emerged on the western slopes of the ridge out of sight of the enemy. Its official name was Cabaret Rouge, but "The Never-ending Road," the title given to it by the men, was a better description, for it took one over two hours to traverse it from end to end. As

ABLAIN ST. NAZAIRE, NOTRE DAME AND VIMY RIDGE

there was practically no shelling of the communication trenches and back roads, the transport and carrying parties had a fairly easy and secure time.

Matters livened up in the sector after the Divisional Artillery [1] had registered, but the enemy appeared to be husbanding his ammunition, and contented himself with trench-mortar bombardments. He stuck to fixed periods. It was remarked that one could wander about peacefully in the sector during the day except between the hours of 2 and 4 P.M.—the time of the trench-mortar interlude. The type used was the "rum jar" —a huge, unwieldy shell that was thrown high into the air—and a man was absolutely safe if he used his eyes and wits. Sentries with whistles kept a lookout, and when a mortar was on the way a whistle-blast gave warning. On such occasions it was easy to distinguish the newcomers from the old hands. On hearing the blast the latter placidly looked up, ascertained where the mortar was likely to land, and acted accordingly; but the former stampeded in a panic for any sort of shelter, content so long as it would cover their heads. After a few experiences, however, most men learned to trust to their eyes and their judgment; for no dug-out, unless it was exceptionally deep, was proof against a trench mortar. A shorter "strafe" took place in the evenings, between six and seven. The officers of one mess, compelled to have dinner in the open, owing to lack of accommodation, often had that meal interrupted, and it was not an uncommon sight to see them leave a course and rush for safety.

The disagreeable element during this period was furnished by the weather. From the end of August

---

[1] In September the artillery were reorganised on a basis of 6 guns per battery, the 53rd Brigade being broken up for this purpose. The Divisional Artillery then consisted of the 50th, 51st, and 52nd Brigades.

scarcely a day passed without much rain, and thus there was the usual constant struggle to keep the trenches from being flooded. There was a grave suspicion, too, that enemy mines were perilously close to our parapet. One curious incident happened. At 10.20 A.M. on the 19th August, the enemy exploded a small mine on the front of the 27th Brigade. Three sappers of the 90th Field Coy. were thrown into the crater caused by the explosion, two being killed, and one buried up to the neck in the débris. Some of the Germans were also buried, and an informal truce was observed while the stretcher-bearers of both sides dug out their comrades. The G.O.C., who was going round the line at the time, ran a narrow escape, as he had just passed the area affected by the explosion. There were however more alarms than events, and casualties were exceptionally low. The customary routine for a battalion was twelve days in the front system, six in brigade reserve, and six in billets in divisional reserve, when a good deal of training could be carried on. While the South Africans were at Frevillers on the 11th August, H.M. the King passed through the village, and dismounting from his car, walked along their ranks.

Apart from trench mortars, the chief thrills were provided by sniping and raids. The prince of snipers dwelt in the Carency sector, and was affectionately known amongst the men as "Cuthbert." He was a deadly shot, and destroyed an enormous number of our periscopes. No man dared show a finger when Cuthbert was on duty; he was never known to miss, so naturally he was the chief object of our snipers' efforts. Numerous posts were erected for his benefit, but no sooner were they ready than Cuthbert sent a few bullets through the loopholes. At last one was constructed that escaped his notice. Too much success had made him careless; he rose from his lair and stretched his arms. That was sufficient. With his disappearance our snipers had it all their own way.

The raids engineered in this sector met with fair success. On two occasions parties of the 12th Royal Scots and of the "Rifles" penetrated the hostile lines but failed to secure prisoners; the former had the satisfaction of killing a few Germans, but the latter found the trenches deserted by the garrison. The biggest capture of prisoners was made by the South Africans. At 4 A.M. on the 14th September, 2 officers and 60 men of the 2nd South African Infantry entered the enemy's trenches under cover of an artillery barrage; they killed at least 12 and brought back 5 prisoners. The only casualties were 2 wounded, one of whom unfortunately had to be left in the German lines. On the evening of the 16th September a successful raid was carried out by the Black Watch and Camerons, and on this occasion the Highlanders satisfied the desire of the G.O.C. for an identification by bringing back a prisoner, but at least 50 had fallen victim to their blood-lust. This last raid was carried out under a Stokes barrage, so terrific that dozens of the enemy were killed, and the remainder paralysed with fright. All the Stokes Guns in the Division had been collected for the operation, and in forty-five minutes they fired 9000 shells, which completely obliterated the opposing front trenches. At one time the 26th Brigade was marked out for something more ambitious than a raid; for the First Army desired to push the enemy off the crest before winter set in, but the scheme was postponed, possibly because it would have used up troops that were needed for the Somme.

On leaving the Vimy Ridge on the 25th September

the Division, after moving first to a training area under the Third Army, joined the III. Corps[1] of the Fourth Army, and on the 9th October the 26th and South African Brigades relieved the Forty-seventh Division in the line near Eaucourt L'Abbaye. The move was made chiefly by route march over wretched roads and in vile weather, but for a portion of the distance buses were available. The 27th Brigade had a trying experience. At 8 A.M. on a chill October morning, all the men were lined up on a road near Barly, waiting for the buses, which did not arrive until 3 o'clock in the afternoon, with the result that units reached the terminus in inky darkness, and some of them had then to march a long distance to their billets.

The Lewis Gunners had a most unenviable time. Battalions had now been supplied with 10 guns, each with its mounting and 44 magazines, each of which contained 49 cartridges. There were also bags with spare parts, gloves for firing the guns when they were hot, jackets[2] for carrying them, and hyposcopes, so that the gun could be fired without the firer being seen. For the carriage of all this material handcarts had been provided in June, but they proved utterly useless except on good roads, and they imposed an intolerable strain on the men who pulled them. All the units altered these carts so that they could be drawn by mules, but even so they were unsatisfactory and broke down continually. When the Somme was reached, so was the limit of endurance. The whole drainage system of the country had been smashed by months of shelling, and the roads, poor at their best, seemed to have no bottom; the ruins of whole villages were thrown into them, but even that never appeared

[1] Commanded by Lieut.-General Pulteney.
[2] The gloves were occasionally used, the jackets never.

to make them any firmer. The battalions of the 27th
Brigade will never forget the march from Lavièville
to Mametz Wood. It was plain sailing as far as the
vicinity of Fricourt Wood. At this point the path lay
along the eastern edge of the wood, but the carts and
mules sank deep in mud, and had to be hauled out and
dragged along by the sweating and blasphemous teams.
This harassing process continued until the carts were
eventually parked in the transport lines on a tableland
on the east side of Mametz Wood. One unit found
the zig-zag path to this tableland completely blocked
by an artillery horse which had fallen and could not
be persuaded to rise. The men were tired and hungry
and not relishing the prospect of a lengthy wait, they
hauled the carts and mules one by one up the face of
a precipice and so reached the transport lines.

In other theatres the outstanding event was the
entry of Roumania on the 27th August as a belligerent
on the side of the Entente. This event, which was
greeted with boisterous and undignified jubilation in
France and Britain, was regarded as a decisive blow
to the Central European Powers, but the tribulation
that the immediate future brought upon Roumania
seemed to indicate that an exaggerated estimate had
been placed on its worth and services. The grievances
of the Roumanians in Transylvania and Hungary, the
ostensible cause of war, led logically to an invasion
of the former province ; and this campaign would
have had a greater effect on the war than the narrow
aims of Italy, had it not been for the gross ineptitude
and short-sighted selfishness of Russia, whose overtures
and representations had the most weight in bringing
the little Balkan state into the field.

In 1915 Russia had been precluded from invading
Bulgaria by the neutrality of Roumania, whose territory

interposed an obstacle and whose declaration of war
now gave her an opportunity of turning the situation
in the Balkans in favour of the Entente.   But
Roumania was allowed to prosecute her campaign
single-handed, and after a few initial successes had
to meet powerful and well-equipped German forces
under Von Falkenhayn and Von Mackensen.   The
ability of Germany to send a strong army to the
Balkans was a disagreeable surprise to the Western
Allies, and showed that our offensive on the Somme
was not so menacing as official bulletins and
press accounts had led us to believe, and that our
calculations of German losses were probably greatly
over-estimated.   The effect of this intervention soon
made itself felt; the Roumanians, opposed and out-
numbered, were compelled to fall back, but their
resistance was neither discreditable nor negligible,
and belated help from Russia, if generously given
and seriously intended, would have endangered the
flanks of Von Falkenhayn and perhaps have exercised
a decisive influence on the war.   But only the most
grudging and limited support was given, and though
an offensive from Salonica under General Sarrail
detained three Bulgarian divisions and eventually
led to the recapture of Monastir, the Roumanians
were pressed back by the 10th October to the borders
of Moldavia.

More than two months had elapsed since the
Division fought at Longueval, and in this period
continuous hammering had brought the British forces
far into the enemy's territory.   The greater part of
the ridge from Thiepval to Combles was now in our
hands, and the Germans had been pushed back
to their fourth system of defences.   With good
weather the speedy fall of Bapaume might be reckoned

on. On the front taken over by us, the principal feature was the Butte de Warlencourt, a mound of chalk about 50 feet high, which stood at the far end of the spur that ran from the main ridge through Flers, and was flanked by the tree-lined Albert–Bapaume road. North-east of this the ground sloped into a depression, which led into the valley of the Ancre, and beyond it lay a spur running from the road towards Morval, on which the enemy had his fourth position.

Behind the British front line lay the vast waste of wilderness created by three months of savage warfare. Its general colour scheme was a dull uniform grey, which changed to a dingy yellow when the sun shone. The whole area was covered with the débris of battle and of camps, but worst of all, from Mametz Wood to the front line were scattered fragments of corpses and a heavy fetid odour pervaded the atmosphere. The work of burying the dead was a slow process and even in Mametz Wood, which had been in our hands for two months, the 27th Brigade found a number of British and German dead still uninterred. The entire area was intersected by rutted roads, which even in fine weather could barely stand the stupendous amount of traffic that passed over them in a never - ending stream. Every available man of the 27th Brigade, which was in divisional reserve, worked daily repairing them, but all the labour served only to keep them passably decent, and when the weather broke down, almost superhuman efforts were required to keep them from collapsing altogether.

The line held by the 26th Brigade on the right, and the South Africans on the left, lay to the north of the Abbey of Eaucourt. On the 7th October the Forty-seventh Division had made an unsuccessful attack, but had established posts in front of its line. The Ninth joined up these posts and formed them into a new front line and a starting-point for fresh operations. These were notified on the 9th October, and the chief object of the attack, which was entrusted to the Ninth and Thirtieth Divisions, was to clear the Butte de Warlencourt. The objectives of the Ninth were two; first, Snag and Tail Trenches, and second, the trench lying to the far side of the Butte de Warlencourt, including the mound itself. Zero was fixed for 2.5 P.M., and the attack was to be covered by a creeping H.E. barrage, moving at the rate of 50 yards a minute.[1] The left flank was to be covered by a smoke-screen, which the Fifteenth Division was to put down between Le Sars and Warlencourt. To deceive the foe, a "Chinese Attack"[2] was arranged for the 11th October.

Brig.-General Ritchie's plan was to attack with the 7th Seaforths, supported by two companies of the Argylls and a section of the 26th L.T.M.B. The former, with two companies in line, each on a two-platoon front, was to advance in four waves. The assault was to be supported by Vickers Guns; one section was to follow the Seaforths, another the Argylls, and a third was to garrison the original front and support lines, the remaining section being in reserve. The arrangements of Brig.-General Lukin were on similar lines. The assault was to be made by the

---

[1] On this occasion the 47th Divisional Artillery and two brigades of the 1st Divisional Artillery supported the attack under the direct command of the C.R.A. 47th Division. Brig.-General Tudor acted as C.R.A. to General Furse.

[2] A "Chinese Attack" was not an attack; but the artillery put down the same sort of bombardment that was the usual prelude to an advance, moving by lifts over the enemy's system and then suddenly coming back to his front line, and so catching his infantry when they were manning the trenches to repel the expected assault.

BUTTE DE WARLENCOURT

2nd South African Infantry, supported by the South African Scottish. Each battalion was to form up in four waves, with two waves of carriers. On the afternoon of the 11th, the "Chinese Attack" caused several hostile machine-guns to unmask their positions and these were reported to the artillery.

Both brigades were formed up early in the afternoon of the 12th October, apparently without arousing the enemy's suspicion. In a drizzle of rain the attack was launched. One minute after zero the enemy[1] replied with a heavy barrage, which cut all the telephone wires and broke off communication between Brigade H.Q. and the assaulting battalions. From that moment obscurity reigned, and for a long time the only reports received by the Division came from the Artillery and the Royal Flying Corps. At the early hour of 2.34 P.M. the former announced that our men had failed to reach the first objective, but a rumour at 3.20 P.M. that some of our men had been seen on the Butte and to the right of it raised hopes that the assailants had overcome their difficulties. Whatever truth there was in that report, it was certain at 8.50 P.M. that the attack on the front both of the Ninth and Thirtieth Divisions had failed, though it was not till later that definite information was received.

At the very start the Seaforths had suffered some casualties by occasional shells from our own guns, which fell into the assembly trenches, and when the barrage became intensive the number of "short" shells increased. The difficulties in the way of artillery observation were immense and as there were many scratches of trenches that were not marked on the map, it was not surprising that during the various

---

[1] Consisting of Bavarians of the 6th Bavarian Reserve Division.

actions fought near the Butte the infantry frequently complained that they were being shelled by their own artillery.[1] The first objective lay several hundreds of yards from our front line, and the ground, which rose from our position in a gentle slope, formed a magnificent field of fire for rifles and machine-guns. The leading waves of the Seaforths advanced in perfect order, but they were swept away by a blast of lead. The supporting companies of the Argylls became involved in the disaster and a mixed party of Argylls and Seaforths dug in on a line about 150 yards in front of our original line. The others struggled back to their own trenches in the course of the evening. The new line was held and strengthened, and the front trenches were taken over by the Argylls. The supporting sections from the machine-gun company and the L.T.M.B. were both knocked out by the enemy's barrage before they could leave the trenches.

A similar series of misfortunes fell to the lot of the South Africans. The attack simply melted away before the enemy's scathing fire and the South Africans were seriously disorganised. Not until the morning of the 13th was the situation fully cleared up, when it was discovered that a party of 60 with 2 officers had dug in close to Snag Trench. It was impossible to reach this force during daylight, but it was safely withdrawn under cover of darkness on the night of the 13th October.

The attack broke down, because the artillery had failed to demolish the enemy's trenches and machine-guns; the barrage, though heavy, was inaccurate, as was proved by the air photographs received after the

---

[1] This was denied by the artillery, who suggested that the shells complained of were fired by the enemy; but many British fuses were found in the front trenches.

action. The whole operation was a rush, and was
carried out in spite of a strong protest by General
Furse to the Corps and Army Commanders. Since
it was important that we should secure the Bapaume
Ridge before winter set in, he urged that a premature
attack which ended in failure would waste much more
time than would be expended in preparations to insure
success, and he suggested that the attack should be
postponed for twenty-four or forty-eight hours to give
his men the chance of really localising the enemy by
reconnaissance, in order that the gunners might have
no doubt whatever as to the position of our infantry
and that of the enemy.

No further operation on a big scale took place until
the 18th October. The intervening period was blessed
with good weather, and more advanced positions were
dug to form a new starting-point. In front of the
South African lines, and on the left of the Snag Trench,
was a small mound, called the Pimple, which was
believed to be occupied by the enemy, as it appeared
to be the key to the trench. Brig.-General Lukin
was instructed to send out a strong patrol to seize
this point, and on the night of the 13th October a
party of the 3rd South African Infantry went out and
reconnoitred it. It found the Pimple unoccupied, but
returned so late that there was no time before dawn
to send out a force to garrison it. However, on the
evening of the 14th October, a strong force under
Captain L. F. Sprenger, who later was wounded, went
out and captured it. No serious endeavour was made
to dispute our possession of the Pimple, but when the
South Africans moved along from it and attempted to
expel the enemy from the junction of Snag and Tail
Trenches, which was known as the Nose, they were
driven back by machine-gun fire. Later on in the

evening the Germans tried in vain to recapture the Pimple, which was further strengthened by being linked up with the South African lines. The position, commanding an admirable view right up to the Butte, formed an ideal place for machine-guns and from it numerous losses were inflicted on enemy working-parties.

Orders for the operation on the 18th October were received from the Corps on the 14th, but the hope of taking the Butte at a stride was abandoned and the objective became the Snag Trench. On the right the attack was to be carried on by the Thirtieth Division. General Furse again entrusted the operation to the 26th and South African Brigades. The Camerons, with four companies in line, each on a platoon front, were to lead the 26th Brigade attack, supported by a company of the 8th Black Watch and a section of the machine-gun company. The Stokes mortars were to co-operate with the artillery in barraging the enemy's front line. On the left front the leading battalion was the 1st South African Infantry, with three companies in line, each on a platoon front, the fourth being in support, and a company of the 3rd South African Infantry in reserve. The hour of zero was 3.40 A.M.

By this date the fine weather had broken down and the attack began in a deluge of rain. Early information was received from the Camerons that they had reached their objective, but great uncertainty prevailed for a time as to the fate of the South Africans. It soon became known that the left half of their attack had been repulsed, but no news came about the right half. At 9.30 A.M. it was learned that a few men of the right company of the 1st South African Infantry had joined hands with the Camerons, who were in touch with a battalion of the Thirtieth Division on the right. Elsewhere the assault had failed.

The Camerons, carrying out their part with great dash, kept close to the barrage and entered the German trench as soon as it lifted. Except for some machine-gun fire from the left, resistance was slight and the garrison of the trench fled precipitately to the Gird Line. Blocks were immediately constructed on the right and left and held by bombers. About fifteen minutes after the capture, the enemy counter-attacked with bombs and forced his way in on the right, but the Camerons, immediately retaliating, killed a large number of the assailants and drove the remainder off in confusion. During this action a Stokes Gun team rendered great assistance by putting down a barrage on the Germans.[1] On the left the Camerons got into touch with a Lewis Gun team of the 1st South African Infantry, but could obtain no information concerning the rest of the battalion. In the afternoon about 300 Saxons were seen to be massing as if for a counter-attack. At once the S.O.S. was sent up and the men in field-grey, peppered with bullets and shell-fire, broke up in disorder and scrambled for shelter. Early in the evening, about 5.30 P.M., the enemy made still another attempt. A party of them left the Gird Trench and, moving round to the left flank, endeavoured to expel the Camerons by a bombing attack, but the garrison had received due warning and easily checked the onset with a Lewis Gun. During the night a company of the 9th Seaforths arrived and dug a communication trench from the old front line to Snag Trench.

The Lewis Gun detachment of the South Africans

[1] These were Saxons of the 40th Division, which had relieved the Bavarians.

M

on the left of the Camerons proved to be the only section of the brigade that secured the objective. The company on the left was held up by wire and came under a withering machine-gun fire. All the officers having been killed or wounded, the survivors were drawn back to their original line. The fate of the other two companies was wrapped in obscurity, and the bare fact is that, with the exception of the Lewis Gun post and a few wounded, none of them ever returned. A wounded South African reported that his comrades got into the German front trench, which was full of dead and wounded, and it is probable that they reached their objective, but, failing to recognise it as the trench had been completely wrecked, had pushed on, only to perish through machine-gun fire from the Butte.[1] A few stragglers made their way back later in the day, bringing with them 19 prisoners.

On learning what had occurred, General Furse sent instructions for another attack to be delivered at 5.45 P.M. The key of the German position was the Nose, which was to be bombarded. The South Africans were ordered to secure it and to establish a block about 500 yards up the Tail, and as the Camerons had already extended their line westwards they were in a position to assist the attack. Owing to continuous heavy rain conditions were appalling. All firmness had been soaked out of the ground, which became a sea of pewter-grey ooze, and even the lightly-equipped runners sank with each step beyond the knees in mud and took fully four hours to struggle over 1000 yards. The attack was entrusted to Lieut.-Colonel Dawson. He arranged for the fourth company of his own battalion to attack from the Pimple, while a

---

[1] Many dead South Africans were seen in front of Snag Trench by the 27th Brigade.

company of the 3rd South African Infantry was to
enter Snag Trench east of the Nose and attack westwards. The assault from the Pimple was made with
bombs, but the trench leading to the Nose dipped into
a hollow which was commanded by machine-guns from
it. Beyond this point all advance was barred to the
assailants. The second party entered Snag Trench
without difficulty and reached a point within 25 yards
of the Nose, but here the Germans were strongly posted
with three machine-guns in action and the advance
came to a halt. The South Africans then withdrew
to their original trenches, but later were ordered to
reoccupy the Snag. This was done early on the
morning of the 19th and a block was established on
the side of the Nose.

Thus in spite of considerable progress the Division
had been unable to complete the whole of its job. The
26th Brigade had done magnificently, but the Nose
had defied all the strenuous efforts of the South
Africans, whose failure had been due to no lack of
dash or determination but solely to the dreadful
conditions. Never did the Division fight on a more
grisly battlefield. The long muddy slope up to the
Butte was thickly strewn with British and German
dead, and in the more forward trenches corpses of
all units lay sprawling, wedged in by the slime that
coated them. In the open near the Snag, a long line
of men of the London Division, each on his face, was
grim evidence of a gallant charge and the accuracy of
the enemy's machine-gun fire. Here and there a body
arrested attention by the peculiar contortion of its
attitude and served as a landmark to guide runners
on their way. The air was rank with the odour of
death. To eye, ear, and nose the whole place was
repellant and it required extraordinary strength of

will even to appear cheerful amid such ghastly surroundings.

For ten days the Highland and South African Brigades had held the line and on the 18th October the G.O.C. instructed the 27th to take over the whole position on the night of the 19th. Before the relief commenced the mud-covered slope was again the scene of furious and bitter encounters. Dawn ushered in a miserable day with torrents of rain lashing down, and at 5.30 A.M. the Germans made a terrific assault, using flammenwerfer. The Black Watch,[1] who had relieved the Camerons during the night, met them in a desperate conflict. The only weapons fit for use were bombs; rifles and machine-guns were clogged with mud and could not be fired. The right company easily held its own and repulsed the invaders. The greatest danger came from the left, for on that flank the flammenwerfer caused much havoc amongst the South Africans, most of whom were driven out of Snag Trench, though a few moved eastwards and joined in with the Highlanders. At their backs followed German bombers who inflicted heavy casualties on the crowded troops, but a vigorous counter-attack by men of the "red hackle" stopped the assailants and forced them back for 40 yards. Captain Taylor of "B" Company hurried up from the support trench to the front line, and grasping the situation made arrangements for an attack. Bombing parties were organised and bombs brought up. Fortunately 2nd Lieut. Gibson of the L.T.M.B. had one Stokes Gun in good working order, and under its barrage the Black Watch regained all their trenches and had even penetrated into the South

---

[1] Commanded by Lieut.-Colonel Sir George Abercromby since the 20th September; Lieut.-Colonel Gordon, D.S.O., was promoted to a brigade in the Forty-first Division.

African sector by noon.   The whole of the defences
were then reorganised, but the enemy did not venture
again to tackle the Black Watch.

The South Africans had been expelled from the
Snag Trench by flammenwerfer, which had inflicted most
dreadful wounds.   But the Germans had not escaped
without scathe; for in the operation they exposed
themselves to the machine-guns at the Pimple, which
quickly thinned out their ranks.   After they were
compelled by the Black Watch to retire many took
refuge near the Nose, but this point was heavily
bombarded by our gunners, and large numbers leaving
the trench darted in the direction of the Butte.   Few
of them reached it; they were mowed down by the
Vickers and Lewis Gun fire of the Pimple garrison,
commanded by Major Ormiston.   Early in the afternoon the South Africans sent forward a party to
reoccupy the Snag and if possible to secure the Nose.
The first part of the scheme was easily accomplished,
but the tenacious machine-gunners ensconced in the
latter stopped all further progress.   For some inscrut-
able reason the wildest reports were sent back to
D.H.Q. that the Nose had been taken and that if
only more bombs could be sent up the Butte could
be captured without difficulty.   Such fallacious reports
are extremely dangerous; they may lead to the useless
sacrifice of many lives.   When the relief of the South
Africans began, General Furse was under the impression
that the Nose had been taken and he instructed the
27th Brigade to exploit the success.

The relief on the night of the 19th October will never
be forgotten by any officer or man of the Ninth who
took part in it.   In the forenoon under a soaking
rain the units of the 27th Brigade marched first to
High Wood, and even there a man sank up to his

ankles in mud.   The 6th K.O.S.B. and the 12th Royal
Scots who were to take over the left and the right
fronts had a terrible time.   The trial came as soon
as the communication trenches were entered.   There
seemed to be absolutely no bottom in them and the
men struggled along waist-deep in mud.   Darkness had
fallen when they reached the trenches near Eaucourt
L'Abbaye and an intense hostile barrage added to
the horror.   With devilish accuracy the shells pitched
near the communication trenches and many plunged
right into them.   Unspeakable was the fate of any
man who was badly wounded that night; he sank
below the mire and the men in the rear pressed on
all unconscious that the welcome firmness, which
momentarily sustained them, was the body of a
comrade.   Progress could be made only with the
greatest exhaustion; a yard seemed a mile.   Every
now and then the men had to halt for a brief space,
resting their elbows on the sides of the trench to
prevent their whole bodies being engulfed in the mud;
without such support it was fatal to stand still.   It
was not surprising that the relief was not complete
until 6 A.M. on the 20th October.

Many horrible tales were told about that relief,
but no invention could beggar the reality.   Men with
rifles and haversacks could scarcely struggle on, but
their lot was easy compared with that of Vickers
and Lewis Gun teams, whose guns had to be carried
up and also ammunition[1] for them.   The magazines
for the Lewis Guns were taken in buckets, like nose-
bags, each holding four.   The usual weight for a

---

[1] Here more might have been done to help the men by divisions in the
line handing over stores to those taking over.   It would have saved trouble
if the ammunition for the machine-guns had been kept in sealed boxes and
handed over; this plan was adopted later.

man was two buckets, but that was a Herculean load on such a night. Tales of distress reached the battalion H.Q. and parties with ropes and spades set out to rescue stranded men. One Lewis gunner of the 6th K.O.S.B. was so firmly embedded beyond the waist in mud that when he was finally extricated with ropes both his ankles were broken. The agonies endured by the Highlanders and South Africans were indescribable. Parties of worn-out men coming down from the front line threw themselves into any shell-hole, too tired to care what happened to them, and it was a kind cruelty that drove them to their feet and forced them on to some safer place. Many Highlanders discarded their kilts as being too heavy, but indeed so glutinous was the abundant mud that it was difficult to tell whether a man wore a kilt or not. Some of the Black Watch dropped down exhausted at the door of a dressing station near High Wood, and their tunics and equipment could not be removed in the ordinary way, but had to be hacked off them before they could be revived.

After their purgatorial march the men of the 27th Brigade were unfit to exploit any success, but the situation did not allow of any such attempt as the 6th K.O.S.B. found when they reached the front line. The enemy still held the Nose, and this was immediately reported by Lieut.-Colonel Connell to Brig.-General Scrase-Dickins, who immediately made arrangements for an attack to be delivered at 4 P.M. Until that time the Tail and the Nose were to be bombarded and at zero the 6th K.O.S.B. were to advance under cover of a barrage, which was to lift 50 yards every time the infantry fired a green light. The attack was to be from Snag Trench by bombing parties, but in the event of this being checked another was to be delivered across the open from the east by a support company an hour later. Lieut.-Colonel Connell supplemented these instructions by ordering the company at the Pimple to be ready to take advantage of these assaults. Both attacks from the east were repulsed by the machine-guns at the Nose. During these actions the garrison at the Pimple observing groups of the enemy retiring from the Tail towards the Butte, inflicted severe losses with machine-gun fire. At the same time, 2nd Lieut. Johnson and a few men rushed across the open, drove out the enemy and occupied the Nose. But the company commander, thinking that his men were too few to hold the whole trench from the Pimple to the Nose, evacuated the position. On hearing this, Brig.-General Scrase-Dickins ordered the 11th Royal Scots in support to send a company to retake the Nose and establish a post about 500 yards up the Tail, but before it arrived the Nose was reoccupied by the 6th K.O.S.B. Under the direction of Lieut.-Colonel Connell, who had gone to the Pimple on learning of the evacuation, a party of the K.O.S.B. retook the position and joined up with the company in Snag Trench. Later the company of the 11th Royal Scots arrived and passed up the Tail, where it established a post.

Thus on the night of the 20th October all the objectives of the attack of the 18th were secured. Till the evening of the 24th October the Division held the line and was busy strengthening its position and digging new assembly trenches for an attack on the Butte. It was the intention of the Corps to employ the Ninth in a battle that was arranged for the 25th October. On General Furse's representations this arrangement was cancelled and the Division was

relieved late on the 24th.[1] Another engagement was
indeed beyond the capacity of the men. Though
casualties were not so high, the nerve-strain and fatigue
were even greater than in July. More men were
lost from illness and exposure than from wounds and
death, and the number of cases of trench feet was
exceptionally large. Many men on being brought
back from the mud of the line took off their boots to
rub their feet, which swelled to such an extent that
they could not be inserted in the boot again.

The work of the R.A.M.C., especially from the
18th October onwards, was evilly affected by the
conditions. A man too seriously wounded to walk
was in a piteous plight; he had to wait for several
hours until men were available to carry him to a
dressing station. The usual number of men for a
stretcher is two, but eight were scarcely sufficient
at the Butte de Warlencourt. It was perhaps inevitable that in a place over which the tide of battle
ebbed and flowed for days and nights, a number of
wounded should have been missed. For several days
after the Ninth took over the line not a few wounded
men of the London Division, the ghastly aftermath
of an unsuccessful attack, were brought in by patrols.
Every man who could be spared was sent to help
the R.A.M.C. and the utmost efforts were made by
the Division to ensure that no wounded man was
overlooked.

The action at the Butte de Warlencourt was the
most dismal of all the operations carried out by the
Division, but it was ennobled by the great qualities
of endurance and heroism displayed by all who had
a share in it. In that waste of mud and water the

[1] The artillery stayed in and supported the attack by the Fiftieth
Division on the Butte.

ground captured, though small in extent, represented no mean achievement. The Butte remained impregnable, guarded by slime and weather, and it was not till the enemy voluntarily evacuated the place that it was entered and held by British troops. It may be questionable if the ground gained was worth the cost, but the mud had proved a more powerful ally of the adversary than had been expected.

CHAPTER VIII

ARRAS

NOVEMBER 1916 TO APRIL 1917

ON the 23rd November the Division was transferred from the Fourth to the Third Army, commanded by Sir Edmund Allenby. Most of the training and re-organisation was carried out in the neighbourhood of St Pol, and during this period several important changes in command took place. On the 21st October, while the Ninth was still engaged at the Somme, Brig.-General Scrase-Dickins was promoted to the command of the Thirty-seventh Division. He had been some-what unfortunate during his career with the Ninth. At Loos and at Longueval his brigade had the bad luck to run into the enemy's defences where they had been least damaged by artillery-fire; but these calamities were due not to lack of foresight or leader-ship, but to circumstances that would have similarly affected any other brigade. The General was noted for his Spartan routine and his extraordinary personal bravery. He was able to subsist on less than most men and limited himself to two meals a day. When his brigade was in the front trenches, he paid a daily visit to the line, and of his gallantry many stories were current. During the fighting in July his H.Q. at Montauban were persistently shelled, but he was never seen to twitch a muscle or dive for shelter; not even under the fiercest bombardment did he forego his daily tub in the open square at Montauban. His departure was viewed with the greatest regret; for he had been with the Ninth since its formation, and he was loved and respected by all who served under him. But his promotion [1] was known to have been thoroughly well earned and he took with him the congratulations and good wishes of the Division. His successor was Brig.-General F. A. Maxwell, V.C., who came from the Eighteenth Division and had the distinction of having led the battalion that took Trones Wood.

There was a change also in the Highland Brigade. On the 4th December Brig.-General Ritchie was appointed to the command of the Sixteenth Division. His service with the Ninth had been attended with almost unbroken success, and both at Loos and the Somme his men had not only shown great brilliancy and dash in securing their objectives, but had proved themselves to be masters of the art of counter-attack. He was succeeded by Brig.-General J. Kennedy of the Argylls.

On the 1st December General Furse [2] was appointed Master-General of the Ordnance. It is safe to say that no name is more closely associated with the annals of the Ninth Division than that of General Furse. In the fourteen months during which he had been in command he had succeeded in effecting that organised co-operation which was the proof of the unity that bound Lowlanders, Highlanders, and South Africans into one complete whole. He loathed water-tight compartments and did his utmost to foster the closest intercourse and co-operation between the various arms—

---

[1] Unfortunately long and constant strain had told on his health, and shortly after his appointment to the Thirty-seventh Division he was invalided to England.

[2] For his services in the war General Furse received the K.C.B. in June 1917.

infantry, gunners, sappers, and mounted men—who only by acting in concert could realise severally their highest fighting efficiency.   The fighting spirit had never been absent, but in training, in trenches, and in battle, he fostered and encouraged it until it became an instinct. He was a reservoir of power and ideas, and he had a natural *flair* for striking phrases.   Anxious and alert to increase the efficiency of his command, he was alive to the necessity of testing all new tactical appliances, and in his numerous conferences the principal motive was "not fault-finding but fact-finding."   An officer of the Division once remarked, "General Furse made the Ninth Division, and the Ninth Division made General Furse," and there is much that is true in the statement.   The leader had every reason to be proud of his men and the men of their leader.   His appointment was viewed with both regret and gratification ; regret, because a tried leader had gone, and gratification because his promotion was regarded as a tribute both to himself and to the Division.   But though his connection with the Ninth was officially severed, he was able in his new capacity to render it useful service.

He was succeeded by Major-General H. T. Lukin of the South African Brigade, the command of which passed to Brig.-General Dawson of the 1st Regiment. Major-General Lukin had won a great name while in command of the South Africans, and much was expected of him in his new position.

In the course of the next five months there were a few changes among battalion commanders.   In the Argylls the new C.O. was Lieut.-Colonel H. G. Sotheby. Lieut.-Colonel Connell was invalided to England after the action of the Butte de Warlencourt, and Lieut.-Colonel G. B. F. Smyth, who had been thrice wounded in the war, left the Sappers of the 90th Field Company

to command the 6th K.O.S.B. In March 1917 Lieut.-
Colonel Fargus went to England, and Lieut.-Colonel
Thorne took over the command of the 12th Royal
Scots. There were several adjustments in the South
African Brigade. Lieut.-Colonel F. H. Heal became
C.O. of the 1st Regiment; Lieut.-Colonel Tanner
returned to the 2nd, and Lieut.-Colonel Christian took
over the command of the 4th.

The training of the men followed the usual lines,
but in one respect there was a significant change. The
bomb had proved to be a very useful weapon, but it
had been cultivated to such excess that the men were
in danger of forgetting how to use their rifles. The
rifle is the principal weapon of the infantryman, and
practice in its use became the foundation of all our
training. The bomb was discouraged, for it had been
noted that a man with a rifle and bayonet in his hands
was more enterprising and aggressive than one with
his pockets full of bombs. About the end of the year a
more efficient protection against gas, the box respirator,
was issued and the men were drilled in the rapid
adjustment of it.

On the 5th December the Division took over the
line north and east of Arras. During the last week
of November the battalions at dusk marched along
the long, straight *pavé* road from St Pol and entered
the city through the majestic pylons of the Baudimont
Gate. Arras had been damaged during the German
onslaught of 1914, but since that time had been scarcely
molested. This quaint old Spanish city, well known
to artists and antiquarians, presented a harmonious
blending of the mediæval and the modern. The eye
was constantly surprised by new aspects that offered
themselves on a ramble through the streets—the old,
narrow, nubbly lanes, overlooked by ancient Hispano-

MAJOR-GENERAL SIR HENRY TIMSON LUKIN, K.C.B., C.M.G., D.S.O.

[Face page 172.

Flemish houses, opening out into spacious and ordered
boulevards with modern and opulent mansions, the
commercial commodiousness of the Petite Place and
the Grande Place, and the ramparts of Vauban. The
natural centre was the two squares, Petite Place and
Grande Place, both now bordered by the ruins of
stately gabled houses and so often intermittently shelled
that they were avoided by all except sightseers and
souvenir hunters. Near them, massive ruins suggested
a nobility and dignity of structure that the intact
cathedral had never possessed. But the greatest
example of German vandalism was the mound of
masonry and dust that marked the site of the Hôtel
de Ville, justly celebrated as a notable example of
Spanish architectural art. Arras, skirted on the north
by the River Scarpe, lay in a gentle hollow, overlooked
on the west by a semicircle of low hills, and on the
east by a ridge, which, farther north, passed into the
Vimy Ridge. From the station the railway ran east
to Douai, a branch swinging north to Lens, while
towards the south it ran into Albert. The Arras–Lens
railway and the eastern ridge were held by the enemy,
whose guns commanded the greater part of the Albert–
Arras line.

At the end of 1916 Arras seemed a city of the
dead. On the long main roads the rumble of wheels
and the clatter of hoofs were seldom heard, and the
streets were deserted except for a few soldiers and
some civilians who skulked along under the eaves of the
houses. Few parts of the town were without the scars
of war. In many houses the jumbled and disarranged
furniture told a story of panic and hurried departure;
in some cases the outside wall had been broken by a
shell, revealing the inside of a house intact, like the
model of a doll's house. Here and there enterprising

civilians ran excellent cafés, where the men could supplement their rations at prices that were not exorbitant. Near the station the Hôtel de Commers was the favourite rendezvous for officers.

The trenches taken over by the Division lay on the western slopes of the eastern ridge and extended from the south of the Scarpe as far north as Roclincourt. The area was divided into three sectors, "I," "J," and "K," from south to north, and all three brigades were in the line, the 26th in "I," the South African in "J," and the 27th in "K." This position, with certain changes, was held by the Division until the 9th April 1917, and the long spell enabled the men to make the trenches as perfect as they could be made. During this time the strictest discipline was maintained and the morning round of the battalion C.O. brought reproof or commendation according as each company did its duty. By 9 A.M. every man had to be washed and shaved, the rifles clean and polished, and the trenches neat and tidy. There was tremendous competition between the various companies in the desire of each to better its neighbour in the provision of comforts for the men; hot soup and cocoa were served late at night and early in the morning to those in the front trenches, but perhaps the last stage of luxury was reached when hot water was supplied for shaving.

Behind the lines the duties of the transport, located near D.H.Q. at Duisans, were neither rough nor unduly perilous. The busiest centre of activity was the Divisional Tactical School, near Givenchy, under the direction of Lieut.-Colonel Croft.[1] The cult of the rifle was assiduously inculcated, and officers and N.C.Os. were divided into sections, which competed with one

[1] In *Three Years with the Ninth Division* Lieut.-Colonel Croft discusses several questions of interest to C.Os.

another in all forms of warlike sport. A great effort was made to banish the deadening effects of trench warfare, and initiative and resource were stimulated by means of tactical schemes. Each course was wound up with a great display, in which the whole school carried out an attack, and the showers of Véry lights (representing the barrage), the rattle of the rifles and machine-guns, the line of flares, and a contact aeroplane gave a very fair impression of a real fight.

Training, however, was not confined to the school or the back areas. Though Arras itself was overlooked by the enemy, there was a wide stretch of dead ground between the city and the eastern ridge, where there were excellent facilities for training. Near Roclincourt a long bank provided a natural butt for Lewis Gun practice from any range up to 300 yards, and the valley offered ample scope for rifle-grenade instruction. More could and should have been done; but, since the days of 1914 when everyone that could be spared was needed to man the trenches, it had been customary to regard trench warfare and training as incompatible. Thus training as a rule had been confined to such periods as the men spent out of the line. As a matter of fact, battalions had often better chances of useful practice when in the line than when in back areas, and in 1917 the more satisfactory system of carrying on training at all times was begun. The vast importance of constant training as a primary factor of efficiency had been long neglected in France, but when the start was made development was continuous. Though belated, the issue of pamphlets which dealt with the action of the platoon (S.S. 143) and of the Division (S.S. 135) in attack, was none the less welcome. Hitherto, officers and N.C.Os. had been guided only by the general principles stated in Field

N

Service Regulations, but the pamphlets provided illustrations showing the application of these principles to
actual problems.   The more junior the commander, the
more desirable it was to make things clear to him by
concrete cases, and in this respect S.S. 143 was invaluable.   The adoption of these pamphlets ensured both a
uniformity in training and organisation throughout the
army and a practical knowledge of the methods of
dealing with the problems of actual warfare.

During the winter, which was the driest one since
the war began, the health of the men remained good.
Every precaution was taken to prevent trench feet;
each battalion in the line arranged for frequent supplies
of clean socks, and each man's feet were rubbed daily
by the stretcher-bearers with whale-oil under the supervision of an officer.   In January and February 1917 a
hard frost set in, the most severe since 1839, and during
this period men in the line were more comfortable than
those in Arras.   There was a great scarcity of fuel,
and the strong temptation of men in windowless and
draughty billets to loot wood and furniture from empty
houses had to be sternly repressed.   With the thaw
came mud and hard work, but the trenches had been
thoroughly revetted and any damage was quickly
repaired.

In November 1916 the sector was reputed to be one
of the quietest on the whole British front.   "Even
more peaceful than the Vimy" was the remark of men
who had gone forward with working-parties, and the
experiences of the first two or three days appeared
to confirm the statement.   The trenches had been
previously held by the Thirty-fifth, a Bantam division,
and were too shallow for people of ordinary stature.
If the enemy had been vindictive, he could not have
failed to snipe a number of our men, but happily he

was not bellicose and was ready to lie low, provided
he was not disturbed.   In the course of a few days the
trenches were deepened, so that one could walk along
the front line without being exposed from his waist
upwards, and after the Ninth Divisional Artillery relieved that of the Thirty-fifth on the 28th December,
the Germans were annoyed to find that the peace of
the sector had vanished.   Peevish and fretful, the foe
retaliated chiefly by means of heavy trench mortars and
lighter ones, variously known by our troops as "aerial
darts," "pine-apples," or "fish-tails."   Though the former
made a terrific din and flattened the trenches, they did
not cause much loss of life, but the latter were very
sinister weapons, and were fired five or six at a time,
so that, though they were visible, it was difficult to
dodge one and avoid running into another.   From these
came most of our casualties, about 30 per week for each
battalion in the front line, a fairly high total for what
was regarded as a tranquil spot.   The duel of hate
however was much in our favour.   The enemy trench
system was divided into sectors for retaliation purposes,
and so admirable was the co-operation between our
infantry and gunners, that when a battalion was pestered
by trench mortars, it only required a single code word
such as "Dora" or "Minnie" to be 'phoned by the
former to the latter to ensure prompt punishment for
the offending sector.

Raids were the most outstanding feature of these
months and they came to be regarded rather as a
matter of course than as an adventure.   Ten raids,
the majority of them successful, were carried out
between the 1st January and the 9th April.   Many
of the enemy were killed and 49 prisoners captured,
while our casualties, chiefly wounded, did not exceed
the number of the prisoners.

By far the most notable raid was that of the
"Rifles" on the 14th February. The credit for the
scheme belonged principally to Major M. N. Forsyth,
M.C., who suggested it to Brig.-General Maxwell.
The ground selected for the operation was well
adapted for a daylight raid; it was east of Roclincourt
and, lying in a shallow dip, could not be observed
from either flank. The most painstaking care was
given to organisation and arrangements. The raiding
party, which consisted of 20 officers and 320 other
ranks under the command of Major Forsyth, was
divided into various groups, each with a special task
to perform, such as clearing dug-outs, demolition of
emplacements, blocking trenches, escorting and searching prisoners, cutting wire, and evacuation of wounded.
No raider carried any identification mark either on
his tunic or in his pocket. A plan of the enemy's
ground was mapped out behind the line, and here
men and officers had a number of rehearsals. The
general scheme was simple. After a one-minute
barrage by the artillery and trench mortars, two groups
were to leave our trenches and enter the enemy's
system through two gaps in the wire previously cut
by trench mortars. The parties were to push rapidly
up the communication trenches bounding the area and
were to meet in the third line, shutting in all the
garrison. Other groups were to follow and clear all
the intermediate trenches and dug-outs. The whole
party after remaining for forty minutes in the German
lines was to withdraw at the end of that time through
three gaps, the third being cut during the raid. While
the raiders were busy, the artillery were to screen the
area from observation by a "box"[1] barrage.

---

[1] The barrage fell along three sides of a rectangle, screening the
infantry from the front and the flanks.

The operation met with the success[1] its careful preparations deserved. At 11 A.M. Major Forsyth led his party across "No-Man's-Land" and entered the opposing trenches. In the skirmish that followed many of the enemy were killed and 43 were captured; 2 machine-guns, 1 trench mortar, and a large number of rifles and other material were brought back. The slight casualties of the "Rifles," who well earned the praise[2] of the Commander-in-Chief, consisted of 2 killed, 15 wounded, and 1 missing.

All other raids, though on a smaller scale, were marked by the same particular care in organisation. At 3.8 P.M. on the 6th January a company of the Black Watch, under 2nd Lieut. Proudfoot, and one of the Argylls, under 2nd Lieut. Pardy, after a heavy preliminary bombardment and covered by a smoke-barrage, penetrated to the enemy's third line and remained in his trenches for half an hour. The whole system was thoroughly smashed by the artillery, and only 4 men were found above ground, of whom 3 were killed and one was captured. The remainder of the garrison, which according to the prisoner consisted of 160 men, had sheltered in the dug-outs, where the greater number must have perished when these were demolished by Stokes shells thrown down by the raiders. This raid was undertaken at short notice by the Highland Brigade, and its objects were to test the efficiency of our heavy artillery in cutting wire, especially in front of the second and third lines,

[1] News from the very start was good. Brig.-General Tudor, who was in the trenches watching the raid, was in touch with the front line by telephone, and the only reports he received were, "One more penny"—"Two more pennies," etc. "Penny" was the code word for prisoner.

[2] The following message was sent by Sir Douglas Haig on the 16th:—
"Congratulate the Ninth Scottish Division, and particularly the 9th Scottish Rifles, on the success of their raid carried out on the 14th."

and to find out if good observation could be obtained from the hostile trenches on to a strong point in the enemy's rear, known as "The Harp," which was likely to be a formidable obstacle to our advance during the offensive that was being planned. These objects were fulfilled, and the general opinion was that the success [1] of the raid was due to the "heavies." The Germans showed their annoyance by subjecting Arras to a gas bombardment so intense that it has been quoted by the gas experts as one of the heaviest concentrations of the war. Equal success attended dashing raids by the South Africans on the 2nd January and the 7th April, and by the 6th K.O.S.B. on the 11th January. The attempts of the enemy were feeble and half-hearted, a significant confession of nervousness and consciousness of inferiority. Between the 6th December and the 21st March four attempts to penetrate our trenches were beaten off with loss.

At the beginning of March, Arras awoke to vigorous life. After nightfall throngs of men jostled each other in the streets of the town, and from the great main roads rose the hum of constant traffic. In the faubourgs and wooded fields round the city numerous batteries of heavy guns, sinister and menacing engines of destruction, were ready in position, and amid bosky recesses and inviting orchards one often stumbled upon fresh emplacements that indicated the expected arrival of many more. The evidences [2] of a projected offensive were

[1] In the Ninth, however, it was thought that the principal factor was surprise, and the raid of the "Rifles" already referred to was undertaken to show that a preliminary bombardment was not necessary for success.

[2] At the end of January a party of the Division proceeding along the road to Arras was accosted by a Canadian soldier. "Hullo, what crowd are you?" "Ninth Division," was the reply, and then came the exclamation, "Huh! the scrappin' Ninth." The Canadian's tone of mingled friendship, admiration, and uneasiness betrayed more clearly than any words his firm conviction that storm-troops were gathering for a battle.

WEST GATE, ARRAS

unmistakable, and these were confirmed by changes on our front. Until the 14th January, the Ninth was under the VI. Corps, but on that date it was transferred to the XVII., commanded by Sir Charles Fergusson. As a result, the 26th Brigade was shifted from the right of the line to "L" sector on the left, which was taken over from the Third Canadian Division, and until the 11th February the Division held the whole of the Corps front from the Scarpe to the Arras–Lille road. That day the Highland Brigade and part of the 27th were relieved by the Fifty-first Division from Roclincourt to the Lille road. On the 24th February the line was still further contracted when the Thirty-fourth Division took over the rest of "K" sector. This left to the Ninth only the "I" sector extending from the Scarpe to St Pancras Trench, lying to the north of the Arras–Bailleul road, the stretch of front amounting to some 1800 yards.

From the beginning of 1917 every man was hard at work on the preparations for the great offensive that had been planned at a conference held at the French G.H.Q. in November 1916. The general idea was to carry on a series of offensives on all fronts for the purpose of "depriving the enemy of the power of weakening any one of his fronts in order to reinforce another." [1] The design of Sir Douglas Haig was to garner the fruits of the Somme struggle by pinching off the salient between the Scarpe and the Ancre, into which the enemy had been pressed as a result of that battle. With this object, a converging attack was to be carried out by the Third Army from Arras and the Fifth Army on the Ancre. Provided the situation remained unchanged, there was good reason to expect that this manœuvre would inflict enormous

[1] Haig's Despatches, vol. i., p. 81.

losses on the enemy and compel him to use up his reserves, and thus offer a greater assurance of success for the main object of the British Field-Marshal, which was to secure the control of the Flanders coast-line before the end of 1917. The attack of the Third and Fifth Armies was to be protected by an operation against the Vimy Ridge, which would also give us the command of the Douai plains and might even lead to the capture of Lens. Apart from these objects Sir Douglas Haig had no desire to carry on a protracted fight in the neighbourhood of Arras.

These important projects were considerably modified at the beginning of 1917. The striking power of the British forces was sensibly diminished by the fact that a considerable portion of the line, extending as far south as Roye, had to be taken over from the French. Again the British plans were made ancillary to those of General Nivelle, now in command of the French armies, who had planned an ambitious campaign in Champagne, and the Arras offensive was expected to assist his schemes by pinning down a large proportion of the German forces. Moreover, the enemy, realising his danger in the Ancre–Scarpe salient, anticipated the British attack by withdrawing from that area to new and formidable defences (the Hindenburg Line) in front of Cambrai, on the construction of which the Germans had worked like beavers during the winter months. This timely retreat largely eviscerated the hopes of the Arras campaign.

The plans of the Western Allies were marked by compromise and strategic vacillation, and this was particularly unfortunate, because 1917 was the period that was expected to produce the greatest disparity between the forces of the Entente and those of the Central Powers in favour of the former. The principal scheme of the British Higher Command was indefinitely postponed, and it would probably have been wise to replace it by another plan, which, while assuring the support promised for the schemes of General Nivelle, would yet offer a prize worthy of a big effort. This end would have been fulfilled by fixing Lens, and perhaps Douai, as the objective of the British Army. If the former place were carried before the summer, its possession by us would probably turn the north end of the Drocourt switch line, and would certainly give us control of the Douai plains and enable us to menace La Bassée from the south. The tremendously high moral of the British Army, stimulated greatly by the common talk about 1917 as the year of victory, deserved to be harnessed to ambitious and even heroic schemes. Events in Russia also, culminating in the Revolution while the preparations for the battle were being carried on, seemed to demand a big effort. It was futile to wait to see what the effect of the Revolution would be, and it was desirable to endeavour to affect it by events in France. An important success at the beginning of the year would probably strengthen the moderate elements in Russia, and preserve it as an effective ally for the Entente. But the Passchendaele project, which undoubtedly held out the most alluring prospects if successful, obsessed the British Higher Command too much to lead to any drastic alteration of plan. It is impossible to doubt the cordiality and genuineness of the co-operation between the British and the French armies, but both the schemes and the events of 1917 demonstrated that the strategical unity of plan necessary for success could be secured only by a single Command directing both forces towards a single end.

A perplexing point in the preparations for the

battle lay in the fact that there was no approach to the trenches except through Arras, which was an obvious mark for artillery. In the town reasonable safety was provided by improving and strengthening the system of underground vaults and catacombs, which were capable of accommodating large bodies of troops. It was not so easy to form roads and routes in sufficient number to allow of a smooth distribution of stores and munitions, but in this respect the work of the Staff was so well performed that there was virtually no delay or congestion. With similar attention to details of organisation, communication trenches were dug and allotted, so that the attacking troops could reach their assembly position without hindrance. By the end of March the preparations on the front of the Division were practically completed with little interference from the enemy's artillery, though numbers of trench mortar emplacements were repeatedly hit.

The rôle of the XVII. Corps was to capture the enemy's third system of defences, running north from the Scarpe at Feuchy through the Point du Jour. After this was accomplished, a further advance was to be made south of the Point du Jour to secure the fourth system and the village of Fampoux. Three divisions were to lead the assault, the Ninth on the south, Thirty-fourth in the centre, and Fifty-first on the north, while the Fourth was to be in reserve. On the right of the Ninth the attack was to be carried on by the Fifteenth Division.

The Ninth was required to take the enemy's third system from the Point du Jour to the Scarpe and to consolidate a line leading from the eastern end of the village of Athies to the Point du Jour. There were three objectives, marked on the map as the Black,

Blue, and Brown Lines.   From our front line the
ground rose gently to the summit of the ridge, on the
reverse side of which was the German main trench
of the first system, protected by a triple row of strong
wire, as our air photographs showed.   This trench,
called Obermayer, extended to the east end of the
village St Laurent-Blangy and formed the Black Line.
From this point the ground dipped to a shallow valley
and rose again to the line of the Arras–Lens Railway
(Blue Line), which on the left ran through a deep
cutting, but towards the Scarpe went over a high
embankment.   From the Railway the ground sloped
up to the plateau of the Point du Jour (Brown Line)
thickly covered with wire.   The fourth objective (Green
Line), which included Fampoux, was to be secured by
the Fourth Division.   The attack, to be covered by a
creeping barrage, was ultimately arranged for the 9th
April and was to be preceded by a preliminary bombardment commencing on the 5th.

All three brigades, the 26th on the right, the South
African in the centre, and the 27th on the left, were
to take part, each on a frontage of approximately
600 yards.   Two battalions in each brigade were to
take the first and second objectives, after which the
other two were to pass through and carry on the attack.
Four tanks were to assist the Division by helping to
clear the two villages of St Laurent-Blangy and Athies.
No battalion was to attack with its full strength.   Since
the time of Loos never more than 20 officers per
battalion had gone into battle, the remainder along
with some men being left at the Transport Lines.   The
pamphlet S.S. 135 laid down the proportion of men
and officers to be left out of action, so that even if
a battalion received a shattering blow in battle there
would be the nucleus of a new organisation.

The preparations of the C.R.A. were marked by unflagging industry and ingenuity. As the result of months of toil, the gunners had constructed positions that enabled the batteries to function under almost ideal conditions. There were no natural hidden positions to serve as emplacements for the guns, so ridges of screens were built up to conceal emplacements, situated in such a way that of the seven[1] brigades under the command of Brig.-General Tudor only one was more than 2000 yards from the enemy's line. Arrangements were also made to construct emplacements in one of the forming-up trenches, so that when the infantry advanced batteries could move up in close support. Moreover, all the guns were virtually square with their tasks, so that the barrage would be formed by shells falling at right angles to the line of advance. The R.F.A. Brigades were in St Catherine, St Nicholas, and Roclincourt Valley.

Ingenuity and initiative were shown in the arrangements for the creeping barrage, which was to be formed by a combination of H.E. and smoke-shell. Brig.-General Tudor had consistently upheld that a smoke-screen offered the best form of support for infantry, and though smoke had received a bad name at Loos owing to men losing direction, he believed that this was due to the fact that on that occasion the smoke had been produced by candles and had necessarily been started on our own parapets. If the smoke-screen could be put down on the enemy's line it would guide our men instead of confusing them, while it would still blind the enemy. At the end of 1915

---

[1]

14th Brigade R.H.A.		52nd Brigade A.F.A. (taken from the Ninth in January).
50th	„ R.F.A.	23rd „ A.F.A.
51st	„ R.F.A.	29th „ R.F.A.
	32nd Brigade R.F.A.	

•

he pressed for the manufacture of smoke-shells, but nothing was really done until General Furse took the matter up; as a result of his importunity smoke-shells were made, and they began to arrive in France about the autumn of 1916. The supply was limited, but as no other division desired them, the Ninth was able to get the whole quantity issued to the Third Army, about 4000 rounds. Smoke-shells were employed by the Canadians to cover their raids, and also by Brig.-General Tudor on the 6th January to support the raid of the Black Watch and the Argylls, but the 9th April was the first occasion on which they were used in a creeping barrage.

Zero was to be 5.30 A.M., and at that hour the barrage was to open 50 yards in front of the German front line trench. Where "No-Man's-Land" was 200 yards or more in extent, the assaulting troops were to leave their trenches and form up in the open. One minute after zero the barrage was to lift on to the front line, where it was to remain for three minutes. The rate of advance between lifts varied from 50 yards every one and a half minutes to 100 yards every four minutes. The infantry was expected to reach the Black Line at 6.4 A.M., and the barrier fire would then advance 300 yards beyond it, where it would remain until 7.36 A.M., by which time the leading battalions would be ready to resume the advance. In similar fashion the Blue Line was to be secured by 8.13 A.M., and the Brown Line by 1.2 P.M. At that time the Fourth Division was to pass through and go on to the Green Line. To prevent the enemy in the rear seeing the creeping barrage and countering it, a distant smoke-barrage was to be formed by two 18-pounder batteries.

The artillery bombardment was to be supplemented

by a trench-mortar and machine-gun barrage. Forty 2-inch and fourteen 9·45-inch mortars and twenty machine-guns were to take part. The Division had been vastly strengthened both in Lewis and Vickers Guns; each battalion had now sixteen of the former, and the arrival of the 197th Machine-Gun Company had brought the Vickers Companies up to four. All machine - gunners had received constant training in indirect fire while in this sector, and during the battle the German positions were to be drenched by showers of machine-gun bullets. One hundred and twenty-six 18-pounders, forty-two 4·5 howitzers, and forty-seven guns of heavier calibre were to support our attack.

While the preparations were being made, it was noticed that the enemy's aeroplanes had become very enterprising and aggressive. Up to the end of 1916 scarcely one had ventured to cross our lines, but from the first days of February there was a disquieting change. On every clear day swarms of German machines patrolled the air and penetrating far over our hinterland, boldly challenged conflict with our planes. Individual combats between the rival airmen were of frequent occurrence, and most of those that took place in the view of the infantry resulted in the triumph of the enemy. The most formidable and audacious of the hostile planes was a very fast one, which, being painted on the underpart with a brilliant red, was generally known as the "Red Belly." It seemed to be much more capable of rapid manœuvre than any of ours, and on one occasion a single-handed "Red Belly" broke up and put to flight a squadron of six British planes. These German machines were believed to belong to Von Richtofen's "Circus," which became very famous in latter days and was moved from one point of the front to another as required; it consisted of from 30 to 50 planes, controlled by expert pilots. Amid these circumstances the persistence with which our airmen in unequally equipped and inferior machines rose daily to meet the enemy and observe his lines, was a convincing proof of their grit and devotion to duty. There was some hope, however, that the conditions of July 1916 would be restored when the new and speedy machines, which were being manufactured in great numbers, were ready to take the air.

The comparatively short line held by the Division after the 24th February provided a welcome opportunity for the training of the men on a more thorough scale than had been possible before any previous battle. While one brigade held the trenches, another located in "Y" huts on the Arras–St Pol road was engaged on work, and the third underwent a course of training near Monchy Breton. This arrangement allowed eight days' training for each brigade in turn. From the photographs taken by the Royal Flying Corps, the enemy's system was marked out accurately on the training area by tapes and shallow trenches made by ploughs, and the frequent practice that the men had over this course gave them a very fair idea of what they were expected to do on the 9th April. Exact models of the ground to be attacked were moulded in clay, and the men thus learned not merely the character of the country, but also the names of the German trenches.

When the preparations were nearing completion, the unwelcome news was received that the enemy had evacuated his positions in the Ancre–Scarpe salient. It was feared that he would evade our blow by withdrawing from his line in front of Arras. Rumours of a retirement had been circulated on the 24th February, and when the Third Division in the south reported on the 19th March that the foe had retired from his front line up to the Arras–Cambrai road, Sir Charles Fergusson resolved to test his strength in front of Arras by a daylight reconnaissance. This was entrusted to the 11th Royal Scots. The operation was timed for 3 P.M. on the 21st March, by which hour the infantry were assembled, but it had to be postponed for half an hour to allow the artillery to finish their preparations. Two or three hostile planes were hovering overhead, but it was impossible to say if they had spotted the assembly. A heavy German trench mortar opened fire during this period but the damage it inflicted was insignificant. The assailants, consisting of two companies commanded by Lieut.-Colonel Croft, jumping over the parapet, swept on under desultory machine-gun fire and entered the opposing trenches. A furious and intricate conflict ensued, and when some Germans counter-attacked across the open, they were shot down by the accurate rifle-fire of the Royal Scots. When at last Lieut.-Colonel Croft gave the signal to withdraw, his men returned to their own line without molestation. Though their losses—amounting to 5 officers and 70 other ranks killed, wounded, and missing—had been heavy, they had fulfilled their mission, and proved that the enemy was holding his line in strength opposite the XVII. Corps.

For the next few days Lieut.-Colonel Croft's men had a surfeit of thrills. At 5 A.M. on the 22nd, after a short preliminary bombardment, the enemy dashed across "No-Man's-Land" and secured 3 men from a Lewis Gun post. On the night of the 23rd, the Royal Scots replied in kind. Lieutenant Matthews with a small party entered the opposing trenches and killed 4 Germans, whose outcry alarmed the garrison.

The raiders, however, did not escape without loss, one man being killed, another wounded, and Lieutenant Matthews was missing. Next day sentries reported that they saw a body believed to be that of Lieutenant Matthews lying in the enemy's wire, and Lieut.-Colonel Croft issued orders for a patrol to go out after dusk and bring it in. 2nd Lieut. Storey, mistaking the instructions, did not wait for dusk, but went out alone in full daylight; though fired at continuously, he was able to crawl near enough to see that what had been taken for a body was only a piece of sacking.

The formations adopted and practised for the attack were the same in all three brigades. The men were to advance in a series of waves, a wave consisting of two lines, and each wave was to be followed by a line of "moppers-up," who were to clear captured trenches and dug-outs of skulking foes, so that no damage might be done after the leading troops had gone on. From right to left the disposition of battalions was as follows: 7th Seaforths, 8th Black Watch, 3rd South African Infantry, 4th South African Infantry, 12th Royal Scots, and 6th K.O.S.B., and these were supported by the 5th Camerons, 10th Argylls, 1st South African Infantry, 2nd South African Infantry, 9th Scottish Rifles, and 11th Royal Scots. The infantry were reinforced by the sappers, machine-gunners, and the trench mortar batteries. The four tanks were to be assembled in the valley just east of the Candle Factory, and the noise of their approach was to be drowned by machine-gun fire. The enemy's front wire had been entirely demolished by the 2-inch trench mortars, and constant patrolling had prevented the gaps being repaired. This wire-cutting feat was a great triumph for the 2-inch trench mortars; many people believed it was impossible for them to cut the wire, but they did it most effectively.

o

On the eve of the battle the men were in high spirits and very confident of success. The notion of a check was never entertained. Since the beginning of December they had achieved a marked and increasing ascendancy over the enemy,[1] who was known to be nervous and much perturbed as to our projects.

[1] The enemy opposing us consisted of the 1st and 24th Bavarian Reserve Divisions.

CHAPTER IX

THE BATTLES OF ARRAS

THE ACTIONS OF 9TH APRIL, 12TH APRIL, 3RD MAY, 5TH JUNE 1917

THE preliminary bombardment of the German entrenched positions opened on the 5th April. Special attention was devoted to counter-battery work, and with the assistance of aeroplane observation and sound - ranging devices, a great many of the hostile guns were knocked out by direct hits. As a result, the reply was extraordinarily weak, and though a few shells were thrown into Arras, little damage was done. Our "Chinese barrages" not only made fine spectacles, but were most useful as the reply they provoked showed us where the German retaliation barrage would fall. The assembly of the Division was completed without difficulty during the night of the 8th/9th. On the front of the 26th and 27th Brigades the leading troops were accommodated in the trenches, but the South Africans made use of small craters, which had been blown by the sappers in front of their line.

Shortly before zero all hope of a fine day was dashed by a gentle drizzle of rain. At 5.30 A.M. our guns opened with a deafening crash. Overhead the rushing steel sounded like a frenzied discord combining the deep boom of the drum with the shrill shriek of the whistle, and where the shells landed, the earth

leaped up in a mad barbaric dance. A gigantic wall
of smoke and fire lay right along the enemy's line, and
sprays of coloured lights, shooting up from his trenches,
betokened the anxiety and distress of the garrison.
The hostile barrage was slow, and when it descended
on our front line, eight minutes after zero, it was thin
and ragged. During the first three minutes of our
barrage the leading waves took up their position for
the advance, the only trouble being on the extreme left,
where the K.O.S.B., forming up, had some casualties
through our smoke - shells falling short. With the
first lift the khaki lines pushed forward. In spite of
their training, the men had the greatest difficulty in
recognising the hostile trenches, which had been so
torn up that they hardly presented a break in the
belt of churned-up soil that marked the devastating
path of the artillery. The only serious resistance was
encountered by the Seaforths, who stormed the Island
near Blangy and killed a number of bombers among the
rubble and cellars of Athies. Elsewhere the advance
was carried on without check. A few casualties were
inflicted by machine-guns, but the smoke-screen was
most effective, and owing to this the enemy's shooting
was very erratic. The ardour of our troops could
scarcely be restrained; flushed with success, they
kept close up to the barrage and in many cases
passed through it. The Bavarians had built up a
worthy reputation during the war, but before they
had time to show fight our men were upon them.
On reaching the Black Line the Black Watch captured
the regimental commander and the adjutant of the
8th Bavarians, who had not realised that a battle was
in progress. On the left, Lieut.-Colonel Thorne of the
12th Royal Scots was killed when leading his men,
but the battalion under Major Hay was irresistible

and easily secured the Black Line.   The K.O.S.B.
shot past the first objective and stopped in a sunken
road beyond it, where they found swarms of the 25th
Bavarians crouching in the dug-outs.   The whole of
the Black Line was secured in the time allotted.
During the advance a few of the South Africans bore
too much to the north, but the Black Watch extended
their left flank and the boundaries between the
brigades were readjusted at the first objective.

Owing to the bad light and the obliteration of the
enemy system, the "moppers" had great difficulty in
recognising the various trenches and in some cases
overran their objectives, consequently there were several
instances of Germans emerging from their shelters and
firing at the backs of our men.   The most serious
mishap took place on the front of the 27th Brigade,
where a machine-gun suddenly came to life and
opened fire on a party of the 9th Seaforths who
had come up to dig a communication trench.   The
men dropped their shovels, picked up their rifles, and
after killing its crew carried off the machine-gun as
a trophy.   The clearing parties found the front system
full of Germans, most of whom had taken shelter either
in the dug-outs or just in the doorway, and they were
killed or taken prisoner.

The drizzle had developed into a steady downpour
while the reorganisation and arrangements for the
second advance were being carried out.   The dispositions of the South African and 26th Brigades remained
unchanged, but in the 27th Brigade the supporting and
leading battalions changed places.   At 7.36 A.M. the
attack on the Blue Line (Arras–Lens Railway) commenced.   The defenders had not yet recovered from their
surprise, and their resistance, considering the strength
of their position, was extremely poor, though a few

stout-hearted groups held out to the last and inflicted casualties before they were killed. The right wing of the 26th Brigade was held up for a time by enfilade machine-gun fire from a post at the Railway Triangle on the front of the Fifteenth Division. But the artillery were prompt to assist, and, covered by an effective smoke-screen put down by "F" Battery R.H.A. from the Railway embankment north of the Scarpe, the Highlanders reached the Blue Line practically without a halt. Equally successful was the attack of the other brigades. The South Africans lost some men from snipers as they were struggling through the gaps in the wire in front of the Railway cutting, but the enemy's machine-guns were dilatory in coming into action and the South Africans easily accounted for them when they reached the cutting. On the left, when the leading battalions of the 27th Brigade advanced into the valley, they came under hostile machine-gun and artillery-fire from the Railway and Maison Blanche Wood. Two of the machine-guns were rushed in the cutting, and two others, which were holding up the advance of the Thirty-fourth Division, were enfiladed by Lewis Guns and driven to earth. Of the garrison on the Railway not one escaped ; all were killed or captured.

The four tanks allotted to the Division were very unlucky. Two were put out of action at the start by artillery - fire ; a third broke down about 200 yards from the Railway on the front of the 27th Brigade ; and the fourth failed to reach the Railway after the officer in charge of it was killed, but the surprise of the enemy was so complete that there was little need for them. South of the Scarpe a tank did good service by helping to clear the Railway Triangle, which had caused a great deal of trouble to the Fifteenth Division.

During the halt on the Blue Line, the only changes
in disposition occurred in the 26th and South African
Brigades, where the Camerons, Argylls, 1st and 2nd
Regiments were placed in the lead. The four hours of
waiting were not without anxiety. An enemy aeroplane
came over our lines and as a result the German artillery
opened on the Railway, 300 yards east of which our
protective barrage was falling at that time. Fortunately
this counter-barrage did not last long, and the majority
of the leading men were already formed up some
yards east of the Railway, but for a short spell nearly
six battalions lay precariously between two fires in
a space of 300 yards. At length the final attack
began at 12.16 P.M. On the right, tough resistance
by the enemy at the Railway Triangle left us with
an exposed flank, and a quick and critical decision
had to be made whether to advance on this wing or
not. Brig.-General Kennedy decided to press on,
and the movement was completely screened by the
smoke-curtain put down by our guns. This prudently
bold policy not merely prevented our own troops from
being checked, but materially assisted the Fifteenth
Division to capture the Railway Triangle. Elsewhere
the last vestige of resistance had disappeared with the
capture of the Blue Line, and the assault on the
Brown Line took the form of an orderly procession.
This was a happy occurrence, since the wire in front
of the Point du Jour trenches had scarcely been
damaged and was penetrated laboriously even by
unmolested men. The spectacle of lines of men
moving steadily forward with their rifles at the slope
seemed more like a Salisbury Plain ceremonial
manœuvre than an attack in grim earnest. As the
troops pressed on, their eyes were gratified by the
sight of scores of Germans fleeing in a wild panic,

Fanned by the breath of victory and keen to grasp all its rewards, they broke into a smart run. The Thirty-fourth Division had been slightly delayed by Maison Blanche Wood, and there was an awkward space on the flank of the 11th Royal Scots, the left battalion of the Ninth, but this was filled by a company of the K.O.S.B. which rushed a machine-gun at the Point du Jour, destroyed the team, and devoured its lunch. With the capture of the Brown Line the Division had accomplished all its tasks.

Half an hour before the commencement of the attack on the Brown Line the leading battalions of the Fourth Division began to arrive. As they came down the slope of the valley from the first objective they suffered some casualties from shell-fire. They reached the Point du Jour–Athies line in good time, and at 3.10 P.M. passing through the Ninth pressed on to the Green Line, which they secured easily and swiftly.

Success had been gained without a check and at very small cost, and the uniform excellence of the work performed by the several arms of the Division was one of the noticeable features of the battle. The Sappers, Pioneers, and R.A.M.C. toiled steadily and efficiently. The infantry, including the wounded, were hyperbolical in their praise of the smoke and H.E. barrage, to which they attributed their own slight losses and the complete surprise of the enemy. The only criticism was that the barrage was too slow for eager men and that there was scarcely enough of smoke. Never at any previous time were the men so jubilant and so confident of a speedy victory. On that day the ground captured and the booty seized far exceeded all that had hitherto been secured in the same period by the British forces in France. In

all, 51 officers, 2086 other ranks, 17 field-guns and
howitzers, 24 machine-guns, and 3 trench mortars were
the spoils of the Division. *84 MGs according to S. African History*

But the decisive nature of the victory was due not
so much to the surprise of the enemy as to the foresight with which arrangements were made to overcome all possible obstacles, and the readiness and
resource which the infantry showed in attacking places
outside their own area.   Typical examples of the latter
were the capture by the Seaforths of the Island and
the storming of the Point du Jour by the K.O.S.B.
It was too often the tendency during the war for a
unit to keep to its own allotted task without making
any effort to help its neighbours, and the facility and
speed with which our men in this battle worked to
their flanks were very important factors in contributing to the rout of the enemy.   General Furse had
repeatedly impressed on the officers of the Ninth
the necessity and advantage of assisting their neighbours, and never was this practice exemplified on
a finer scale by the Division than on the 9th of
April.

It is impossible to praise too highly the forethought
shown with regard to the Railway Triangle.   Brig.-
General Tudor learned just before our advance from
the Black Line was resumed, that the Fifteenth Division was held up by the Triangle and had not won
its first objective. Realising the disastrous result
of this for the Ninth, since the enemy south of the
Scarpe would see our infantry north of the river and
would enfilade them with numerous machine-guns, he
turned on a battery, which he had standing by for
such an eventuality, to blind that enemy to our
movement.   This not only enabled the Ninth to make
its advance undisturbed from the right, but further

enabled its right brigade, after seizing the Blue Line, to turn its machine-guns and some infantry against the northern wing of the enemy opposing the Fifteenth south of the river, thus combining a flank with a frontal attack on that portion of the enemy and compassing his defeat and the advance of the Fifteenth Division. Without this prearrangement the whole fight would have been far less successful and far more costly.

The action of the 9th April was a very great triumph for British arms. Compared with the gigantic advances made after August 1918, the ground gained may seem insignificant and the number of prisoners meagre, but the true comparison is not with 1918 but with 1916. In 1917, as in the Somme fighting, the moral of the Germans was high and their resistance formidable, and there is substantial reason for regarding, as Professor Pollard[1] does, the capture of the Vimy Ridge and the advance to Fampoux as amongst the finest achievements of the war. But the impetus of our attack came to an end on the same day. It is possible that the magnitude of the first day's success was so much more extensive than had been expected that the preparations for supporting it lagged in arrear, and that the Germans were able to concentrate more quickly for the defence than we were for the renewal of the onset. Wet weather, which figures so constantly in Sir Douglas Haig's despatches as the marplot of British projects, was made chiefly responsible for our failure to follow up our victory, but though it greatly increased our difficulties, it is probable that ineffective Staff work rather than weather may have been the chief cause of our disappointment. The possession

[1] *A Short History of the Great War*, p. 257.

of the Vimy Ridge, the disengagement of Arras, and the obligation of the enemy to draw on his reserves had largely fulfilled the intentions of the Higher Command, but it is never satisfactory to lose chances of exploiting success. For a time the Germans were badly shaken, and Ludendorff admitted that the opening of the Arras Battle caused him considerable uneasiness. If cavalry had been available to go through on the afternoon of the 9th April they could not have failed to bring in many more prisoners, but they made no advance until the 11th, and by that time it was too late; the enemy had recovered from his fright and had brought up reserves. Nor were there large reserves of our infantry at hand to resume the attack at once. The infantry had become the handmaid of the artillery, and vexatious delays occurred until the latter could move up their guns.

Till late in the evening of the 9th the bulk of the Division remained in the trenches on the Brown Line, but after all danger of a counter-attack had passed, the battalions were withdrawn to the Blue and Black Lines. The weather, which had shown signs of improvement during the afternoon, utterly broke down, and blizzards of snow and sleet swept the ground. The wearied men spent a wretched night, as there was not sufficient shelter for all, and many had to lie in the open, unprotected from the drenching sleet. The next day was spent in cleaning rifles, replacing kit, and salvaging the battlefield. On the 11th, the Fourth Division was instructed to secure the slopes of Greenland Hill, a small ridge lying to the east of the village of Roeux, and the South African Brigade was sent up to support it. The attack was repulsed, and the Ninth was ordered to renew the attempt the following day.

The line, which was held by the Fourth Division, lay some distance east of the original Green Line [1] and included the village of Fampoux on the north bank of the Scarpe. From it a number of roads ran to the north-west and north, while the continuation of the Main Street joined the Roeux–Gavrelle road near the Station, close to which lay the Chemical Works of Roeux. The Railway crossed the Scarpe south-east of Fampoux and ran along a high embankment in a north-easterly direction to Douai. To the south of it the Scarpe broadened out into marshes and lagoons, which made approach to Roeux impracticable except from the north ; beyond the Roeux–Gavrelle road the country ascended in a gradual rise to Greenland Hill. The line held by the enemy was the Roeux–Gavrelle road, and he had installed numerous machine-guns in the Chemical Works, the Station, and an Inn about 1500 yards north of it.

The Division received orders to capture this line from the Inn to the village of Roeux inclusive. There were two objectives. The first, to be carried by the South African and 27th Brigades, consisted of the ground north of the Railway embankment, and comprised the Station Buildings, the Chemical Works, and the line of the road as far as the Inn ; the second, which fell to the 26th Brigade, entailed the capture of Mount Pleasant Wood, and the village of Roeux. There was to be the usual creeping barrage, which, commencing at 5 P.M., was to move forward at the rate of 100 yards every two minutes. The orders reached the brigades late during the night of the 11th, so that

[1] The original Green Line consisted of the strongly-wired trenches immediately west and north of Fampoux. Shortly before the attack on the 9th April the final objective was altered so as to include the hostile positions just west of the Roeux-Gavrelle road and the village of Fampoux.

the time for preparation was very limited. It was understood that all the buildings held by the enemy were to be demolished by the fire of the heavy guns.

The enemy's position was reconnoitred by brigadiers and battalion commanders on the morning of the 12th. A reference to the map suggested that the best place to form up was in the valley at the east end of Fampoux. But this was found to be out of the question, for the road lay under direct observation from the Chemical Works and was thickly sprayed with shells on the appearance of even the small reconnoitring party. The South Africans, being the right brigade, had really no choice except the village as an assembly place, but it was eminently dangerous, since it was a favourite target of the hostile guns. The 27th Brigade was compelled to choose the German trenches immediately north of Fampoux, which were sited on the horizon, and the approach to which from the west had to be carefully reconnoitred to find lines of advance that would reduce the probability of the oncoming troops being seen by the enemy. It was an evil position, for it entailed the advance of the brigade for 1700 yards down the slope into the valley in full view of the foe on the opposite slope, but there was no alternative. Brig-General Maxwell recognised that to screen the movement, a barrage, with smoke if possible, would be necessary, but he failed to get into communication with General Lukin in time. As the barrage was to fall along the enemy's line at zero, the 27th Brigade had to commence its advance from its forming-up position half an hour before zero, so as to reach the front held by the Fourth Division just before the barrage opened.

The action that followed was calamitous. The firing of the heavy guns during the day never rose to the intensity of a bombardment, and the large collection of buildings round the Station remained quite intact, only one shell being seen to fall near the Chemical Works. There was absolutely no chance of success from the outset, and the uncomplaining heroism of the men was on that account the finest feature of the battle.

Shortly before the attack was delivered, the Division learned from an air reconnaissance that the enemy had dug-in to the west of the Roeux–Gavrelle road, but this news was received too late for action to be taken, and our barrage dropped behind the enemy's front trench. On the right, the 2nd and 1st South African Regiments were in the van, with the 4th and 3rd in support and reserve. The assembly of the brigade in the shell-swept village of Fampoux was a costly business, but in spite of heavy losses the men were remarkably steady. As soon as the South Africans emerged from the shelter of the houses their ranks were scourged by accurate rifle and machine-gun fire, and it was possible to advance only about 200 yards from the positions held by the Fourth Division.

On the left the attack was carried on by the 11th and 12th Royal Scots[1] and the "Rifles," the K.O.S.B. being in reserve. The advance of the brigade began at 4.25 P.M., and with incredible coolness the infantry pressed through the enemy's barrage and reached the line held by the Fourth Division a few minutes before zero. At 5 P.M. our barrage opened and was excellent, but our men were checked almost at the start by very heavy machine-gun fire. In these circumstances nothing could be gained by throwing the 26th Brigade into the battle and the forward troops were accordingly withdrawn. The collection and evacua-

[1] Major Sir J. Campbell commanded the 11th, and Major Macpherson the 12th Royal Scots in this action.

EAST OF ARRAS. BATTLE GROUND OF APRIL 1917

tion of the wounded proved a difficult and harassing job, but this was accomplished before dawn through the untiring and unselfish efforts of the infantry and R.A.M.C.

Little can be said in defence of this battle, which the Division fought with great reluctance. The preparations and arrangements were hurried to a culpable degree, and though the basis of the action was understood to be the bombardment of hostile machine-gun emplacements by the Corps' heavy artillery, the heavies might as well have remained silent for all the assistance they gave. Apart from the fact that the time for reconnoitring the enemy's position, particularly by the artillery,[1] was miserably inadequate, defeat was practically inevitable when the 27th Brigade had to be formed up in full view of the enemy and at a distance of more than 1000 yards from the barrage line. Much of the haste was undoubtedly caused by D.H.Q.[2] being too far back, the time necessary for the issue of orders and the arrangement of preparations being thus unduly extended. The only possibility of success lay in the Ninth taking over the front line from the Fourth Division on the night of the 11th, but this was not done, because it was considered expedient to let the worn-out men have a good night's rest.

After the battle the Ninth was withdrawn from the line and was concentrated in billets near Hermaville. The high spirits of the men, which had been at fever-pitch on the 9th, had been somewhat damped by the events of the 12th, but a short rest served to illustrate once more the amazing recuperative capacity of the

---

[1] Brig.-General Tudor, who was assisting the Fourth Division, received news of the battle so late that he had no time to reconnoitre.

[2] On the 9th April D.H.Q. were at Etrun ; they moved forward to St Nicholas only on the 12th April.

British soldier. The South African and 27th Brigades had been hardest hit. The weakness of the former occasioned grave concern as its losses exceeded its drafts, and it was clear that, if its identity was to be preserved, it could not be available for immediate action.[1] More drafts were forthcoming for the 27th Brigade, which by the end of the month was ready for the field.

In the latter part of April strenuous fighting took place near Roeux and the Chemical Works, both of which, though we gained a good deal of ground, remained in the hands of the enemy. While the South Africans were employed on work at Arras, the other brigades relieved the Thirty-seventh Division on the nights of the 28th/29th and 29th/30th April. On the last day of April the Division lost Colonel F. A. Symons, the popular and efficient A.D.M.S., who was killed by a shell near Athies; Colonel Elsner of the 27th Field Ambulance was appointed his successor. There was now a welcome change in the weather, brilliant sunshine and warm breezes giving promise of a glorious summer. On the 2nd May instructions were issued for an operation on the 3rd. This was to be undertaken with the Fourth Division on the right, the Ninth in the centre, and the Thirty-first on the left, and the First and Fifth Armies were also to attack. It was believed to be of unusual importance, for on the evening of the 2nd the Division received a message that the battle was to be the biggest in which the British armies had yet taken part.

The 26th Brigade, with the Camerons and Black Watch in front, the Argylls in support, and the Sea-

[1] General Lukin on 18th April suggested that the South African Brigade should be withdrawn from the Division on account of its weakness and its lack of reinforcements.

forths in reserve, was on the right ; and on the left was the 27th, with the "Rifles" and K.O.S.B. in front, and the 11th and 12th Royal Scots in support and reserve. In place of the South Africans the Division was supported by the 52nd Brigade, which was located at the Blue Line. The objectives were the line of trenches Weed–Weak and the Biache–Gavrelle road. The attack was to be under the customary creeping barrage, which was to open 200 yards east of our front line and, after a pause of four minutes, was to move forward at the rate of 100 yards every two minutes, while a machine-gun barrage was to keep 400 yards in advance of it. The time of zero, 3·45 A.M., was made known to the Division only a few hours before the battle.

The position held by the enemy lay on the western slopes of Greenland Hill and consisted of shell-holes and stretches of trenches hastily excavated after his defeat on the 9th April. His trenches therefore were not of the same elaborate and formidable nature as those he occupied on that date, but owing to their comparative indefiniteness they offered neither a clear target for the artillery nor an easily recognisable land-mark for the infantry.

The night of the 2nd May was clear, with no hint of dawn when the hour of zero approached, though by the mellow sheen of the stars and the setting moon one could see about 50 yards along a path. At 3·45 A.M. the air reverberated with the crash of thousands of guns, their flashes forming an almost solid glow. On striking the dry earth the shells threw up a thick cur-tain of smoke and dust, which, owing to a north-east wind, drifted back towards our lines. At the same time, the Germans sent up showers of coloured lights and rockets in a wild appeal to their artillery for assistance.

P

As a result of the darkness, intensified by dust clouds, the attacking troops lost direction almost at the beginning.   The Germans replied immediately with heavy machine-gun fire from trenches and organised shell-holes, which were closer to our front line than we expected and had escaped our barrage.   The Camerons, misled by hostile lights sent up from short entrenched lines echeloned in depth, swung so much to the right that they crossed the front of the 2nd Essex Regiment (Fourth Division), who fired on them.   The Black Watch also lost cohesion and only a few groups managed to reach the enemy's front trench.   The Argylls in support, who became heavily involved in the fighting, suffered serious casualties when they moved forward, and were subjected to persistent bombing attacks from the vicinity of the Gavrelle–Plouvain road. Most of them were compelled to take cover in shell-holes, from which they gradually worked their way back to our line.   One company of this battalion, maintaining direction throughout, went straight to the first objective, but being unsupported and cut off only a few survivors managed to return.   This effort was really a brilliant performance.   In a second attempt the Black Watch succeeded in expelling the enemy from Charlie and Cuthbert Trenches, but they were unable to remain there owing to accurate machine-gun fire from the Railway embankment and the Chemical Works.   When the 26th Brigade was reorganising in its original line, German aeroplanes displayed great audacity ; three of them hovered persistently over our front until one was brought down by machine-gun fire.

The task of the 27th Brigade was complicated by the fact that the left battalion, the K.O.S.B., occupied a position beyond the " Rifles." Before advancing, the former had therefore to wait for five minutes until

the latter came into line, and as a guide to the
"Rifles" a lamp was shown on the right flank of
the K.O.S.B.   When at zero the "Rifles" left their
trenches they failed to pick up the lamp, which was
to guide their left, and in spite of compass-bearings the
two assaulting companies swerved to the right, with the
result that the right flank reached Cuthbert Trench
earlier than was intended.   This trench, which had
been scarcely damaged, was strongly manned, and
here a stern hand-to-hand contest was waged.   Some
of the "Rifles" succeeded in pressing forward, but
practically none of the two leading companies returned,
the great majority being killed, wounded, or taken
prisoner.   When the supporting companies attempted
to advance they came under heavy machine-gun fire
and dug themselves in 200 yards beyond the front
trench.   The 11th Royal Scots, unable to see what
was happening, pushed up two companies, which joined
with the supporting companies of the "Rifles," and
dug-in along with them.

The K.O.S.B. after waiting five minutes for the
arrival of the "Rifles," went on without them,
according to orders.   Three companies crossed the
enemy's front trench and passed on towards the
objective.   Lieut. - Colonel Smyth,[1] with a view to

[1] While this chapter was being written, news came of the cold-blooded
murder of this officer in the County Club, Cork, on the 17th July 1920 by
a dozen so-called patriots.

If ever a man lived who deserved a fair field and a fair fight it was
Colonel Smyth.   A more gallant and honourable gentleman never lived.
As a captain in the Royal Engineers he commanded the 90th Field Coy.
R.E. in the Ninth Division till October 1916, when he was promoted to
the command of the 6th K.O.S.B.   In October 1918 he commanded the
93rd Brigade in the Thirty-first Division as a Brig.-General.

Major-General H. H. Tudor, when given command of the Police Forces
in Ireland in June 1920, found Colonel Smyth in command again of a
Field Coy. R.E. in Ireland, and, knowing his worth, secured his appointment as one of his deputy commissioners.

protecting his exposed right flank, sent out a platoon from the remaining company to block the south end of Wit Trench, but it was practically annihilated on leaving the parapet, though the Lewis Gun was brought back owing to the splendid coolness of Sergeant C. Hawthorn. A serious disaster had occurred, and Lieut.-Colonel Smyth, who was badly wounded in the shoulder, was unable to do anything to help the three forward companies; for the front of the 27th Brigade was swept from both flanks, and the position here was almost hopeless unless the 26th Brigade and the Thirty-first Division could clear the enemy in front of them. Later Lieut.-Colonel Fulton, commanding the "Rifles," and Major Hamilton of the 90th R.E., ignorant of the check experienced by the rear companies of the "Rifles," went up to the right of the K.O.S.B. in Wish Trench, and observing a party of 50 Germans, whom they took to be prisoners entering Wit Trench, sent an officer and two men to bring them in. These were fired at and hit. It was thus manifest that the enemy had reoccupied Wit Trench and that he now interposed between us and the three companies of the K.O.S.B. Some of these penetrated as far as Square Wood, but their plight was beyond hope and most of them were killed though a few were taken prisoner.

The only tidings to reach D.H.Q. were those of failure. Oppy on the north defied all assault, and the Thirty-first Division was driven back and counter-attacked by the Germans, who gained a footing in the outskirts of Gavrelle. Accordingly at 8.39 A.M. instructions were issued that the general onset was not to be pressed. Brig.-General Maxwell asked for artillery-fire to be directed on the portion of Wit Trench opposite his front, in the hope of clearing out the

Germans, and so opening a way of retreat for the men who had been cut off. Unwilling to leave troops who had managed to advance, unsupported and cut off, he decided to attack Wit Trench with the object of holding it during the night to allow the K.O.S.B. to return under cover of darkness. Accordingly one and a half companies of the 12th Royal Scots were ordered to undertake this operation at 8 P.M., while the light was still good; they were to be covered on each flank by a barrage of artillery and machine-gun fire. These men, 150 in all, made a most determined charge, but though a few reached Wit the attack was broken by machine-gun fire. Only 30 of them returned, but their noble sacrifice enabled a considerable number of K.O.S.B., mostly from the right company, to come in.

The battle of the 3rd May showed up the training, especially of officers, in a bad light. The customary gallantry and keenness were exhibited in full measure, but the high degree of training essential for efficient leadership was absent. The difficulties of keeping direction were undoubtedly enormous, and had they been foreseen, would have given well-trained officers the opportunity of overcoming them by the application of knowledge and intelligence. But these difficulties had to be faced by officers and N.C.Os. without adequate warning. Word of the sudden decision of G.H.Q. on the 2nd May to launch the attack before instead of during daylight, as originally planned, was received by the Division only a few hours before the time of assault, when it was impossible to make the necessary arrangements for maintaining direction in the dark, and this ill-advised eleventh hour change was largely responsible for the failure of the attack. The battle also revealed a lamentable decline in initiative, largely due to the excessive dependence of the infantry on the artillery, fostered by the method of the limited objective and months of trench warfare. After the initial check the barrage was lost, and the men in general remained where they lay without making any serious effort to push on. This was strongly commented on by Brig.-General Kennedy in his notes on the battle. In the old Regular Army the men had been accustomed to help themselves and others to make headway by the skilful use of their rifles and by taking full advantage of folds in the ground, and it was now clear that subsequent training should be directed towards the recapture of this lost standard.

These remarks about the Division have a similar application as regards the attack generally. At a prodigious sacrifice the only places of importance carried were Fresnoy, Chérisy, and Roeux, and of these the two latter were regained by the enemy during the day. There was no doubt that the action cost the assailants many times more lives than it did the defenders. The short summary in Sir Douglas Haig's despatches somewhat disguises the seriousness of the defeat, for the 3rd May was assuredly a black day for the British Army.

The action however was fought under constraint. The far-reaching designs of General Nivelle had fallen short of accomplishment, and the primary function of the British forces was to ease the pressure on the front of their allies. The surest method of effecting this was by means of an operation, and similar subsidiary enterprises had been undertaken in connection with the Battles of Loos and the Somme. But this method, while gaining its end, has the drawback of involving a sacrifice of men, and it is possible that the British Army, now that it was adequately equipped with guns and munitions, could have secured its object by the employment of artillery battle preparations without an infantry assault. In face of a vast concentration of guns and men, an enemy, who had the hardihood to hold his defences thinly, would expose himself to a deadly stab, but so profound was the dejection caused in France by the disappointment of her hopes that it would have been folly to take risks. The restoration of the nerve of France was worth a big sacrifice.

The Ninth remained in the line until it was relieved by the Seventeenth Division on the nights of the 9th/10th and 10th/11th May, and was employed during this period in improving trenches and communications. The 27th Brigade was assisted by a composite battalion of South Africans under Major Webber. On relief, the Division proceeded to billets near Ruellecourt, where it rested, drilled, and was reorganised. The training area at Monchy Breton was visited on the 26th May by General Allenby, who presented ribbons and decorations to officers and men.

At the end of May and beginning of June the Ninth once more returned to the line in relief of the Fifty-first Division. Those scenes of fierce encounters, Roeux and the Chemical Works, were now in our hands, and Arras was rapidly assuming a more settled and less minatory aspect, for many of the bigger emplacements were now empty and others showed preparations for removal. At this time the activity and boldness of the German aeroplanes were very marked. The bombing of Arras and its environs, which had been occasional, was now a regular practice ; and after dusk the dove-tailed planes of the enemy flying low over our hinterland dropped light bombs and fired machine-guns on our infantry and transport lines. In such enterprises our airmen had been the pioneers, but the Germans were

quick to imitate them.   At first, the men regarded these
new disturbances as an amusing entertainment, but as
the raiders became more proficient and expert, they
realised that a fresh and deadly terror had been added
to modern warfare, and the "purr" of the "Albatross"
became a signal to rush for shelter.   Anti-aircraft
mountings for Lewis Guns were issued, and they
enabled the infantry to keep the enemy's machines at
a respectable height.

We still retained the ascendancy in artillery, but the
enemy was alert and pugnacious, and his retaliation
came almost as the echo of our practice barrages.   On
the 5th June a minor operation was carried out by the
27th Brigade and the Thirty-fourth Division on its
left.   The object of the former was to advance its line
up the western slopes of Greenland Hill on a front of
850 yards.   It was in trenches north and south of the
Arras–Douai Railway, which divided its front into two
equal parts.   Cupid Trench was to be taken north of
the Railway, and south of it the line of the sunken
road (leading from Roeux), while outposts were to be
established on a more or less undefined shell-hole line
occupied by the enemy some 200 to 250 yards beyond
the objective in each case.   The advance was to be
covered by a creeping barrage, moving at the rate of 50
yards a minute, supplemented by a machine-gun barrage
and a Stokes mortar bombardment.

The battalions detailed for the operation were the
11th and 12th[1] Royal Scots.   The assembly was very
difficult ; entry into the front system could be effected
only by night, on account of the almost continuous
artillery-fire by day between it and the rear system, and
because the traffic in the trenches, which were poor,

---

[1] Major Macpherson was wounded in the action of the 12th April, and
the command of the battalion was taken over by Lieut.-Colonel Ritson.

was visible to the field-grey observers. As the attack was timed for 8 P.M., not only had the units, additional to the ordinary garrison, to be brought up to the front line on the night of the 4th/5th, but they had to remain crowded in its limited accommodation throughout a scorching day, and hidden as far as possible from the view of hostile air patrols. The question of concealment was of first-rate importance, since any shelling of the congested trenches must have caused heavy loss and would have rendered any operation difficult, if not impossible. To provide cover for the extra men, scoops were made in the parapets and wooden shelters were installed ; fish-net screens were then hung in front of each hole, and the troops were allowed to emerge one at a time in turn from 4 A.M. till five minutes before zero, when they turned out in full strength.

To deceive the enemy, they waited for twenty seconds before going over the parapet. This raid ruse was eminently successful, since the enemy, seeing no infantry move with the barrage, took it to be a " Chinese Attack " and. lay low. The men accordingly crossed " No-Man's-Land " without a casualty, though subsequently there was brisk fighting, during which some gaps in our ranks were made by the more spirited of the defenders.

The right company of the 11th Royal Scots, on the south of the Railway, went up the sunken road and endeavoured to push out a strong post about 150 yards north-east of the bend in it, but, encountering a strong machine-gun nest, was brought to a halt. Ultimately this post fell to a combined attack by the company, assisted by two platoons of the reserve company, considerable havoc being wrought among the enemy's garrison by volleys of rifle-grenades. The centre and the left companies reached their objective, the shell-hole line about 200 yards east of the sunken road, and two platoons went on to establish forward posts.   One, moving along the Railway, pursued a body of retiring Germans and overshot its mark, but later withdrew to its proper position; the other, farther north, whose function it was to mop up an organised shell-hole area just east of the road, had been so slow in moving up that the enemy had time to recover his nerve and brought it to an abrupt halt, but a liberal dose of rifle-grenades, accurately directed, put the garrison out cf action, 11 Germans being killed and 2 wounded.

North of the Railway the 12th Royal Scots attacked on a two-company front.   There was no opposition except at the junction of Cambrian and Cupid Trenches, where the fighting was severe, for the unit on the left, detailed to attack Curly Trench, lost direction, and coming behind our left occupied Cupid along with the Royal Scots.   The left company with great difficulty cleared the north end of Cupid and part of Curly, but about 70 of the enemy remained in the latter till next day, when they were induced to surrender to the Thirty-fourth Division, assisted by physical persuasion from the Royal Scots.   Two advance posts were established, one on the Railway immediately opposite that held by the 11th Royal Scots and one farther north.

Under cover of darkness the 9th Seaforths arrived through a formidable barrage and dug trenches on the captured positions, with communication trenches to connect them with the original front line.   In spite of persistent shelling and many casualties this most efficient battalion accomplished all its tasks.   On their return the Seaforths had to pass through a gas barrage, and lost a number of men.

During the night the Germans made two spiritless

thrusts against the 11th Royal Scots, but they were easily driven off by the fire of the advanced posts. Some of them lay out until dawn, presumably with a view to making another attempt. At 3.30 A.M. they retired, but by a stroke of ill-luck the barrage that had been arranged for that hour was cancelled, and they escaped with only the punishment that Lewis Guns and rifles could inflict in a poor light. On the night of the 6th/7th two further efforts at counter-attack, preceded by artillery - fire, were made. The first was broken up before the Germans had actually made a move, but the second along the Railway was determined, and succeeded in driving in the strong post on the Railway. But its impetus was so disturbed by the accurate shooting of the advanced posts that it failed to reach the main line of defence. The enemy withdrew in the early morning when our barrage came down, and the Royal Scots reoccupied the Railway posts.

The action of the 5th June was extremely satisfactory, for while our losses were slight, those of the enemy were exceptionally heavy for the forces engaged. The 11th Royal Scots considered that they had killed more Germans in this fight than they had in any previous engagement of the war. The barrage was perfect, and the machine-guns and trench mortars co-operated admirably with the infantry. Tactically, the most noteworthy feature of the operation was the effectiveness of rifle-grenades, when fired by volleys, in knocking out machine-gun posts.

A little more ground was gained in the neighbourhood of Greenland Hill by the Division, but this was done by peaceful penetration. Covered by the K.O.S.B.,[1] a large party of the Black Watch dug a trench to extend the line of Cuthbert and Cod south of

---

[1] Commanded since the 3rd May by Major A. R. Innes Browne.

the Railway before midnight on the 10th.   On the 12th and the 13th the Ninth was relieved by the Fourth Division and marched to billets near Ruellecourt.   The Division had spent its last day in the Arras sector, where it had experienced in almost equal measure the elation of triumph and the depression of defeat.   Over 5000 casualties, chiefly among the infantry, had been suffered during the months of April and May, and the men were sorely in need of rest.   There was some fear that the Division would lose the South African Brigade, as three fresh battalions [1] had been attached to it for instruction, but happily a prolonged stay behind the lines enabled the South Africans to fill up their war-worn ranks once more and take their place beside their Scottish comrades.

[1] These were the 3/10th Royal West Surrey Regiment, 3/10th Royal West Kent Regiment, 3/10th Middlesex Regiment.

CHAPTER X

PASSCHENDAELE, 1917

Actions of the 20th September and the 12th October

From the 13th June till the 26th July, the best part of the summer of 1917, the men remained out of the line, and this unusually long and welcome rest enabled the Division to regain its old efficiency. As it was necessary to convince the infantry that progress was possible even when artillery support was unavailable, training was directed not merely to develop a high standard of efficiency in musketry, but to foster initiative and resource among the subordinate leaders. The value of the rifle-grenade had been demonstrated on the 5th June, and practice in its use was taught by means of shell-hole attacks. An area of country was cratered by the sappers to present the appearance of a shell-torn battlefield, and marks to indicate machine-gun posts having been placed on one side of it, the infantry advanced from the other. Under cover of rifle-grenades, fired in volleys, riflemen and Lewis Gun teams moved forward by rushes, till they were able to make a converging assault from a short distance under a final grenade barrage. This form of training realised as nearly as possible the actual conditions of warfare, and new men thus became accustomed to the distracting noise of battle and gained confidence in their own powers. A few casualties were caused by "short" bursts, but no one was seriously wounded, and the trifling cost was more than counter-balanced by the assurance and keenness inspired in the men.

On the 25th July the Division was transferred to the IV. Corps, whose area embraced the devastated country lying east of Bapaume. The completeness and care with which the demolition had been carried out showed how thoroughly the foe had made his detailed preparations for retreat. Desolation reigned everywhere, no village possessed a roofed building, and even the trees had not escaped, their bark being partly stripped off so that the sap would dry up. From the rubble of ruined houses, billets and stabling accommodation could be constructed, but food to supplement rations could be obtained only from canteens and consisted mainly of tinned products.

The front line was taken over from the Fifty-eighth Division on the night of the 26th by the 26th Brigade, the South African and 27th Brigades coming in on its left on the 28th and 30th. The sector held at first lay south of the Canal du Nord at Havrincourt, but on the 4th August the 27th Brigade was transferred from the south of the line to the north. The country was undulating, with ridges and alternate valleys lying north-north-east. The excavated channel of the Canal du Nord, which after an easterly course turned off in a northerly direction past Moeuvres, formed the boundary between the 27th and the other two brigades. South of the Canal the line lay on the slopes of the spurs that ran out from Havrincourt Wood under observation of the enemy, though the wood itself provided a covered approach to within 1500 yards of our front line. Some of the spurs had

HAVRINCOURT

originally formed part of the forest, but they had
been cleared by the enemy, who used the timber for
engineering purposes, and they were now covered with
a low thick scrub, which afforded concealment for
small groups. On the southern bank of the Canal
was a spoil heap which, as the greater part of it was
in our possession, gave us observation along our
entire front. The position was well adapted for
defence, since machine-guns, placed on a spur, could
bring flanking and cross-fire to bear on the adjoining
spurs. The trench system consisted of outpost, front,
support, and reserve lines.

On the front of the 27th Brigade, the Canal, of
which the channel was more than 50 feet below the
surface, separated friend from foe except at a spoil
heap on the west bank, which the enemy held as an
outpost to his main system. Havrincourt village,
red-tiled and attractive in the sun, occupied a commanding position, while to the north-east behind the
German front line could be seen the dark cloud of
Bourlon Wood. The enemy's defences along the
whole front were strongly entrenched and lavishly
wired.

A comparatively uneventful month was passed in
this quiet spot, less discomfort being caused by the
enemy than by the unusually heavy rainfall of August.
The most active of the brigades was the 26th, and
it afforded some diversion by carrying out a number
of raids. Several posts, which the enemy held only
during the night, were located, and on the 18th August
a patrol of the 7th Seaforths, crossing the wire
guarding one of these by means of a sheet of expanded metal, lay in wait for the garrison, who,
though taken unawares, put up a stiff fight. Four of
the enemy were killed or wounded and one was

taken prisoner, the casualties of the Seaforths being
one wounded and two missing. After dusk on the
same evening the Argylls sent out strong patrols,
which met with strenuous resistance; several Germans
were killed and one was captured, while the Argylls
had two officers and eleven men wounded, and one
officer and three men missing. The object of the
patrols had been to sweep the enemy from his position on the spoil heap, and though they failed to
accomplish this, the Germans were so shaken that
they evacuated the heap, which was found to be
clear when the Argylls made another raid on the
30th. The scope for adventure by the 27th Brigade
was necessarily limited to the hostile positions on
the west bank of the Canal, and on the 25th, 2nd
Lieut. Mosscrop with three men of the "Rifles"
entered a night post shortly after dusk and captured
one of the garrison when it arrived. The prisoner
belonged to the 89th Grenadier Regiment (17th Division), a *sturm truppen* lot, and this seemed to indicate
that the enemy had aggressive designs on hand, so
the troops were warned not to relax their vigilance.

A proposal by the IV. Corps that the Division
should undertake a big raid against the main entrenchments of the enemy was vetoed as impracticable,
since the amount of gun-fire necessary to cut the wire
was bound to advertise our intentions. It led however
to an interesting suggestion by Brig.-General Tudor,
which he submitted to the Corps after satisfying
himself, with Brig.-General Kennedy's help, of its
practicability on this front, and it formed the basis
of the scheme carried through in the same region
by Sir Julian Byng during the Battle of Cambrai
in November 1917. Artillery preparation, he pointed
out, could be dispensed with if tanks were employed,

and thus surprise, the value of which had been fully grasped by the Ninth, might be obtained. The tanks, protected by a smoke-barrage, would cut the gaps to allow the infantry to enter the enemy's positions, and the probability was that the Germans would be so completely surprised that large captures would be made and much ground gained at a trifling cost. The infantry were to advance towards Flesquières Ridge, but half of the tanks were to wheel to the north and roll up the German front system to the Scarpe, the aim being not to break through in depth but to destroy the enemy's forces on a wide front. This, with some modifications, was the plan carried out by the Third Army in the following November.

But the Division was not destined to participate in the Cambrai offensive. By the end of August it was relieved by the Thirty-sixth (Ulster) Division, recently engaged in the Battle of Passchendaele, and this spot the Ninth surmised was to be its next destination. The first sojourn was in the shell-torn region near Achiet le Grand, where the nature of the training gave the men a fair idea of what would be expected of them later, and on the 12th September the Division moved north by rail to camps between Poperinghe and Ypres in the V. Corps'[1] sector.

As already indicated, the principal campaign planned by Sir Douglas Haig was in the north. His design was to carry the Passchendaele Ridge and secure the command of the Belgian coast, as this would threaten the enemy's communications, and at the same time restrict appreciably his submarine warfare. But the British Field-Marshal was favoured with little luck, and it was not till the beginning of May, after the failure of General Nivelle's offensive in the Aisne, that

[1] Commanded by Lieut.-General Sir E. A. Fanshawe.

Q

his plans were approved at a conference held in Paris on the 4th and 5th May. This comparatively late start proved to be a fatal handicap, and in other theatres the rosy hopes of the beginning of the year were dispelled by the tragic events in Russia. The Revolution eliminated Russia as a German enemy, rendered the position of Roumania practically hopeless (though in the days of its stress it fought with admirable and heroic resolution), and prevented General Maude from garnering the full fruits of the fine campaign that had resulted in the capture of Bagdad on the 11th March. The Egyptian offensive broke down at Gaza, the Salonica front remained stationary, and Italy, engrossed in Trieste and Albania, was scarcely pulling her weight. Moreover, as the Germans were cognisant of our aims, and had made dispositions to defeat them, it was regrettable that G.H.Q. did not excogitate a fresh plan, which, carried out in the same manner as the Cambrai offensive later, would have disconcerted the foe and led to extensive gains without a heavy sacrifice of life.

The preliminary of the attack on Passchendaele was the capture of the Messines–Wytschaete Ridge, which overlooked our lines and a large portion of the hinterland. This was brilliantly accomplished by the Second Army on the 7th June, the enemy's position being blown into the air and the ridge passing into our hands with slight loss. The preparations for the assault on Passchendaele were then taken in hand, but for some yet unexplained reason the first blow was not struck till the 31st July. During the interlude the Germans, delivering on the 10th July an attack against the bridgehead north-east of the Yser between Nieuport and the coast, were so far successful that they prevented the projected co-operation between the

Fourth Army and the Navy, which they dreaded above all things.

The first assault launched by the Fifth Army began well, and the greater part of the ridge over-looking Ypres was stormed, but the German scheme of defence, based on holding their forward positions lightly, depended chiefly on counter-attack, and before the end of the day many of our gains, including St Julien and Westhoek, were recaptured. Above all, the key of the enemy's position on the Menin road remained in his hands. On the same day the fatal rains made their appearance, and torrential downpours transformed the battlefield into a quagmire. The con-tinuance of the wet weather, which made August of 1917 one of the most disastrous months in the war, was all in favour of the Germans; it delayed our preparations, and should indeed have led to the abandonment of the campaign; but with the pertin-acity of the true gambler, the British resumed the attack on the 16th August, but made little progress south of St Julien, the Germans defying all our efforts in the neighbourhood of the Menin road.

The defence, which was directed by General Sixt von Armin, who had achieved great fame as a tactician during the battles of the Somme, was distributed in depth. Trenches being impossible in a swamp, the defenders were placed in the ruins of barns and farmhouses; these, strongly concreted to an average thickness of three feet, offered a small mark for artillery and were proof against all except the heaviest of our projectiles. These fortified farms, or "Pill-boxes" as they were called by the men, were so situated that each could support its neighbour by cross- and enfilade-fire and was a veritable fortress in itself. They were of various sizes, according to the

extent of the ruins on which they were erected; some
had several apartments, and were capable of accommodating a whole company of men. They were
admirably adapted to break up and delay the line
of an attack, and even if they were carried and the
objective taken, the worn-out assailants would have
to meet a counter-blast from the fresh German reserves
in rear. Up to the 16th August no satisfactory means
had been found of dealing with these fortifications.

Apart from these strongholds the great problem
was how to keep rifles and machine-guns clean; on
more than one occasion our men had been forced to
give ground, because their rifle-bolts jammed owing to
mud so that the rifles could not be fired. It was also
clear that " Pill-box " fighting demanded skilful leading
and resource on the part of subordinate commanders.
The series of waves, so successful in the Arras battles,
was not suitable to meet the new conditions. Accordingly it was planned that the attack should be carried
out by lines of sections, each section being in file and
separated from its neighbours by about twenty yards.
This gave an opportunity of overwhelming a " Pill-box "
by the co-operation of the nearest sections while the
others made headway, and each part was to be cleared and
garrisoned before the sections involved continued their
advance. The plan ensured the attack being carried
on with the greatest expedition and the least fatigue,
and, provided the leadership was good, it held out
reasonable prospects of success. This was the form
of training practised in the devastated area near
Achiet le Petit, the ground being marked out by tapes
in facsimile of the actual country where the assault
was to be made.

The next phase of the Passchendaele Battle was
arranged for the 20th September, and the assembly line

of the Division lay along the crest of the Frezenberg
Ridge.   The span of front allotted to the Ninth, fully
1500 yards in all, consisted of a number of posts placed
at intervals along a road roughly at right angles to that
on which stood the hamlet of Frezenberg.   So battered
and ravaged was the country by continuous shell-fire
that no trace of the road could be discerned.   From the
ridge the ground sank to the valley of the Hanebeek
stream, which trickled through the gaunt and melancholy remains of Hanebeek Wood and meandered
northwards past the Ypres–Roulers Railway.   From
the hollow the ground rose gently to another ridge,
higher on the right where the main point was Anzac
Redoubt, and gradually sank on the left to a flat
swamp.   Beyond this was another valley, covered by
the spur on which stood the ruins of the Station
and the village of Zonnebeke.   The ordinary landmarks
indicated by the map did not exist; the only one
remaining that the eye could pick up without much
effort was the Ypres–Roulers Railway.   All vestige of
roads had been obliterated, and even the Hanebeek
brook had ceased to flow.   Its banks had been blown
in by months of relentless gun-fire and a zigzag trail of
shell-holes, rather deeper and more full of water than
the others, alone gave evidence of its former existence.
A bleaker and more repellant battlefield it is impossible
to imagine, and even the sun served only to throw into
stronger relief the dreadful ghoulishness of the landscape.   If a personal reconnaissance was impossible,
the one safe way to gain a knowledge of the country
was by a study of the excellent air photographs
furnished by the R.F.C.   Apart from the Railway, and
to the south of it, the most prominent guide was
Hanebeek Wood, which housed a number of "Pill-
boxes."   Clusters of these forts lay along the Railway

and to the north of it, the most important being
Beck House, Borry Farm, and a strong group called
Potsdam.

The attack was allotted to the 27th and South
African Brigades. The former had two objectives; the
first (indicated on the map as the Red Line) ran from
the eastern half of Hanebeek Wood up to Potsdam;
the second (Green Line) was Zonnebeke Redoubt on the
ridge running north-west from Anzac Redoubt. The
6th K.O.S.B.,[1] 9th Scottish Rifles,[2] and 12th Royal
Scots were to take the former, and then the first two
battalions were to go on to the latter. The South
Africans had three objectives; the first (Red Line) was
in prolongation of that of the 27th Brigade; the second
included Bremen Redoubt (Yellow Line); and the third
carried on the Green Line from the Frezenberg–
Zonnebeke road to the Zonnebeke stream. The leading
battalions were the 3rd and 4th[3] Regiments, and these
were supported by the 1st and 2nd.[4] The assault was
to be on the "Leap Frog" system; when any hostile
work was met it had to be occupied and held while the
line immediately behind the attacking one was to pass
through and carry on to the next objective. The Ninth
was flanked on the right by the Second Australian
Division and on the left by the Fifty-fifth.

There were few novices in the Ninth in the art
of mounting an attack, but Passchendaele demanded
special and anxious consideration. The enemy's powerful artillery swept all the back areas and the approaches
to our line unceasingly, and roads and camps beyond

[1] Now commanded by Lieut.-Colonel H. D. M. Maclean, the original
C.O. of the battalion, who returned to France in August.

[2] Lieut.-Colonel W. Lumsden succeeded Lieut.-Colonel Fulton at the
end of July.

[3] Commanded since April by Lieut.-Colonel Macleod.

[4] Temporarily commanded by Major Cochran.

ZONNEBEKE FROM FREZENBERG

the effective scope of shells were persistently bombed by fleets of Gothas.   There were no roads or communication trenches to guide troops on their way to the front line, and along the ridges of craters zigzag routes constructed with duckboards became a mark for hostile gun-fire, but they could not be deserted except at the risk of death by drowning or suffocation, which was the melancholy fate of more than one poor man and animal. These routes required the most careful preliminary reconnoitring, as the chances of taking a wrong turn were too numerous to be neglected.   Casualties on the march to the assembly area were regarded as inevitable, and there was nothing for it but to trust to luck. Everything was done to ensure that the wounded would be properly attended ; numerous aid posts were established and the staff of stretcher-bearers was greatly increased by large parties from the infantry. The problem of conveying stores and ammunition was colossal, and so, in order to be independent of carrying parties as far as possible, the men were to take rations for forty-eight hours and extra water-bottles.   Rifles were covered with sand-bags, so that they would be in good working order when the operation commenced, and each man carried a spade.   For dealing with the "Pill-boxes" a liberal quantity of phosphorous bombs was issued.

The attack was to be carried out after a preliminary bombardment of twenty-four hours and under cover of a creeping barrage.   The shell commonly used in the Second and Fifth Armies was shrapnel, and it was due solely to the insistence of General Lukin that the Division was given reluctant permission to use that combination of smoke and H.E., which had given so much satisfaction at Arras.   During these weeks the gunners had a dreadful time, for our artillery supremacy had been boldly challenged by the foe, and day and night our battery positions were fiercely bombarded. Hostile bombing machines played their part by night and frequently interrupted the laborious toil of bringing up the ammunition for the guns; hence the work of our gunners was carried out under much greater difficulties than usually fell to their lot. The creeping barrage of smoke and H.E. was to open 150 yards in front of the leading line and move at the rate of 100 yards every four minutes for the first 200 yards; then it was to pass on to the first objective at the rate of 100 yards every six minutes. The infantry, who were expected to arrive at the Red Line in twenty minutes, were to wait there for an hour, protected by barrier-fire. On the resumption of the advance the rate of the barrage was to be 100 yards every eight minutes, till the final objective was reached. A searching barrage of shrapnel was to precede the creeping one and sweep the open country 500 yards in advance of it. The combination of H.E. and smoke allowed certain refinements to be introduced which would have been impracticable with shrapnel. The most prominent obstacles were kept under fire while the barrage moved on, so that the infantry could surround them on all sides when the fire lifted. This was most conspicuously illustrated in the case of Hanebeek Wood, bristling with "Pillboxes" and machine-guns. To allow the K.O.S.B. to come to grips with the defenders before they could open effective fire, Brig.-General Tudor arranged for the barrage to be maintained on the wood, while a lane was to be left clear for men to move up and get to its rear; thus when the fire lifted the infantry would be able to attack the wood simultaneously from all sides.

Machine-guns also had an important rôle to play.

They were to barrage the final objective until the infantry began their advance from the first, and then they were to lift on to an S.O.S. line in front of the Green Line. The machine-gun was expected to be of great assistance in defence, and several were to be taken up with the assaulting brigades to support them against the expected counter-stroke.

Until the 12th September the Ninth was in camp near Ypres, and on the 16th and 17th it relieved the Forty-second Division on the Frezenberg Ridge, the 27th Brigade taking over the right sector and the South African the left. Unhappily, a deplorable incident occurred. When the 11th Royal Scots,[1] who were conveyed to Ypres by rail, were detraining near the Asylum, a shell landed among the men, causing 51 casualties in killed and wounded.

The responsible task of taping out the assembly areas was satisfactorily accomplished by both brigades. On the night of the 19th the assaulting battalions made the purgatorial march along the slippery trench-board tracks to the forming-up points. Heavy rain descended for nearly three hours, but by rare good fortune the enemy's guns were unusually quiet and comparatively few casualties were suffered; this was taken as a good omen. By 5 A.M. on the 20th the assembly of the Division was completed.

At zero the light was perfect, being sufficient for the assailants to distinguish their objectives, but rendering them only dimly visible to the enemy. Under a first-rate barrage the leading lines advanced, one company of the K.O.S.B. halting near the west margin of Hanebeek Wood, which appeared like a gigantic furnace shooting

---

[1] Lieut.-Colonel Croft was promoted to the command of a brigade a few days before the battle, and the battalion was now commanded by Lieut.-Colonel Sir J. Campbell.

up blazing roots and trunks to an enormous height.
To the left of it another company, advancing along a
lane flanked by two walls of smoke and fire, took up
a position on the rear, having intercepted and killed
on the way a party of Germans who were moving up
to reinforce their comrades in the wood. When the
barrage lifted the wood was rushed from front and rear,
and the terrifying combination of lusty Australians and
dour Scotsmen was invincible. The Germans were
allowed no time to bring their machine-guns into
action, and the wood yielded up four machine-guns
and about 50 prisoners. Our casualties were few
and were caused chiefly by rifle-fire and by our own
shrapnel which was used on the right flank of the
wood.

On the flank of the K.O.S.B. the right company
of the "Rifles" encountered very feeble opposition
and reached the first objective in good time, but the
left company, being seriously delayed by machine-gun
fire from a "Pill-box" on the Railway, gained the
objective only in time to go forward with the advance
to the Green Line.

The Railway line was a formidable fortress, as it was
defended by several strong "Pill-boxes," R1, R2, R3,
R4, and R5, and was flanked by the fire of the Potsdam
group on the left. A company of the 12th Royal
Scots was detailed to seize the "R" "Pill-boxes" up
to the first objective, but its onrush was checked at
the outset by bombs and machine-gun fire from R1,
so Lieut.-Colonel Ritson sent up two platoons from
his reserve company to attack it from the south. This
manœuvre, attracting the attention of the enemy, gave
the platoons on the Railway the opportunity of rushing
the "Pill-box" and overcoming the garrison, of whom
40 were taken and three machine-guns. This practi-

cally ended the resistance on the Railway, and the right company of the Royal Scots soon arrived at the Red Line. The task of the left company was to capture "A" and Potsdam. The defenders of the former were wideawake, and their raking machine-gun fire made the assailants very uncomfortable, but Captain Reynolds and six men managed to move close up to the "Pill-box," where they were safe from the hostile fire. They tried to put a Mills bomb through the loophole, but this the garrison blocked with a pack while still keeping the machine-gun firing. There was a real danger of the attack in this sector being held up by the obstinate "Pill-box"; but Captain Reynolds, showing extraordinary bravery and resource, under a storm of lead contrived to squeeze a phosphorous bomb past the obstruction through the loop-hole; the explosion set the place on fire and smoked out the garrison, who immediately surrendered, 7 prisoners and two machine-guns being the result of this lively episode.

At Potsdam two machine-guns were in action in the open. While two platoons of the Royal Scots made a frontal assault, a third, assisted by some South Africans, attacked from the north, and another platoon from the south. Before this converging onslaught the defenders were overpowered, and 70 prisoners and two machine-guns were captured.

During the pause on the first objective the K.O.S.B. and the right companies of the "Rifles" reorganised their forces. In each case the supporting companies had now to lead the attack, but as the right supporting company of the K.O.S.B. had already suffered severely from the enemy's barrage, Lieut.-Colonel Maclean was obliged to put his whole battalion in the front line, and he asked Lieut.-Colonel Sir John Campbell to

support him with two companies of the 11th Royal
Scots.   On the left, Lieut.-Colonel Lumsden, owing
to the late arrival of his left companies, resolved to
swing his right companies towards the Railway, and
to keep in touch with the K.O.S.B. by means of one
platoon.

The operations against the Green Line caused very
little trouble.   The K.O.S.B. encountered one machine-
gun in a shell-hole right out in the open, but the men
worked round it and bayoneted the team.   At the
Zonnebeke Redoubt the enemy made no show of a
fight, and 40 prisoners were taken.   Equally swift
progress was made by the "Rifles."   The two left
companies, moving up rapidly, caught up the barrage
and joined in the action ; except for slight opposition
from two " Pill-boxes " all was plain sailing.

Brig.-General Maxwell, who reached the Green
Line just after its capture, selected the line to be
consolidated, and this was done by improving shell-
holes and then forming short lengths of trench by
connecting them up.   The workers were covered by
a number of advanced posts, each with a Lewis Gun,
but the enemy made no attempt at a counter-stroke.
At the same time half of the men cleaned their rifles
while the others kept guard, and machine-gun sections
arrived and took up positions.   While the consolidation
was in progress a hostile aeroplane, flying low up and
down our line, roughly indicated the position to the
German gunners who sent over a few shells.

On the South African front the Red Line was
carried almost without a check, and the 4th Regiment
on the left entered Borry Farm, isolated in the same
manner as Hanebeek Wood, and Beck House, before
the Germans had time to resist.   The only trouble
was on the right, where the 3rd Regiment sustained

several casualties from Potsdam, but an assault by
Captain Sprenger with a few men materially assisted
the 12th Royal Scots to overcome this stronghold.
At the first objective the supporting battalions took
the lead, and at 7 A.M. the 1st and 2nd Regiments
moved against the Yellow and Green Lines. The
former reached its objective without opposition, but
the latter had to fight nearly every yard of the way.
From Waterend House, Tulip Cottages, and Hill 37,
all in the area of the Fifty-fifth Division, machine-
gun fire scourged the flank of the South Africans, and
created a gap between them and the troops on the
left. When the 2nd Regiment eventually carried
Zevencote and Bremen Redoubt, a defensive flank
was thrown out on the south bank of the Zonnebeke
stream, and the garrison of Mitchell's Farm was
augmented. So heavy had been the losses of the
South Africans that they had to be reinforced by
the Camerons. Late in the evening the Fifty-fifth
Division succeeded in clearing Hill 37, and thus
closed the gap between it and the South Africans.

At the fall of night all the objectives of the
Division had been secured and consolidated. A
counter-thrust was expected and even hoped for,
but it did not come. A terrific barrage along our
line about 5 P.M. seemed to be the prelude to an onslaught, and our men, surging forward out of the
shelled zone, peered eagerly into the mist for a sight
of the field-grey foemen, but all attempts of the
enemy to mass were broken up by our artillery-fire.
So accurate and stupendous was our barrage that it
seemed like a solid, impenetrable barrier.

The nature of the fighting lent itself to individual
exploits, and two V.C's. were given to the Division, one
being awarded to Captain Reynolds and the other to

Lance-Corporal W. H. Hewitt of the 2nd South African Regiment. He tackled a "Pill-box" single-handed, and on attempting to enter the doorway was severely wounded by the defenders; undaunted, he crawled to a loophole, and though wounded again pushed a bomb through the embrasure, the explosion of which dislodged the Germans. Numerous feats of a similar nature were performed by the men of all battalions, and the excellent understanding between the members of sections was a source of legitimate gratification to all responsible for the training of the men.

The line captured was held by the Division until the 24th September. The "Pill-boxes" provided a welcome shelter during the fierce gusts of artillery-fire; but their interiors were disgustingly squalid, and the floors were a foot or more under water. The Argylls and Camerons relieved the 2nd and 1st South African Regiments on the left, while the "Rifles" and K.O.S.B. held the right front. During this period there were violent storms of artillery-fire but there was no infantry action.

A deep gloom was cast over the whole Division by the news of the death of Brig.-General Maxwell on the 21st. Since taking over the command of the 27th Brigade in October 1916 he had been one of the outstanding personalities in the Ninth. Daring to a fault, he was a soldier with real gifts of generalship, and it was a sad calamity that death prevented his brilliant talents receiving fuller scope in a higher command. He was one from whose manner and bearing all plucked courage and confidence; in the glamour of his presence, his unfailing courtesy, and the opulence of his ideas lay the secret of the love and respect with which he was regarded by all his subordinates. Too great a disregard of personal danger led to his death; in his anxiety to ascertain that all was right on his front he exposed himself freely, and was shot by a sniper at 40 yards' range. His habitual hardihood had been a constant source of anxiety to his staff, but it was one of the qualities that raised him above criticism in the eyes of the men. Courage begets courage, and within a few weeks of his coming Brig.-General Maxwell had made the 27th one of the finest fighting brigades in France. His spirit lived among the men after his death, and his teaching and training remained a fount of inspiration to all ranks of the 27th Brigade.

The action of the 20th September was one of the most satisfactory in which the Ninth took part. Though the number[1] of prisoners taken was not large and the space of ground gained inconsiderable, the operation was the first to reap satisfactory results against Von Armin's system of defence, and it encouraged the Higher Command to continue the campaign in spite of the lateness of the season. Communications throughout the battle had been wonderfully good, and though telephone wires could be maintained only with difficulty on account of shellfire, messages were received by means of pigeons, lamps, and runners. The arrangements of the R.A.M.C. were effective and adequate, and the extra stretcher-bearers furnished by the infantry enabled the wounded to be rapidly evacuated from the forward areas. The H.E. and smoke-barrage required no justification in the eyes of the Ninth, but its success attracted the attention of higher authorities and led to its being employed by the Third and Fifty-ninth Divisions in the engagement of the 26th September.

[1] 32 officers, 312 other ranks.

On the 24th September after being relieved by the Third Division, the Ninth moved to Arneke and neighbouring villages, where the men were practised for their next engagement, which, if all went well, was expected to bring us near Westroosebeke. The new leader of the 27th Brigade was Brig.-General Croft, who was recalled from the brigade to which he had been appointed just before the September battle. As C.O. of the 11th Royal Scots he had been with the Division since December 1915; and no man was more likely to keep the high standard which his predecessor had set. Realising the value of a distinctive name, he caused his brigade to be known by the term "Lowland" as well as by its number. The spell of good weather that set in during the latter part of September did not last, and rain fell almost continuously from the 6th October onwards. On the 5th the Division was ordered to concentrate in the area of the XVIII. Corps,[1] and under the most depressing conditions it was transferred to the vicinity of Brake Camp, the infantry arriving late on the night of the 9th. For many of the men there was no shelter from the rain, and bivouacs and tents had to be hastily erected on the sodden ground. No camps in the whole British line were more dismal than those round Ypres, sloppy with mud and persistently bombed by the enemy's aeroplanes. So serious were the effects of bombing that all tents and horse lines were encircled by ramparts of earth to localise the explosions. On the night of the 10th/11th the Highland Brigade relieved the 144th (Forty-eighth Division) in the line near Poelcapelle, and the Ninth received orders for an attack on the 12th October.

The scene of battle was the low, flat country

[1] Commanded by General Sir Ivor Maxse.

near the northern end of the Passchendaele Ridge.
Along the left boundary of the Division ran the
Lekkerboterbeek stream, and though the whole area
was studded with fortified farms and houses, there
were no clear landmarks. Since the 20th September
performance had lagged far behind programme, and
Westroosebeke lay beyond our immediate grasp. There
were three objectives[1]; the first two (the Yellow Dotted
and the Blue Dotted Lines) were to be taken by the
Highland Brigade, and the final one (the Dotted Purple
Line) by the Lowland. The leading battalions of the
26th, the Black Watch[2] and Argylls, each on a two-
company front, were to capture a subsidiary objective
(Green Line) and the Yellow Dotted Line, after which
the Seaforths and Camerons[3] were to pass through
and go on to the Blue Dotted Line, while the final
attack was allotted by Brig.-General Croft to the 12th[4]
and 11th Royal Scots. The assault was on a very
wide frontage for a brigade, and necessitated considerable gaps between sections. The barrage was to move
at the rate of 100 yards every eight minutes, with
a pause on the first and second objectives, and 16
Vickers Guns were to form a machine-gun barrage
and were also to support the infantry with covering-
fire. On the flanks of the Ninth the attack was to be
carried on by the New Zealand Division on the right
and the Eighteenth Division on the left. Zero was
5.35 A.M.

About midnight on the 11th, the weather broke
down completely, and the march of the battalions of the
27th Brigade under torrents of rain along the slippery

[1] See Map.

[2] Commanded by Lieut.-Colonel R. W. Hadow since September.

[3] Commanded since the beginning of October by Lieut.-Colonel
A. G. M. M. Crichton.

[4] Commanded in this action by Major Scott.

R

duckboards to their assembly positions was one prolonged ordeal.   The forming-up positions were heavily
barraged with gas and H.E. by the enemy's guns;
many of the taping parties were killed or wounded,
and all had to wear their respirators for several hours.
The assembly was in consequence a difficult matter,
and slight confusion arose before the men were placed
in their correct positions.

At 5.35 A.M. our barrage opened, but was thin and
ragged.   The leading men lost direction almost at once,
owing to the wide frontage and the execrable condition
of the ground.   The right company of the Black Watch,
by the aid of skilful Lewis Gun and rifle-fire, rushed
Adler Farm, captured several prisoners, and though
some casualties were sustained reached its objective on
the Green Line.   But the left company ran into our
own barrage, and inclining to the left, made a gap
between it and the right company; it was under fire
the whole way and was compelled to dig-in a few
hundred yards in front of our original line.   The
company, which was to pass this one on the Green
Line, also swung to the left to such an extent that it
came up on the left of the leading company; from the
very commencement it was in trouble, and its commander and H.Q. were all knocked out in an attempt
to rush a "Pill-box."   Meantime the right rear company, passing through its front one, reached Source
Trench near the Yellow Dotted Line.

The first company of the Seaforths, sadly depleted
by fire from parties of Germans[1] in organised shell-
holes, advanced and filled the space between the two
leading ones of the Black Watch.   The 12th Royal

[1] The enemy opposing the division on this occasion was the Sixteenth
Division, which had the honour of being classed by our G.H.Q. as a first-
rate division.

ARTILLERY HEAD-QUARTERS NEAR ST. JULIEN

Scots, following close behind, became mingled with the Seaforths. There was some opposition from Inch Houses, and in numerous cases clusters of Germans offered resistance until they were taken in flank; in one case two of our sergeants, both of whom had been wounded, charged a group of nine and killed every one. Small parties of our men were seen in the dim light to pass Banff Houses and Source Trench, and some may even have reached Source Farm and Vat Cottages. A mixed body of Black Watch, Seaforths, and Royal Scots entered the eastern end of Wallemolen, but being heavily enfiladed from both flanks had to fall back on the Cemetery–Inch Houses line.

On the left, matters were even worse; for the ground in some places was impassable, and as a consequence the Argylls were unable to keep pace with the barrage. The right company and its supporting company maintained direction, but the others swung to the left and some of the men, crossing the Lekkerboterbeek, so churned up by shell-fire that it was unrecognisable, entered the sector of the Eighteenth Division. On the right a "Pill-box" near the front line stopped the leading company and held up the whole advance, with the result that parties from the rear battalions, the Camerons, 11th Royal Scots, and 6th K.O.S.B.[1] became involved in the firing-line. A combined assault by men of all units on the "Pill-box," the occupants of which had shown the white flag but continued firing, eventually mastered the defence, the garrison being killed and four machine-guns captured. But by this time the barrage was far ahead, the troops were exhausted and disorganised, and the leading ranks were able to proceed only 150 yards or so from the "Pill-box," where they consolidated a line of shell-holes. The men of the left

---

[1] Commanded in this action by Major A. R. Innes Browne.

company who crossed the Lekkerboterbeek advanced
for some 80 yards, but were stopped by machine-gun
fire from Beek and Meunier Houses. The left rear
company, which could make no headway, formed a
defensive flank and gained touch with the Eighteenth
Division on its old front line.

Except on the extreme right the advance had come
to a halt about 100 yards from the starting-point.
The New Zealanders on our right flank had made some
progress, but the Eighteenth Division, as was the case
with our left battalion, had been handicapped by the
spongy nature of the ground and was back in its original
position. Several unfortunate men had been drowned
in the deep, water-filled shell-holes, and rifles and
machine-guns were clogged with slime. The barrage
having gone far ahead, nothing was to be gained by
persisting in the attack, and the line taken up by the
Ninth at the close of the battle ran from the Cemetery
near Wallemolen in front of Inch Houses, thence to
Oxford Houses and back to our original front system.
Though the 26th and 27th Machine-gun Companies had
been roughly handled during the action, they were able
to provide efficient protection for the position now held.

During the night the front was reorganised in three
sectors ; the right, garrisoned by the 12th Royal
Scots, the Seaforths and Black Watch, the centre held
by the Camerons and Argylls with the "Rifles" in
support, and the left occupied by the 11th Royal Scots
and K.O.S.B. Patrols were sent out during the dark
hours with orders to join up with the leading men of
the Black Watch, who had been seen near Source Farm,
but not until next day was touch established with a few
of them in Source Trench, and these were relieved
during the night of the 13th/14th. On the same night
the South Africans took over the whole of the front,

and the 26th and 27th Brigades were withdrawn from the line.

Rain and mud constitute the chief explanation for the failure of the Division in this battle, which should not have been fought; no man could progress at more than a snail's pace, and sheer exhaustion was a factor more potent than the enemy in bringing the advance to a standstill. The breakdown in communications was understandable and largely unavoidable, since the pigeons were unable to fly against the strong wind that prevailed, and the men who had charge of the messenger dogs all became casualties. The barrage was not up to the usual standard of the Divisional Artillery, but its lack of density and its raggedness were due to the short period that had elapsed since the last action and to the weather. Many of the guns stuck in the mud, all the men were dead-beat, and Brig.-General Tudor could not get the quantity of the smoke-shells he wanted. Since the horses could not leave the roads, it was only by means of light railways that field-guns could be brought into action off the roads and supplied with ammunition. The Sappers, under Lieut.-Colonel Hearn, always a strong advocate of the light railway, gave the greatest possible assistance to the gunners by constructing a very useful railway system east of Springfield.

Serious errors were undoubtedly committed by the infantry, but when officers and men were engaged in a long and cruel struggle against ineluctable conditions, cool leadership could scarcely be expected. As on the 3rd May, there was a deplorable loss of direction at the very start leading to confusion of units, but at the same time the vast length of the attacking frontage— 1500 yards for two battalions—with wide gaps between each section, and the absence of conspicuous landmarks

made the maintenance of direction a difficult matter.
Leadership, marked more by valour than by discretion,
caused an unnecessary number of battalions to be
involved in wasteful and confused fighting. If the
mixing up of the supporting and leading units of the
26th Brigade can be understood and condoned, it was
none the less regrettable, but there was less reason for
throwing the battalions of the 27th into the fight. Of
battalion commanders Lieut.-Colonel Lumsden alone,
seeing that the attack of the 26th Brigade had been
checked, kept his men back, and the net result of
over-zealous leading was that General Lukin, instead
of a brigade, had only one battalion intact. But even
in this respect there was some excuse. It was at least
a venial fault that officers and men refused to accept
a check without making a desperate effort, and Lieut.-
Colonel Sir J. Campbell and Major Innes Browne
regarded our line as unsatisfactory, if not untenable,
while the " Pill-box " that caused the left of the attack
so much trouble remained in the hands of the Germans.
Possibly heroism on a grander scale has never been
shown than in the brutal fighting on the foul quag-
mires of Flanders. Often neck-deep in mud, the
men floundered forward until their overtaxed limbs
could no longer support them, and to wrest victory
under such appalling conditions was a task beyond
the power of man.

Few people at Passchendaele had a more thankless
and trying time than the Sappers and personnel of the
R.A.M.C. The former were constantly engaged in
maintaining the shelled duckboard tracks, making
plank roads, repairing paths and constructing shelters
and tramways. Three hundred infantry had been
attached to the latter for stretcher-bearing; they were
all needed, and it was only by sheer hard work and much

nervous strain that the wounded were satisfactorily evacuated from the dreary swamps of Passchendaele.

The line was held by the Division until the 24th October and during this time the hostile artillery periodically barraged the back areas and approaches, causing serious losses to reliefs and working-parties between St Julien and the front trenches. A great deal of material was carried up to the front for the Sixty-third (Naval) Division and many yards of cable were buried to ensure a rapid and reliable signal service. Advance posts were thrown out by the 27th Brigade, and the assembly areas for the Sixty-third Division were marked by tape. On the 22nd a feint attack in our sector, carried out by men of the XVIII. Corps Cyclist Battalion who manipulated dummy figures, assisted the Eighteenth Division in bringing its position into line with that of the Ninth. On the 24th the 27th was relieved by the 188th Brigade (Sixty-third Division) and the Ninth [1] was concentrated in the various camps near Ypres.

[1] On leaving the Fifth Army the Division received the following message from General Sir Hubert Gough :—

"The Ninth Division has fought splendidly while it has been in the Fifth Army and maintained the great reputation of the Scottish Divisions in France. The Division achieved a very notable success on 20th September and played a gallant part during the severe fighting of 12th October. In spite of the casualties sustained and the demands made upon the men's endurance during the past six weeks, the Division's moral remains as high as ever. Well done, everybody !"

CHAPTER XI

PREPARATIONS FOR DEFENCE

October 1917 to 21st March 1918

THE operations of the 12th October concluded the share of the Division in the fighting of 1917. It had played an important part in all the big battles except Messines and it had been too recently in action to be employed in the operations near Cambrai, which began in November. The Ninth was frequently engaged in the travail of battle; its rôle during the year had been rather that of storm troops than of mere occupants of the line, and though this had entailed great hardships and a heavy casualty list, some compensation had been derived from the comparatively long interludes spent in rest and training. Through gain and loss, hope and fear, officers and men had shown that splendid and invincible cheerfulness which made the Ninth so terrible in battle. The general standard of physique was perhaps not so high as in earlier years, but the spirit of the Division remained as unconquerable as ever despite the disappointing nature of the recent operations.

The situation at the close of the year contrasted sadly with the soaring hopes entertained at the beginning. Russia, whose claim to be the protector of the Balkan Slavs had been the occasion of the war,

had been ignominiously driven from the field, and her
military collapse involved the sacrifice of Roumania.
Near Salonica, the Entente had been able to do little
more than hold its own, and the greater part of Serbia
was in the hands of Bulgarians.   The Italians, unable
to wrest the coveted port of Trieste from the Austrians,
were in October dispersed in rout at Caporetto before
a combined army of Austrians and Germans, and the
allies in the West had hurriedly to send reinforcements
to stiffen Italy's resistance.   In Flanders the Passchendaele offensive dragged on beyond the limits sanctioned
by sagacity or prudence until November, and its only
result was to secure us less than five miles of ravaged
soil without effecting any important strategical gain.
The Belgian coast was still firmly controlled by the
enemy and our military efforts had signally failed to
contract his submarine campaign.   Audacity and
originality, exhibited in the intelligent employment
of tanks, achieved on the 20th November our most
remarkable victory and all but led to the capture of
Cambrai, but we were either slow or unprepared to
extend our success, and what had been our greatest
triumph was counterbalanced by our gravest defeat.
Ten days later the German counter-stroke made
Cambrai secure and rent a gap in our line near
Gouzeaucourt and Gonnelieu.

Even at sea there was cause for concern.   Though
the Battle of Jutland on the 30th June 1916 had
rendered the German Navy negligible, the submarine
activities of the enemy wrought serious havoc among our
merchant shipping, and compelled the British Government to adopt a system of rationing to conserve the
food supply.   Till the end of the year it was estimated
that we were losing ships faster than we could build
them, and it was not till the beginning of 1918 that

we made any real headway against the submarine menace.

Only in Mesopotamia and Egypt had the tide of fortune turned definitely in our favour. In the former, General Marshall pushed our conquests far beyond Bagdad, though it was impossible without Russian help on his flank to make any ambitious movement against Aleppo. General Allenby had been transferred to Egypt in June 1917, and in a vigorous and masterly campaign carried Gaza and gained possession of Jerusalem before the end of the year.

But if the year ended in humility and disappointment the future was not without a gleam of hope. The entry of America far outweighed the defection of Russia, and gave complete assurance of ultimate victory. Nevertheless the immediate situation was not happy. Though American troops had taken their place in the line by December, great numbers of trained men could not be expected to reach the Western Front from the United States until well on in 1918, and it was certain that Germany would make a supreme effort to snatch victory before their arrival. For such an emergency the British forces in France were perilously short of men, yet on the plea of home defence, which was absurd while the Navy controlled the seas, the Government retained in this country large bodies of troops urgently needed by Sir Douglas Haig as reinforcements. And at this juncture the British Commander became responsible for an additional stretch of 28 miles of front, taken over from the French in deference to a decision of the Versailles Council against the expressed opinion of the British military representative.

On leaving the disagreeable and constantly bombed camps near Ypres, the Division moved on the 25th

NIEUPORT BAINS, LOOKING TOWARDS THE GERMAN LINES

October to the Wormhoudt area, and on the following morning to the coast in the Nieuport sector. Here two days later the 26th Brigade relieved the Forty-first Division in the line. After the stress and turmoil of the Salient the Belgian coast was a veritable haven of rest, the only storm centre being Dunkirk, which was nightly bombed. Even in the trenches there was little to disturb the harmony of life, and when our gunners in accordance with their usual practice began to liven up matters, they were ordered by the XV. Corps to assume a quieter attitude. Behind the lines the broad, firm expanse of sand fringing the coast offered ample scope not merely for the manœuvring of troops but for such forms of recreation as polo and football.

The sojourn in this sector, where preparations were made for a long period of useful training, came to an abrupt end. On the 11th November General Lukin was informed that his command was to be transferred to the X. Corps of the Second Army. Further orders were received that the 9th Seaforths were to be sent ahead of the Division, and on the 19th they moved to the area of the VIII. Corps. After relief by the XXXVI. French Corps, the Ninth concentrated near Fruges. Then on the last day of the month the Germans delivered their counter-thrust near Cambrai, and the whole Division was hurried by rail to Péronne. On the 3rd December it came under the III. Corps, and two days later relieved the right brigade of the Guards' Division and the Second Cavalry Division in the sector extending from Gauche Wood to Chapel Crossing.

On its flanks were the Twenty-first Division on the right and the Sixty-first on the left. All three brigades were in the line, the 26th and 27th in the north and south respectively, and the South African in the centre. With feverish energy the trenches were strengthened, improved, and protected by wire entanglements. On the 15th December the Ninth came under the control of the VII. Corps.[1] Two days later, when the fear of an immediate attack was dying away, at a conference the brigadiers agreed that it would be a gain to hold the sector with two brigades, allowing the third to work and train, and it was also decided to hold our front with an outpost line with a buffer line running through Gouzeaucourt, while the main line of resistance was to be the reserve system. From the 17th December there were heavy falls of snow, but in spite of the inclement weather the enemy launched an attack early on the morning of the 30th against the Sixty-third Division, which had relieved the Sixty-first on our left. After a violent barrage he broke into its trenches, and two parties taking the position of the Highland Brigade in the flank were repelled by the Argylls only after a desperate conflict, in which the enemy sustained heavy losses. During the afternoon a counter-attack of the Sixty-third Division succeeded in recapturing part of the lost trenches. At dawn next morning the enemy shelled the 26th Brigade with gas and H.E., but made no infantry attack on our front, though he delivered a fruitless assault against the left division. Fine cold weather prevailed during the opening days of 1918, but in the middle of January a thaw set in and our parapets melted away in liquid snow and mud. The greatest vigilance and alertness were maintained by both sides, and patrols found few opportunities of effecting surprise. Alarms still continued, and a message picked up from the Germans seemed to indicate that an attack would

[1] Commanded by Sir W. Congreve, V.C.

be made on the 19th, but nothing out of the usual occurred until the 23rd, when an enemy patrol was repulsed in an attempt to rush the trenches held by the 11th Royal Scots. Towards the close of the month the relief of the Ninth by the Thirty-ninth Division was begun, and was completed on the first day of February.

For almost six weeks the Division remained out of the line, the time being spent in training and in work on the railways and rear defences. During this period our waning strength in man-power was responsible for infantry brigades being placed on a three- instead of a four-battalion basis, and in accordance with this rearrangement the Argylls were sent to the Thirty - second Division and the "Rifles" to the Fourteenth, while the 3rd South African Regiment was broken up and its members allocated to the remaining battalions of the brigade. This alteration not merely affected the strength of the Division, but to some extent its fighting efficiency, because the new grouping of units was one with which the British Army was unfamiliar, and new methods of tactical handling had to be acquired. At this time also the 9th Seaforths were reorganised as a three-company battalion.

The training was on the old lines of the open warfare system. It was known that the Germans were receiving special training for a supreme effort, and the best means of countering it was by securing an equal efficiency. There was nothing new or original in the methods of Ludendorff; he wished to recapture the old flexibility in movement and method that dis- tinguished the Germans in 1914, but had been lost through the routine of trench warfare. An army of the same experience as that of "The Contemptibles" would have had no difficulty in coping with Ludendorff's

sturm truppen, but the New Armies of Britain through
sheer lack of opportunity for training were much
below that standard. Using picked troops the
Germans intended to press on without halting to
adjust irregularities in their line, pockets of resistance
being compelled to withdraw or surrender by the
pressure on their flanks. This method was well
known to the British Army, and was distinctly
emphasised in the manual on Infantry Training, 1914,
in which the men were told that the best way to help
a neighbour forward was to push on themselves.
Though the time was short every moment was fully
utilised, and the infantry of the Ninth had reached
a very satisfactory stage of efficiency when they returned
to the line. The artillery, now at Bray under Brig.-
General Tudor, underwent a course of training, the
value of which was soon to be shown.

On the 1st March a further reorganisation took
place with regard to machine-guns. Each division
was equipped with a machine-gun battalion of
4 companies with 16 guns each, and the 3 companies attached to the infantry brigades now formed
part of the 9th Machine-gun Battalion under Lieut.-
Colonel Chalmers. This rearrangement strengthened
the discipline of the Machine-gun Corps by the introduction of senior officers, and a more intense *esprit
de corps* followed. It also permitted greater co-ordination and co-operation in the use of machine-guns.
There was a great increase in the number of Lewis
Guns; each battalion now possessed 36, with an additional 4 for anti-aircraft work.

At the beginning of March, General Lukin [1] was
appointed to a command in England. During his

---

[1] Later General Lukin was awarded the K.C.B., an honour which gave
much gratification to the Division.

period of command the Ninth had gained numerous outstanding successes, particularly those of the 9th April and 20th September 1917, and had developed steadily the reputation so firmly established at Loos. He had served with the Division for nearly two years and had won the esteem and confidence of all ranks. His successor was Major-General C. A. Blacklock, who arrived on the 13th March. The Division had also a new G.S.O.I.; Lieut.-Colonel P. A. V. Stewart, who had served with the Ninth since March 1916, left it in December 1917, and was succeeded by Lieut.-Colonel T. C. Mudie.

On the nights of the 11th/12th and 12th/13th March, the Ninth returned to the line in relief of the Thirty-ninth Division. The sector extended from about a thousand yards west of Villers-Guislain to about the same distance north-west of Gonnelieu, and, except that Chapel Hill was now included in the sector of the Twenty-first Division, was the position held before February. The hill should have been left in the area of the Ninth because it formed the key to the greater part of its defences.

The Ninth was on the left flank of the VII. Corps of the Fifth Army, and on its left flank was the Forty-seventh Division of the V. Corps of the Third Army. Since the junction of different armies is always a tempting mark for a hostile attack, the position of these divisions was one of particular importance; on the liaison between them depended the liaison of the Fifth and Third Armies. Of these two armies the former was by far the weaker; General Gough was responsible for a front more than forty-five miles in extent, and the forces at his disposal numbered only 14 infantry and 3 cavalry divisions, while opposing him were 46 strong German divisions. General

Byng with slightly over twenty-six miles of front
had 19 divisions (11 in line and 8 in reserve). Sir
Douglas Haig probably anticipated that the heaviest
blow would fall on the Third Army, and he furnished
it with a comparatively large body of reserves. The
Fifth Army holding less vital ground had ample scope
for manœuvre and was therefore provided with fewer
troops. But the position of General Gough was not
a comfortable one, as the first shock of attack would
absorb his few reserves, and after that he would have
to rely on his neighbours for help.

The country comprised in the Ninth's area was
undulating, with rolling downs dotted here and there,
with a few scattered woods and ruined villages. The
main tactical features were the low ridges on the east
and west of Gouzeaucourt, which joined about Chapel
Hill, one and a half miles south of the village. We
held Quentin Ridge, east of Gouzeaucourt, as far north
as Quentin Redoubt, from which point our front line
ran along the western slopes of the ridge to Fifteen
Ravine, which was the boundary between the Ninth
and Forty-seventh Divisions and the Fifth and Third
Armies.

The area was organised into three zones for
defence. The defences of the first or Forward Zone
consisted of a continuous front line supported on the
right and centre by Gauche Wood and Quentin
Redoubt, a well-wired, anti-tank field, an intermediate
line running due north from Chapel Hill, and including the village of Gouzeaucourt, and the Red Line
stretching from Chapel Hill west of Gouzeaucourt to
Beaucamp Ridge, where it joined the second zone
defences at the Divisional boundary.

The second or Battle Zone consisted of two continuous trenches — called the Yellow System — two

GONNELIEU FROM GOUZEAUCOURT

or three hundred yards apart, starting on Chapel
Hill and lying roughly north and south along the
ridge west of Gouzeaucourt, and a continuous trench
(the Brown Line) leading north-west from Railton
about one mile south-west of Chapel Hill. The
Brown Line was the only one which would not
be seriously compromised by the loss of Chapel Hill.
Numerous strong points had been made between the
Brown and the Yellow Systems, and the support line
of the former was in course of construction. A switch
line from the Yellow System along Revelon Ridge to
the Brown Line was begun when the blow fell, but
Revelon Farm, which was to have been in this switch,
was strongly defended and permanently garrisoned.

Behind this lay the Rear Zone. The villages of
Heudecourt, Sorel and Fins were intended to form
centres of resistance, but their fortifications had scarcely
been commenced at the time of the attack. Beyond
these was a continuous trench, the Green Line, running
north and south through the village of Nurlu, which
formed a centre of resistance. The sector for the
defence of which the Ninth was responsible lay between the north end of Epinette Wood and the south
end of Equancourt; it was thus echeloned in rear of
the right flank of the Battle Zone. This point requires
notice; for the enemy's penetration of the Division on
our right on the first day of the battle, and later the
failure of the troops on our left to extend to their
southern boundary, were causes of great trouble during
the retreat.

The general scheme of defence may be summarised
thus : The men in the Forward Zone were to maintain
their ground, but no counter-attack on a large scale
was to be made to recover any part of it that might
be lost. But all the resources at the command of the

s

Division were to be engaged, if necessary, to retake any part of the Battle Zone invaded by the enemy, and the artillery positions were chosen primarily with a view to the defence of the Battle Zone.

The South African Brigade [1] on the right and the 26th [2] on the left held our front. In each of these one and a half battalions were detailed for defence and local counter-attack within the Forward Zone, and the remainder was entrusted with the defence of the front of the Battle Zone. The 27th Brigade,[3] the 9th Seaforths, and the Divisional Engineers were in reserve. The 11th Royal Scots were quartered in Heudecourt, the 12th Royal Scots in Dessart Wood, and the K.O.S.B. and the 9th Seaforths in Sorel. The Divisional Reserve was to be ready to counter-attack within the Battle Zone or to man the Brown System. Of the Machine-gun Battalion, three companies were deployed in depth in the Forward Zone and in the Yellow System, and all guns were sited for direct fire, but where possible they had also been given an indirect S.O.S. line. The remaining company was in reserve at Heudecourt. The machine-gun barrage was designed to cover the valley between Gonnelieu and Villers-Guislain and the ground in front of Fifteen Ravine on the extreme left. Gun positions in the Battle Zone behind the Yellow

[1] The 2nd Regiment was now commanded by Lieut.-Colonel Christian. Lieut.-Colonel Tanner was promoted to the command of the 8th Brigade (Third Division).

[2] Lieut.-Colonel Horn of the 7th Seaforths took over the command of the Army Musketry Camp on the 18th October; the battalion was commanded by Major P. C. Anderson during the retreat.

Lieut.-Colonel Crichton left the Camerons in March, and was succeeded by Lieut.-Colonel J. Inglis.

[3] Lieut.-Colonel Sir J. Campbell being on leave, the 11th Royal Scots were commanded by Major A. C. Campbell during the retreat.

Lieut.-Colonel Maclean left the K.O.S.B. in October 1917, and was succeeded by Lieut.-Colonel Smyth, who returned to France at the end of September.

System had been reconnoitred, and this proved of great value later, for guns hastily taken up to the south of Revelon Farm on the first day of the battle did great execution.

The Divisional Artillery, reinforced by the 65th and 130th A.F.A. Brigades, covered our sector, and the barrage-fire of the field-guns was concentrated in front of Gonnelieu and Villers - Guislain. Alternative and rear positions had been prepared, and it was noted that four batteries, which had moved into their alternative positions during the week before the attack, were not shelled during the German bombardment.

Concerning the intentions of the enemy there could be no doubt. From the beginning of March fresh indications of an impending blow were reported daily in the Intelligence Summaries of the VII. Corps and Fifth Army, though long before this the construction of railways, roads, and bridges over the Canal de St Quentin had aroused speculation. The fact that several German divisions[1] had been put in the line about the middle of February, and taken out again at the end of the month, presumably for a final rehearsal, seemed to point to the middle of March as the probable time for the beginning of the offensive. On the 12th March the Corps Intelligence Summary stated that during the last four days the enemy's preparations had been extended to the forward area and were being carried on rapidly, noticeably north of Gonnelieu, while from the statements of prisoners it appeared probable that the attack would commence between the 14th and the 16th.

Up to this date all the information on which an estimate of the enemy's purpose could be based came

[1] The 18th Division, for example, after holding the Villers-Guislain-Gonnelieu sector for fourteen days was relieved on the 3rd March by the 107th Division, a prisoner from which said that his division had undergone intensive training for an attack and break through.

from higher authority. Not a sign of the coming thrust could be discerned by the men holding the line. The only suspicious circumstance lay in the failure of the hostile artillery to retaliate after the heavy bombardment carried out by our gunners at dawn every morning. On the 13th, 14th, and 15th, our left and the right of the Division on our left were subjected to severe gas bombardments; but apart from this the silence of the enemy's artillery was significant. Nothing unusual occurred till the 16th, when an extraordinary amount of movement was reported by our observers, and it was noticed that our heavy artillery "shoots" caused a surprising number of explosions.

During these days of suspense Brig.-General Tudor was in command of the Ninth, General Blacklock having gone on leave on the 16th. The Corps Summary for the 19th stated that the attack was to be expected on the 20th or 21st. It would have been impossible for anyone to detect any trace of nervousness among our troops, and a remark in the diary of the Highland Brigade on the 6th March that "the enemy is supposed to be going to attack here" reflected in its cheerful unconcern the attitude of the men. But the strain of waiting was beginning to tell on them physically, since the need for unremitting vigilance and frequent "stand-to's" materially curtailed the time for sleep. Hence the stroke of the enemy was longed for more than feared.

The German plan of attack is described in *Meine Kriegserinnerungen* by Ludendorff. The enemy had two fronts[1] of attack; the northern extending from Croisilles to Moeuvres; the southern from Villers-Guislain to a point on the Oise near the junction of the

---

[1] The northern attack was entrusted to the 17th Army, the southern to the 2nd and 18th Armies.

French and British fronts. The position of the Ninth
was exceptionally complicated; the southern half of its
area was included in the German southern front of
attack, but the northern half lay in an area comprising
the Flesquières salient, which projected between the
two zones of the hostile operations, and against which
it was no part of Ludendorff's plan to push home an
attack. In addition to the northern wing of the Ninth,
the salient was held by three divisions of the V. Corps,
and provided that the pressure north and south of it
met with success, Ludendorff had good reason to
expect that the whole of the garrison would be cut off
and forced to surrender. It is important to note that
the Ninth's line of retreat, plainly indicated on the map,
lay south-west, while the direction of the enemy's
southern advance ran due west. Thus it was clear that,
should the German attack compel a retirement, the
Division would be in danger of being cut off, since its
line of retreat took it across the enemy's front.

CHAPTER XII

GERMANY'S SUPREME EFFORT

21st to 29th March 1918

THE 21st March 1918 was big with destiny; on that day began the battle on the issue of which depended the fate of Germany and the world. At first the omens seemed favourable to the enemy, for a thick mist, hovering over ridges and valleys, allowed his grey-clad men to leave their trenches without detection. At 4.45 A.M. the masses of guns concentrated by Ludendorff on the British front spoke with an ear-splitting noise, and our lines were robed in smoke and flame. The bombardment of the Forward Zone, particularly on the front of the 26th Brigade, was not exceptional, but battery areas, Dessart Wood, and the villages of Heudecourt and Sorel were heavily shelled. Nurlu, where General Tudor had his H.Q., was the special target for a high velocity gun, and as such marked attention to a D.H.Q. was a luxury reserved for great occasions, it served to give early warning that the supreme crisis had arrived. Large quantities of gas were sent over, compelling the battalions at Heudecourt and Dessart Wood to wear respirators for two hours. Shortly after 5 A.M. telephonic communication between the two front brigades and D.H.Q. was broken, the line to the 26th

being invariably cut immediately after repair. But
General Tudor remained in constant touch with Brig.-
General Croft at Sorel, and when the bombardment
terminated, the lines to the South African and Highland
Brigades were quickly mended. At 9.53 A.M. news
was received that German infantry had been seen
advancing on Gauche Wood and Quentin Ridge behind
a smoke-barrage, and this information was reported at
once to the VII. Corps and the S.O.S. sent out by
wireless.

In the sector of the Highland Brigade there was no
infantry attack ; small parties of Germans were seen to
make a show of advancing from Gonnelieu, but an
assault, if it had been intended, was prevented by our
tremendous concentration of artillery - fire on the
village. But a serious thrust was made against the
South Africans and between 8 and 9 A.M., under cover
of a smoke-screen, strong hostile parties marched
against Gauche Wood, which was garrisoned by a
company of the 2nd Regiment holding three strong
points with another in the open on the south-west side
of the wood. Captain Green, who was in command,
was assisted by two machine-guns and a section of the
brigade T.M.B. Some Germans attacked the wood
fiercely from the east, and others, screened by the fog
while threading their way through our outposts in the
north, entered it from that direction. A desperate
resistance was offered by the posts, and great rents were
ruthlessly torn in the ranks of the invaders, but yard by
yard the Germans tightened their hold. The garrisons
of two of the posts were almost completely blotted out,
but Lieut. Beviss and half a platoon hacked their way
out and dug in immediately west of the wood. Captain
Green with the men of the third post fought his way
back to join his troops near the south-west margin.

Prodigal of life, the pursuing Germans charged in mass at 50 yards' range, and whole sections were shot down by the vengeful fire of the South Africans.   Brought to a sudden halt, the assailants commenced to dig themselves in on the western edge ; still the unerring bullets of Captain Green's men took heavy toll of them, and they retired within the shelter of the wood, but even there they found no safety, for Brig.-General Dawson, on hearing what had happened, directed all the artillery at his disposal to bombard it.   Gauche Wood was all that the Ninth yielded on the first day of the battle.

The first confirmation that General Tudor received of the enemy's attack was at 11 A.M., when he learned that German infantry were advancing between Vaucellette Farm and Gauche Wood.   Half an hour later, he heard from the Twenty-first Division that the farm had been lost, and from the South Africans that the Germans were occupying the wood.

Up to noon the situation seemed to be fairly satisfactory.   To the north, the right of the Forty-seventh Division had been unmolested, while on our right the Twenty-first Division, according to its reports, still held Cavalry Trench, east and south-east of Chapel Hill.   But at that time sinister tidings arrived, a divisional observer reporting that the infantry of the Twenty-first had withdrawn from the Hill on Revelon Farm at 11 A.M.   From noon, gnawing anxiety was the constant companion of the Division.   As we have seen, Chapel Hill formed the southern buttress of our defence scheme, and accordingly General Tudor ordered Brig.-General Dawson to ascertain at once if the Hill and Chapel crossing were still in our hands, and, if not, to concert measures with the brigade on his right for the reoccupation of these vital positions.

The South Africans' commander was fully alive to the

seriousness of the situation, for the loss of Chapel Hill might mean the sacrifice of his two forward battalions. He promptly ordered the troops holding Lowland Support (the rear trench of the Yellow System) to turn about and face south, thus forming a defensive flank between Chapel Hill and Revelon Farm, and this flank he strengthened by sending forward a company of the 2nd Regiment; it however met the enemy in the trenches on the north slope of the hill and could make no further progress. The task of recapturing Chapel Hill was entrusted to a company of the South African Scottish; at 5.30 P.M., advancing with great dash, the men chased the Germans from the crest, took the trenches on the southern and south-eastern slopes and linked up the position with Genin Well Copse.

But farther south matters were becoming exceedingly grave. The Germans bored a passage to the vicinity of Genin Well Copse, where they were rudely checked by the fire of a machine-gun section at Railton, while the South African Scottish raked them with flanking-fire, and C/51 Battery under Major Sawder at Revelon Farm engaged them over open sights with deadly effect. Patrols of the 11th Royal Scots entering into the fray, dislodged the enemy's snipers from the copse and captured an officer and 33 men.

On the afternoon of the 21st March the situation on the front of the Ninth was satisfactory. No serious assault, except on the right, had been made against its entrenchments, but the Germans had in store for it perils more desperate than those that come from a frontal attack. So far, our main source of anxiety was the south, where the chief shock of the onset had been felt, but the possession of Chapel Hill, Lowland Support, Revelon Farm, and Railton, gave reasonable security to our flank and kept us in touch with the

Twenty-first Division, which, according to our patrol reports, was holding the Brown Line south of Railton. The ominous news in the Corps Summaries of disaster farther south, and the fact that our line of retreat to the Green Line, which ran south-west, was already jeopardised by the enemy's penetration to a depth of fully 2000 yards on the Twenty-first Division's front necessarily kept the attention of General Tudor focussed on our right flank.

Information from the north had been reassuring, the Forty-seventh Division having reported at 4.40 P.M. that no alarming thrust had been made on its front. It therefore came as a huge surprise to General Tudor when he was ordered to withdraw his men during the night to the Battle Zone, in order to conform with the retreat of the V. Corps to the Red Line (a continuation of our Yellow System). This was due to events on the front of the Third Army, where the Germans had scored a greater measure of success than could have been anticipated. The loss of Doignies and the penetration of hostile infantry as far as Beaumetz and Morchies imperilled the Flesquières salient and compelled General Byng to withdraw his men on the right to Highland Ridge, and thence westwards along the Hindenburg Line to Havrincourt and Hermies. But a more extensive withdrawal involving the abandonment of the whole of the salient would probably have been our wisest policy, since it would have forestalled the enemy's designs.

Warning orders, immediately sent out to brigades, prevented Brig.-General Dawson from carrying out an attempt, which he had in mind, to recapture Gauche Wood. Instructions were also received for the Ninth to take over the defences of Chapel Hill from the Twenty-first Division; this had actually been done, but parties of the Twenty-first still on Chapel Hill and between it and Revelon Farm were relieved by the South Africans during the night. In order that the extra territory then taken over might be adequately guarded, the 11th Royal Scots were sent up to reinforce the South Africans, who established a continuous line from Chapel Hill in front of Revelon Farm to Railton, a trench being dug on it after dark by the Sappers and 9th Seaforths. With the approach of dusk the withdrawal from the Forward Zone began and was carried out without molestation, the night passing quietly except for slight gas shelling of Dessart Wood. Cheering news filtered through at midnight; the Twenty-first Division had retaken the Yellow Line from south of Chapel Hill to the Railton–Peizière Railway, and the prospect at the close of the first day's fighting seemed distinctly good.

With the second day, trials and troubles for the Ninth accumulated and grew in magnitude as the enemy's attack was pressed, and during the following days only consummate leadership and indomitable gallantry enabled the Division to extricate itself from the dangers that threatened it on all sides.

When dawn came, gelid shadows of mist drifted over the landscape, bringing poor comfort to men who, half-numbed with cold, had passed a long, sleepless night. There was no change in our dispositions, the Battle Zone being held by the South African Brigade on the right and the Highland Brigade on the left, each being deployed in depth between the Yellow and Brown Systems. At 7 A.M. General Tudor was informed by the Corps Commander that as the weight of the enemy's assault was expected to be in the south, he must be prepared to take over the front of the Twenty-first Division as far as the Railton–Peizière Railway by

10 A.M., and orders for this relief were issued at 8.35 A.M. But before they could be carried out heavy fighting had recommenced.

Enshrouded by fog, the Germans brought up undetected numerous trench mortars, with the fire of which they hammered our positions from Chapel Hill to Railton. Brig.-General Dawson, now established at Sorel, had not the same control of communications as on the previous day, and was less able to assist his infantry effectively with artillery-fire. The persevering and tenacious Germans gradually mastered the Hill, as the garrison became weakened by fatigue and casualties. General Tudor, having realised that there was little prospect of the Twenty-first Division establishing any line in front of the Brown System, which ran south from Railton Station, instructed Brig.-General Dawson to hold the Reserve Switch, which connected the front and rear lines of the Yellow System along the line of the Revelon Farm–Gouzeaucourt road. But our strained right flank was still locked in conflict, and General Tudor contemplated an attack by his reserves to relieve the pressure on the South Africans, but he was instructed by the Corps Commander, in view of the situation farther south, to form a switch from the Yellow System on the left to the Brown System on the right.

Scrupulous care and timely anticipation marked the actions of the G.O.C. In the forenoon he had sent one of his staff officers to acquaint the Forty-seventh Division with the critical state of affairs on our front, and at 12.15 P.M. he warned it by telephone that there was a possibility of our being ordered to retire to the Brown Line, and that as this withdrawal would necessarily be in a south-westerly direction, the length of the front of the Forty-seventh would be greatly extended. The situation on our right flank was precarious enough in itself, and General Tudor was anxious to assure his left.

In the afternoon matters developed rapidly. The policy of the Fifth Army was to fight a rearguard action to delay the enemy, and the Ninth was instructed to withdraw at once to the Brown Line; but before this order was issued another message commanded a retirement to the Green Line. The South African and Highland Brigades were accordingly told to move back to the Brown Line at 4.30 P.M., and from it to the Green Line at 7.30 P.M. The 12th Royal Scots already occupied the Green Line north of Nurlu, and the Black Watch, the reserve battalion of the 26th Brigade, were withdrawn at once, and taking up a position on the left of the Royal Scots held the Green Line as far north as the Fins–Equancourt Railway, with the details of the 26th Brigade on their left. Brig.-General Croft directed the K.O.S.B. to hold the high ground between Sorel and Lieramont, and two companies of the 11th Royal Scots were posted south-west of Heudecourt. The 150th A.F.A. Brigade was withdrawn and came into action south of Sorel. It was hoped by these dispositions to secure the Green Line and cover the southern flank of the South Africans and Highlanders during their retirement, which in the case of the former at least was bound to be of exceptional difficulty, since by 4 P.M. the enemy in the south had entered Guyencourt and threatened to cut across the Division's line of retreat.

The first stage of the retirement was accomplished successfully. When the Germans noticed our movement they advanced in dense formations past Revelon Farm, until they were broken up in confusion by heavy fire from the 2nd South African Regiment. The retreat

to the Green Line was one long struggle against frantic
odds and deadly perils.   Farther south the plodding
Germans, still making ground, had pierced before dark
the Brown Line south of Railton in the sector of the
Twenty-first Division, and, commencing to roll up our
line, burst into Heudecourt from the south-east at
6.30 P.M.   This manœuvre threatened the right wing
of the Ninth with destruction, and all three battalions
of the South African Brigade were in imminent danger
of envelopment.   Safety depended on the successful
checking of the enemy until the friendly mantle of night
gave the several units an opportunity to retire.   General
control was impossible, but section and subordinate
leaders handled their men in a manner that must have
excited the admiration even of their skilful adversaries,
and the bulk of the South African forces succeeded in
reaching the Green Line.

While the retirement of the artillery was taking
place, throngs of hostile aeroplanes flitting above them
sprayed the teams with bullets and engaged our
infantry.   In the dim light, the South Africans could
see in Sorel the sad evidences of an army in ·retreat;
streams of wounded, guns, and details of departmental
units were hurrying through the streets, while the enemy
was pressing on towards the village in large numbers.
It was imperative to stop him until our retiring troops
and guns had reached safety, and Brig.-General Dawson
manned the trenches west of Sorel with the personnel
of his staff.   The K.O.S.B., already in position, were
engaged with the Germans, and with the help of Brig.-
General Dawson's staff brought them to a halt.   Before
they had time to organise an attack the last guns had
left the village, and Brig.-General Dawson with his
H.Q. drew off into divisional reserve at Moislains.
The remnants of his three battalions withdrew north

to Fins, which they left as the advance parties of the enemy entered it, and thence they retired without interference behind the Green Line.   A few of the South Africans missed their way in the darkness and did not rejoin the Division until some days later.

The retirement of the Highlanders was attended with many thrills.   In the morning they had been undisturbed and patrols had remained till noon in Gouzeaucourt, which was spasmodically shelled by the Germans, who seemed to be unaware that our men had left the Forward Zone.   Fortunately there was no frontal pursuit ; for the Germans advancing from Gonnelieu walked into our anti-tank minefield and exploding some of the bombs hurriedly retired.   The route of the Seaforths and Camerons ran through Fins to Etricourt, but the enemy had already taken possession of the former, and the Highlanders had to make a wide detour to the north in order to reach Etricourt, where they spent the night, part holding the line with the Black Watch and part in brigade reserve.

The flames of burning huts fired by the Sappers, with the dark silhouettes of retiring troops, formed an awesome and romantic spectacle.   From Nurlu ascended clouds of brick-dust, like the genie from the brass bottle, and shell dumps belched forth volumes of thick black smoke and glowing flames, while every now and then a heavy shell exploded with a deafening crash, and green, red, white, and blue rockets soared through the air like fairy fountains.

> " That night, a child might understand,
> The Deil had business on his hand."

Amid such turmoil and desperate haste it was inevitable that several parties should go astray, and material should be lost.   The South African company

of Captain Green near Gauche Wood and a company of
the 11th Royal Scots at Revelon Farm had never a
chance of escape and were overwhelmed. A platoon
of the Seaforths under Lieut. Cameron had been left
in the Yellow System by mistake, but at 10 P.M. with
amazing coolness this young officer piloted his men
through groups of the foe and brought back 18
prisoners, including an officer. The guns, which had
covered the withdrawal up to the last moment, firing
over open sights, had caused dreadful havoc among the
hostile infantry, and were all brought out except
a forward anti-tank gun, one which was bogged, and
ten field-guns of the two batteries of the 150th A.F.A.
Brigade, the teams of which failed to turn up in time.
All the abandoned pieces were rendered useless.

During the night the K.O.S.B., the remaining three
companies of the 11th Royal Scots, and the 63rd and
90th Field Companies occupied Nurlu and the Green
Line, as far south as Epinette Wood. The 9th Seaforths
and the 64th Field Company moved into divisional
reserve in Vaux Woods, north of Moislains.

General Tudor, who had transferred his H.Q. to
Moislains at 3 P.M., had extricated his force from one
danger only to be confronted by another equally
critical. He had been most punctilious in his reports
to the Forty-seventh Division in order to avoid any
misunderstandings about his left flank, and to give
that division timely warning of the measures to be
adopted to maintain liaison. But in spite of his pre-
cautions complications arose. The staff officer he
had sent to inform it of our withdrawal to the Green
Line returned with the message that the Forty-seventh
was going to retire to the Brown Line only, and was
not prepared to accept responsibility for connecting
up its right on the Brown Line with our left on the

Green Line. This was a most awkward *contretemps*, and General Tudor at once informed the Corps Commander, who promised to arrange matters with the V. Corps, to which the Forty-seventh belonged. Shortly before 7 P.M. the point was again referred to, when the Ninth was advised that the Third Army was also to withdraw to the Green Line. Accordingly at 7.30 P.M. the exact position of our troops was reported to the Forty-seventh Division, which informed us that the 99th Brigade was at Manancourt and Equancourt in reserve. This brigade was placed under the orders of the Ninth at 9.10 P.M., and one of its battalions was ordered to extend from the left of the 26th Brigade to a point about 1000 yards north of Fins. The stretch of front held by the Division, with the 99th Brigade attached, on the night of the 22nd/23rd amounted to 7500 yards. No touch was established with the units on either flank, but the V. Corps promised that its troops would link up with the 99th Brigade at 5 A.M. on the 23rd, while the Twenty-first Division stated that it was holding up to the north-eastern end of Epinette Wood.

Thus the prospects on the night of the 22nd were uncertain and disquieting. The onus of anxiety had hitherto come from the south, but from now onwards the gate[1] between the Fifth and Third Armies began to be pressed open, and offered a glorious chance of sweeping victory to the enemy. And the course of events forced the Ninth to become the guardians of the door, which it held by the gallantry of its men and the skill of its leaders, until reinforcements were

[1] For a clear, full, and concise account of the boundary question between the Fifth and Third Armies, see article in the April (1920) number of the *National Review*, entitled, the "Epic of the Ninth Division," by W. S. Sparrow.

T

available. On the evening of the 22nd the divisions
in the Flesquières salient had been violently attacked
at Villers-Plouich and Havrincourt, and though the
assaults had been beaten off with great slaughter
they hindered the retreat of the Third Army in a
south-westerly direction. The V. Corps, pushed
away from its boundary, failed to link up with the
Ninth at 5 A.M. on the 23rd as arranged, so that
a co-ordinated retirement by the two armies was
impossible.

It must be borne in mind that throughout the
retreat the men suffered constantly from want of sleep,
and supplies being inevitably irregular, they had to
endure frequently the pangs of hunger and thirst.

Unfriendly mist again bathed the battlefield at
dawn on the 23rd. Orders were received at 5.26 A.M.
to hold the Green Line with rearguards only, and
to withdraw the remainder to a line east of Moislains
and along the eastern edge of Vaux Woods, the
retirement of the rearguards to conform with that
of the troops on our right. The movement was
necessary owing to a breach in the Green Line farther
south, but it added enormously to the territory of
the Ninth, which, being obliged to keep in touch with
the Forty-seventh Division west of Fins, now had
the vast frontage of 11,000 yards.

Before the orders for retreat reached the front line
troops, the enemy launched a resolute assault against
the Green Line under an artillery and trench-mortar
barrage. On the left it was repulsed, but the right
of the Division was turned by Germans who swarmed
through Epinette Wood, and only a brilliant rearguard action by Captain Cockburn enabled the
K.O.S.B. to extricate themselves from a critical position. The South Africans retired undisturbed to

divisional reserve on a ridge east of Bouchavesnes, but the Highlanders and Lowlanders passed through a fiery ordeal.

The retreat had to take place in broad daylight under strong pressure and without the support of the guns, which had to be conveyed across the Canal du Nord, but it was slowly and skilfully carried out, and appalling losses were inflicted on the pursuers. The men behaved like veterans, and the Sappers took their place with the infantry. Brig.-General Kennedy never received the orders to retire, and his Highlanders commenced to retreat only when the enemy was in Nurlu and shared the same trenches. Admirably covered by two companies of the Seaforths and two companies of the Camerons, the brigade shook itself free. The covering force counter-attacked the Germans, and the Seaforths meeting them with the bayonet hurled them back into Nurlu. As a result of this fine effort, the Highlanders successfully effected their retirement to the ridge behind Equancourt and Manancourt which extended from the Beet Factory to Hennois Wood. For the 26th Brigade there was only one bridge at Manancourt across the Canal, which here was full of water, and some of the Black Watch had to swim, but by 2 P.M. the whole Division was safely behind the Canal du Nord from Moislains to the Beet Factory north of Etricourt, with the 99th Brigade, about 750 strong, continuing the line to the north of Fins, where it was in touch with the Forty-seventh Division. The position was a strong one and had been reconnoitred the previous evening by General Tudor, but the vast extent of front could not be held as a continuous line, and touch between the various units was at all times precarious.

The whole of the 99th Brigade and most of the 26th, the right of which was just east of Hennois Wood, were in Third Army territory, and this was pointed out to the VII. Corps. An attack on this weak and far-stretched flank was to be dreaded, since it might drive these brigades north and north-west and break the front of the Division. Accordingly, General Tudor, having obtained permission from the V. Corps to order the right brigade of the Forty-seventh Division to take over our front north of Fins to north of Equancourt, delivered these instructions to it at 11.15 A.M. In the afternoon the 99th Brigade was transferred to the V. Corps, which was to extend its right flank down to the boundary between the Third and Fifth Armies, west of Manancourt.

In the afternoon the Germans launched a furious attack against the 26th and 99th Brigades, and succeeded in penetrating some distance between Brig.-General Kennedy's Highlanders and Brig.-General Croft's Lowlanders. The Twenty-first Division fell back to the south of Bouchavesnes, and the South Africans took up a position on the ridge east of that village to cover the right rear of the Ninth. Orders were then received from the Corps to take up a line from Bouchavesnes along the eastern edge of St Pierre Vaast Wood to a point south-east of Saillisel on the Third and Fifth Army boundary. This gave the Ninth a span of 6000 yards, and all three brigades were required to hold it because casualties had been numerous and the men were tired out by continual marching and fighting. General Tudor thereupon visited the South Africans, and gave orders to Brig.-General Dawson to retire after dusk from the Epine de Malassise to the ridge just west of Bouchavesnes, requesting him to tell Brig.-General Croft to withdraw his men to the east of St Pierre Vaast Wood. The new line was to be held at all costs. This message was never received by Brig.-General Croft, and when the South Africans commenced their retirement between 7 and 8 P.M. the right of the Lowland Brigade, thus left unprotected, was heavily attacked. At the same time the left wing of the Lowlanders was threatened by the enemy's advance from Manancourt, and was out of touch with the Highlanders, whose right in the course of fierce fighting had been compelled to give way, and who, with their ammunition practically exhausted, were now occupying a line extending from a mile south of Mesnil-en-Arrouaise to a point 1000 yards west of the Beet Factory.

On leaving the South Africans, General Tudor hastened to see Brig.-General Kennedy, whose brigade he found in a critical position. Envelopment of both flanks appeared imminent, but as a withdrawal by daylight meant destruction, he instructed Brig.-General Kennedy to retire by 4 A.M. to a line in front of Saillisel. Returning to H.Q., he reported his action to Fifth Army H.Q., the VII. Corps then being on the move, and pointed out that, unless the Third Army could take over the front as far as its southern boundary according to arrangement, a gap would exist between the two armies after 4 A.M.

The crisis of the battle was swiftly approaching. The whole line of the Fifth Army was in flux, for General Gough, with weak and battered forces and no prospect of reserves, dared not risk an engagement, and the Germans seemed confident of victory, their infantry onslaughts being heralded by many "Hochs!" and bugle blasts. But our men showed marvellous control; time after time the enemy was allowed within 50 yards of our line, and then on the word of command a shower of well-aimed bullets abruptly halted him. During the night, in compliance with orders, the Lowland Brigade, with the 9th Seaforths attached since the 23rd, moved back to St Pierre Vaast Wood, where it repulsed with many losses several attacks before midnight. During this conflict the K.O.S.B. lost their commander, Lieut.-Colonel Smyth being wounded for the fifth time in the war. The hazardous and complicated move of the Highlanders was attended with wonderful fortune, and they came into line on a position extending from the northern corner of the wood across the ridge, on which stood the village of Saillisel. The Third and Fifth Armies were now separated, there being a space of fully 3000 yards between them. Nothing had been heard of the 99th Brigade since it had been attacked in the afternoon, but after midnight it was learned that it had been withdrawn to Rocquigny and Le Transloy. No troops arrived to hold the ground between Mesnil and the left of the Ninth, and fruitless efforts were made to establish connection with a brigade of the Seventeenth Division, which had been ordered by the V. Corps to take up a position west of Saillisel.

The great activity of the enemy on the night of the 23rd utterly precluded sleep. About 2 A.M. the troops of the Twenty-first Division on the right of the South Africans reported to Brig.-General Dawson that Cléry was in the hands of the enemy and that they were about to make a further retirement. The South Africans were on the right of the Ninth on the ridge west of Marrières Wood, the Lowlanders at St Pierre Vaast Wood and the Highlanders on the left. There was no reserve except the details of the Divisional R.E., and our front measured 9500 yards.

Before dawn the Highlanders, acting on a false report that the Lowland Brigade had been withdrawn,

retired to the line of the Bapaume–Péronne road in
order to secure touch with it. The message with this
news took five hours to reach D.H.Q., now at Maurepas.
Three tanks, which were at Combles, were ordered to
proceed to a point between Marrières Wood and
Rancourt to prevent the enemy penetrating between
the South African and 27th Brigades. But it was
too late.

At 8 A.M. vast hordes of Germans assailed the
Lowland Brigade in front and on both flanks. The
weight of attack was on the right wing, but the
K.O.S.B., in brigade reserve south of Rancourt, were
able to delay the enemy's turning movement long
enough to allow the other battalions of the brigade to
be withdrawn from St Pierre Vaast Wood to a position
covering Combles. This position had been rapidly
taken up by details of the Divisional R.E. under the
orders of Brig.-General Croft, and these troops aided
by the three tanks helped to cover the retirement of the
Lowlanders, and held their ground for over an hour.
From there, greatly harassed by bombs and machine-
gun fire from aeroplanes flying low and bearing British
colours, the brigade withdrew first to Guillemont Ridge,
and then to a position between Maricourt and the
Somme, already occupied by the 9th Provisional
Battalion.

Meanwhile the enemy delivered a series of blows,
growing in fury, upon the South Africans from 9 A.M.,
and Brig.-General Dawson reported at 11.10 A.M. that
he was being heavily attacked from south and west,
but that his line was still intact. This was the last
message received from the brigade.

When the South Africans were posted near Marrières
Wood, they succeeded in gaining touch with the left
of the Twenty-first Division, but, except for a company

of the K.O.S.B., they failed to find the 27th Brigade. Brig.-General Dawson's last instructions were to hold the position "at all costs," and he explained to his battalion commanders the full significance of these words. The position contained one good trench and one or two poor ones, and there was a large number of shell-holes. The ground sloped downwards towards the east, and then rose to another ridge about 1000 yards from the front line. The men had each 200 rounds of ammunition and there was a fair supply of Lewis Gun drums, but the four Vickers Guns had only four belts, and three of these with their teams were accordingly sent back to the Transport. The strength of the brigade was only 500 all told, including the personnel of H.Q. and a detachment of the Machine-gun Battalion, while all ranks had been three nights without sleep, and were in a state of extreme fatigue from their physical exertions and the strain of the previous days.

At 9 A.M., heralded by machine-gun and artillery-fire, the enemy onsets began. At the first essay the hostile infantry kept a respectful distance, and did not venture to assault. But an hour later a dangerous attack developed on the left front and flank from the north-east. Under a smoke-screen, formed by setting fire to the dry grass, the Germans skilfully picked their way up to a point between 200 and 100 yards from our front line, but further advance was baulked by unerring marksmanship, the South Africans husbanding their ammunition and firing carefully. Foiled but persistent, the assailants wheeling a field-gun forward by hand tried to bring it into action, but a Lewis Gunner of the 1st Regiment shot down the team before it could be fired. Some hours later another gun was brought up at the gallop, but, under the accurate fire of the same Lewis Gunner,

men and horses went down in a struggling mass, an
inspiring sight greeted by the South Africans with
jubilant cheers.

About noon the troops on the right and left of the
brigade retired, and the movement misled an officer and
about 30 men of the South Africans who, thinking
a withdrawal had been ordered, began to fall back, but
no difficulty was experienced in bringing them in. The
exposed left flank was protected by Major Ormiston
with 25 men. No wounded, except those who could
not handle a rifle, were allowed to quit the brigade area,
but none complained or gave the slightest evidence of
any desire to leave their comrades; the corporate
heroism of the South Africans was beyond all praise.
Every round was collected from casualties, and men not
in the front line or not having occasion to use their
rifles passed their ammunition to those who required
it. By 2 P.M. the South Africans were completely
surrounded, and were being fired at from the west as
well as from the south and east.

Rescue was now impossible, and the South Africans
grimly set themselves to sell their lives at the highest
price. Between 2 and 3 P.M. German troops in the
north were seen to retire, and wild hope surged through
the men that the Thirty-fifth Division, which was
known to be coming up, was now within reach; but
the enemy had come under his own machine-gun fire
from the west and was merely withdrawing from the
danger zone. About 4 P.M. only 100 worn-out, dust-
covered men remained and the ammunition was all
but finished, while batteries of field-guns and several
trench mortars were now in action against them. The
faint chance of effecting an escape under cover of night
was extinguished when, half an hour later, the enemy in
great strength and dense formation surged down on the

survivors.   Only a few scattered shots greeted this, the
final charge, and then the tiny groups were swallowed
up in a sea of Germans and Brig.-General Dawson and
his small band of heroes were prisoners.

The glorious stand of the South Africans was the
most dramatic and arresting episode of the retreat, and
has already achieved a prominent place in the annals
of the British Empire.   Throughout all lands of the
British race it silenced craven panic and roused that
strong pride of race which is ever the parent of
valorous deeds.   The story [1] reported by Captain
Peirson, the B.M. of the 48th Brigade of the
Sixteenth Division, reveals the effect on the enemy,
which was not confined to moral results.   As Brig.-
General Dawson was taken behind the German lines
he saw the roads blocked with a continuous double line
of transport and guns from west of Bouchavesnes to
Aizecourt le Haut; for over seven hours the South
Africans had kept back, in addition to the infantry, all
the artillery and transport which were to advance by
the Bouchavesnes–Combles road, and the delay was
of inestimable value to our troops in rear.

[1] "After being captured at La Motte, near Corbie, I was taken to the
German Battalion H.Q. for examination by an intelligence officer.   In the
course of this examination the officer asked me if I knew the Ninth
Division; he said that the fight it put up was considered one of the best
on the whole front, and particularly the last stand of the South African
Brigade at (I think) Moislains, which, he said, was magnificent.   Both
men and officers fought to the last against overwhelming odds, the
brigadier himself being taken, firing a machine-gun whilst his brigade
major was killed beside him.

"After this conversation I was sent to Le Cateau, and on the way many
German officers spoke to me and all mentioned the splendid fight put up
by the South Africans.

"On reaching Le Cateau, I met two officers (British), who said that
whilst their party was being marched to this place, they were stopped by
the Kaiser, who asked if anyone present belonged to the Ninth Division.
The Kaiser then said that had all divisions fought as well as the Ninth
Division he would have had no more troops to carry on his attack with."

Meantime the 26th Brigade, which remained on Sailly Saillisel Ridge, north-west of St Pierre Vaast Wood until 11.30 A.M., retired through Guillemont and Maricourt. A stand was made on the Morval–Combles Ridge, where the enemy experienced a rough handling, and later the brigade held the ridge behind Leuze Wood to Combles for a considerable period until the Lowlanders had established their position. During the murderous combat that ensued here Brig.-General Kennedy had his horse shot under him, and the stubborn Highlanders were hard pressed to stem the savage onrushes of the Germans. The most heroic assistance was rendered by the Divisional Artillery, whose alternate battery retirement was magnificent, and they killed vast numbers of the enemy at point-blank range; in numerous cases they remained in action until the enemy's infantry were swarming on them. C/51 and D/51 Batteries catching the Germans coming down the slopes towards Combles, inflicted enormous casualties and kept on firing till the last possible moment. All the guns were safely withdrawn, though the last gun-team of D/51 was slightly delayed by a direct hit from a "dud" 4.2 shell, which went right through the wheel horse. Skilfully, Brig.-General Kennedy withdrew his men, but in the keen and close encounters the brigade became split up into three parties. The bulk of the Highlanders after a brief halt at Maricourt proceeded to Montauban, where a position was taken up in support of the First Cavalry Division, which was then maintaining a line in front of Bernafay Wood.

The second group, consisting of about 150 Camerons on the left flank of their battalion, had been the last to retire. These men drew off in the direction of Les Bœufs and finding it occupied by Germans marched to Flers, where they joined the 52nd Brigade of the

Seventeenth Division. They went with the 52nd
Brigade as far as Martinpuich, where they attached
themselves to the Sixty-third Division on the 26th,
but having received permission to go back to the Ninth,
succeeded in rejoining it later in the evening. Another
party of Camerons, about 100 in all, in attempting to
keep touch with the troops on its left became separated
from the rest of the brigade and attached itself to the
142nd Brigade, Forty-seventh Division, and on the
25th, after reaching Albert, formed a part of Lieut.-
Colonel Hadow's force.

The third group, consisting of 300 Black Watch
under Lieut.-Colonel Hadow, remained on Morval
Ridge until its flank was turned, and it was compelled
to retreat northwards. This force, growing in numbers
as it collected stragglers from all units, was 2000
strong on the 26th; as "Hadow's Force" it was
organised into two battalions and under the orders
of the VII. Corps, took up a position from Mericourt
L'Abbé to Sailly le Sec. There it remained until
relieved by the 43rd and 38th Australian Brigades on
the 28th, after which the men of the 26th Brigade
rejoined their battalions.

Sunday, the 24th March, was one of the most
dismal days of the retreat. In the south General
Gough's men did not fare so badly; for though the
Péronne bridgehead had been lost on the 23rd the
enemy did not make much progress between the
Somme and the Oise. But the terrific fighting along
the entire front all but shattered our defences. On the
Third Army front the enemy attacking on the right
flank of the V. Corps won Combles, Morval, and Les
Bœufs, compelled the Third Army to surrender the
whole of the old Somme battlefield, and threatened the
liaison between the Third and Fifth Armies. Fissures

appeared between the units of the V. Corps, which was forced away from its boundary, and when darkness fell, its right flank, which should have been south of Montauban, rested near Bazentin.

The Ninth now under General Blacklock, who had returned from leave in the afternoon, and reinforced by the 12th H.L.I. of the Thirty-fifth Division, remained in ignorance of the misfortunes of the V. Corps until after midnight. In accordance with instructions from the VII. Corps it took up at 8.30 P.M. a position extending from an east and west line through Harde-court to the Guillemont–Montauban road. The 12th H.L.I. formed the outpost; the main position was held by the 27th Brigade and two composite battalions of the VII. Corps Reinforcement Training Camp under Lieut.-Colonel Hunt, the 18th H.L.I. being in reserve. The 26th Brigade was at Montauban and D.H.Q. were at Billon Wood. The fragments of the South African Brigade, consisting of the men who had been separated from their brigade on the 22nd, were collected during the night near Maricourt and formed into a battalion under the command of Lieut.-Colonel Young, who had been in charge of the South African details. A dismounted cavalry brigade under General Legard, composed of remnants of the First Cavalry Division, occupied a position between Montauban and Bernafay Wood. Persistent efforts were made to establish touch with the left, and at 1.20 A.M. General Blacklock learned that the right of the Forty-seventh Division was at Bazentin. The Forty-seventh was now as far behind as it had been in front of us in the morning, and there was a gap of two and a half miles between the two armies.

The boundary question had obtruded itself in a fashion that could not be neglected. At all costs the breach between the armies had to be filled if Ludendorff's

plans were to be thwarted.   The first step of G.H.Q.
was to transfer all the troops north of the Somme
from the Fifth to the Third Army; in other words,
the smaller army holding the longer stretch of front
had to provide reinforcements for the stronger force
with the shorter front.   Nothing can illustrate more
clearly than this the absurdity of the story, once widely
circulated and even yet largely credited, that the Third
Army would have had no need to retire at all had it
not been for the retreat of the Fifth.   The territory of
the latter army was not curtailed in compensation for
the loss of these troops.   If the Third Army had been
able to keep to its southern boundary, General Gough
could have assisted the hard pressed XIX. Corps in
the south with units of the VII. Corps.

In accordance with this arrangement the Ninth along
with the rest of the VII. Corps now came under the
Third Army.   The boundary between the V. and
VII. Corps was fixed as follows: the Railway south
of Montauban, thence along the road Montauban–
Mametz–Le Carcaillot, all inclusive to the former.

These measures did not and could not fill the gap,
but it was expected that if the V. and VII. Corps
were put under the same Army Commander, he would
succeed in securing better co-operation.

Early on the 25th the Lowland Brigade was relieved
by the 106th Brigade, 35th Division, and assembled at
Talus Boise, whence it marched to Etinehem to rest and
reorganise.   After daybreak the 26th Brigade occupied
a position on the south-west of Montauban to protect
the left flank of the cavalry.   On the withdrawal of
the Lowlanders the line was held by the 18th H.L.I.
and the 9th Provisional Battalion, along the western
edge of Favière Wood to the southern margin of
Bernafay Wood, where the 106th Brigade was con-

nected with the cavalry near Montauban. The 12th
H.L.I. were on outpost from the north of Harde-
court to the south of Trones Wood. On the right the
Thirty-fifth Division, to which the Ninth was now
attached, held from Hardecourt to Curlu, its H.Q.
being at Bray.

The transference of the VII. Corps to the Third
Army maintained liaison between General Gough and
General Byng, but there was still an awkward opening
between the VII. and V. Corps. In the morning of
the 25th the enemy launched repeated attacks against
the Ninth's front, and a resolute effort was made to
turn its left flank, Bernafay Wood being lost and
recaptured in the course of the fighting. By 10 A.M.
the reserve consisted of only two companies, and still
no connection had been established on the left with
the Seventeenth Division, which was said to be moving
in on the right of the V. Corps. A welcome reinforcement, a battalion of the 104th Brigade, arrived and was
sent to strengthen the 106th Brigade.

At 1 P.M. the VII. Corps reported that the Seventeenth Division was holding a line from north of
Bernafay Wood to a point 700 yards south-east of
Bazentin-le-Grand, and that two of its brigades were
reorganising east of Fricourt, but attempts to establish
touch were still fruitless. Shortly afterwards, however,
information was received that the Twelfth Division
had been commanded by the VII. Corps to move as
rapidly as possible to the line Montauban–Bazentin,
and to link up with the Seventeenth Division.

About 2 P.M. the Germans in great strength de-
bouched from Ginchy and moved against Trones Wood,
and though our gunners swept their ranks with accurate
and withering fire, they drove the 12th and 18th H.L.I.
back to the line of the road running from west of

Maricourt Wood to the Briqueterie south-west of Bernafay Wood. By a fine counter-attack men of the D.L.I., 106th Brigade, regained Favière Wood. More reinforcements came up, consisting of tired fragments of the Twenty-first Division, and at 4 P.M. one battalion was ordered to join the 104th Brigade at Maricourt and the other two the 106th. Still the enemy continued his onslaughts, but though he gained a footing in the Briqueterie south-west of Bernafay Wood he was summarily ejected.

Until about 6 P.M. there was comparative quietness, but after that hour frequent reports were received that hostile infantry had been seen north of Montauban, and even as far west as Mametz Wood. In the evening a withdrawal to the line of the Bray–Albert road was ordered by the VII. Corps, the retirement to be covered by rearguards, which were to maintain their position until 2 A.M., while the retirement of the artillery was to be accomplished gradually, harassing fire being kept up all night to conceal the retreat, and to prevent as long as possible any noticeable diminution in the volume of fire. The new front of the Ninth extended from east of Meaulte to Albert, and the 27th Brigade was instructed to occupy it at once. This was a most fatiguing day for the 26th Brigade. After fighting continuously all day the men trekked to Etinehem, just in time to receive orders to march by night on a compass-bearing to Dernancourt. The South Africans, now formed into one battalion, moved to Ribemont sur L'Ancre. The last battery did not retire until 3.30 A.M. on the 26th.

After a night march the Lowland Brigade garrisoned the Ninth's sector with the 11th and 12th Royal Scots in line, the 9th Seaforths in support, and the K.O.S.B. in reserve. The dispositions had scarcely been completed when the vanguards of the Germans approached

from Fricourt, but were checked by our outposts.   At
1 P.M. an attack in force was delivered against the
right of the line, a hostile battery coming into action
on a ridge in front of it.   The assault withered away
before the careful, well-controlled fire of the 12th Royal
Scots, and the enemy's battery was quickly compelled
to withdraw.   The co-operation between our artillery
and infantry was wonderfully good, and the Germans
in Becourt Valley, where an attempt to concentrate
was crushed by our fire, suffered innumerable losses.
This repulse quietened the enemy on our front, but
farther south where troops had retired he gained the
high ground between our right flank and Bray, and
brought up machine-guns, with which he enfiladed our
line.   To meet this danger Brig.-General Croft formed a
defensive flank with the 9th Seaforths, but no sooner was
this wing guarded than the left was jeopardised by the
retreat of the Twelfth Division across the Ancre during
the afternoon.   This made it necessary for the 27th
Brigade to conform, and the retirement over the river
was carried out in perfect manner, although the 12th
Royal Scots lost heavily in passing through Meaulte.

Meanwhile the 26th Brigade, with the South African
composite battalion attached, after a few hours' rest
occupied about 1 P.M. a position behind the Ancre
between Dernancourt and Moulin du Vivier, the South
Africans holding the former, still apparently a thriving
village.   The 9th Machine-gun Battalion, which had
been withdrawn during the night of the 25th/26th to
Mericourt L'Abbé, where it was reorganised into two
groups with 10 guns each, covered our line west of the
Ancre.   After crossing the river, the Lowland Brigade
was posted along the line of the Railway between the
left of the 26th Brigade and the Albert–Amiens road,
where it was in close touch with the Twelfth Division.

U

The enemy on noticing our retirement advanced towards the river in considerable force, but was caught by our barrage when moving down the slopes, and the few who succeeded in crossing were easily dealt with.

At the commencement of the 26th, the fighting strength of the Division was approximately as follows: Highland Brigade 300, Lowland Brigade 800, South African Battalion 320, Sappers 120, two Machine-gun groups with 10 guns each, a total of 1340 rifles and 20 machine-guns. Brig.-General Croft's men had lost cruelly during the day, and it was doubtful if the line now occupied, over 3000 yards in length, could be defended next day against a strong attack.

During the night of the 26th/27th alarming reports of a break through on the Albert–Amiens road came in, but nothing serious had actually happened, and the few troops who had given way were quickly rallied. A machine-gun on the left of the Lowland Brigade was a source of much annoyance to the 11th Royal Scots until a smart counter-attack organised by Major A. C. Campbell put it out of action. Unfortunately Major Campbell, who had led the 11th Royal Scots with great skill and sterling courage during the retreat, received wounds which proved fatal.

The 27th was a critical day for General Gough's army; for the Germans forced the line of the Somme from Chipilly to Cérisy, and took Lamotte on the great Amiens road, about 9000 yards behind the fighting line of the Fifth Army. There was more stability on our front, though some of our troops were reported to be retiring near Albert. This was due to furious shelling, and to bombing by aeroplanes with British colours, but the retrograde movement was stopped and an outpost line established along the Railway with Lewis Gun

posts in front. During the day there was a violent
artillery and trench - mortar bombardment of our
positions, and at 10.30 A.M. German infantry were seen
entering the valley north-west of Meaulte. Later, great
clusters of the enemy coming down the slopes of the
Ancre were hotly engaged by our artillery and machine-
guns, and did not venture to assault. Here and there
clefts appeared in our thin line, but were promptly
closed by swift and skilful local counter-attacks. Undoubtedly the most disturbing factor was the persistent
bombing of our positions by large numbers of aeroplanes, British by their marking.

With the close of the day the long travail of the
Ninth terminated. The infantry were relieved by the
4th Australian Division, and after moving to the
neighbourhood of Baizieux, ultimately concentrated in
the Bertangles area on the 29th. For two days more
the artillery remained in action with the Australians
and were then withdrawn.

The retreat imposed a heavy burden on the
R.A.M.C., but Colonel Elsner's staff met their difficulties with untiring devotion and conspicuous success.
Many wounded among the forward troops inevitably
fell into the hands of the enemy, but stretcher-bearers
and motor parties often ventured up to the fighting
line in their search for casualties. The selection of
routes for the evacuation of the wounded called for
careful consideration, in order to avoid congestion on
roads blocked with transport and guns, but Colonel
Elsner was eminently successful in making the best
working arrangements possible. Gallantry and resource
among the R.A.M.C. were too common to be remarked
on, and motor-drivers as usual braved all the difficulties
of the roads with the air of phlegmatic boredom that
seemed to be their natural expression. Every means of

conveyance was requisitioned, and the whole of the work during the retreat strikingly revealed the efficiency of the R.A.M.C.

Equally difficult and important was the task of keeping the men supplied with rations and ammunition. The regular transmission of stores was naturally affected by the constant movement, but our organisation withstood the strain, and the A.S.C. performed its duties in a manner worthy of its high traditions.

Never perhaps did the Ninth render such vital services to the Empire as during the Somme retreat. It had covered not merely its own territory, but had extended its line far beyond its northern boundary, and in the arduous and critical fighting till the 24th March, its success in blunting the deadly German thrust between the Third and Fifth Armies did much to save the British forces from what might have been an irretrievable disaster. Adroit leadership and dogged pluck were the qualities that steered it through the labyrinth of dangers that beset it at every turn. Officers of all ranks had shown throughout the conflict surprising resource and initiative; the coolness and foresight of General Tudor during the most critical days led one writer[1] to declare that his name "should be as well known as are Wellington's best generals, Crauford, Colborne, and Picton."

Ably led, the men had brilliantly performed the most difficult operation in war—a withdrawal in face of the enemy. Men who after rough buffetings can at the end of a retreat turn round and confront the foe with unshaken nerve and steadfast courage have proved their manhood indeed, and this, the acid test of the true soldier, had been accomplished by the men of the Ninth. In a general sense, it is true that the gain or

[1] W. S. Sparrow in "The Epic of the Ninth Division."

loss of ground is insignificant in comparison with the destruction of an army, but for the individual the surrender of many miles of territory, painfully won after more than three years of costly strife, cannot fail to rouse the most sombre reflections, and only the best of troops can overcome the leaden despondency caused by a continuous backward movement. Valour alone would not have availed to stem the enemy's advance ; discipline was required to direct and control it, and disciplined valour was, in fact, the characteristic of the Division during the retreat. The six weeks of training in February had helped to make the Division more than a match for the pick of Ludendorff's storm-troops.

Since the time of the Cambrai operations in 1917, G.H.Q. had renewed the custom, abandoned after Loos, of mentioning by name the divisions that had particularly distinguished themselves. The retreat was the first operation in which the Division had participated since the resumption of this practice, and it earned the proud honour of a special mention[1] by Sir Douglas Haig.

[1] " Great gallantry has been shown by the troops engaged in the fighting in this area and to the south of it. The Nineteenth and Ninth Divisions have distinguished themselves by the valour of their defence."

(*Extract from Communiqué published by the Press on the* 25th *March.*)

CHAPTER XIII

THE GERMAN OFFENSIVE IN FLANDERS

APRIL 1918

IN spite of their success in forcing the passage of the Somme on the 27th March, the Germans had shot their bolt, and though they had secured the most extensive acreage ever taken in any one offensive since trench warfare began, they had failed in their strategical design — the capture of Amiens and the severance of the French and British forces. Their front had been worn to a fine point by the 27th, and an attempt to widen it by a stroke against Arras was shattered by the glorious defence of the northern wing of the Third Army on the 28th March. No effort on their part could prevent our thin line in front of Amiens gaining in strength and stability. Throughout the retreat General Gough had shown sound generalship and admirable control, but the strain on him and his staff had been so constant and severe, that Sir Douglas Haig replaced the Fifth Army Staff by that of the Fourth under General Rawlinson. This arrangement unfortunately appeared to strengthen the impression created by the Prime Minister's unjust remarks in the House of Commons on the 9th April, implying that General Gough was responsible for our disasters at the Somme. These were

primarily due to the failure of the home authorities
to keep our line in France adequately supplied with
men.   About this time, the conference at Doullens
arrived at the vastly important decision which led
to the appointment of Marshal Foch on the 26th
March as the Generalissimo of all the forces on the
Western Front.

After the relief of the Ninth, General Blacklock
was transferred to another division, and he was succeeded by Major-General H. H. Tudor.   There could
have been no more popular promotion.   The new commander, since he joined the Division in February 1916,
had exercised an important influence in its councils,
and his conduct of the operations from the 21st to
the 24th March had marked him as a leader of outstanding skill.   Brig.-General H. R. Wainwright
succeeded General Tudor as C.R.A.

During the retreat from Gouzeaucourt to the
Ancre, our losses exceeded 50 per cent. of the infantry,
but the rest were in good heart.   In the fighting
of the last few days there had been an element of
sport which appealed to the men, and though they
were the hunted they had killed an enormous number
of the pursuers.   Consequently the Division was
exhilarated rather than disheartened by its recent
experiences, and its moral was all that could be
desired, when, on the 1st April, it entrained for the
north, where it expected to take over a quiet sector
on the front of the IX. Corps in the Second Army.
On the 2nd and 3rd April it detrained at Abeele and
Hopoutre, D.H.Q. being established at Scherpenberg.

On the night of the 3rd/4th April, the Highland
and Lowland Brigades relieved the 3rd Brigade of
the 1st Australian Division in the area extending from
Hollebeke (inclusive) across the Ypres–Comines Canal

to the south end of Bulgar Wood, a stretch of some
3000 yards. Here there were no indications of an
impending attack, and General Tudor was told that his
first duty was to prepare his command as speedily as
possible for the "second round of the Third Somme
Battle," which, it was generally believed, would be
continued. This involved a great deal of preparation.
Although individual soldiers recovered remarkably
quickly from exhaustion, units could not recover with
equal rapidity, as there was a lamentable dearth of
trained leaders and instructors. Very large drafts, consisting chiefly of youths of eighteen and nineteen years
of age, were received almost daily by the 26th and 27th
Brigades, but they could not be brought speedily to the
same level of efficiency as that exhibited by the veterans
of the Somme, while the process of absorbing so
many new officers and men, which would have been
slow at any time, was rendered even more difficult
by the fact that both brigades were in the line. The
physique of the drafts that joined the Division at this
time was excellent. They were largely composed of
lads who had been taken at the age of seventeen, and
were splendid examples of the beneficial effect of
good feeding, regular exercise, and military discipline
on young Scotsmen. The South African Brigade [1]
about 1300 strong, and now under the command of
Brig.-General Tanner, appeared to have no immediate
prospects of obtaining reinforcements, and while the
several regiments meanwhile maintained their identity
the question of forming it into one battalion was under
consideration. Too weak to man a brigade front, it
was stationed in divisional reserve in the vicinity of
Ridge Wood, 1000 yards north of Vierstraat.

[1] The 1st Regiment was commanded by Lieut.-Colonel Young; the
2nd Regiment by Captain Jacobs; and the 4th Regiment by Captain Reid.

In order to hasten reorganisation as much as possible General Tudor decided to hold the whole of his line with the 27th Brigade, while the 26th was withdrawn to absorb its numerous reinforcements. This arrangement however was upset by Corps orders to take over from the Nineteenth Division 500 yards of line to the south of Hollebeke on the night of the 10th/11th. The Highland Brigade was instructed to do this, but on the morning of the 9th, the enemy made his surprise attack against the XV. and Portuguese Corps, which for some time jeopardised our grip on the Channel Ports, and the Division was required to carry out the relief on the night of the 9th/10th, and take over the remainder of the Nineteenth Division front on the night of the 10th/11th. Accordingly, the Lowland Brigade was ordered to relieve the 26th and garrison also the 500 yards of front in the Nineteenth Division's sector on the night of the 9th/10th. The new area was a featureless and desolate waste of shell-holes, where it was hard enough to locate one's position in broad daylight and with the aid of a map, and was therefore all but impossible in darkness. Yet in spite of the impossibility of reconnaissance through lack of time, and a heavy bombardment of the trench system and battery area with H.E. and gas, the relief was duly carried out, though it was after daybreak on the 10th before our outposts were in position. The satisfactory accomplishment of this relief was a very fine feat on the part of the 27th Brigade. To move in the dark over the most barren country in Europe under a really heavy bombardment, without losing cohesion, was an achievement that would have done credit to the finest soldiers of " The Contemptibles."

Brig.-General Croft's Brigade had a span of 4000

yards astride the Ypres–Comines Canal, with its right
about 800 yards south-west of Hollebeke, and its left
approximately 1200 yards east of Klein Zillebeke.
As this sector formed the extreme right flank of
the Passchendaele salient, the general direction of
the lines of defence ran from south-west to north-
east. The whole front was covered by a line of
posts, some of which were in "Pill-boxes," and 300
to 800 yards behind this and overlooking it was a continuous trench from the northern divisional boundary
to 500 yards from the Canal, where the ground was
swampy. From 300 yards south of the Canal another
continuous trench ran as far as the Hollebeke road.
In the part taken over from the Nineteenth Division
there were no defences immediately in rear of the
posts, except some 100 yards of trench leaning in a
northerly direction.

Our position north of the Canal appeared the part
most likely to be attacked, since it formed the hinge
of the Passchendaele salient, while the Klein Zillebeke
Spur and Hill 60 offered tempting objectives to the
enemy, who could make his arrangements and concentrate his forces under cover of the Zandvoorde Ridge.
South of the Canal the reserve line defences consisted
of a strongly-wired line of posts stretching in a
south-westerly direction to the Stables, and supported
by the defences of White Château, a former residence
of Leopold of Belgium, which, as it occupied a
commanding position, was now tunnelled with dug-
outs and held a permanent garrison. From the Stables
two massive belts of wire extended south-south-east
and south-west. Behind these were a few posts which
it was impossible to man adequately, owing to the
length of the brigade front and the necessity of holding
in strength Hill 60, The Bluff, and White Château.

No switch protected the right flank of the Division,
but a section of machine - guns covered the space
between the right of the support line and the
Stables.

The front was covered by the 50th and 51st
Brigades R.F.A.   In divisional reserve were the
26th Brigade, south-west and north-west of Vierstraat,
the South African Brigade between La Clytte and
Scherpenberg, and the 9th Machine-gun Battalion (less
two companies) about 1000 yards east of Ridge Wood.

The heavy cannonade, which had commenced at
1 A.M., slackened about two hours later.   On this
morning the tide of battle flowed north, and the
right flank of the IX. Corps being hotly engaged, the
South Africans were sent by the Corps to positions
of assembly south of Neuve Eglise, there to be in
Corps reserve.   Brig.-General Kennedy was instructed
to be ready to move his brigade at thirty minutes'
notice, and the line along the eastern slopes of the
Messines–Wytschaete Ridge was to be held at all costs.
Early in the afternoon the situation near Wytschaete,
which was held by the Nineteenth Division, was very
obscure, and Brig.-General Kennedy sent a patrol of
Camerons to ascertain the relative positions of the
enemy and of our troops.

Between 1 and 2 P.M. the Ninth entered the battle.
After a terrific bombardment the Germans rushed our
outpost positions south of the Canal held by the 11th
Royal Scots, and attacked the support position, but the
enemy's ranks were swept away by rifle and machine-
gun fire, and by the accurate fire put down by the 27th
L.T.M.B. under the direction of Captain Drummond
Shiels.   Unfortunately success farther south enabled
the Germans to threaten our flank, and the next assault,
developing from the south and extending as far west as

the Stables, would have broken our defences but for the
timely arrival of two companies of the 12th Royal Scots,
who prolonged the defensive flank formed by the 11th
Royal Scots.   Considering the exceptionally fatiguing
relief, the fine resistance of the 27th Brigade was a
magnificent effort.   Nevertheless the situation was
decidedly alarming.   All touch with the troops to the
south had been lost, and as the Highland Brigade had
been placed under the Nineteenth Division, the 9th
Seaforths, now the only infantry General Tudor had
in reserve, were despatched to reinforce the Lowland
Brigade and were posted on the Dammstrasse, echeloned
in rear of the right flank of the Lowlanders.

About 3 P.M. the order placing the 26th Brigade
under the Nineteenth Division was cancelled, and the
58th Brigade (the left of the Nineteenth Division)
together with its front was transferred to the Ninth.
It was uncertain what ground was held by that
brigade, but some of its troops were believed to be
in Wytschaete, which was also occupied by the Cameron
patrol, and so the Highland Brigade was sent up to
establish a line between the left of the 58th and the
right of the 27th Brigade.   At 5.30 P.M. the situation
was believed to be as follows :   The 58th Brigade was
holding the line L'Enfer–Pick House–Torreken Corner ;
the Black Watch were in Grand Bois, the Seaforths
moving on Dammstrasse, and the Camerons in reserve
south-west of Vierstraat, while the 9th Seaforths and a
detachment of Sappers were in the Dammstrasse ; the
27th Brigade was holding the line from the Stables
to Hollebeke, thence along the support position to the
Canal and its original line north of the Canal.

At 8 P.M. the 26th Brigade, which had established
itself on the line Stables–Delbske Farm–Ravine Wood–
southern edge of Denys Wood–Guedezeune Farm,

WYTSCHAETE FROM VIERSTRAAT

reported that Wytschaete had been evacuated by our troops. Having received as reinforcements the 62nd Brigade (less one battalion but with one battalion of the 146th Brigade attached), General Tudor sent two battalions to strengthen his line, and these passing through the Cameron detachment, which had already reoccupied the village, established a line east and south-east of Wytschaete. The Black Watch also advanced and held a line along the eastern edge of Onraet and the western margin of Oosttaverne Wood, connecting the left of the 62nd Brigade with the right of the 7th Seaforths[1] and the 9th Seaforths in the Dammstrasse. The 4th and 11th M.M.G. Batteries, being sent to the Ninth, were retained in reserve near Scherpenberg.

South of our positions the Germans made disquieting progress during the day; they compelled our troops to evacuate Armentières, and crossing the Lys in strength occupied Estaires, Steenwerck, and Ploegsteert, and threatened the Messines Ridge. So very grave was the crisis that the weak South African Brigade was thrown hurriedly into the battle. On the front of the Nineteenth Division the Germans had penetrated our defences between Messines and Pick House on the Wytschaete road, and the South Africans along with the 57th and 58th Brigades of the Nineteenth Division were ordered to retake this portion of the ridge. With the 1st and 2nd Regiments leading and the 4th in support, the South Africans moved forward to the attack at 5.45 P.M. On their right was the 57th Brigade. Only two F.A. Brigades were available for artillery support, and the enemy's riflemen and machine-gunners in shell-holes and "Pill-boxes"

---

[1] Commanded since the 7th April by Lieut.-Colonel the Honourable David Bruce.

were able to inflict numerous casualties on the assailing
troops, but in spite of the difficulty of keeping touch
in the mist, the South Africans pressed on, expelled
the enemy from his shell-holes and "Pill-boxes," and
established a line along the western outskirts of
Messines–Middle Farm–Four Huns Farm–Lumm Farm,
with a defensive flank thrown back to L'Enfer. The
1st Regiment, dashing through Messines, by a fine
bayonet charge drove the enemy down the eastern
slopes of the ridge, but the village was an awkward
place to hold, and though in a series of stubborn hand-
to-hand combats the 1st Regiment kept its ground,
the village was eventually abandoned and a line was
established just west of it.

In the small hours of the 11th the Germans resumed
their efforts, and strong forces attempted to break
through our defences on the Dammstrasse and the
right flank of the Lowland Brigade from the Stables
to the southern end of the support position, but the
hostile concentration had been observed and our rifle,
machine-gun, and artillery-fire, cutting deep lanes in the
dense field-grey hordes, beat back the foe in tumultuous
and terror-stricken disorder. The Seaforths, taking full
advantage of the panic, counter-attacked with a small
party under Sergeants Tait and Jeffries, and rounded
up 17 Germans and 3 machine-guns. The young
soldiers who had joined the Division behaved with
admirable courage and coolness, and our gunners earned
the gratitude of the infantry by the rapidity and
precision with which they engaged every favourable
target.

On the front of the Ninth the enemy had been too
severely punished to risk another enterprise, and no
incident interrupted the rest of the day. A counter-
attack was even contemplated with a view to clearing

the high ground west and north of Oosttaverne, but the project was given up on account of German inroads farther south. Advantage of the lull was taken to reorganise the line, the 62nd Brigade now holding from Pick House to Somer Farm, the 26th to the Hollebeke–St Eloi road, and the 27th in its original sector, the total frontage amounting to nearly 9000 yards. During the evening the Division and its sector were transferred from the IX. to the XXII. Corps.

On the same day Messines Ridge was wrested from our grasp. During the night of the 10th/11th the South Africans tried to gain touch with the Ninth near Pick House, but this place consisting of three "Pill-boxes" was found to be strongly manned by the enemy and defied every attempt to overpower it. At daybreak the 108th Brigade moved up in support of the South Africans, and the forenoon passed without event. Early in the afternoon, however, the Germans, attacking the left wing of the South Africans in great strength, expelled the 2nd Regiment from the crest, and though a resolute counter-stroke, led by Captain L. Greene, regained the lost ground, the enemy's turning movement on our left flank forced the South Africans to retire to a line some 200 yards east of Hell Farm. This position was maintained in face of heavy losses and incessant attacks throughout the remaining hours of daylight.

Owing to German penetration in the south the right flank of the Second Army, pivoting on Wytschaete, was obliged to withdraw in the night to a line passing through Kruisstraat Cabaret and a point east of Wulverghem. When this movement was completed the right wing of the 62nd Brigade rested on the Bogaert Farm–Pick Wood Spur, and a defensive flank was formed along the Wytschaete–Peckham road.

The retirement was naturally more pronounced in the case of the Nineteenth Division, and in conformity with the rest of that formation the South Africans were drawn back to a line N. Midland Farm–Kruisstraat Cabaret–Spanbroekmolen–Maedelstede Farm.

From the 12th to the 15th there was a lull in the fighting on the front of the Ninth, but merciless artillery-fire caused many casualties. During this period of comparative peacefulness General Tudor made several rearrangements. The 64th Brigade (less one battalion) took over the front from Somer Farm to Dome House in relief of the 26th, which continued to hold the Dammstrasse, and the 9th Seaforths and the 58th Brigade were withdrawn from the front trenches, the latter rejoining its own Division on the 13th. Meantime reinforcements were gathering in the rear; the South Africans returned to the Ninth on the night of the 13th/14th and two battalions of the 39th Composite Brigade (late Thirty-ninth Division) were moved by the Twenty-first Division to Ridge Wood to be available if required. All our defences were strengthened and the Sappers and 9th Seaforths laboured steadily on the Vierstraat line, which the 62nd and 26th Brigades were ordered to garrison, each with a battalion. A prolongation of front on the evening of the 15th obliged the 62nd Brigade to take over the front of the Nineteenth Division as far as Spanbroekmolen. The success of the enemy also forced us to surrender our dearly-bought gains of the Passchendaele campaign, and in conformity with the withdrawal round Ypres, the left flank of the Ninth from the north-east end of the Dammstrasse to the northern divisional boundary was brought back to the Corps line.

This line, leaving the Dammstrasse, east of Eikhof

Farm, crossed the Canal just east of The Bluff, where, turning east - north - east, it passed over the Klein Zillebeke Spur, 500 yards north-west of the hamlet of the same name. The White Château and Klein Zillebeke were thus given up, but The Bluff and Hill 60 were retained. With a view to shortening our front, and so economising troops, a more extensive retirement —to˙ the Vierstraat line—was contemplated ; but on General Tudor urging that this position, besides offering inadequate protection against artillery - fire, was completely overlooked from the Spanbroekmolen– Wytschaete Ridge, and was a poor substitute for the valuable observation afforded by our present position, the idea was abandoned.

The stretch, for which the· Ninth with its attached troops was responsible, amounted to 9000 yards. The portion of the Corps line, occupied by the Lowland Brigade, consisted of a string of cleverly camouflaged posts protected by heavy and continuous belts of wire, and had previously been reconnoitred by Brig.-General Croft and Captain Duke, his brigade major. The retreat was skilfully carried out on the night of the 15th/16th under cover of patrols, which, going out as usual after dusk, were so enterprising that the enemy failed to realise that a withdrawal was in progress. All next day the Germans violently shelled the vicinity of the Corps line, but the posts were so well concealed that little damage was done, and even low flying aeroplanes were unable to detect our new positions. Our far-reaching observation served us handsomely ; the enemy frequently presented excellent targets as he advanced, and the accurate and galling fire of our Stokes mortars and machine-guns stationed on The Bluff shattered a hostile concentration near the Canal.

On the 16th a huge enemy effort was directed

X

against Wytschaete.   About 5 A.M., after a hurricane bombardment which broke down all communications in the sector, the Germans, screened by a mist, carried the battered site on which had stood Spanbroekmolen Mill, the 64th Brigade being forced to throw out a defensive flank 500 yards north of the former on the line Somer Farm–North House–Black Cot, whence it was continued to the Vierstraat line by two companies of the Black Watch.   The South Africans were hastily brought up, and manned the southern sector of the Vierstraat from La Polka to Desinet Farm, while the Lowland Brigade occupied the northern sector from the Vierstraat–Wytschaete road to Snipers' Barn.

About noon a furious attack developed against the Camerons in the Dammstrasse, but was repulsed by rifle and machine-gun fire, and the Germans withdrew to Pheasant Wood, leaving their wounded where they fell.   An hour later an attempt of the enemy to debouch from the wood was easily frustrated.

The loss of Wytschaete was no light matter, and an operation for its recapture was quickly planned. French reserves having been sent up, one division was to attack with its left flank parallel to and 500 yards north of the Kemmel–Spanbroekmolen road, and the Ninth was to co-operate by retaking Wytschaete.   Our available forces consisted of two battalions of the 62nd Brigade, the 7th Seaforths, and two companies of the 39th Composite Brigade, and the objective was the line Pick Wood–Bogaert Farm, the cutting 300 yards south of Wytschaete–Staenyzer Cabaret–Somer Farm.   The French however were unable to complete their preparations, and at 7.30 P.M. the Ninth attacked alone under cover of a creeping barrage.   Just as the German barrage began our troops moved forward.   The dash of the Seaforths was superb.   An irresistible charge

carried them right through Wytschaete village, and
during a combat where many feats of valour were
performed, Captain Reid and C.S.M. Jeffries singled
themselves out by the daring with which they rushed
a "Pill-box" on the ridge and captured 14 prisoners
and 5 machine-guns. But the extreme left of the
attack was checked by machine-gun fire from North
House, and though on the right the men of the 62nd
Brigade reached the line Petit Bois – Maedelstede,
they failed to capture the craters at the two latter
places owing to machine-gun fire from Spanbroekmolen
and Peckham, which the French were to have attacked.
The result of the operation was that success on the left
had been gained on a narrow front, while on the right a
line had been established which could not be held by
daylight unless Spanbroekmolen were taken.

The French therefore agreed to assault the village
at 5 A.M. on the 17th, when the 62nd Brigade was to
co-operate by attacking Wytschaete Wood. To support
the Seaforths in Wytschaete village the South Africans
were placed under the orders of Brig.-General Kennedy,
and the 4th Regiment, followed by the 1st, moved up
to the village. By dawn the line occupied ran from
Somer Farm through North House and the Hospice to
Black Cot. The French effort against Spanbroekmolen
was unexpectedly feeble, only one company being used,
and nothing was achieved, with the result that the 62nd
Brigade had to withdraw to the line La Gache Farm—
eastern edge of Petit Bois.

From the 17th to the 24th no infantry attacks took
place, but relentless artillery-fire persistently swept our
trench system and back areas. On the 18th an unlucky
shell struck the 26th Brigade H.Q., causing the deaths
of Lieut.-Colonel Horn, on his way to rejoin the Seaforths, Major Rose, the B.M. of the artillery, Captain

Somers Cocks, the Staff Captain, and the Rev. C. G.
Meister. The German advance, which had given the
enemy possession of Wytschaete, Wulverghem, Neuve
Eglise, Bailleul, and Meteren, had now brought him
close to the Kemmel–Mont des Cats Ridge, the retention of which was vital to the security of our grip on
Ypres and Poperinghe. A weighty blow had been dealt
against the British forces, whose organisation had been
gravely affected by the necessity of throwing piecemeal
all available reserves into the battle line, and Ludendorff
might have realised his dreams if he had returned to
the main strategical design with which he began the
year. But his gains at the Lys had so far exceeded his
expectations that he was tempted to carry on in the
north in the hope of securing the Channel Ports, and the
two schemes, by offering conflicting prizes, began to lose
all measure of co-ordination in the German plans.

During this period the French, relieving the Nineteenth Division, joined up with the Ninth on the right,
and on the night of the 19th/20th our front north of
Eikhof Farm was handed over to the Twenty-first
Division. This included the whole of the front originally
held by the Ninth Division, and, although the portion
south of the Canal had been heavily attacked time after
time, no part of the ground had been lost, except that
portion in front of the Corps line which was evacuated
in conformity with the army plan. On the 19th the
62nd Brigade was relieved and joined its own division,
while the H.Q. and two half battalions of the 146th
Brigade came under the orders of General Tudor. The
remaining two halves arrived on the 21st and 22nd, and
two battalions of the 39th Composite Brigade were
transferred to the Twenty-first Division. Other reinforcements arrived ; the 4th Tank Brigade (less one
battalion and without tanks), consisting of the 5th

Battalion, with 30 Lewis Gun detachments, and the 13th Battalion with 47. On the 22nd the South African Brigade, for lack of drafts, became a battalion styled the South African Composite Battalion,[1] and the remaining units of the brigade, which retained its distinctive name under Brig.-General Tanner, were made up of the 9th Scottish Rifles and the 2nd Royal Scots Fusiliers. The former battalion was thus retransferred to its old division from the Fourteenth, while the latter, a Regular battalion originally in the famous Seventh Division, came from the Thirtieth Division, in which it had served since December 1915.

Another stroke against Wytschaete in co-operation with the French was planned for the 26th, but was anticipated by a great German thrust on the 25th. As was not unusual with the Ninth, its line formed a pronounced salient, and on the evening of the 24th was held from right to left by the 27th Brigade from La Gache Farm to Black Cot, by the 146th Brigade to North House, and the 64th to Dome House, and thence by the 26th (with the "Rifles" attached) to the northern divisional boundary at Eikhof Farm. The 27th Brigade was practically facing south. The Vierstraat line and another from 800 to 1000 yards in rear of it, known as "The Cheapside line," had been assiduously strengthened, and they were divided into three sectors, of which the right was allotted to the 27th, the centre to the 146th, and the left to the 26th Brigade. Each sector was held by one battalion, deployed in depth in and between the two lines, two companies of each battalion being earmarked as garrison, and the remaining two being at the disposal of brigade commanders for counter-attack. On the right the 12th

[1] Under the command of Lieut.-Colonel H. W. M. Bamford of the 2nd Regiment.

Royal Scots held the line with the K.O.S.B.[1] in close
support and the 11th Royal Scots in reserve. Thirteen
Lewis Gun detachments of the 5th Battalion (Tank
Brigade) were stationed by Brig.-General Croft on
supporting positions on Vandamme Hill. The South
African Brigade, now in process of reorganisation, and
the remainder of the 4th Tank Brigade were in divisional
reserve, the former about Hopoutre and the latter
half-way between Reninghelst and Poperinghe. The
XXII. Corps H.Q. company, also under General Tudor,
was composed mostly of men unfit for active operations,
and was in reserve.

Our boundary on the south gave to the French the
low ridge running east from Mount Kemmel to Spanbroekmolen, without leaving to them sufficient space in
which to deploy troops for its defence. It was unfortunate that this ridge was not in the area of the Ninth;
for while it was of little account as regards the defence
of Kemmel, it was essential for the protection of our
right flank. During the week 18th to 26th, although
no serious attack developed, the troops were subjected
to great strain owing to incessant and severe shell-fire,
and the casualties amongst those in and behind the
Vierstraat line were numerous.

Between midnight and 1 A.M. on the 25th a prisoner
captured by the French stated that a big onslaught was
imminent and would probably take place on the 25th.
Before daybreak a thick mist straddled the ground, and
at 2.30 A.M. a violent hostile bombardment of gas and
H.E. opened along the whole front. Telephonic communication between General Tudor and Brig.-General
Croft was sundered at the outset, and the S.O.S. was

---

[1] The K.O.S.B. had been commanded by Major Innes Browne since the
24th March; he was killed at Hill 60 on the 10th April, and was succeeded
first by Lieut.-Colonel Chamberlain, and then by Major H. J. Wilkie.

KEMMEL AND YPRES FROM THE FREZENBERG RIDGE

seen to go up on the French front. At 3.20 A.M. the
4th Tank Brigade was ordered to send up immediately
two companies to the Cheapside line, and the South
Africans were instructed to be ready to move at fifteen
minutes' notice.

At 4.50 A.M. news came from the French that
the enemy's infantry were attacking, and half an hour
later the S.O.S. signal was reported from the front
of Wytschaete. Kemmel was wreathed in smoke and
large numbers of enemy aircraft circled over both
it and Wytschaete, but no definite information reached
D.H.Q. until 6.40 A.M., when a belated message
arrived from the 64th Brigade to the effect that up
to 5.15 A.M. no infantry attack had developed on its
front. A few minutes later the C.R.A. reported that
the enemy's barrage had moved forward considerably,
and that one of our aeroplanes had dropped word
that it extended along the whole front from Luden-
hoek to the south-west end of the Dammstrasse. At
7.15 A.M. another message from the C.R.A. stated
that the Germans were within 300 yards of Siege
Farm, about 2000 yards north-west of our right flank
troops at La Gache Farm. This information came
as a complete surprise, since no news of an infantry
attack on our front had yet reached D.H.Q.

The enemy's onset in the first instance was directed
about 3 A.M. against the Twenty-eighth French Division,
and the right of the Ninth held by the 12th Royal
Scots. At 5 A.M. there was a determined frontal assault
on the 12th Royal Scots, and at one time a lodgment
was effected between the centre and right companies,
but after bitter fighting the Royal Scots drove off
the assailants. About 7 A.M. the K.O.S.B. in the
Vierstraat line received word from the Royal Scots
that their front was intact, and this information was

the more amazing in as much as the K.O.S.B. were themselves hotly engaged with the enemy, while French prisoners under escort were observed in their rear. The Germans had been foiled in their frontal attack, but their onrush had pierced the French on our right and enabled them to turn our flank from the south.

The 12th Royal Scots were entirely cut off, and about 8.30 A.M. the battalion fighting desperately to the end was engulfed by a flood of Germans, here and there a whirling eddy testifying to the fury of a last stand. Only a few isolated groups escaped the clutch of the foe and fought their way through many perils to the Cheapside line. On the left of the Royal Scots, the 1st East Yorks Regiment (64th Brigade) was forced back to Grand Bois, where, encircled by hordes of Germans, it put up a gallant fight. The K.O.S.B. also suffered seriously from the enemy's turning movement; the two forward companies were virtually annihilated after a fierce resistance, and the battalion H.Q. were surrounded and captured. The remainder of the battalion took up a position on the Cheapside line, which was also held by the 9th K.O.Y.L.I. (64th Brigade), and by Lewis Gun detachments of the 4th Tank Brigade. Two companies of the 11th Royal Scots, the Black Watch, and the 9th D.L.I. were sent up in succession to support and continue this line back towards La Clytte.

In this manner the dangerous thrust was parried. The Black Watch, moving up from Ouderdom, crossed the Cheapside line, and engaging the enemy captured 67 prisoners at small cost to themselves. The K.O.S.B. in a brilliant counter-attack directed by Captain Cundle, now in command of the battalion, inflicted severe losses and secured 58 prisoners.

Throughout the action our machine-gunners earned

noteworthy distinction by the doggedness with which they kept their guns in action till the last possible moment. Most of the company with the 27th Brigade shared the fate of the 12th Royal Scots, but made the enemy pay a heavy price for his victory. One gun directed on the Steenbeek valley, fired 1500 rounds before it was put out of action; other two were silent until the Germans reached the wire in front of them, when the crews suddenly opened fire and mowed them down. Only after one gun was knocked out, and the other withdrawn through lack of ammunition, did the enemy succeed in penetrating the wire. Of the teams at Vandamme no man returned; at Vandenberghe the guns were kept in action until the last belt was fired and were then destroyed, since it was impossible to withdraw them. In the Vierstraat line, a whole section became casualties. Two sections of another machine-gun company supporting the 1st East Yorks opened fire on the valley of the Wytschaete Beck with three guns between 5 and 6 A.M., and continued firing at intervals, until 9 A.M., when two of the guns were withdrawn to cover the right flank of the infantry, and remained in action for two hours without tripods. Of these sections there were only six unwounded men at the end of the day.

On the left of our line the storm beat violently against the Dammstrasse, but failed to break the defence of the Highlanders, who held the position with the Camerons and the Seaforths. Up to half an hour before noon all hostile attacks were repulsed, our infantry, machine-gunners and the personnel of the 26th L.T.M.B. co-operating most effectively. When ammunition began to run short, several of the men dashed forward to deserted dumps in full view of the enemy, and brought back bandoliers of cartridges. Between 11.30 and 1.30 P.M. shells fell without ceasing, and the Camerons in the forward posts were practically wiped out, but our position through Piccadilly Farm–The Mound proved invulnerable to every attack for the remaining part of the day. Under Captain H. E. Bennet the men of the 26th L.T.M.B. fired off all their Stokes ammunition into the dense masses of the Germans, and after destroying the mortars used their rifles with deadly effect against the hostile infantry and transport. The machine - gunners with the Highlanders handled their weapons with such skill and enterprise that the infantry voluntarily collected ammunition and kept up the supply, while parties of the "Rifles" in the Vierstraat–Snipers' Barn line were organised for belt filling.

After darkness fell, a line in rear of the Highlanders having been established and manned by fresh troops of the Twenty-first Division, the Camerons and Seaforths with the other detachments extricated themselves and were drawn back to a camp 700 yards north-east of Ouderdom. The stone-wall defence of the Highlanders had put a final stop to the enemy's northern onrush, which had rolled up the front and immediate supports of three brigades, and threatened our hold on Ypres.

The shattered fragments of the Ninth, with the exception of the South African Brigade and the artillery, were relieved by the Forty-ninth Division at 11 A.M. on the 26th. The brigade remained in the sector until the night of the 5th/6th May, and all three battalions, though constantly harassed by artillery-fire, inflicted enormous casualties on the enemy when on the 29th he strove to take advantage of his possession of Mount Kemmel. Rarely has heavier artillery-fire heralded an attack. On that day, the Royal Scots Fusiliers signally distinguished themselves. They were deployed in, in front of, and behind the Cheap-side line, and suffered horribly from the bombard-ment; but of their eight Lewis Guns, which were out in front of their position, only one was knocked out, so that when the enemy's infantry advanced they were immediately checked, and then our barrage came down on the top of them. First a few rose up and bolted, and then the remainder fled in panic, where-upon the Royal Scots Fusiliers fairly took toll of them with their rifles and Lewis Guns. The enemy's attack was utterly defeated.

That date marks the failure of the German designs in Flanders. The value of Kemmel proved to be less vital than had been anticipated; the enemy failed to carry the valleys that separated it from Scherpenberg, and here, as in front of Amiens, the battle line became stabilised. The diversion had caused anxious tremors at G.H.Q., and for some time our organisation showed signs of giving way. The situation was too critical to be glossed over by misleading communiqués, and Sir Douglas Haig's famous " Backs to the Wall " Order,[1]

[1] " Three weeks ago to-day the enemy began his terrific attack against us on a fifty-mile front. His objects are to separate us from the French, to take the Channel Ports, and destroy the British Army. In spite of throw-ing already 106 divisions into the battle and enduring the most reckless sacrifice of human life, he has as yet made little progress towards his goals.

" We owe this to the determined fighting and self-sacrifice of our troops. Words fail me to express the admiration which I feel for the splendid resistance offered by all ranks of our Army under the most trying circumstances.

" Many amongst us now are tired. To those I would say, that victory will belong to the side which holds out the longest. The French Army is moving rapidly and in great force to our support. There is no other course open to us but to fight it out.

" Every position must be held to the last man. There must be no retirement. With our backs to the wall and believing in the justice of our cause, each one of us must fight to the end. The safety of our homes and the freedom of mankind depend alike upon the conduct of each one of us at this critical moment."

(*Special Order issued by Field-Marshal Sir Douglas Haig on 12th April.*)

issued to all ranks on the 12th April, was a bracing and salutary warning to the British Army of what had to be done to deprive the Germans of victory. But Ludendorff, by using too much strength to exploit his initial success, had converted the diversion into a major operation, and had been unable to turn it into account in front of Amiens. The Flanders offensive instead of supplementing had supplanted the enemy's main scheme of the year, and from this moment the projects of the German Higher Command show both uncertainty and nervousness.

Considering how sadly the Ninth had been depleted as a result of the Somme retreat, the unwavering resistance it offered in April is little short of marvellous. Since the 21st March it had enjoyed virtually no rest, and yet it had retained all its high fighting qualities unimpaired; this was largely due to the excellent spirit shown by the young boys who formed a large proportion of each unit. The Ninth's protracted defence of Wytschaete had not merely added another glorious record to its lengthy list, but had helped almost as much as the retention of Givenchy by the Fifty-fifth Division to set a limit to the German gains in Flanders, and earned for it another "mention"[1] from G.H.Q. It

[1] "Farther north a heavy attack launched by the enemy this morning against our lines in the neighbourhood of Wytschaete and Hollebeke (the Messines Ridge) was completely repulsed by the Ninth Division with great loss to the enemy."

(*Extract from the official Communiqué of the* 11th *April.*)

Before this appeared the Corps Commander informed the G.O.C. that Sir Douglas Haig and Marshal Foch fully appreciated the valuable work performed by the Division. This was communicated to units in the following message :—

"The Corps Commander wishes it to be known that the Commander-in-Chief, in course of conversation with him, said that it was mainly due to the stubborn resistance of the Ninth Division that the Army was now in a

is worth noting that here, as during the Somme retreat, the enemy never succeeded in wresting any ground from the Ninth by a frontal attack, and it was only when its flanks were turned that any territory was surrendered. The infantry had shown throughout incomparable tenacity and endurance, and the work of the trench-mortar batteries and the machine-gun battalion was invaluable. It is doubtful if the 26th L.T.M.B. ever did finer work than on the 25th April, while no reputation was more thoroughly established than that of the 9th Machine-gun Battalion, and the prestige won in these turbulent April days gave a tremendous stimulus to the *esprit* of this recently formed unit.

The successful resistance of the Ninth was due to sound generalship as well as the valour of its troops. On the critical 25th April the Highland Brigade being on the inner flank had time to send two companies up from the reserve to form a defensive flank facing south, and it was this measure that stopped the spread northward of the German turning movement until the troops along the Dammstrasse could be withdrawn to the Piccadilly Farm–Mound position, and then at night behind the Vierstraat–Snipers' Barn line. In holding up the onslaught on the Cheapside line and eventually in consolidating themselves in it, when Mount Kemmel, which looked right along it, was in the hands of the enemy, the men of the Ninth accomplished an almost incredible performance. The action is a conspicuous example of the value of defence deployed in depth ; for the fact that the Germans never broke through the

position to hold on to the present line. If the Ninth Division had not held on there would have been no alternative but to retire a long way back. He also stated that General Foch fully appreciated what had been done by the Ninth Division."—No. A. 9837/12, 17/4/18.

Division, although their first attack completely outflanked the front and support lines and even the front
reserve line (Vierstraat line), was due, apart from the
courage of the troops, to the great depth of the original
deployment of the Division.

By its prowess in March and April the Ninth
thoroughly earned the flattering message [1] received
later from Sir Douglas Haig. It was now widely
known even beyond Scotland, and shared with the
Fifty-first Highland Territorial Division, the rare distinction of appearing in a leading article of *The Times*.
This publicity was the theme of an amusing conversation between the popular Padre Brown and a Padre
of another division.

" Oh, you belong to the Ninth Division, do you ? "

" I do."

" You seem to have a very good Press."   (This,
of course, nettled Padre Brown.)

" Yes, we have."

" How do you manage it ; have you got a special
correspondent ? "

" Oh yes."

" Really ; and he seems to accompany you wherever
you go."

" Yes, he does."

" I say, do tell me who he is."

" Oh, his name is Haig ! "

---

[1] " Please convey to General Tudor and to all ranks of the Ninth
Division my deepest appreciation of the great gallantry displayed by them
during many days of severe fighting north of the Lys. In the stubborn
struggle for the Ridge at Wytschaete, with which their name will always
be associated, as well as on many other occasions, they have shown the same
high qualities which distinguished them throughout the Battle south of
Arras, and have most worthily upheld the traditions of the British Army."

(*Ninth Division*, No. A. 9827/28.)

CHAPTER XIV

METEREN AND HOEGENACKER RIDGE

MAY TO SEPTEMBER 1918

THE moral of our troops was a subject of frequent notice in the Press during March and April, and it was so persistently stated that it had not been affected by reverses and disasters that suspicions were aroused about the value of a moral which required so much loquacity to convince people of its soundness. As a matter of fact the men in France were calmer and less nervous than our "Home Front," as the Germans would call it. It is true that both in March and April there had been instances of unseemly panic, but this was inevitable in an army numbering many thousands. But though here and there a few weaklings succumbing to exhaustion and despair lost heart, the vast majority of the men of the Fifth, Third, and Second Armies never faltered; they fully realised that on their devotion and sacrifice depended the fate of civilisation. Greater nervousness was in fact apparent after the crisis had passed, and during the summer of 1918 there was a regular epidemic of self-inflicted wounds, but it was very noticeable that practically all the culprits were fresh soldiers who had never been in any fighting, and a few weeks' careful training in the trenches led to' a rapid diminution of this feeble-hearted device.

A clear gain early in 1918 was the greater reliability of our official communiqués. The garbled and mis- leading accounts of the battles since the time of Loos were not calculated to elevate the moral of those fighting in France, and men who had taken part in such an action as the "3rd May" 1917 were exasperated to find it reported in the Press as a great British victory. "British official," formerly the hall-mark of truth, became a dubious phrase, and the practice of soothing the timid by toning down reverses was more than counterbalanced by a loss of faith in the veracity of the British Government. The method now adopted of publishing full accounts of events was as whole- some as it was satisfactory, and undoubtedly helped to improve the moral of the Army.

The Germans in two offensives had seized a vast extent of territory, and made huge captures in prisoners and material, but they had failed to overwhelm the British forces and to break our liaison with the French. During the panic in March and April the British Government extended the scope of the Military Service Act, and sought, without adequate considera- tion, to introduce conscription into Ireland. From these measures no real gain was to be expected; for the men in Britain now drawn into the Army were more necessary for the upkeep of industry at home, and were too old to be of much service as soldiers, while the attempt to bring Ireland under conscription delivered the country to the Sinn Feiners, and com- pelled the Government to divert to that island large forces which could have found more useful employment on the Western Front. A more solid compensation was derived from the energy and celerity with which America came to the assistance of the Entente, and the rapid and continuous transportation of its soldiers

across the Atlantic to France was the most signal
illustration of the failure of the German submarine
campaign. Unless Germany could intercept American
reinforcements her position was hopeless; and her
capacity for interference was at least curtailed by the
dashing naval operations which blocked the harbours
of Ostend and Zeebrugge.

Even success on land added to her embarrassments;
for her length of front had been greatly augmented
and portions of her line, especially in the north, were
difficult and costly positions to defend. Moreover, the
attack had taxed her strength to the utmost, and it
was not till the end of May that she was able to strike
a fresh blow. The new offensive directed against the
Chemin des Dames with the object of widening the
German front towards Paris, marked the final abandonment of the strategical conception with which Ludendorff
had commenced the campaign, though our front near
Amiens probably remained for the enemy the most
profitable point of attack. The rush on the 27th May,
which chiefly affected the French, at first swept everything before it, and by the end of the month the enemy
had reached the Marne between Château Thierry and
Dormans. Near that point the line became stabilised,
and the resistance of the French was supported by
British and American troops.

During the greater part of May, the Ninth after
leaving Poperinghe was resting and reorganising near
St Omer. D.H.Q. were at Blaringhem, and the brigades
were in neighbouring villages except the 27th, which
was in a camp at Lumbres. After three weeks of
constant training and good weather, the Division, now
largely composed of youths little more than eighteen
years of age, was ready to return to the line, and on
the night of the 25th May the 26th Brigade with the

Y

9th Scottish Rifles attached, relieved the Thirty-first Division near Meteren. On the following day the South African Brigade took over the right sector from the 26th.

The position held by the Ninth was essential for the safety of the important railway centres of Hazebrouck and St Omer, and had therefore to be maintained at all costs. The main feature was the narrow isolated ridge of the Meteren Hill running north and south from Fontaine Hoek towards Meteren; on the east it overlooked the French and German lines towards St Jans Cappel and Bailleul, and on the west the valley of the Meteren Becque as far as the Flêtre–Roukloshille Ridge which lay behind the Hill. The enemy was in possession of the village, which, standing on high ground, afforded him observation of all approaches to the west of Meteren Hill and almost all the ground in our area east of the Flêtre–Roukloshille Ridge, thus preventing any movement on the part of our men in daylight.

In the early summer the initiative still remained with the enemy, and there was anxious speculation as to the place where his next blow would fall. Prince Rupprecht was known to have large forces in reserve and the Mont des Cats and Hazebrouck seemed to offer tempting prizes. Our aeroplane observation showed that extensive preparations for an attack had already been made, and throughout May and June our vigilance was never suffered to relax. Rows of trenches were dug back to St Omer; in the forward area a continuous front trench was excavated, covered by isolated advance posts, while there was a strong support line hinging on Phineboom and a reserve position near Flêtre. On the 27th May the "Rifles" secured a wounded prisoner, who informed us that the enemy was going to make a big attack on the 29th, but that day passed without any untoward occurrence. The German operations near the Chemin des Dames were now in full swing, but the foe on our front continued to form dumps and depots, and not until the end of June was it clear that his projected offensive on the Mont des Cats and Hazebrouck had been given up.

On the whole, the Ninth found the sector a very pleasant one to hold and our casualties from the enemy's artillery-fire were not very high. The landscape was typically agricultural and consisted of wide fields of long waving corn, coloured in patches by the bright red of the poppy, with a few substantial farmhouses interspersed here and there. So hurried had been the flight of the civilians from the district that at many of the farms some live-stock had been left, and in one portion of the line two cows were regularly handed over on reliefs as part of the trench stores.

The attitude of the Division was one of active defence. Patrolling was assiduous; screened by the tall corn, small parties left our lines every day to examine the enemy's positions. Raids for the purpose of securing identifications were constantly carried out, and as the youngsters of the Division gained experience and learned the lie of the country they became adepts in the art of surprising posts. Abortive attempts to take prisoners were made by the K.O.S.B.[1] on the night of the 2nd/3rd June, the 12th Royal Scots[2] on the 10th, and the Black Watch on the night of the

---

[1] After the fighting near Kemmel Lieut.-Colonel J. Colchester Wemyss commanded the battalion until Lieut.-Colonel Smyth returned at the end of May.

[2] In June Lieut.-Colonel Ritson left for England and the battalion from the time it went into the line near the end of May was commanded by Lieut.-Colonel J. Murray.

14th/15th, but during these forays several Germans were killed and wounded. On the 15th, however, the "Rifles" captured a prisoner, and on the 20th a party of the 11th Royal Scots under Lieutenant Keen took three Germans of the 81st Reserve Division. Two days later, a smart piece of ·stalking by Sergeant Smith of the K.O.S.B. realised a bag of three prisoners belonging to the same division.

In June alarm was caused by a distressing outbreak of trench fever which affected the whole Division; numerous officers and men were removed to hospital, but the attack proved to be as short as it was sharp, and in the majority of cases the patients were able to rejoin their units after a fortnight's absence. In the same month several officers and N.C.Os. from the American forces were attached to the Ninth for instruction in trench warfare; they were agreeable companions and enthusiastic workers and willingly joined in enterprises carried out by the units to which they were attached.

Our neighbours at this time were the French on the left and the Australians (First Australian Division) on the right. The latter had won a big reputation by their success in stalking Germans, and there was scarcely a Corps Intelligence Summary which did not record some Australian captures. On the night of the 2nd June a minor operation surprised the enemy in the middle of a relief and the Australian haul consisted of 5 officers and 250 other ranks. At 12.30 A.M. on the 24th a joint enterprise by two companies of the South Africans and two companies of the 1st Australian Brigade advanced our line on a front of 2000 yards to a maximum depth of 500 yards. The attack took place astride the Meteren Becque under cover of an artillery and trench-mortar

METEREN

barrage, and the South African share of the spoils amounted to 29 prisoners and 4 machine-guns.

From the end of June the Germans were daily harassed by Scotsmen, South Africans, and Australians. The captures on the front of the Ninth were smaller than on the right, but our difficulties were greater, the country in our sector being thickly streaked with dense hedges often profusely wired. On the night of the 11th/12th July three successful raids bringing in 7 prisoners were made by the 12th Royal Scots to the north-east of Meteren, and by the Royal Scots Fusiliers and the South Africans to the south of the village. Two nights later, a German N.C.O. was surprised and surrendered to the K.O.S.B.

On the 19th July Meteren was attacked. The commanding ground on which the village stood and its proximity to the line, for the protection of which the Ninth was responsible, rendered it desirable that our front should be advanced beyond the village. During May and June when the enemy was expected to strike, it was inadvisable to attempt the operation but preparations for it were made. Our experience of Longueval suggested the necessity of thoroughly demolishing Meteren; it was therefore systematically bombarded to prevent the consolidation of the position by the enemy and to level the walls and so allow a creeping barrage to go through the village without danger to the assailants. For a fortnight previous to the attack, "heavies," field-guns, and trench mortars poured a never-ending stream of missiles into Meteren and completely flattened it.

As it had been decided that the infantry would attack under a smoke-barrage, bombardments with H.E. and smoke, accompanied by the discharge of gas from projectors, took place from time to time with a view to leading the enemy to associate our use of smoke with gas. It was originally intended to wait for a wind favourable for smoke, but later it seemed politic to carry the operation into effect as soon as possible in order to ascertain the enemy's designs and to delay his preparations for an offensive if one was contemplated. Arrangements had therefore to be made to attack without too much dependence on a favourable wind, and batteries were moved into positions more directly in rear of their tasks. In calculating the amount of smoke and the placing of it on or beyond the barrage line, the velocity and direction of the wind were to be taken into account. The artillery barrage was to be reinforced by the action of trench mortars and machine-guns.

Zero was arranged for 7.55 A.M., as that was an unusually late hour for an attack and the enemy might therefore be expected to be off his guard. The assault was entrusted to the South African and 26th Brigades, the former attacking with the South Africans and the Royal Scots Fusiliers, and the latter with the Camerons and Black Watch. The "Rifles" and Seaforths were in support. The infantry were in their assembly positions before dawn, and in order to avoid detection before zero, the trenches were covered with cocoanut fibre matting, along which a black streak eighteen inches wide had been painted so as to simulate the appearance from the air of an empty trench. As the enemy's centre formed a prominent salient, the men in our centre were to advance at zero, but those in the wings had to remain in their trenches for a few minutes until the middle portion of the barrage came on an alignment with the flanks.

The assault began under the most inauspicious circumstances. On the previous day the battle stores of the South African Brigade were destroyed when the farm in which they had been dumped was burned to the ground, and fresh stores were obtained only in time to be issued to the men when in their assembly positions. Then a Stokes mortar detachment moving to the left brigade sector strayed into the enemy's lines five hours before zero, and one man was captured. The wind was unsteady and unfavourable for smoke. Finally, some guns on both flanks opened five minutes too soon, and while this mistake proved to have no bad consequences on the right flank, it probably served to put the enemy on the alert on our left.

In spite of these mishaps the operation met with almost complete success. The South African Brigade easily subdued all opposition except on its extreme left, where a pocket of Germans in a shallow trench behind a wired hedge offered a stout resistance, but this was adroitly overcome by the Royal Scots Fusiliers. The whole objective on the right was secured to time, numerous losses being inflicted on the enemy, especially behind the hedges running north and south on the west side of Meteren. Fortunately the course of the advance took the hedges in flank and discounted the protection which the Germans hoped to obtain from these obstacles. When the protective barrage ceased a company of South Africans advanced and captured an enemy trench running north-east from the Meteren Becque towards Alwyn Farm.

The Highland Brigade had a more strenuous time. The Camerons clearing the German front passed on through the ruins of Meteren, where the enemy was found holding a hedge in considerable force. After a brisk combat they seized the hedge and reached their objective in time. But the Black Watch on the left were not so happy. A portion of the right company won its objective along with the Camerons, but the remainder of the battalion was at once checked by a thick hedge on the left flank. Previously a successful raid had been effected at this place, but the enemy had since then appreciably strengthened the defences, and now there was a belt of wire behind as well as in front of the hedge covering the hostile infantry and machine-guns. Lying too near our lines to be bombarded by the gunners, it had been dealt with by Stokes mortars, but these had failed to cut the wire. Dogged pluck and persistent efforts were of no avail against this strong point, and after serious losses the left half of the Black Watch retired sullenly to their original trenches. The gap between the two portions of the Black Watch was filled by two platoons of the Seaforths, who on the following day turned the enemy's defences by advancing from the west and drove him from the hedge.

After the capture of the objective, patrols moved forward as soon as the protective barrage ceased. Near Alwyn Farm and the hedges north and east of it there was some spasmodic resistance, but our patrols during the 19th and 20th succeeded in establishing a line on a slight ridge south of the Brahmin Bridge–Gaza Cross Roads. The battlefield was rapidly cleared, but the stretcher-bearers had great difficulty in finding the wounded, who were hidden by the corn. In the days following the attack, the 26th Brigade gained all its objectives, and came into line with the advanced troops of the South African Brigade.

The operation of the 19th July was a brilliant triumph, and increased immensely the enthusiasm and confidence of the young soldiers, to whose dashing fearlessness the victory was mainly due. Our losses, with the exception of the Black Watch, were small compared with our gains ; many of the enemy had been killed, while 6 officers and 348 men, with a considerable amount of material,[1] fell into our hands. The Germans had been taken entirely by surprise. They had become so accustomed to bombardments of H.E. and smoke accompanied by gas that they regarded our barrage of the 19th July as another of the same, and a great many of the prisoners were wearing their gas-masks when captured. The unusual hour of zero was another factor in the surprise, and prisoners stated that all expectation of an attack that day had been abandoned after "stand-to." Our enterprise apparently anticipated a hostile offensive on our front ; the enormous quantity of trench-mortar ammunition which was found close in rear of the enemy's front positions clearly indicated that the Germans were preparing to deliver an attack in this sector.

The capture of Meteren was the last operation of the Highland Brigade conducted by Brig.-General Kennedy. He had led the brigade through some of the stormiest and most critical fighting of the war, and of his many fine achievements perhaps the most outstanding was his daring and skilful handling of his men during the very trying days of the Somme retreat. After three years of continuous strife he had well earned the rest which an appointment in England now secured for him. His successor was Brig.-General the Hon. A. G. A. Hore Ruthven, V.C., who came from the Staff of the VII. Corps with a reputation already established, and assumed command on the 27th July.

The right sector was now taken over by the Lowland Brigade. Before daybreak on the 25th the enemy

---

[1] 1 field-gun, captured at Gaza Cross Roads ; 6 heavy trench mortars ; 6 light trench mortars ; 11 heavy machine-guns ; 36 light machine-guns ; 1 stick-bomb thrower.

sought to gain some compensation for his recent reverse by raiding our lines. At 2 A.M., under cover of a trench-mortar and artillery bombardment, hostile parties attacked trenches held by the K.O.S.B. and 11th Royal Scots. The raid was utterly repulsed, and the enemy left behind two corpses and two unwounded prisoners. From the identifications we learned that the Germans had relieved the battered and demoralised 81st Reserve by the 12th Division, which had a good fighting record. An even more formidable raid was made in the early hours of the 26th. But the Germans were driven off by the K.O.S.B., and though on the right they succeeded in entering a trench held by the 11th Royal Scots, they were expelled by an immediate counter-attack, nine prisoners being taken.

The period from the 26th July till the 18th August was marked by raid and counter-raid. On the 30th July the Australians took Merris. On the 31st a raid by the K.O.S.B. just failed to secure prisoners, but Lieut. C. Campbell and Sergeant Smith killed nearly a dozen of the enemy in a fierce hand-to-hand encounter. Next day the Germans made a strong effort to seize a post held by the 12th Royal Scots, but were easily repulsed. On the 3rd August Captain Grant and a party of Camerons rushed a hostile post, and after killing six and wounding one other, returned without loss to our lines. On the 5th and 14th other raids made by the Germans were driven off.

Since the fear of a hostile offensive was fading away battalions out of the line enjoyed quite a comfortable time. Training, especially of officers, carried on diligently and uninterruptedly, produced a marked improvement in efficiency and discipline. Occasionally, however, the ordinary routine was broken. On Sunday the 4th August, the fifth anniversary of the entry of

Britain into the war, a Parade Service, attended by detachments of all divisions in the Second Army, was held at Terdeghem, the detachments of the XV. Corps being under the command of Lieut.-Colonel Smyth of the 6th K.O.S.B. At this time the Ninth adopted the practice, generally followed by most divisions in France, of distinguishing its personnel by a special mark. This consisted of a white metal thistle on a small circular disc of royal blue cloth worn on the upper part of both arms, and the first unit to be completed with the sign was the 6th K.O.S.B., who had the honour of marching past His Majesty the King near La Brearde on the 6th August. Most fortunately this ceremony saved the Lowland Brigade some casualties; for while a company of the 12th Royal Scots lined the road a shell passed through its vacant billets.

Hoegenacker Ridge, lying beyond Meteren, was clearly the next task of the Division, and instructions for its seizure were received from the XV. Corps on the 10th August. A general plan of attack had been drawn up previously, and was in fact being practised by the Lowland Brigade then in reserve. Since the Meteren Becque was an awkward obstacle to an advance from the west it was decided, while simulating preparations for an attack from this direction, to make the assault from the north. The Ninth was to take the ridge and all the ground east of the Becque as far south as Terrapin House; but as this would give it a frontage of 3000 yards on the objective, while the space for forming-up amounted to only 1500 yards, two companies of the Twenty-ninth Division were to follow in rear of the right flank of the Ninth and take over the front from the Becque to Terrapin House as soon as it had been captured. The Twenty-ninth Division by means of patrols was to follow up any success gained, and if possible secure the village of Outtersteene.

The attack was to be supported by machine-guns and trench mortars and was to be covered by the favourite Ninth barrage. A German document had been captured in which the enemy, attributing our success at Meteren to the use of smoke, instructed his machine-gunners to open fire at once on our parapets when a smoke-barrage came down. It was therefore necessary to give the foe as little time as possible to bring his machine-guns into action, and our barrage was to be put down at one minute after instead of one minute before zero, as originally intended, while the infantry were to count ten after the barrage came down before leaving their trenches.

The assault was to be carried out by the Lowland Brigade with the K.O.S.B., 11th Royal Scots, and "Rifles," each attacking on a two-company front, the first wave in skirmishing order and all succeeding waves in file. In the hope of effecting a tactical surprise, 11 A.M. on the 18th was fixed as zero, and the camouflage device so successfully employed at Meteren was adopted to screen the assembled troops. To ensure that none of the enemy were lurking within our barrage line the 12th Royal Scots established four new posts in six days, and held them against all efforts of the Germans to eject them. These posts were withdrawn before dawn on the morning of the attack.

The operation met with gratifying success. On the right the K.O.S.B. suffered losses from a heavy counter-barrage put down by the enemy between his outposts and his line on the ridge; near the Becque, too, there were some obstinate encounters in which a German machine-gun was knocked out by a Lewis Gun fired from the hip. On the left little opposition was experienced, the enemy being utterly surprised. In their impetuous eagerness our men more than once overran the barrage, some casualties being incurred in consequence. The whole objective of the Division was gained in fine style, and one company of the K.O.S.B. pressing on as far as Outtersteene returned with two heavy machine-guns.

So demoralised was the enemy that a great deal more ground could have been won, but though the men were impatiently anxious to go on, it was not considered advisable to leave the ridge for the low swampy ground beyond. The enterprise had been exceedingly satisfactory, no hitch having occurred at all. Ten officers and 287 other ranks had been captured along with a quantity of material.[1] The ground secured was of real importance as it dominated the whole sector, and unless the enemy had abandoned all hope of an offensive in this district he was bound to counter-attack. But nothing happened; the Germans had their hands too full with our counter-offensive in front of Amiens to contemplate ambitious projects in other parts of the war zone. Four days after the capture of Hoegenacker Ridge the Germans commenced a retreat on this front which did not close until they had abandoned the whole of the Lys salient. This step was probably chiefly due to events farther south, but the loss of the ridge, which afforded wonderful facilities for observation, undoubtedly precipitated the enemy's retirement.

The Ninth remained in the line until the 24th. Terrapin Farm was not taken over by the troops of the Twenty-ninth Division until the 19th, probably because the amount of ground gained by exploitation

[1] 20 heavy machine-guns, 22 light machine-guns, 342 rifles.

was greater than had been expected.   On the 22nd the
Black Watch, in conjunction with a brigade of the
Thirty-sixth Division which was now on our left,
advanced their line about 150 yards without opposition.
On the same date a patrol of the Camerons encountered
a hostile post, which it summarily wiped out ; it was
then attacked from different directions and retired after
shooting two officers who were leading enemy parties.
On the 24th and 25th Hoegenacker Ridge was taken
over by the Thirty-first Division and the Ninth was
withdrawn to rest near Wardrecques.

At the end of August the South African Composite
Battalion moved to the Lumbres area preparatory to
leaving the Division, its connection with which officially
ceased on the 13th September.   Heavily engaged
throughout 1918 it had once been practically demolished, and it was clear that there was no chance
of bringing it up to the strength of a brigade until it
was withdrawn from the line.   It was only fitting that
the Union of South Africa should be represented in
France by a force stronger than a battalion ; but the
severance of the connection thus rendered necessary
was a great blow to everyone in the Ninth.   The trials
and hardships borne by Scots and South Africans at
the Somme, Arras, Passchendaele, and the fierce ordeal
of the German offensives in March and April had
forged a bond, consecrated by common sufferings and
triumphs, that will ever link in sympathy such distant
parts of the Empire as the misty land of Scotland and the
Dominion that extends from the Cape of Good Hope
to the Zambesi.   The departure took place without fuss
or ceremony in the same fashion as tried friends say
farewell when duty bids them part.   The final greeting [1]

[1] "I wish to express to you and to your officers, warrant officers,
N.C.Os. and men of the brigade under your command my great regret

of General Tudor to the men who had played such an eminent and distinguished rôle in the Division reflected the sincere feelings of the Scots.

There was some consolation in the report that the place of the South Africans was to be filled by Ian Hay's battalion, the 10th Argylls; but it was not immediately available, and another battalion of Colonial troops, the Newfoundlanders, tough fighters and good comrades, joined the Ninth under the command of Lieut.-Colonel T. G. Matthias. The 28th Brigade thus reconstituted was placed under the command of Brig.-General J. L. Jack.

Before the end of August the war had taken a turn that was as unexpected as it was gratifying. The German offensive in May and June towards Paris had been foiled by the doughty resistance of French and American troops, and Ludendorff, seeking an easier quest, dealt on the 15th July his final and hazardous blow against Rheims. Marshal Foch's skilfully excogitated tactics were more than a match for the storm - troops who, lying in a sharp salient near Soissons, Château Thierry, Epernay, and Rheims, experienced a jarring shock when attacked on the

---

that the exigencies of the Service prevented me seeing you all personally before you were transferred from the Ninth Division in order to say good-bye. For two and a half years your brigade has shared the fortunes of the Ninth Division. At Delville Wood, at Arras, at Ypres, in the Somme retreat, and finally at Meteren, it has fully contributed in establishing and maintaining the glorious record of this Division. The South African Brigade bore the brunt of the attack on the divisional front in March 1918, and its final stand at Bouchavesnes on 24th March, when it held out all day until all ammunition was exhausted, will live as one of the bravest feats of arms in the war. The cheery keenness and comradeship with which the South African Brigade has always worked and fought will be very much missed by me personally and by all the Ninth Division. We wish you and your brigade the best of fortune, and know that you will always fully maintain the splendid name you have earned."

(General Tudor's Letter to Brig.-General Tanner.)

18th July by a French force under General Mangin who had collected it under cover of the forests of Compiègne and Villers-Cotterêts. The Germans were driven from the salient, Soissons was recaptured by the French, and on the 3rd August the enemy was pushed back across the River Vesle.

General Mangin's stroke on the 18th July was the turning-point in the campaign. Ludendorff's hope of victory was broken, and the ultimate triumph of the Entente was definitely assured. But few people were prepared for the sequence of brilliant victories that attended the Allies' arms, and the autumn of glorious hope that succeeded the gloomiest spring of the war. On the 8th August the British Fourth Army struck so shrewd a blow that it disengaged the city of Amiens, and reduced Ludendorff to despair. The resistance of Germany began to crumble, and her forces were driven back in a retreat, which was rapidly developing into a rout, when the Armistice put an end to hostilities. The line of battle extended to the north when, on the 21st August, the British Third Army attacked between Albert and Arras. On the 29th Bapaume fell to the Third, and on the 31st Péronne to the Fourth Army. The First Army, joining in, stormed the formidable Drocourt–Queant line. These events emasculated opposition farther north, and Bailleul, Mount Kemmel, Ploegsteert Wood, and Lens were evacuated. Before the end of September the Germans had lost all their conquests of the spring, and were endeavouring to gain time behind the entrenchments of the Hindenburg Line.

With Germany in the toils all pith and sting dropped from her allies. In the Balkans, General Franchet d'Espercy, now in command of the Entente forces in that area, commenced on the 15th September an attack which in ten days forced the Bulgarians to sue for peace. With the collapse of Bulgaria the Central Powers lost their grasp on the Balkans, and there was no force of any consequence to make even a fight for Serbia. Turkey was now isolated, and suffered a series of catastrophic reverses from the armies of General Allenby, whose cavalry campaign mopped up the greater part of the Turkish soldiery, and eventually with the co-operation of General Marshall from Mesopotamia compelled the Sultan to accept our Armistice terms on the 30th October.

In France the admirable discipline of the enemy's troops had so far prevented anything like a rout, but every day increased the embarrassments of the German General Staff. Reserves had to be thrown in hastily to stem our advance with no time to consider how they might be employed most usefully. Within Germany itself the rigours of our naval blockade caused acute discomfort, and the failure of the military effort raised murmurs ominous of the Revolution that was to sweep the Hohenzollerns from the Imperial Throne.

Thus the general situation towards the end of September was full of promise for the Allies, and Marshal Foch and Sir Douglas Haig, realising that a continuation of our pressure was bound to overwhelm the armies of the adversary, arranged for four simultaneous and convergent attacks against his sagging line.

The first was to be delivered by the Americans, who had already flattened out the St Mihiel salient, and was to be in the Woeuvre in the general direction of Mezières; the second by the French west of the Argonne with the same general goal as the Americans; the third on the Cambrai–St Quentin front by the Fourth, Third, and First British Armies in the direction

z

of Maubeuge; and the fourth on the 28th September
by the Belgian and Second British Armies in the
direction of Ghent.

The Ninth, being in the Second Army, was thus to
take part in the Flanders campaign. In billets, first
near Wardrecques and later in the neighbourhood of
Esquelbec, the men for over three weeks were resting
and training, but the elation caused by their triumphs
near Metern and the daily reports of fresh victories
made them burn to join in the final onset. On the
11th September the Division was transferred from the
XV. to the II. Corps, and the 26th Brigade took
over the front between the Ypres–Menin and Ypres–
Zonnebeke roads from the Fourteenth Division on the
20th September.

Our front line ran approximately from Hell-fire
Corner on the right to Mill Cot, rather more than a mile
east of Ypres. East of this line the ground was low-
lying and marshy, but rose gradually on the right
to Bellewarde Ridge, and thence to the Westhoek–
Frezenberg Ridge, which extended across the divisional
front from south to north. From Stirling Castle, a mile
south of Westhoek, the main Passchendaele Ridge ran
north of Broodseinde to the village of Passchendaele.
Between the Frezenberg Ridge and the Noordemdhoek–
Broodseinde sector of the main ridge, two small but
important underfeatures ran north-west; these were
known as Anzac Ridge and Glasgow Spur, the former
being separated from the Frezenberg Ridge by the tiny
stream of the Hanebeek in a very boggy valley, which
had been heavily wired. Since the desperate battles
of 1917, the sector had experienced unusual repose,
and the wilderness of shell-holes was now covered
by long rank grass.

The Ninth being on the left flank of the Second

Army was in close liaison with the Belgians. The co-ordination of artillery arrangements naturally presented complications, but ultimately it was decided that while the Belgians should open with a three hours' preliminary bombardment before zero, the Ninth would attack under cover of its customary creeping barrage, commencing at zero. There was less difficulty as regards the Twenty-ninth Division on our right, though a pause of fifteen minutes after the capture of Bellewarde Ridge was necessary to allow that division after passing through Sanctuary Wood to reorganise, preparatory to storming Stirling Castle.

The final objective of the Ninth for the first day extended from the southern end of Polygone de Zonnebeke to a point about 500 yards south of Broodseinde. Before this line was reached a series of ridges had to be secured, Frezenberg, Anzac, and Glasgow Spur. Batteries of artillery were to move forward as each height was taken, so that an effective barrage might be maintained throughout the advance. The assailing troops were the 28th Brigade on the right and the 26th on the left, the former with the "Rifles" and the Royal Scots Fusiliers in line, and the latter with the Seaforths and Black Watch [1]; the Newfoundlanders and Camerons were in reserve. Lieut.-Colonel Lumsden of the "Rifles" was ill and had a very high temperature on the eve of the battle, but this officer, who had never missed an action since he crossed to France with the Division in 1915, refused to go sick. The 27th Brigade was to follow in support, and its rôle was to depend on the situation at the close of the day. Each brigade had a company of the Ninth Machine-Gun Battalion attached to it, the remaining company being in divisional reserve. Zero was at 5.25 A.M.

[1] Commanded by Lieut.-Colonel French since August.

A big victory was expected and with good reason. Defeats in the south had caused the enemy to thin the garrison in front of Ypres, but the nature of the ground with frequent " Pill-boxes " and scattered belts of wire was likely to retard our advance. The Germans who opposed us were the 11th and 12th Bavarian and the 10th Saxon Divisions; they were alert but nervous, and numerous low flying aircraft carried out reconnaissances over our front system. There was a regrettable mishap on the 26th. A stray shell hit the H.Q. of the Camerons; Lieut.-Colonel Inglis was wounded, and Major Cameron, Captain Fraser, the adjutant, and six others of Battalion H.Q. were killed. Lieut.-Colonel A. W. Angus then joined the Division, and was sent up to command the Camerons. Since the 9th April 1917 our men had never been in better spirit, and when the troops assembled for the attack on the night of the 27th/28th September, they were full of confidence.

CHAPTER XV

FROM YPRES TO LEDEGHEM

28th September to 14th October 1918

Three hours before zero on the 28th September the Belgians commenced their preliminary bombardment, which on our front provoked little retaliation. Heavy rain was falling and it was the dark hour before dawn, when at 5.25 A.M. our leading infantry advanced to the attack over the slippery and shell-pitted ground. The 28th Brigade was on a front of 700[1] yards and the 26th on one of 1200.

The whole operation went like clockwork, although at the start progress was somewhat impeded by the darkness and the churned-up soil, now rendered more unstable by the continuous rain. A smoke-barrage[2] was at first unnecessary owing to the very early zero[3] hour, but as dawn broke and a south-west breeze sprang up, its great value became apparent and the tunnelled dug-outs and "Pill-boxes," which strewed the

[1] The 28th Brigade was given a narrower front in the advance to the first objective in order to ensure that a sufficient force would still be in hand, after Frezenberg Ridge was reached, to press home the attack along the main ridge, most of which lay within the right brigade sector.

[2] Owing to the small number of field-guns per yard (one gun to about 45 yards) the Division had to depend chiefly on smoke for the barrage, and the guns fired two rounds of smoke to one of H.E.

[3] A great deal of trouble had been taken to arrange the right hour for zero, but all the calculations of the Divisional Staff were completely upset by the fact that the morning was cloudy with drizzling rain.

Bellewarde and Frezenberg Ridges, were isolated and captured with greater ease than might have been expected.   By 6.45 A.M. the northern end of the Frezenberg Ridge was taken; by 8 A.M. the whole of it was in our hands, and patrols from the Highland Brigade had pushed on towards the Hanebeek, in conjunction with the Eighth Belgian Division.

The Sappers and Pioneers, who had bridged the stream at Potijze during the night of the 27th/28th, followed immediately behind the infantry, and set to work without delay on the Ypres–Zonnebeke and Hell-fire Corner–Zonnebeke roads.   Their rapid improvements rewarded all the forethought and labour which had been expended in the accumulation of suitable material, and enabled the forward movement of the divisional artillery to begin at 8 A.M.   By 8.30 A.M. our first howitzer battery came into action in its new position, but the Ypres–Zonnebeke road soon became congested with Belgian artillery and the progress of our remaining batteries was slow.

Advance from the Frezenberg Ridge was resumed at 8.35 A.M.   The dispositions of the 28th Brigade remained unaltered, but in the 26th the Camerons passed through the Seaforths and Black Watch.   The plan now entailed a partial wheel to the left, in order that the high ground might be secured before the low ground farther north was crossed.   This manœuvre was accomplished with the aid of a H.E. barrage, into which the Field Artillery joined, battery by battery, as they reached their new position west of Frezenberg Ridge.   The first real opposition encountered by the infantry was near Anzac Ridge, where dense strands of wire and groups of "Pill-boxes" enhanced the natural strength of the position, but nothing could arrest the momentum of our men, and half an hour before noon all the main ridge from the Polygone de Zonnebeke to Broodseinde was in our possession.

Thus our final objective was won with surprising ease and at trifling cost; the only matter now to be settled was the part to be played by the 27th Brigade.

This brigade had moved up from camps west of Ypres early on the 28th, and proceeded steadily over the heavy ground to the Polygone Butt. Brig.-General Croft had been ordered to be prepared for any one of three courses; to assist either of our assaulting brigades during the advance to Broodseinde Ridge, or to advance north from Broodseinde in the event of the Belgians finding the low and boggy ground on their front impassable, or to exploit success by an advance towards Becelaere.

Accordingly General Tudor and Brig.-General Croft went forward to the Broodseinde Ridge, and by 12.30 P.M. had ascertained beyond doubt that it was firmly held by the Belgians as well as by our own men. The resistance of the German infantry was feeble, and their artillery-fire practically negligible. Gheluvelt had already fallen to the Twenty-ninth Division, and the Highland Brigade and the Eighth Belgian Division were in close touch several hundred yards east of Broodseinde Cross Roads.

The Lowland Brigade was therefore instructed to advance against Becelaere. Owing to a breakdown of the visual signalling arrangements there was a delay in the transmission of the orders, and the two assaulting battalions, the 12th and 11th Royal Scots, did not leave their position of deployment near Polygone Butt until 2.30 P.M. Stern opposition was encountered at once, chiefly on the left of the 11th Royal Scots, and increased perceptibly as our men approached Becelaere. Just north of the village three hostile batteries came into action in the open, and it was only after a strenuous combat that the 11th Royal Scots, assisted by a section of "B" Company of the Machine-gun Battalion, took possession of one of these batteries and silenced the others. The enemy's machine-gunners were still full of fight, but all virtue had gone out of the infantry, who, though present in large numbers, took no part in the operation. The 11th Royal Scots mastered the Molenhoek Ridge, and the high ground north of the village of Becelaere was taken by the 12th Royal Scots about 4 P.M.

The seizure of the village set a limit to our advance that day. At nightfall the situation was as follows: the Twenty-ninth Division was believed to be holding the line Nieuwe Kruiseecke Cross Roads–Poezelhoek, but no connection had yet been secured with it; the 27th Brigade, holding Becelaere, was in touch at Judge Cross Roads with the 26th, which was linked up with the Belgians east of Broodseinde Cross Roads, each brigade having two battalions in line and one in brigade reserve; the 28th Brigade lay in divisional reserve near Polygone Butt with one battalion pushed forward to protect the right rear of the 27th. Our casualties had been slight, and in that one day considerably more ground had been won than during months of furious fighting in 1917. Nothing could have revealed in a stronger light the unmistakable change that had come over the character of the war.

Our greatest trouble was the opening up of decent roads from Ypres to the ridge. The one route of any consequence—the Ypres–Zonnebeke road—was ready for wheeled traffic as far as Zonnebeke by 1 P.M., and by dusk all three [1] artillery brigades were in action behind the Broodseinde Ridge. But it was

---

[1] The 28th Brigade A.F.A. was attached to the Division.

the one highway fit for use, and during the hours of darkness it was thronged with Belgian and British limbers, some of which remained out on the road all night. These difficulties had been foreseen by Lieut.-Colonel Jeffcoat, who had organised a small column of pack animals for each brigade, and under the personal supervision of the brigade staff captains the rations for the men were brought up on the night of the 28th.

Early in the afternoon of that day General Tudor was informed that the Thirty-sixth Division, in Corps reserve, was to come into line between the Ninth and Twenty-ninth Divisions, and the 153rd A.F.A. Brigade was to be under its command. About midnight orders were received to continue the push next day by daylight. The Thirty-sixth Division, which was to take over Becelaere from the 27th Brigade, was to advance on Terhand while the Twenty-ninth Division was to carry Gheluwe. The Ninth, covering the left flank of the Thirty-sixth Division, was to conform on its left to the Belgian Army, by moving in close touch with it to the vicinity of Keiberg Spur.

The brigadiers received their orders in person from General Tudor. The 28th Brigade was to lead the attack; the 27th and 26th, following in rear of the right and left of the 28th respectively, were to reinforce and carry on the assault without waiting for orders in the event of progress being checked. To give the men as much rest as possible and to allow the Thirty-sixth Division to come up into line, 9 A.M. was the hour fixed for the resumption of the forward movement.

The steady downpour under which the attack had begun was still falling at 9 A.M. on the 29th. The autumn night had been not only wet but very cold, and as practically no shelter was available great discomfort

was endured by the men. Fortunately the sky showed
signs of clearing when the 28th Brigade, with the
"Rifles" and Newfoundlanders in line, and the Royal
Scots Fusiliers in reserve, passed through the outposts
of the 26th Brigade and began its advance on the
Keiberg Spur. There was no creeping barrage, but
our guns fired smoke to cover the movement of the
troops across the shallow valley separating Keiberg
from Broodseinde Ridge. Amid desultory shell and
considerable machine-gun fire Brig.-General Jack's men
pressed on, and by 10 A.M. the Newfoundlanders with
the Belgians on their left had captured the Keiberg and
had broken through the Passchendaele–Terhand line;
by 11.25 A.M. they were reported to be entering
Waterdamhoek. One section of the 50th Brigade
R.F.A. reached the Spur and was soon followed by
the remainder of the battery.

From the outset the "Rifles" met firm opposition
and were constantly enfiladed by machine-gun fire
from the south, though the Thirty-sixth Division had
gone through the outposts of the 27th Brigade about
9.30 A.M. For a brief space our men were checked
by the Passchendaele – Terhand line, but this was
quickly carried, and about 1 P.M. both the "Rifles"
and Newfoundlanders were facing a strongly - wired
line running east of Moorslede and Waterdamhoek,
and west of Strooiboomhoek and Dadizeele, called
the Flanders I. Stellung. Here they suffered grievously
through machine-gun fire from the front and from the
right wing, where Terhand had not yet been captured.
There was now a gap between the 28th Brigade and
the Belgians, and the Highland Brigade was ordered
to send a battalion to fill it.

The Camerons accordingly moved forward, but
after they had passed well over the Keiberg Spur,

the Belgians, who were experiencing obstinate resistance near Moorslede asked for assistance, and General Tudor commanded Brig.-General Hore Ruthven to use his whole brigade if necessary, and press on south of Moorslede with the utmost speed.

Meanwhile Brig.-General Croft had instructed his battalion commanders to follow close behind the "Rifles" and to join in the attack if the advance showed any sign of being checked. Finding that the leading troops had been brought to a standstill, Lieut.-Colonel Smyth, who had been reconnoitring well ahead of the brigade, consulted with Lieut.-Colonel Sir J. Campbell, and they sent forward two companies each of the K.O.S.B. and the 11th Royal Scots. The additional momentum thus thrown into the onset carried the whole line forward about 2.30 P.M. On a front of nearly 4000 yards men of the 27th and 28th Brigades broke through the Flanders I. Stellung position and entered Dadizeele about 4 P.M., just as the enemy was hurriedly evacuating it. Pushing forward, they established themselves on the Menin–Roulers road as dusk was falling. North of them the Highlanders, whose dash had materially assisted the Belgians to carry Moorslede, took up a position about 300 yards west of the Menin–Roulers road, extending north almost to St Pieter, which the Belgians wrongly reported as being in their hands. The latter did not forget the assistance given them by the Highlanders on this day, and it was referred to in terms of great appreciation by the King of the Belgians when he reviewed the Division on the 5th November.

This concluded the operations for the day. On our right the Thirty-sixth Division, encountering stiff opposition, did not secure Terhand until 3.45 P.M., and at night the enemy was still holding Wijfwegen and Hill 41, a very important tactical feature, which

dominated our right flank. On our left the Belgian
line ran back for fully 1000 yards parallel to and south
of the St Pieter–Moorslede road, north of which they
had failed to penetrate a thick belt of wire.

The line of the Ninth was thus well ahead of that
held by the divisions on both wings, our frontage
being about 3500 yards, 1500 of which were south of
the divisional boundary. Owing largely to the skilful
leading of regimental officers casualties had on the
whole been few, the " Rifles " being hardest hit. Lieut.-
Colonel Kelso of the Royal Scots Fusiliers was blown
up by a shell, but though severely shaken refused to
leave his battalion. In the evening the 28th Brigade was
withdrawn into divisional reserve about Potterijebrug,
with the exception of three and a half companies which
were left in the line until the following night to reinforce the 27th Brigade.

After a dry spell, rain commenced again at 6 P.M.
and continuing to fall throughout the night added
enormously to the difficulties of keeping open the
Ypres–Zonnebeke road, where traffic was constantly
blocked by huge Belgian drays, slowly hauled along
by one or two miserable horses.

Orders were received from Corps to resume the
advance on the 30th, but in view of the fact that the
Ninth was already holding a difficult salient, General
Tudor decided to await news of the attack by the
divisions on our wings before giving any orders.
Brigades, however, were instructed to be ready to
move at 9 A.M.

At 8 A.M. General Tudor presided over a conference
of brigadiers at Waterdamhoek. Our patrols had
reported strong opposition east of the Menin–Roulers
road, and he therefore ordered his brigade commanders,
pending news from the divisions on our flanks, to look

for weak parts in the hostile line and to push on if opportunity offered.

Neither the Thirty-sixth nor the Eighth Belgian Division attacked in force on the 30th. The former, under a smoke-screen put down by the 50th Brigade R.F.A., captured Hill 41 about 4.30 P.M., but was almost immediately expelled by a counter-attack. During the day it took over the line up to Klephoek Cross Roads from the 27th Brigade, which even after this adjustment was still holding 1000 yards south of the divisional boundary. The Belgians failed to secure St Pieter, and the Black Watch who co-operated were also stopped by severe machine-gun fire; thus by night the situation was unaltered, the Ninth continuing to occupy a sharp salient.

During the morning the artillery brigades sent forward one or two guns to give close support to the infantry, and one gun of B/51 Battery near Slypshoek was almost up to the front line. Between noon and 2 P.M. the 50th and 51st Brigades R.F.A. were in action in the area Strooiboomhoek–Slypskappelle–Spriethoek. The route taken by the 50th Brigade to reach its position was in full view of the enemy's lines, but the movement was carried out without much interference. Constant and heavy rain fell throughout the day, and consequently there was complete dislocation of traffic on the Ypres–Zonnebeke road, with the result that no artillery ammunition could be brought up, and the ration wagons of some units remained on the road all night.

The troubles that beset us were now becoming formidable, and it was also clear that the enemy was rushing up fresh troops to dispute our further progress. General Tudor, convinced that isolated attacks were a mistake, as the experience of the Thirty-sixth Division and the Belgians on the 30th showed, rode over to see General Detail, G.O.C. of the Eighth Belgian Division, who agreed that if an attack was to be made it should be along the whole line. At the same time, General Detail declared that his division would not be able to make an assault for some days. Shortly afterwards orders arrived for a general onset at 6.15 A.M., the Ninth Division having as objective Ledeghem, thence due east to Cuerne and Harlebeke. The first objective of the Corps consisted of the villages of Ledeghem and Menin, and the line of the Railway between them. The frontage allotted to the Division was from Klephoek, east of Dadizeele, to St Pieter. The Ninth was ready, but, as shown above, the Belgians were unable to attack so soon. This was represented to the Corps, but communications were defective and very slow, speaking on the telephone was impossible, and time did not permit of a complete report of the situation reaching Corps H.Q. in time to postpone the operation. Knowing that the Belgians could not attack, though, as always, they were eager to help us in any way in their power, General Tudor acquainted them with the situation, and they agreed to safeguard our flank by conforming later if our efforts were successful. He also instructed Brig.-General Hore Ruthven, who was very anxious about his northern wing, to seize and consolidate the line of the Railway, but to go no farther unless the Belgians joined in the battle.

The position on our right also caused great uneasiness; so long as Hill 41 remained in German hands our advance on this flank was bound to be a precarious business, but it was understood that the Thirty-sixth Division would storm the Hill at 5.45 A.M.

The weather was still very disagreeable when at 6.15 A.M. on the 1st October, the assault was launched under cover of a smoke-barrage. It was delivered by the 27th Brigade, with the K.O.S.B., the 12th Royal Scots and a company of the 11th Royal Scots, and by the 26th Brigade with the Seaforths and Black Watch. On our right the enemy put down a heavy bombardment, but fortunately it fell principally behind the 27th Brigade. A few field-guns had been brought up to within 400 or 500 yards of the front line to engage Ledeghem and some scattered farms close to our front. The fire of these guns at short range, combined with the smoke-barrage, proved of immense value in helping the infantry to overpower the stout resistance which was at first encountered in and around the farm buildings. When that had been quelled, progress was continued with great rapidity, and for a time all opposition collapsed. The Lowland Brigade carried the whole of Ledeghem and speedily arrived at the line of the light railway 500 yards east of the village. On the left the Highland Brigade captured what turned out to be one of the last groups of German "Pill-boxes," and also reached the light railway, while the Black Watch advancing as far as Rolleghem Cappelle penetrated the village and engaged hostile guns caught in the act of limbering up.

The opposition in front was insignificant, but the enemy, who had brought up fresh troops,[1] was quick to detect and take advantage of the weakness on our wings. On the right the K.O.S.B. had been harassed continuously from the start of the battle by machine-gun fire from Hill 41, which increased in volume as the Menin-Roulers Railway was approached. The Thirty-

---

[1] The 6th and 7th Cavalry Divisions, consisting of men of fine physique, who, according to their own statements, were known as the "War-prolongers" because they remained full of fight while the resisting power of other German troops was diminishing.

sixth Division had postponed its attack on the Hill, with fatal consequences to our right wing, and Dadizeelehoek, less than 1000 yards south of Ledeghem, appeared to be bristling with machine-guns. Lieut.-Colonel Smyth with admirable promptitude swung two of his companies to the right, with the intention of clearing Hill 41 from the north. But the manœuvre was foiled by an almost solid flow of lead from hostile machine-guns, and Lieut.-Colonel Smyth was obliged to use the greater part of his battalion in forming a defensive flank, while a field-gun, with bullets pattering against its shield, was brought up ready to fire at point-blank range as soon as the enemy counter-attacked.

On the left, as the Belgian forces had not yet advanced, Brig.-General Hore Ruthven had to employ his reserve battalion, the Camerons, in forming a defensive flank under scourging machine-gun fire.

At the outset of the battle the situation appeared to offer a distinct opportunity for cavalry [1] exploitation to widen the breach that had been made in the enemy's line, but no force was available to move up immediately and the chance was lost. Very anxious about his left, General Tudor sent messages to the French Cavalry leader and the commander of the Eighth Belgian Division, requesting the former to send up without delay a regiment to Brig.-General Hore Ruthven's H.Q. at Slypskappelle, and the latter to fill the gap that now existed between our left and its right. Word was also despatched to the Corps suggesting that any available troops should be sent up behind the Ninth to follow up success, and protect its flanks. At the same time General Tudor commanded the 28th Brigade, which since the 28th September had been out of the

---

[1] The cavalry in reserve consisted of the 3rd French Cavalry Brigade, which, however, was not under the orders of the G.O.C. Ninth Division.

"PILL-BOX" NEAR LEDEGHEM

p. 350

fighting line for little more than twenty-four hours, to be ready to guard the right flank.

The hostile pressure on our exposed flanks was steadily augmented. By 11 A.M. the Highlanders after suffering severe losses were obliged to withdraw to the main Menin–Roulers Railway, which they held for a distance of 1000 yards north of Ledeghem, whence their line ran back to a point about 500 yards south of St Pieter. This difficult retirement was carried out with the utmost coolness. Lieut.-Colonel French of the Black Watch, with great personal courage formed a defensive flank with his men and prevented the Germans from breaking our line. The French Cavalry Regiment arrived later, but the opportunity for its profitable employment had passed. The Belgians attacking at 11 A.M. took St Pieter, but failed to advance more than 100 yards east of it. Farther north their assault did not succeed, and their line ran in a north-west or west-north-west direction from the village. The machine-gun company in divisional reserve was moved up to reinforce the 26th Brigade, which had gained about 1000 yards on its right, while its left sloped back to the southern end of St Pieter.

On our right at 10.30 A.M. a hostile counter-attack from the south-east, gallantly led by mounted officers, withered away before the fire of four Lewis Guns in Ledeghem Cemetery, but two hours later a second attempt from the north-east as well as from the south-east expelled our troops from most of Ledeghem. An immediate counter-thrust by the 11th and 12th Royal Scots retook the northern end of the village, west of which the K.O.S.B. established a line along the Railway with their right flank thrown back to Manhattan Farm. From an observation post about 100 yards behind his

2 A

front line, Lieut. - Colonel Smyth saw the Germans
collecting troops for a great counter-stroke, and the
K.O.S.B. were bracing themselves for a desperate
resistance at Manhattan Farm, when the timely arrival
of the 1st Inniskilling Fusiliers, who made a most
heroic attack on Hill 41 from the north, scared the
enemy and turned his efforts solely to defence. Though
the Inniskillings failed to capture the Hill, their plucky
effort probably saved the K.O.S.B., and so great was
the admiration of the latter and the troops of the Ninth
Division who witnessed the attack, that the G.O.C. at
their request wrote at once to the Thirty-sixth Division
expressing the admiration and thanks of the officers and
men of the Ninth.

Throughout the whole of that trying time when
the Division was fighting single-handed, the close
and fearless support of the infantry by our gunners
proved of inestimable value in breaking up counter-
attacks. In spite of the continuous rattle of bullets
on the shields, Lieut. Gorle of the 50th Brigade R.F.A.
led two guns up to Ledeghem, and on four separate
occasions under a veritable hail of lead brought single
guns into action within a few hundred yards of the
enemy. Providentially, though his tunic was combed
with bullets, he escaped the death that seemed inevitable, and for his most opportune heroism he was
worthily awarded the V.C.

Our gains on the 1st October were insignificant
compared with those on the 28th and the 29th
September, but in the old days of trench warfare
they would have represented a very creditable achievement. And there is little doubt that they would
have been much more remarkable but for the lack
of co-operation which prevented a simultaneous attack
along the whole front, for the Ninth had been stopped

only by the want of support on its wings. Nevertheless, since the 28th September the Division [1] had crossed the tragic Passchendaele Ridge, left behind it the blighted wilderness created by more than four years of grisly strife, and established itself on the fringe of a landscape yet unscarred by war. In all, ten miles had been traversed since the beginning of the battle, and many prisoners and countless trophies had fallen into our hands.

The operations of the 1st October mark the end of the first phase of the Flanders offensive. It was clear that the enemy had strengthened his front, and that time would be saved and success more assured if the advance was resumed under cover of a thoroughly organised artillery-barrage. This involved a certain amount of delay, as our advance had outstripped our facilities for sending forward stores and supplies, and roads and routes had to be constructed through the

[1] A tribute greatly cherished by the Division was received from General C. W. Jacobs in a Special Order issued on the 3rd October :—

"As the first phase of the operations which began on the 28th September 1918 is over, I wish to express to you and all ranks of the Ninth Division my gratitude and thanks for the splendid work which has been achieved.

"The Ninth Division was specially selected to carry out the attack on the left flank of the British Second Army and to cover the right flank of the Belgian Army attack. The objectives given were rather more distant than those we have attempted hitherto in Flanders, but, owing to the splendid leading of yourself and the officers of all units, not only were all those objectives gained, but you broke right through the enemy's line to a depth of 9¼ miles. In 1917 it took our Army over three months to get only half that distance, and at great cost. The Ninth Division has done it, and a great deal more, in twenty-four hours. What further evidence is required of the magnificence of this exploit?

"The Ninth Division has done splendidly all through the war, but these last operations will be considered by history to have eclipsed all their previous performances. In the last few days the conditions have been trying and you have had to beat off many counter-attacks. The weather has been bad and shelter has been very scanty. Yet the spirit of all ranks has always kept at a high level and you have upheld the splendid traditions of the British Army and of the Division in particular."

trackless jungle of the desolated region before heavy guns and ammunition could be brought up. Fortunately the line held by us was so well furnished with " Pill-boxes," that during the lull our troops were more comfortably housed and protected than could have been anticipated.

Reverses in Flanders formed only a portion of the humiliations that were crowding on Germany. Before September had closed the Hindenburg Line, and with it all the hopes of the Fatherland, was broken by British forces, and the German armies were drawn back to the Selle. This success, together with the advance in Flanders, compelled the enemy to evacuate the Lys salient and draw back his front towards Lille and Douai. In the Woeuvre and Argonne, American and French forces were waging a grim struggle ; for here the foe's resistance was necessarily desperate, since the collapse of this flank was bound to involve the utter destruction of the German forces in France. But steady progress was made, though the Americans were hampered by commissariat difficulties, and it became exceedingly doubtful if the enemy could maintain the line of the Meuse, upon which his last chance of safety rested.

The result of the fighting till the 14th October was that deep dents had been made in the opposing line, which was left with inconvenient salients in the north round Lille and Douai, and farther south between the Oise and the Aisne. With a view to saving Lille and its industrial environs from the ravages of war, the policy of the Allies was to encircle the city and so cause its abandonment. To this end a further attack by the Belgian and British forces was planned for the 14th October.

In this operation the task assigned by the II. Corps

to the Ninth was the Courtrai–Lendelede Railway, after reaching which, the Division was to make good the crossings over the Lys between Courtrai and Harlebeke. The railway was 9000 and the river 14,000 yards from our line. Since the 1st October the Division had experienced a fairly quiet time, but the Royal Scots Fusiliers had the bad luck to lose their C.O., Lieut.-Colonel Kelso being badly wounded by a shell; the command of the battalion was taken over by Major A. King.

On the 3rd the Germans counter-attacked under cover of a heavy bombardment, but were repulsed mainly through the agency of the Newfoundlanders, who, in their anxiety not to miss a fight, left their positions in the support line and hurrying forward to the front used their rifles and Lewis Guns with such effect that the attack lost all its sting. The New-foundlanders had already proved their mettle on the first two days of the battle, and their prowess on the 3rd won them the sincere homage which good soldiers always pay to a brave feat of arms. The clannish Scots were proud to have them as brothers-in-arms.

While preparations for attack were steadily pushed on, each brigade was drawn back in succession for a short rest in the camps west of Ypres. The 104th Battalion of the Machine-Gun Corps, which had been attached to the Ninth since the 28th September, was reorganised into three companies, two of which were attached to the Twenty-ninth and Thirty-sixth Divisions respectively. Various minor changes were made on our front, which on the night of the 13th/14th extended from the north end of Ledeghem to a hundred yards south of the cross roads in St Pieter, the Twenty-ninth Division having again come into line on our right and taken over the position facing the village. Our chief annoyances during the period were caused by hostile area "shoots" and aerial bombing which did much damage in the transport lines, seventy-six artillery horses being killed in a single night. There were suspicions that the Germans were withdrawing, but constant and daring patrol work proved our fears to be groundless.

The boundaries within which the Ninth was to advance consisted of two parallel lines running slightly south-east from the flanks of our sector, and giving us a frontage of 1500 yards; but as our left wing was bent back and faced north-east, the jumping-off line measured nearly 2000 yards. It was therefore advisable to straighten the line and this could best be done by bringing our left up to the Menin–Roulers Railway, along which our right already ran. But to eliminate the risk of the right being barraged by the enemy while waiting for the left to come up, it was arranged that the whole line should advance simultaneously, and that the right would pause for thirty minutes on the light railway, 1000 yards east of the main railway, to enable the left to come into line and to give the Twenty-ninth Division time to clear the village of Ledeghem.

Apart from the enemy, the greatest obstacles seemed likely to be the Wulfdambeek stream, the village of Rolleghem Cappelle and dense masses of wire. Information about the width and depth of the stream was conflicting and scanty, but in order to run no risks eight light foot-bridges were prepared and carried by infantry parties, but, as it happened, they were not required, all the bridges having been left intact. The German wire was intensely strong; close in front of the left flank a belt over 100 yards in depth protected Mogg Farm and one or two "Pill-boxes" near it, and behind Rolleghem Cappelle four continuous bands stretched across our front from south-west to north-east. A similar barrier of equal depth extended along the reverse slope of a low but prominent ridge 4000 yards from our right flank. This ridge could be clearly seen from our line, and was at the extreme range at which the infantry could be covered by the gunners from their original positions; for this reason it was given as the first objective of the Ninth. Whether further progress could be made without artillery support would depend upon the tactical situation after the ridge was won. The advance to the objective was to be covered by the Ninth's usual barrage. A forward section of 18-pounders was detailed to work with each of the two assaulting battalions, and two 6-inch trench mortars, mounted for the first time on wheels, were to operate in conjunction with the infantry.

The attack was entrusted to the 28th Brigade, with the Newfoundlanders and Royal Scots Fusiliers in line, and for the purpose of maintaining liaison with the Belgians, a company of the Black Watch was to operate on the left of the 28th Brigade. The 27th Brigade was in reserve. One company of the 9th Machine-Gun Battalion was attached to each infantry brigade, the remaining one and a company of the 104th Battalion being detailed to barrage certain points to cover the infantry advance, and then to form part of the divisional reserve. The assault was to be delivered at 5.35 A.M.

On the night of the 12th/13th the 28th Brigade A.F.A. and four guns of each battery of the 50th and 51st Brigades moved up to forward positions, the rest of the sections following on the night of the 13th/14th. All the battery positions were within about 1500 yards of the front line, and forward guns of the 51st Brigade were to deal with "Pill-boxes" and farms at a range of 700 yards. Supplementary to the two mobile 6-inch trench mortars, five others were placed in position. The 27th Brigade moved up by battalions from the rest area near Ypres to Keiberg Spur on the 13th, and that night the 28th took over the line except the portion held by the liaison company of the Black Watch. There was great artillery activity during the relief, the enemy sending over a good deal of gas, and the Newfoundlanders and the Royal Scots Fusiliers had over fifty casualties on the way up to their assembly positions.

CHAPTER XVI

FROM LEDEGHEM TO THE SCHELDT

14TH OCTOBER TO 27TH OCTOBER 1918

THE barrage opened at 5.32 A.M. on the 14th October and three minutes later the infantry moved forward. The Black Watch company and the left of the Royal Scots Fusiliers experienced sharp fighting from the beginning. Mogg Farm, wire-bound, was obstinately defended, but regardless of losses the Black Watch pressed on and ejected the enemy from this stronghold. The wind was light and from the south-east, and the smoke of the barrage, adding density to the haze of a fine autumn morning produced an impenetrable fog about 500 yards from our line. As a result our troops found it difficult to keep direction, and some confusion arose but was speedily rectified. Though our troops lost the barrage it had a most salutary effect upon the enemy, and after the first resistance had been overcome the infantry made rapid progress. Rolleghem Cappelle, the first belt of wire, Neerhof, and the Wulfdambeek were carried with much less trouble than had been expected, and the abject failure of the Germans to offer any opposition worth the name behind such defences was a convincing proof of their loss of moral.

At the conclusion of the initial barrage the 28th Brigade A.F.A. reverted to Corps reserve, while the

50th and 51st Brigades moved forward to give further support to the infantry. Owing to difficulties of observation and communication they were not able at first to take much part, but the mobile trench mortars dealt effectively with a single field-gun and machine-guns which were opposing our troops on the east bank of the Wulfdambeek. No sooner were the infantry checked on the ridge south-west of Steenen Stampkot than the 50th Brigade came into action and helped them to capture the ridge by 9.30 A.M., and all the field-guns were moved up behind it.

On our left the 26th Brigade gradually became involved in the battle, partly by reason of the vigorous resistance offered by the German garrison of Mogg Farm, and partly owing to a gap developing between the 28th Brigade and the Belgians. North-east of Rolleghem Cappelle the Highlanders had a stiff time and during their advance several field-guns, firing over open sights, were enveloped and taken. Shortly after the capture of the ridge by the 28th Brigade, which was in touch with the Twenty-ninth Division, the Highlanders and Belgians entered Winkel St Eloi. By this time the Camerons as well as the Black Watch were in the fighting line.

About noon the infantry resumed their advance, supported at close range by the 50th and 51st Brigades R.F.A., but the enemy had rushed up a reserve division (6th Cavalry) to hold Laaga Cappelle Wood and Steenbeek and a desperate combat ensued. Forward patrols of the Newfoundlanders pressed the enemy so closely that they came under our own rifle-fire — luckily escaping casualties—and forced the Germans to continue their retirement. Hostile groups could be seen retreating through Laaga Cappelle Wood, and towards the north a solitary German, mounted and towing a machine-gun cart behind him, helped to fill in the landscape. The Highlanders, passing partially through the left of the 28th Brigade, which, after its long advance of the morning, was naturally somewhat exhausted, fought their way forward, with all three battalions in line, gained a footing in the wood and established a line on the western slope of a low hill to the north of it, but beyond this point progress was barred by fire from Hill 40, 500 yards east of the wood. Near the village of Steenbeek, amply furnished with machine-guns, the enemy managed to stem the advance of the 28th Brigade, the right flank of which was now ahead of the Twenty-ninth Division and was exposed.

During the severe fighting experienced by the Newfoundlanders one of their number won the V.C. Early in the push, when the attack was temporarily checked by the fire of a German battery at point-blank range, Private T. Ricketts went forward with his section commander and a Lewis Gun, with a view to outflanking the battery; but when they were still 300 yards away from the enemy they ran short of ammunition, and the Germans, hoping to save their guns, brought up the teams. Thereupon Private Ricketts darted back under a fierce fire from machine-guns with the battery, procured more ammunition, and returned at the double to the Lewis Gun, which he fired with such accuracy that the Germans with their gun teams were compelled to take refuge in a farm. The rest of the platoon was now able to press on without casualties, and 4 field-guns, 4 machine-guns, and 8 prisoners were taken. Subsequently a fifth field-gun was intercepted by our fire and captured.

The artillery supported the infantry with magnificent dash, and Brig.-General Wainwright must have been very proud of the work accomplished by his

gunners. Our batteries going into action presented
the most sensational and picturesque spectacle of the
advance, and introduced into the war a tinge of the
glamour and romance that seemed for ever to have
departed from it. Tearing along at full gallop, C/50
Battery under Major Hoggart plunged almost into the
infantry firing line, quickly unlimbered and at 800
yards' range turned its guns against the foe in Steenbeek with a rapidity and precision that amazed and
thrilled the infantry. The disgruntled Germans bringing
up a field-gun had the great fortune to wipe out one
team. A/50 Battery, coming up in gallant style, joined
C/50 and their combined fire forced the enemy out
of the village, but owing to the low trajectory our
guns could not touch him in his cleverly chosen
position at the eastern edge of Laaga Cappelle Wood.
Two batteries of the 51st Brigade dashed over the
ridge just in rear of our infantry, but were unable
to come into action because of the hostile shelling of
Steenen Stampkot.

By 3 P.M. the 27th Brigade was concentrated behind
the ridge west of Steenen Stampkot, and the 12th
Royal Scots were sent forward to support the 28th;
but since it was clear that the Germans were occupying
in force a naturally strong position, and that nothing
but a properly organised assault was likely to succeed,
it was decided to postpone the attack until next day,
when the troops would be fresher and more artillery
ammunition available. In the evening, the 28th Brigade
took over a part of the line held by the 26th, thus
making a front of 1200 yards, while the Highlanders
continued to hold the remaining 300 and fully 700
yards of line in Belgian territory. The Third Belgian
Division, under General Joostens, on our left had
fought with admirable courage and *élan*, and at the end

of the day had its right ahead of our left. Ever since
the 28th September the co-operation with King Albert's
army had been excellent, and the Ninth never desired
on its flanks better troops than the Belgians proved
themselves to be.

Every preparation was now made for the renewal of
the attack. The 28th Brigade A.F.A., which was
again attached to the Division, joined the 50th and
51st Brigades in the line, and two 60-pounder batteries
and three sections of 6 - inch howitzers came into
position. "B" and "C" Companies of the Ninth
Machine-Gun Battalion took up barrage positions on
the ridge south-west of Steenen Stampkot. Zero was
arranged for 9 A.M., because it was impossible to bring
up an adequate supply of ammunition before that hour
and it was essential that the men should have a good
night's rest. The objective was the same as on the
previous day, and after its capture the Division was
to exploit towards the Lys. The operation was to be
carried out by the 11th and 12th Royal Scots, who were
to pass through the two brigades in the line.

Punctually at 9 A.M. on the 15th the 11th Royal Scots
advanced at the double under a smoke-screen against
Hill 40 to the north, but owing to the exact position
of our forward posts being uncertain the barrage was
placed beyond this hill. The comparatively late hour
of attack and the wonderfully heavy barrage which
the artillery and machine-guns were able to provide,
took the enemy unawares. Nevertheless the 11th
Royal Scots suffered an unexpected jar at the start;
raking machine-gun fire was opened on them from
the hill behind Laaga Cappelle Wood. But the assailants, adroitly and boldly led, after clearing the wood,
advanced towards Hill 40. The slight delay gave two
machine-gun groups on the Hill time to prepare, and

their fire drove the Royal Scots to earth. At this juncture Corporal Elcock, valiantly braving death, rushed forward with a Lewis Gun and killed the two men manning one of the guns, then diving into their shelter he turned his gun against the other group and knocked it out. A V.C. was awarded for this heroic and timely feat, which allowed the whole line to press on and capture the Hill. On the heels of the 11th followed Lieut.-Colonel Murray with the 12th Royal Scots who, after passing the wood, swung south and ejected the enemy from Steenbeek village and Hill 40 to the south.

The line was then reformed under cover of a protective barrage put down by our guns on Heule Wood and Gemeenhof. Resuming the pursuit, the 12th Royal Scots mopped up the enemy posts in Heule Wood and reached the Snephoek–Heule road, where a slight pause was made until touch was obtained with the divisions on the wings, both of which were making good progress. By 11.30 A.M. the Royal Scot battalions had won the objective on the Heule–Ingelmunster Railway, all opposition from trench mortars and machine-guns having been overcome by the infantry with the assistance of our forward guns. For a short time our men on the Railway were harried by two hostile field-guns, but Captain Brock of the 12th Royal Scots after a fine piece of stalking shot the crews and captured the guns.

Behind the 27th Brigade came the 1/1st Yorks Cyclists, commanded by Lieut.-Colonel Thomson, and the 11th Motor Machine-Gun Battery; under the orders of Brig.-General Croft they now passed through the infantry. The cyclists displayed extraordinary pluck and daring, and their close pursuit prevented all chance of German reorganisation. One company stormed

Stokerij and then pushed on to the Chapel north of Abeelhoek, where it was finally stopped by machine-gun fire from the ridge between Abeelhoek and the Lys. Other cyclists, after occupying Le Chat, dashed into Cuerne about 2.45 P.M., just as the Germans were hurriedly evacuating it. There were several skirmishes, and amongst the victims were two Uhlan officers. Making for the river, the cyclists came under heavy machine-gun fire from the east bank of the Lys, and took up positions covering the southern and eastern outskirts of Cuerne. A stream of hostile transport was moving in panic haste along the Courtrai–Harlebeke road, and the cyclists and the men of the motor machine - gun battery enjoyed effective shooting at targets it was almost impossible to miss.

The infantry followed the more mobile groups. A short distance from the Railway the 27th Brigade had some trouble on the left, because our immediate neighbours, the Third Belgian Division, did not advance at first beyond the objective, as Ingelmunster farther north had been retaken by a German counter-attack. Consequently the 11th Royal Scots were enfiladed from Heetje, and were obliged to attack the village. It was captured only after a severe fight, and the Royal Scots were so far delayed that they did not reach the ridge between Abeelhoek and the Lys till dusk. Their attempt to storm this position was unsuccessful, but the Germans withdrew in the course of the night. Eventually Heetje was taken over from the 27th Brigade by the Third Belgian Division, whose left wing was thrown back to the Railway. The aggressiveness of the enemy near Ingelmunster seemed to point to a counter-attack from the north-east, so the 28th Brigade, which had advanced to Cappelle St Catherine was ordered to be ready to protect our left wing.

The situation on this flank improved greatly during the night, when the Belgians, pressing on, seized Bavichove and Hulste.

On our right there was not the same anxiety, and the 12th Royal Scots and 6th K.O.S.B. moved steadily forward, the leading troops of the former entering Cuerne between 3 and 4 P.M., and the latter relieving the cyclists about 6.30 P.M. Cuerne was not in the Ninth area, but the Twenty-ninth Division had tough work to clear Heule, and was slightly in rear. It was known to be moving forward, but the Ninth was prevented from securing the crossings over the river that day by the fact that until after dark the situation on our left was unsatisfactory and on our right uncertain. The 6th K.O.S.B. and the 11th Royal Scots held the divisional front during the night.

From the hour in which Ledeghem was captured, every village disgorged a number of Belgian civilians, and Cuerne was filled with them. They were warned that it was dangerous to remain, but stating that the Germans had promised not to shell Cuerne, the great majority of them refused to leave their abodes. During the night the village was heavily gas-shelled by the enemy, and the sufferings of many of these poor people must have been dreadful. Posts were pushed close to the river after dark, but all the bridges had been destroyed by the enemy.

On the 16th Brig.-General Croft drew up his plans for forcing the passage of the Lys. Guns, both field and heavy, were moved into position to cover this operation, and arrangements were made for the construction of bridges. The 51st Brigade R.F.A. took up positions on the general line of the Heule–Stokerij road, each brigade sending forward two guns in close support, while four howitzers of the 50th Brigade went into action in Cuerne.   The 28th Brigade A.F.A. was active in rear of the 50th and 51st, and twelve 60-pounders and eight 6-inch howitzers of the 59th R.G.A. had opened fire by the evening.   At 2 P.M. and again at 5 P.M. all the Field Artillery Brigades shelled the Courtrai–Harlebeke road where the K.O.S.B. had observed numerous parties of Germans, and excellent work was accomplished by our forward guns in silencing machine-guns firing from houses in Harlebeke, a large and substantial village.

Brig.-General Croft's plan arranged that the river, about seventy feet wide, should be crossed at two places simultaneously; on the left, the 11th Royal Scots with the aid of the 90th Field Coy. R.E. were to throw a bridge over the ruins of the Hoogebrug Bridge on the Harlebeke–Stokerij road and attack the village of Harlebeke; on the right, the K.O.S.B. were to pass over by boats and improvised bridges in the loop of the river south-east of Cuerne, secure the Courtrai–Harlebeke Railway with the high ground east of it, and effect a junction with the 11th Royal Scots at the level-crossing in Harlebeke.

The attempt was made at 8 P.M.   On the left, it was completely repulsed in spite of the gallant and costly efforts of the Royal Scots and sappers of the 90th Field Company, who were swept away by machine-gun fire at close range.   On the right, Lieut.-Colonel Ker sent three companies across a boat bridge erected by the sappers of the 64th Field Company.   Under a powerful barrage of H.E. and smoke, the K.O.S.B. scrambled up the marshy slope of the east bank, and reaching the Courtrai–Harlebeke road where several Germans were captured, pushed out towards the Railway. The left company then moved north towards Harlebeke but met with obstinate resistance, and the battalion was

2 B

ordered to maintain the ground it had won, holding the loop of the river with an outpost line on the Railway.

A half-hearted counter-stroke during the night against the right flank garrison of the bridgehead was easily defeated. Before dawn the Sappers had constructed a relief bridge close to the first, and by these two bridges, two sections of the 9th Machine-gun Battalion and two platoons of the 2nd Hampshire Regiment (Twenty-ninth Division) crossed. The left company of the K.O.S.B., which had suffered severely in the attempt to force Harlebeke, was relieved by the reserve company and drawn back to the west of the Lys.

Owing to the failure on the left the operation had fallen short of complete success. It was suggested that the rest of the brigade should be taken over the river during the hours of darkness by the K.O.S.B. bridges, and an assault made on Harlebeke at dawn with a view to extending the bridgehead, but it was ultimately decided to consolidate the ground that had been gained. Our position on the east of the river could hardly be considered satisfactory, and it was doubtful if under the conditions of modern war it could be regarded as a bridgehead in the true sense of the term, since the enemy's guns in Harlebeke commanded the river and were in a position to demolish the bridges when daylight came; in fact, if the Germans had possessed a tithe of the spirit that animated them before April there would have been good reason to dread the utter destruction of our forces on the east of the Lys. The attempt was made because it was evident that the enemy's moral was on the wane.

The 17th October was a day of acute anxiety. At 5.10 A.M. the Germans barraged the Courtrai–Harlebeke road and a few minutes later their infantry

advanced to the attack. The centre of the K.O.S.B.
was pierced and four machine-guns were knocked
out, but the flanks held firm and a timely bayonet
charge by the reserve of the right company under
Captain White put the enemy to flight. At the same
time the centre company was rallied by Major
McDiarmid of the 9th Machine-gun Battalion, who
had swum the river under heavy fire, and it reoccupied
its position. On the first news of the attack two
companies of the 12th Royal Scots, who had been
warned to be ready to reinforce, crossed the river
with fine steadiness under intense artillery-fire which
speedily sank both bridges. This addition to the
garrison now made our position on the east bank
reasonably secure ; for the dismal failure of the enemy's
counter-stroke showed clearly that he was losing heart.
Over thirty dead Germans were counted after the
bayonet charge, and of those who fled many were
shot down by our riflemen and Lewis Gunners.

But though the attack had been brilliantly repulsed
and was not renewed, the position of the K.O.S.B. and
the Royal Scots caused Brig.-General Croft the keenest
concern. The slightest movement provoked machine-
gun fire, and as both bridges had been sunk the men
could be neither reinforced nor withdrawn during daylight without enormous losses and the risk of virtual
annihilation. Nevertheless it was necessary to keep the
garrison supplied with ammunition and rations, and two
platoons of the 12th Royal Scots, in single file, working their way along the wreckage of the bridges and
wading over their waists in water under a constant
fusilade of bullets, crossed the river with supplies
of ammunition. In similar fashion, runners succeeded
in maintaining communication between the troops on
both sides of the Lys. Aeroplanes were also employed

and carried over abundant rations and ammunition, which they dropped by means of parachutes. Thus with ample provisions the men on the east bank were in good heart, and later when they were withdrawn they declared that they had never been so well fed in all their previous war experience.

About noon instructions were received from the II. Corps to make no further attempt to establish bridgeheads across the Lys. Our efforts were to be devoted to the reconnaissance of suitable crossing places and to the collection of bridging material. If it were practicable the K.O.S.B. bridgehead was to be maintained, and this matter was left to the discretion of the G.O.C. But since the Ninth was now to take over the front north of Hoogebrug as far as the junction of the Vaarneuykbeek with the Lys northeast of Bavichove, the decision as to the bridgehead was left to the Twenty-ninth Division, which relieved our troops on the east bank after dusk by means of boats and bridges constructed by the Sappers of the 63rd Field Company. Brig.-General Freyburg, who went over in person, decided to abandon the bridgehead, and the 27th Brigade on being drawn back was concentrated in the vicinity of Laaga Cappelle Wood.

The operations[1] in Flanders had fully realised the expectations of Marshal Foch and Sir Douglas Haig. The enemy was obliged to relinquish his grip on the Flanders coast and to withdraw his forces to the neighbourhood of Ghent, and farther south he was compelled to abandon Lille on the 17th October and soon after the industrial centres of Tourcoing and

---

[1] These earned another " mention " for the Division. " In these successful operations the Ninth Division, forming part of the command of General Jacobs' II. Corps, has again fought with great distinction."

(*Extract from official Communiqué*, 16*th October*.)

Roubaix. It was necessary to follow up our successes and to press our advantage. Accordingly preparations were made on the 18th and 19th for crossing the Lys on a large scale, and the night of the 19th/20th was fixed for the attempt. New gun positions were selected and ammunition brought up, and the 26th and 28th Brigades with the Sappers reconnoitred all possible crossings.

The boundary between the Ninth and the Twenty-ninth Division stretched from Hoogebrug – south of Ingoyghem – to the Scheldt south of Trappelstraat. On our left was the Thirty-sixth, which had relieved the Third Belgian Division, and the boundary on this flank ran from the junction of the Plaatsbeek and the Lys – south of Beveren – north of Vichte and Ingoyghem – to the Scheldt north-west of Berchem. Our first objective was the line running north-east and south-west about 500 yards east of the Lys, and the attack was to be carried out by the 26th and 28th Brigades. Divisions were allowed to choose their own time for crossing the river and securing this objective, but all had to be ready to take part in a general advance from it at 6 A.M. on the 20th. The objective for the next advance was the St Louis – Vichte road, but, if the army on our left did not move forward, then the line St Louis–Belgiek about four miles from the Lys.

The Sappers of the 63rd and 64th Field Companies, assisted by two companies of the Pioneers, were responsible for the bridging and ferrying arrangements on the front of the Ninth. Each field company was to throw two single duckboard barrel bridges sufficiently strong to take infantry in file, and to launch and navigate two half pontoons and three rafts, each capable of taking eight men. Lieut.-Colonel Hickling's task was far from enviable; all the pontoons of the

Division were at the bottom of the Lys and all the material to make bridges had to be collected without delay. Since on our front the left bank of the river was exposed for a distance of several hundreds of yards, it was impossible to place the bridging material in position before dark. As it was calculated that our preparations would not be completed till 11 P.M., this was the hour arranged for the launching of the pontoons and rafts. The Ninth and Twenty-ninth Divisions agreed to go over simultaneously, but the Thirty-sixth decided to cross earlier. The first troops were to be ferried over, and it was hoped that the light bridges would be ready by 11.15 P.M.

In effecting the passage of the leading troops, surprise [1] was of course aimed at, and for that reason no artillery-fire was to open until 11.15 P.M., though forward guns were to be prepared to fire at point-blank range at two farms, which being near the crossings might be troublesome. From 11.15 P.M. to 11.45 P.M. an artillery barrage, thickened by machine-guns, was to be put down to cover the forming-up of the infantry on the line of the Harlebeke–Beveren road, after which it was to move forward to a line in front of the first objective. In order to avoid close range machine-gun fire from the houses in Harlebeke, no passage was to be attempted south of the junction of the Vaarneuyk-beek and the Lys, and an enfilade smoke-barrage was to blind the northern end of the village while the crossing was being effected. In the afternoon the various divisions were ordered by the Corps to accelerate the passage of the river; in the case of the Ninth this was impossible, but the Twenty-ninth and Thirty-sixth both went over before the hour originally fixed.

---

[1] This however was practically impossible when the crossing was not to be carried out simultaneously by the attacking divisions.

The enemy's bombing planes and artillery were uncommonly active during the evening and Stokerij and Heetje, important centres of communication, were subjected to concentrations of gas-shell at intervals and to steady harassing fire from 9 to 11.30 P.M. There was also considerable shelling of our forward areas, due probably to the alarm caused by the crossing of the divisions on our flanks. The enemy was thoroughly roused, and with his guns and trench mortars fired vigorously but somewhat aimlessly on our bank of the river.

On our right the Camerons were the first to go over, two companies passing on to the first objective while the remainder mopped up Harlebeke. The Seaforths followed, coming up on the left of the Camerons. On the sector of the 28th Brigade the enemy's fire was heavy and accurate; one bridge was broken and the other badly damaged, while both pontoons were holed and the launching of the rafts was delayed. The casualties sustained and the confusion caused were undoubtedly due to the fact that a simultaneous crossing by all the attacking divisions had not been arranged. Nevertheless the "Rifles" and Royal Scots Fusiliers were concentrated on the right bank of the river half an hour after midnight. This very creditable achievement under continuous fire was a convincing demonstration of the fine discipline and resource of the infantry and sappers concerned. By 1 A.M. the Thirty-sixth Division had two battalions over the Lys and the Twenty-ninth one, a second having been stayed by machine-gun fire. Though the two attacking battalions of the 28th Brigade had crossed, they experienced so much difficulty in securing connection with each other and with the Thirty-sixth Division that for several hours it was uncertain

if it would be possible to continue the advance at
6 A.M.; but by 5.15 A.M. all four of our front line
battalions were in touch with one another on the
first objective except on the left, where our line was
about 300 yards behind, owing to the resistance of
Beveren.

Both brigades moved forward at 6 A.M. on the 20th
under cover of a barrage of H.E. and smoke. The Royal
Scots Fusiliers had a brisk engagement at Beveren,
which they helped the men of the Thirty-sixth Division
to master, but apart from this there was little opposition
at the start. By 8 A.M. Deerlyck fell into our hands,
and as soon as the barrage ceased, the 7th Motor
Machine-gun Brigade and the 1/1st Yorks Cyclists,
who had been ferried across on rafts, passed through the
infantry. The machine-gun brigade and two companies
of the cyclists moving straight down the Deerlyck–
Vichte road entered Belgiek, but were brought to a
standstill a short distance beyond it by machine-gun
fire. Another cyclist company, taking the road running
south-east from Vichte, captured 4 field-guns, 40
prisoners and much material, knocked out the team
of another field-gun who were attempting to escape,
and finally took up a position on the St Louis–Vichte
road. Other cyclists on our left wing compelled the
enemy to abandon a heavy howitzer near Knock and
drove him into the village; four more heavy howitzers
were afterwards found abandoned just south of Belgiek
cross roads.

It was on the wings that the infantry had most
trouble. The country over which the Highlanders had
to progress was marshy and in parts flooded, but by
9.30 A.M. they had reached the Railway where a German
field-gun engaged them at close range. Two guns however of the machine-gun battery went to their assist-

ance, and a steady advance was maintained despite
ever-increasing opposition.   Meantime the Sappers had
completed a pontoon bridge south-east of Bavichove,
and by 9.50 A.M. one battery of the 50th Brigade
R.F.A., followed by the mobile medium trench mortars
and later by the rest of the divisional artillery, had
crossed the Lys.   At 10.30 A.M. both the 26th and 28th
Brigades were believed to be on their objective and a
further advance was ordered to be made at 12.30 P.M.

By that time German resistance had stiffened.   St
Louis was in our hands, but the 26th Brigade was
being subjected to flanking fire from the Wolfsberg,
which our gunners dared not shell as they did not
know the exact position of the troops of the Twenty-
ninth Division, in whose area it was.   In the centre,
Vichte Station was captured after stubborn fighting
by the Newfoundlanders, and this gave rise to an
erroneous report that the village, which lay 1000 yards
to the east of it, was also in our possession.   As a
matter of fact a company and a half of the Royal Scots
Fusiliers [1] did force their way into that village but were
surrounded, and it is significant of the moral of the
enemy that he did not venture to press his advantage.
Some of our men broke through the German cordon
after dark ; others sheltered in cellars with the Belgian
civilians until the village was taken two days later,
when they rejoined their battalion.   A French force
was now on the left of the Second Army, but on this
day it made such slow progress that the Thirty-sixth
Division was compelled to hold a very extended line,
stretching from Straate to the Gaverbeek north-west
of Belgiek, and this strain on the Thirty-sixth inevitably

---

[1] Major King who was commanding the Royal Scots Fusiliers was
wounded near Belgiek, and the command of the battalion was taken over
by Captain J. S. Glass.

reacted on our left wing, which was much exposed. On our right the Twenty-ninth Division, being held up, was consolidating on the line St Louis–Krote–Pont Levis No. 2, while the division on its right was some distance behind it.

To allow the units on the flanks to come up in line with them, the Ninth and Twenty-ninth Divisions undertook no operations on the 21st. The sector occupied by the Ninth was a very unpleasant one as it was overlooked by the enemy, who shelled one farm after another, devoting, it seemed, particular attention to those occupied by Brigade and Battalion H.Q. The 12th Royal Scots were unlucky enough to lose their popular and gallant adjutant, Captain McKinley, who was hit by three successive shells. On the night of the 21st/22nd the Twenty-ninth Division took over St Louis from the 26th Brigade, which was now able to hold its reduced front with the Black Watch alone. On the same night the 27th relieved the 28th Brigade with the 12th Royal Scots.

The objectives of the Ninth for the 22nd were Vichte, Hill 50, and Ingoyghem, and the assault was to be delivered by the 11th Royal Scots and 6th K.O.S.B. at 9 A.M. The former were to clear Vichte and Hill 50, at which point the latter were to pass through and exploit in the direction of Ingoyghem. The Highland Brigade was ordered to be ready to support the attack and was concentrated north-east of the St Louis–Vichte road.

There was delay at the start, and some confusion was caused by a dense fog produced by hostile gas-shelling and by the smoke of our barrage drifting back on the infantry. The fog however blinded the Germans in Vichte, and the 11th Royal Scots entering the village surprised the garrison and then moved on

INGOYGHEM AND OOTEGHEM. 'THE LAST RIDGE'

towards Hill 50 ; a few posts were missed but these
were accounted for by the K.O.S.B. On leaving
the village the Royal Scots came under heavy fire
from Klijtberg and Hill 50 and were checked. For
a time the situation was very obscure, and Lieut.-
Colonel Ker, who had led his battalion along the railway to the bridge south-east of Vichte, had the greatest
difficulty in ascertaining the whereabouts of the leading
Royal Scots. Our gunners exhibited once more the
daring that had characterised their efforts throughout
the advance, and the guns of B/50 Battery were already
in action east of the village. Boldly reconnoitring on
horseback Captain Andrews located a farm near Hill
50 from which the enemy was firing, and suggested
to Lieut.-Colonel Ker, who had already ascertained
that Hill 50 was firmly held by the Germans, that
covered by the fire of the gunners his battalion should
assault the Hill. This was done, and shortly after noon
the K.O.S.B. stormed Hill 50. But any movement
towards Ingoyghem was out of the question ; losses
had been heavy and the hostile machine-gun fire from
the village and buildings near it was accurate and
severe.

The Black Watch, who were now temporarily
attached to the 27th Brigade, filled a gap of 1000
yards between its right and the left of the Twenty-ninth
Division at the end of the day's fighting. By nightfall
our line ran from the road junction a mile east of
St Louis to Hill 50, and thence to the south-east of
the Klijtberg, and the troops were in touch with the
divisions on both flanks. There were rumours of a
German retirement in the north, but on our front the
enemy showed great activity and bombarded our area
savagely from time to time with gas. The Twenty-
ninth Division was now relieved by the Forty-first, and

the 27th Brigade by the 26th and 28th Brigades on the night of the 24th/25th.

At 9 A.M. on the 25th the 26th and 28th Brigades with the Camerons, Seaforths, Royal Scots Fusiliers,[1] and the "Rifles" in line, resumed the operations against the Ooteghem–Ingoyghem Ridge in conjunction with the Forty-first and Thirty-sixth Divisions. The attack was made under cover of a creeping barrage of smoke and H.E., which was more intense than usual because our artillery had been augmented by the 17th Brigade R.F.A. (Twenty-ninth Division) ; two companies of the 9th Machine-gun Battalion and one company of the 104th Machine-gun Battalion also supported the infantry by firing concentrations on certain points and by barraging roads in rear of the enemy's position. The German artillery-fire had been so violent during the evening that four gun teams of a company of the 9th Battalion were completely wiped out before the attack commenced.

On the fall of the barrage our infantry immediately dashed forward but met with most stubborn opposition. The enemy seemed resolved to dispute every inch of ground, and shortly after zero he put down a fierce counter-barrage on our leading troops and swept the ranks of the 28th Brigade with gusts of machine-gun fire ; but in spite of grave losses the infantry made headway and by 10.30 A.M. some of them were on the objective from Klein Ronsse Hill to the Chapel near Ingoyghem. But all the ground had not been cleared ; every farm with its steading was a centre of resistance and furious conflicts were being waged in rear of the objective. The leadership was excellent. Brig.-

---

[1] On the 23rd Lieut.-Colonel R. Campbell, D.S.O., who had seen a great deal of service with the Fifty-first Division, took over the command of the battalion.

General Hore Ruthven and Brig.-General Jack were constantly in the stormiest parts of their sectors. Lieut.-Colonel Campbell of the Royal Scots Fusiliers was ubiquitous; clad in his jerkin, since the day was warm though the night had been cold, he was perspiring profusely from the kit he carried, his rapid pace, the distance he had covered, and the discomfort of one or two nasty crawls, but he seemed to be absolutely tireless. On our left the Thirty-sixth Division had failed to carry the slopes of Kleineberg, and word was received that the right division had also been checked. It was therefore inadvisable to press on from the ridge and the infantry were commanded to consolidate the ground which they had won at no slight cost.

Our gains had been substantial; they comprised the entire Ooteghem–Ingoyghem Ridge, the last commanding position in the Ninth's area of operations. During the afternoon and evening our position was subjected to galling artillery and machine-gun fire from the east and north-east. The enemy clung tenaciously to the Kleineberg, from which an attack by the Thirty-sixth Division at 5 P.M. failed to dislodge him. During the night of the 25th/26th the Germans surrendered their last hold on Ooteghem and a patrol of the Camerons pushing past Klooster Hoek and Langestraat gained the banks of the Scheldt at Waermaerde; on its return it met and attacked a party of the enemy, driving it out of Okkerwijk. On the left patrols of the 28th Brigade went out but could not make much progress since the enemy still occupied Meulewijk and Bergwijk, which dominated all the country east of Ingoyghem.

The men were keen to follow up their victory, but they had now reached the limit of physical endurance. Our losses, though insignificant compared with the results achieved, had been serious, for practically no

reinforcements had arrived to fill up gaps. There had
been no contraction of front to balance our diminishing
numbers and consequently each successive advance
entailed increasing effort. On the 25th October
battalions could muster scarcely 200 bayonets, and
daily it was becoming more doubtful if the Division
would have sufficient weight to carry it forward against
anything like a resolute defence. Hence the weakness
of the units and the exhaustion of the men rendered
it desirable, if not necessary, to withdraw the whole
Division for a rest; and its relief by the Thirty-first
Division took place on the nights of the 26th/27th and
27th/28th, when it went back to the area near Harlebeke and Cuerne.

This was the last operation of the Division in the
war. Since the 28th September it had covered over
twenty-six miles of ground and advanced from Ypres
to the banks of the Scheldt. It had captured over
2600 prisoners and many guns,[1] but the trophies gained
were more numerous than were recorded; the advance
was so rapid that there was no opportunity of making
a proper search of the battlefield. And our losses
suffered during this amazing march, involving constant
fighting, amounted to only 188 officers and 3604 other
ranks, just 1000 more than the number of prisoners
captured. It was certainly the most spectacular of
the Ninth's many successes. Throughout the advance
the admirable co-operation of all branches of the
Division had been the principal factor in contributing to
this glorious result. The spirit of the Division was
nowhere more typified than in the personal example
of General Tudor and his staff, Lieut.-Colonel Mudie,
the G.S.O.I., with his thoughtful, cool head, and
Lieut.-Colonel Jeffcoat, the A.A. & Q.M.G., with his

---

[1] Prisoners captured, 54 officers, 2555 other ranks; guns captured, 64.

typically exact "Q" arrangements. The G.O.C. during
the battles was invariably in or very near the front
line, at the top of insecure church spires survey-
ing the landscape, or on horseback in shelled areas,
and could always decide with personal knowledge.
Incorrigibly dapper, he was invariably calm, quiet,
human, and entirely regardless of his own safety; it
was no wonder that the Division trusted him implicitly.
In similar fashion Brig.-Generals Hore Ruthven, Croft,
and Jack were never far from the hottest encounters
and the ready judgment of these experienced officers
was of the utmost value to the G.O.C. The leading
of the infantry had been daring and skilful, while
the men responded to every demand of their officers
with unfailing cheerfulness and determination. As had
always been the case in the Ninth, infantry and gunners
worked splendidly together, and the former will never
forget the intrepid dash of the latter who assisted them
with such admirable and dexterous promptitude. Nor
must the assiduous though less showy efforts of the
Sappers, the Pioneers, the R.A.M.C., and A.S.C. go
unmentioned; its very best work was freely given by
each branch and was necessary for the common success.

CHAPTER XVII

CONCLUSION

28TH OCTOBER 1918 TO 15TH MARCH 1919

AT the beginning of November 1918 Germany stood alone against her enemies. The tottering empire of Austria soon shared the fate of Bulgaria and Turkey. The Italian armies, which during the critical summer months had remained inactive, in the late autumn hastened to join in the general onslaught against the crumbling resistance of the Central European States. On the 23rd October the offensive began, and four days later the Piave was crossed by British and Italian forces. As a result of this blow the mouldering edifice of the Hapsburg dominions immediately collapsed, and on the 3rd November Austria[1] accepted the armistice terms of General Diaz.

The military position of Germany was utterly hopeless. While maintaining for a time her grasp on the Meuse against the Americans, she was wholly unable to arrest the progress of the British armies on the northern wing of the far-flung battle front. In the Battles of the Selle, 17th to 25th October, the British

---

[1] Near the end of October a staff officer of the Ninth went to the Divisional Signals Office to find out if there was any news. The answer was "Yes, sir, Austria has thrown in her 'mit.'" It was thus that a phlegmatic Scottish soldier announced the fall of the ancient Empire of the Hapsburgs, the oldest reigning family in Europe and heirs of the Holy Roman Empire!

forced the passage of the river, and advanced to the line of the Sambre. Bankrupt of hope and device Ludendorff surrendered to the logic of events, and resigned on the 26th October. Surmounting their commissariat difficulties the Americans broke the enemy line on the southern flank of the battle, and this disaster destroyed all chance of the German army being safely withdrawn behind the Rhine for the protection of the Fatherland. The Allied forces were rapidly converging on the hostile lines of communication, and after the great British victory of the 4th November, when the Sambre was crossed and large numbers of prisoners were captured, the retreat developed into a rout. Though the pursuit was retarded by difficulties of transport owing to roads and railways having been mined by the enemy, it was beyond doubt that but for the Armistice on the 11th November the German forces would have been compelled ignominiously to lay down their arms. The Armistice was in fact a capitulation.

During these fateful days the Ninth was reorganising near Harlebeke. After a short spell of rest the troops recovered their wonted vigour and the drawn, haggard look disappeared from the faces of officers and men. On the 5th November the whole Division was reviewed by H.M. the King of the Belgians. After the ceremony H.M. the Queen of the Belgians requested General Tudor to cut from his sleeve the divisional sign (a silver thistle on a blue background); he did so, and then she pinned it on her breast. Ever after the G.O.C. wore only one badge. Every preparation was made for the Division to return to the front line, but as the days passed it became increasingly doubtful if it would see any more fighting; for it was known that the Germans were negotiating for terms, and even the consistent pessimists of all ranks admitted that there was a chance of the war being finished before Christmas. The spread of social agitation within the Fatherland and the flight of the Kaiser to Holland on the 9th November made it impossible for the enemy to do anything but surrender. On the evening of the 10th the news filtered through to the men that Germany had accepted the Armistice terms and that hostilities were to cease on the next day at 11 A.M. The event occasioned the wildest rejoicings and all units in the Division celebrated it by a special divine service on the 11th.

During the following days camp gossip was chiefly concerned with the question as to which British divisions would have the honour of marching through Germany to the bridgehead, which in accordance with the terms of the Armistice was to be formed across the Rhine. There was great jubilation when it became known that the Ninth had been chosen as the left division of the Army of Occupation. It was the only division of the New Armies to take part in the triumphal march.

The march began on the 14th November. Until the 4th December our route lay through the occupied portion of Belgium, and the troops received an exuberant welcome from the officials and inhabitants of the villages and towns through which they passed. Usually the main streets were spanned by arches gaudily decorated with streamers and the flags of the Allies. Here and there effigies clad in the familiar field-grey and suspended from gibbets, revealed clearly the intense hatred of the Belgians for the vanquished foe. The liberated people frequently evinced a childish delight in displaying the ornaments, goods and wines which they had succeeded in concealing from the

invaders during the four years of war. Every place
gave evidence of the universal respect and affection of
the people for their heroic monarch, and there were
tremendous rejoicings when on the 22nd November
King Albert made his formal entry into the capital.
On that occasion the Division was represented by
the massed pipers of the Highland Brigade and a
company of the same brigade, with platoons from
each of the three battalions and the 9th Seaforths.
Officers and men were also given an opportunity of
visiting the city, and so overwhelming was the welcome
of the citizens that they had the greatest difficulty
in tearing themselves away from the attractions of
Brussels.

On the 4th December the Ninth left the friendly
soil of Belgium and entered the unravaged territory
of the enemy, most of the battalions passing the
boundary post to the tune of " A' the Blue Bonnets
are over the Border." The atmosphere here was icy
compared with that of Belgium. A few of the German
civilians, well versed in military customs, tested the
temper of the men by attempting to break through the
ranks, but so rough and unpleasant were their experiences that they found few imitators. Apart from this
show of bravado there was no expression of hostility.
Several of the inhabitants showed signs of terror,
evidently anticipating reprisals for the outrages which
their soldiers had committed in Belgium and in
France, but they were soon reassured when it became
apparent that our men were neither vindictive nor
malicious. Some of our wilder spirits regarded German
shops and cafés as places that might be legitimately
looted, but that practice was peremptorily repressed,
and as a whole the troops showed the same scrupulous
regard for the property of the enemy as for that of

their allies.[1] Owing to the Revolution in Germany and the consequent collapse of regular government, riots broke out in the large towns, and in order to save Cologne the 28th Brigade was sent up there by rail at the request of the German authorities. The stately city of the Rhine was reached by the remainder of the Division on the 9th and 10th December.

Here three days were spent in cleaning up kit and polishing brass; then on the 13th December the Ninth crossed the Rhine by the boat bridge at Mulheim. Several of the units had to march a long way to reach the starting-point, and there was slight confusion which was regrettable, as it was the intention of our authorities to impress[2] the enemy with our discipline and organisation. The salute was taken by the British Military Governor, Sir Charles Fergusson, but the ceremony was spoiled by the torrents of rain which descended all day. By the 15th the Division had taken up its position on the perimeter of the bridgehead near Solingen, Wald, and Haan, D.H.Q. being established at Ohligs.

Thirty-two days had been spent in proceeding from Harlebeke to the perimeter. On fifteen of them no advance was made in order to allow the Supply Services to bring up rations and stores which had to be conveyed by motor lorries since all the railways had been damaged. During the other days, an average of $11\frac{1}{2}$ miles per day was covered; the total distance was 193 miles.

It was eminently desirable that the men should

[1] The fact that some Germans were relieved of their watches may have been due to a custom that had sprung up during four years of war, or to some confusion of mind about the " Watch on the Rhine "!

[2] The sight of a field ambulance racing through the streets of Cologne, with the R.A.M.C. men running breathlessly behind it, in order to reach its position in time is believed to have enormously impressed the citizens.

realise in some tangible form that they had won the war. Only first-rate billets were accepted, and burgomasters and their staffs were badgered until these buildings were satisfactorily equipped with beds, cooking ranges, and up - to - date sanitary arrangements. Halls were taken over for concerts and reading-rooms, and cinematographs were run for the entertainment of the men. Parties were granted permission to visit Cologne, and every unit was given an allotment of tickets for the Opera House; but the boon most cherished by the men was the liberty to travel by tram or rail without payment. If there was little friendliness between the troops and the inhabitants, there was practically no friction, and the discipline of the soldiers and the fairness of their behaviour were gratefully acknowledged by the townspeople. The first great difficulty of "Q" was the provision of the Christmas dinner. Germany had barely sufficient food to feed her own people, and supplies had to be drawn from the rear areas. Unfortunately as the railway system over the devastated regions required a great deal of repair to put it in good working order, the provisions were delayed, but luckily they turned up in time for the 1st January, an appropriate date for a Scottish Division.

Bridgehead duties were not onerous. The troops certainly enjoyed the power of being able to subject the Germans to restrictions which they themselves had for more than four years imposed on Belgian and French people. The inhabitants were forbidden to be out of doors between 9 P.M. and 6 A.M. without a pass. In the small hours of the 1st January, a Royal Scot officer was proceeding to his billet after the Hogmanay celebrations when he met a civilian in the streets of Haan. This open disregard of our regulations was not to be tolerated, and the officer curtly asked the German for his pass; he was completely nonplussed by the bland query—"Is it not that we are permitted to circulate after 6 A.M. ?"

Certain specified goods were not allowed to be taken across our frontier, and our most exacting task was the repression of smuggling. All sorts of ingenious devices were resorted to, but they were quickly detected as our men gained experience. The craft of Teutonic and Jewish traders in exploiting the innate chivalry of the British soldier by using their womenfolk to convey prohibited goods, the British authorities countered by sending up officers of the W.A.A.C. and soon it became as difficult to smuggle goods past our posts as it is to deceive the Customs officials at Dover. Periodic raids were made upon trains, and while W.A.A.C. officers searched the German women the troops searched the men and explored the engine and compartments; usually a surprising amount of contraband was brought to light, on one occasion several cases of whisky being found under the coals in an engine tender.

The defect of the Teuton is that as a rule he has no sense of humour, but he had one good score against us. A report from a German source reached our authorities to the effect that a certain citizen of Wald was manufacturing air bombs. The secret manufacture of munitions within our area was of course forbidden, and a party of soldiers of the 27th Brigade raided the offender's house. He was found to be a paralytic old gentleman, unable to move about, and a thorough search of his premises failed to disclose any sign of the bombs. Ultimately the officer in charge asked him where he stored his weapons. At first the old man looked puzzled, then light seemed to dawn on

him and he directed the party to a small cabinet in a
drawer of which lay the air bombs.   The feelings of
the officer on picking one up can be better imagined
than described ; it consisted of a tiny pole with a
paper flag attached to a small leaden contrivance which,
when fitted with a cap of the sort used to discharge
toy pistols and dropped on the ground, caused the flag
to rise gently into the air to a height of over ten feet.

Those who infringed our regulations were tried by
a summary court presided over by an officer of field
rank.   The maximum fine which such a court could
impose was 7000 marks, and the maximum period of
imprisonment was six months.   All accused had the
right of appeal to the Military Governor, and the
more serious cases were tried by a special court
equivalent to a court-martial.   The fines and penalties
depended upon the gravity which the officer ascribed
to a particular offence, and naturally throughout the area
of occupation there was for a time considerable dis-
crepancy between the penalties imposed for the same
kind of offence.   Gradually only officers with legal
training were placed over these courts, and a regulated
scale for each particular type of offence was laid down.

Demobilisation was the question of greatest moment
for one and all.   Having viewed the enemy's country,
officers and men were eager to return as soon as
possible to their civilian occupations.   There would
have been practically no trouble if a definite scheme
had been issued, and a date assigned for the commencement of demobilisation.   But demobilisation was
begun at once, with the result that many soldiers who
had seen little or no active service were demobilised
either because they happened to be at home on leave at
the time, or because they were classified as " pivotal."
The " pivotal " clause was grossly abused, and under this

pretext mere youths of eighteen years of age, who had never heard a gun fired in anger, were allowed to go home. Such anomalies created much restiveness and irritation among the older men, and not until they were removed and a smooth-working system devised was the general discontent allayed.

The military authorities acted with tact and sympathy. Training was mostly recreational with a view to keeping the men interested and in good health. After a time those waiting for demobilisation were collected in special camps and separated from those who were to form part of the Army of Occupation. Education was a useful safety-valve during the period of irritation; it kept the men employed and was probably more congenial to them than ceremonial drill. Owing to lack of trained teachers and constant changes of personnel it could scarcely be said that the standard of instruction within units was very high, but all who were really anxious to study were taken from the various units and concentrated in the Ninth Divisional College, where the best teaching ability at the disposal of the Division was available. This College was opened at Ohligs before the end of December 1918, and there much excellent work was carried out.

In the month of February Colours were presented to the various Service Battalions; to those of the 26th Brigade at Solingen by General Plumer, to the 27th at Wald, and to the 28th at Benrath by General Jacob. The Division preserved its identity till the 15th March 1919, but long before that date the vast majority of the officers and men who had fought with it had been demobilised. After the 15th, divisions were reformed under different designations. When the well-tried and trusted leaders of the Ninth were transferred to other posts and new and unfamiliar officers took command it was clear that a new era had begun. The units of the Highland Brigade were transferred to another division and battalions who had not shared in the Ninth's brotherhood of arms took their place.

The history of the Ninth Division ends with the formal disappearance of its title on the 15th March. In the chronicle of its achievements attention is inevitably focussed mainly on the doings of the infantry and the gunners. But just as a good Quartermaster is a blessing to his battalion, though his name rarely occurs in the story of its battles, a division cannot expect to be successful without efficient "Q" and administrative work. The Ninth had good reason to be proud of its special branches, the Sappers, Pioneers, R.A.M.C., A.S.C., and Ordnance; their skilled help, generously given, was a factor of first-rate importance in giving the Division its prominent name among the British forces in France. Their work was assiduous and unremitting and was often carried on under conditions of great strain and extreme peril, particularly in the case of the Sappers, Pioneers, and R.A.M.C. A more trying ordeal can scarcely be imagined than that of digging under a heavy bombardment. The preparations for every battle involved an enormous amount of toil on the part of the Pioneers and the Sappers, and a slight idea of it may be gathered from the summary of their preparations prior to the 9th April 1917 given in Appendix VI.

The Ninth was exceptionally fortunate in its "Q" Branch; no division could have had more efficient or painstaking officers than Lieut.-Colonel McHardy and Lieut.-Colonel Jeffcoat. Details were worked out with a precision and care that ensured success, and a promise of "Q" was equivalent to a fulfilment. Even when the

Division was encamped in the most desolate regions "Q" was able in a surprisingly short space of time to furnish baths, laundries, changes of clothing, and all the other comforts that helped to make the war endurable, and its arrangements for the transference of the troops from one spot to another were such as to cause the minimum of discomfort and inconvenience to the men. Ever since the time of Lieut.-Colonel McHardy, "Q" showed the same concern for the welfare of units attached to the Ninth as for its own troops. This system was carried on and expanded by Lieut.-Colonel Jeffcoat, and the most convincing testimony of its value was that A.F.A. Brigades liked to be attached to the Division.

The unit that had perhaps most reason to complain that the worth of its labours was never fully appreciated by the infantry was the Ordnance Department, which, consisting of an officer and 13 men, had to satisfy the needs of 16,000 men, 3750 horses and mules, and numerous vehicles and bicycles, in everything except food, light, and fuel. The excellence of the work performed by this Branch was largely the explanation why it was so much taken for granted; if it had proved less competent in furnishing and repairing munitions it would have been better though less favourably known to the infantry. The Ordnance people averred that they toiled harder than any other section in the Division; when units were in the line they were busy meeting their fighting needs and when they were out they were busier still re-equipping them. Undoubtedly a vast amount of very useful work was done by the Ordnance and some idea of it may be gleaned from the list quoted in Appendix VII.

In a more subtle and impalpable fashion the Padres contributed to the efficiency of the Division by keeping before the men the lofty principles for which they were fighting, and by emphasising the moral basis of the war. Those attached to battalions were of enormous assistance to C.Os. in organising services, concerts and entertainments for the men, and never did they withhold comfort and advice from those who sought their help. Many men who took part in the Longueval fighting had cause to bless Padre Johnston and his coffee stall.[1] Padre Oddie was one of the personalities of the Division and he was noted for the assiduity with which he cultivated his "parish" both in and out of the trenches. All rendered yeoman service in the sad task of burying the dead, and Padre Smith MacIntosh treasures as one of his most cherished possessions a letter he received from Brig. - General Maxwell thanking him for his labours in this respect near the Chemical Works.

The popular Padre Brown was best known from his connection with "The Thistles" concert troupe, whose entertainments were as beneficial as a tonic to men just drawn from battle. The members of this troupe performed these duties in addition to their ordinary army work. But death made sad havoc among their ranks; the loss of Sergeant Peart of the 28th Field Ambulance at Passchendaele in 1917 was a great blow; he was the most charming lady impersonator that the Ninth ever possessed, and his death was mourned by the whole Division.

The battle record of the Ninth in the war is one to be proud of. It was engaged at Loos, at the Somme twice, four times at Arras, and twice at Passchendaele; it played a conspicuous part in breaking up the German offensives in March and April, and after two minor actions at Meteren took part in the final operations from the 28th September to the 27th October. On the

[1] See Appendix VIII.

few occasions on which it failed, as at the Butte de
Warlencourt on the 12th October 1916 and at St
Julien in 1917, the power to win success was beyond
human means.

A soldier prizes no praise more highly than that of
another soldier, and such praise is most practically
shown when a division is frequently employed in
important engagements.   During its service in France
the Ninth missed only two major actions—Messines
and Cambrai.   Although on neither occasion was it fit
for action, there was a murmur of regret amongst all
ranks because it had no share in these conflicts.   For
while individually officers and men realised the awful
tragedy and pain of battle, their intense pride in their
Division made them fiercely jealous lest the omission
to employ it sprang from a poor appraisement of its
worth.

The Division had the great fortune to be commanded
by a succession of leaders outstanding for character as
well as knowledge, who with their fingers ever on its
pulse, knew well how to direct and control it to the best
advantage.   But the true value of the Ninth depended
not upon the pre-eminence of a few individuals, but upon
the co-operative ability shown by all ranks and depart-
ments to work together.   Each officer and each man
contributed to a common stock, and while he might pass
away his spirit was absorbed by the Division.   The
group is always stronger than the individual.   While

> " 'Tis that repeated shocks, again, again,
> Exhaust the energy of strongest souls,
> And numb the elastic powers,"

after each devastating battle the Ninth rose Phœnix-
like from its ashes, and at the end of the long struggle
exhibited the same keenness and purposeful vigour it
had ever shown since its formation.

MAJOR-GENERAL H. H. TUDOR, C.B., C.M.G.

[Face page 394.

The splendid arrogance of the Division, its well-founded faith in its own prowess, rested on the sure foundation of the fervent belief of each man in the righteousness of the cause for which he was fighting. To die for it if need be was the simple duty that animated all. The qualities that created the Empire are equally necessary to maintain it, and the security of a heritage depends essentially on the sense of duty of those who hold it. War still remains the supreme test of a nation's efficiency, and it is the glory of democracy that it did not shirk that test when challenged. In keeping with the national spirit the Ninth Division had ever before it the injunction received from H.M. King George V. on the 10th May 1915, and its greatest honour is that from beginning to end it faithfully and loyally carried it out.

" Officii fructus sit ipsum officium."

As the war recedes into the past and as the emotions roused by it subside, the tendency is to linger on the splendid and spectacular advances of the latter part of 1918, and to exalt them at the expense of the previous battles. If the war is to be viewed from the proper angle, it should never be forgotten that after August 1918 the Germans were men without hope, and to deduce our lessons of the war from the last four months of fighting would be the height of folly. None knew better than those who fought at Loos, the Somme, Arras, and Passchendaele, and who also took part in the victorious advance, that in the last months we were able with confidence to take risks which it would have been rash to take in 1915, 1916, and 1917. Those whose active service was confined to the fighting after August 1918 never experienced the same deadly nerve-rack and the fierce acuities of emotion that sprang from the pitiless shelling and desperate strife of the previous campaigns. The wearing-out battles, when the foe was encountered at the zenith of his strength, with all their disappointments and mistakes alone made possible the gigantic advances at the end. A glance at the Division's casualty list [1] shows clearly that the heat and burden of the day fell principally upon those who faced the enemy during the campaigns fought between September 1915 and the close of 1917. And the dead of the Ninth in the long chain of battles from Loos to the Lys had by their valour and sacrifice paved the way for the triumphal onset that carried the Division from Ypres to the Scheldt. The countless graves that strew the battle-line of France and Flanders contain the flower of the British race, and furnish silent but eloquent evidence of the robust qualities and manly faith without which the British Empire and all that it stands for must have passed away.

> " *Qui procul hinc*—the legend's writ,
>   The frontier grave is far away ;
> *Qui ante diem periit,*
> *Sed miles, sed pro patriâ.*"

---

[1] See Appendix IV.

APPENDIX I

TABLE SHOWING ORDER OF BATTLE OF THE NINTH (SCOTTISH) DIVISION

CAVALRY

" B " Squadron, Queen's Own Royal Glasgow Yeomanry.
Transferred to Corps, May 1916.

CYCLISTS

9th Division Company.   Transferred to Corps, May 1916.

ROYAL ARTILLERY

R.F.A. BRIGADES

L.	LI.	LII.	LIII.	9th HEAVY BATTERY.
		Became A.F.A. Bde. 8/1/17.	(Howitzer).	Transferred to Corps, June 1915.

In April 1916 D/L., D/LI., and D/LII. were taken away from their own Bdes. and formed into the LIII. Bde. R.F.A. The first three Bdes. had thus one Howitzer and three 18-pounder batteries.

All batteries were then on a 4-gun basis.

(Howitzer). One battery sent to the 27th Div. 9/6/15. Reconstituted April 1916, the three batteries exchanging with D/L., D/LI., and D/LII. Bde. broken up 11/9/16 to complete L. and LI. to 6-gun batteries.

ROYAL ENGINEERS

63rd, 64th, and 90th Field Companies.   9th Signal Company.

INFANTRY

26TH HIGHLAND BRIGADE

8th Bn. Black Watch (Royal Highlanders).
7th Bn. Seaforth Highlanders (Ross-shire Buffs, The Duke of Albany's).
8th Bn. The Gordon Highlanders. Transferred to 15th Div. 7/5/16.
5th Bn. The Queen's Own Cameron Highlanders.
10th Bn. Princess Louise's (Argyll and Sutherland) Highlanders.
    From 27th Bde. 3/5/16.   Transferred to 32nd Div. 15/2/18.

27TH (LOWLAND) BRIGADE

11th Bn. The Royal Scots.   12th Bn. The Royal Scots.
6th Bn. The Royal Scots Fusiliers. Transferred to 15th Div. 8/5/16.
10th Bn. Princess Louise's (Argyll and Sutherland) Highlanders.
    To 26th Bde. 3/5/16.
6th Bn. King's Own Scottish Borderers. From 28th Bde. 6/5/16.
9th Bn. The Scottish Rifles (Cameronians). From 28th Bde. 6/5/16.
    Transferred to 14th Div. 5/2/18.

28TH BRIGADE

6th Bn. The King's Own Scottish Borderers. ⎫ Transferred to 27th
9th Bn. The Scottish Rifles (Cameronians). ⎭ Bde. 6/5/16.
10th Bn. Highland Light Infantry. ⎫ Transferred to 15th Div.
11th Bn. Highland Light Infantry. ⎭ 14/5/16.

The 28th Bde. was broken up 6/5/16, and replaced by the

SOUTH AFRICAN BRIGADE

1st Regt.   2nd Regt.   3rd Regt.   4th Regt.   South African Infantry.
            Disbanded   (South African Scottish).
            3/2/18.

On 24/4/18 the 1st, 2nd, and 4th Regiments were amalgamated, and formed the South African Composite Battalion; and the brigade, composed of this battalion, the 2nd Bn. The Royal Scots Fusiliers from the 30th Div. 25/4/18, and the 9th Scottish Rifles from the 14th Div. 13/4/18, was known as the 28th (South African) Brigade. The South African Brigade left the 9th Division in September 1918 and its place was taken by the

28TH BRIGADE (reorganised September 1918)

2nd Bn. The Royal Scots Fusiliers.
9th Bn. The Scottish Rifles.
1st Bn. The Royal Newfoundland Regiment. From L. of C. 13/9/18.
    Previously with the 29th Division.

PIONEERS

9th Bn. Seaforth Highlanders (Ross-shire Buffs, the Duke of Albany's)

MACHINE-GUN CORPS

26th Company, 27th Company, 28th Company, 197th Company,
formed 1/1/16. formed 22/12/15. formed 1/1/16.   joined from
England 13/12/16.

9th Battalion, formed 1/3/18.

ROYAL ARMY SERVICE CORPS [1]
104th, 105th, 106th, and 107th Companies.

ROYAL ARMY MEDICAL CORPS

27th   28th   29th Field Ambulances.

Replaced April 1916 by the South African
Field Ambulance, which in September 1918
was replaced, first by the 76th (25th Div.),
and then by the 2/1st (East Lancs.) Field
Ambulance.

[1] The A.S.C. became R.A.S.C. 25/11/18.   A.O. (362/1918.)

2 D

APPENDIX II

TABLE SHOWING THE PERIODS SPENT IN THE LINE FROM THE
9TH MAY 1915 TILL THE 11TH NOVEMBER 1918

1915

May. Landed in France (9th to 13th).

June. Out.

July. In line at Festubert.

Aug. „ „ (till 18th).

Sept. „ N.E. of Vermelles.

Oct. „ S. of Zillebeke (from the 5th).

Nov. In line E. of Zillebeke.

Dec. „ „ (till the 20th).

1916

Jan. Out till the 26th.

Feb. In line at Ploegsteert.

Mar. „ „

Apr. „ „

May. „ „

June. Out.

July. Attacked on 3rd at Bernafay; then in line at Montauban. Attacked on 14th (Longueval and Delville Wood); engaged till 20th; then out.

Aug. In line at Vimy Ridge (from the 15th).

Sept. In line at Vimy Ridge (till the 26th).

1916

Oct. In line near Butte de Warlencourt (from the 9th). Attacked on 12th, 18th, and 19th; out from 26th.

Nov. Out.

Dec. In line E. and N.E. of Arras (from 4th).

1917

Jan. In line E. and N.E. of Arras.

Feb. „ „ „

Mar. „ „ „

Apr. „ „ „
Attacked on 9th and 12th, reaching Fampoux and Roeux; out from 16th to 28th.

May. In line E. of Arras. Attacked on 3rd; out from 12th.

June. In line near Roeux. Attacked on 5th; out from 14th.

July. Out till 25th.

Aug. In line, Trescault-Havrincourt - Hermies (till 30th).

Sept. Out till 15th. In line N.W. of Zonnebeke.

1917

Sept.   Attacked on 20th; out from 26th.

Oct.   In line near St Julien from 10th; attacked on 12th; out 25th to 28th.

Nov.   In line at Coast till 17th; then out.

Dec.   In line at Gouzeaucourt (from 6th).

1918

Jan.   In line at Gouzeaucourt.

Feb.   Out from 3rd.

Mar.   In line at Gouzeaucourt (from 12th); engaged in Somme Retreat 21st to 27th.

1918

Apr.   In line near Hollebeke (from 4th); fighting 10th and 11th, 16th and 25th; out from 26th.

May.   Out till 24th.

June.   In line at Meteren.

July.   ,,   ,,
  Meteren captured 19th.

Aug.   In line at Meteren. Attacked on 18th; out from 26th.

Sept.   In line E. of Ypres (from 20th). Attacked 28th to 30th.

Oct.   Attacked 1st, 14th, 20th, 22nd, and 25th; then out.

APPENDIX III

LIST SHOWING (*A*) Commanders and Staff of the Ninth (Scottish) Division; (*B*) Battalion Commanders; (*C*) Artillery Brigade Commanders; (*D*) Field Company Commanders; (*E*) Field Ambulance Commanders from Formation in September 1914 to the Armistice, 11th November 1918.

Notes.—(1) The dates given in these lists indicate the periods during which Commanders were serving with the Division.

(2) Decorations mentioned are those held or awarded during service with the Division.

(*A*) COMMANDERS AND STAFF

DIVISIONAL COMMANDERS

Maj.-Gen. C. J. Mackenzie, C.B.	. .	. to Oct. 1914
,,	Sir C. Fergusson, C.B., D.S.O., M.V.O.	,, March 1915
,,	H. J. S. Landon, C.B. . .	. ,, Sept. 1915
,,	G. H. Thesiger, C.B., C.M.G. .	. ,, Sept. 1915 (Loos)
,,	Sir W. T. Furse, K.C.B., D.S.O.	. ,, Dec. 1916
,,	Sir H. T. Lukin, K.C.B., C.M.G., D.S.O. . . .	. ,, 13th March 1918
,,	C. A. Blacklock, C.M.G., D.S.O.	. ,, 28th March 1918
,,	H. H. Tudor, C.B., C.M.G. .	. ,, Armistice

G.S.Os.I.

Lt.-Col. C. H. de Rougemont, D.S.O., M.V.O.	. to July 1915
,,	F. A. Buzzard . . .	. ,, Sept. 1915
,,	S. E. Hollond, D.S.O. . .	. ,, March 1916
,,	P. A. V. Stewart, D.S.O. .	. ,, Dec. 1917
,,	T. C. Mudie, D.S.O. . .	. ,, Armistice

A.A. & Q.M.Gs.

Col. A. V. Payne	. . .	. to Feb. 1915
Lt.-Col. R. F. Uniacke	. . .	. ,, May 1915
,,	A. A. McHardy, C.M.G., D.S.O. .	. ,, Aug. 1916
,,	A. C. Jeffcoat, C.B., C.M.G., D.S.O.	. ,, Armistice

402

C.R.As.

Brig.-Gen. E. H. Armitage, C.B.   .   .   . to Feb. 1916
    ,,   H. H. Tudor, C.B., C.M.G.   .   . ,, March 1918
    ,,   H. R. Wainwright, D.S.O.   .   . ,, Armistice

C.R.Es.

Lt.-Col. H. A. A. Livingstone, C.M.G.   .   . to Sept. 1915 (Loos)
    ,,   C. M. Carpenter, D.S.O.   .   . ,, Jan. 1916
    ,,   E. Barnardiston .   .   .   . ,, July 1916 (Somme)
    ,,   G. R. Hearn, D.S.O. .   .   . ,, Feb. 1918
    ,,   H. C. B. Hickling, D.S.O., M.C. .   . ,, Armistice

INFANTRY BRIGADE COMMANDERS

26*th Brigade.—*
     Brig.-Gen. H. R. Kelham, C.B. .   .   . to Nov. 1914
          ,,   E. St G. Grogan, C.B.   .   . ,, May 1915
          ,,   A. B. Ritchie, C.M.G.   .   . ,, Dec. 1916
          ,,   J. Kennedy, C.M.G., D.S.O. . ,, July 1918
          ,,   The Hon. A. G. A. Hore Ruthven,
               V.C., C.B., C.M.G., D.S.O. . ,, Armistice

27*th Brigade.—*
     Brig.-Gen. W. Scott Moncrieff .   .   . to Jan. 1915
          ,,   C. D. Bruce   .   .   . ,, Sept. 1915 (Loos)
          ,, (' W. H. Walshe .   .   . ,, March 1916
          ,,   G. F. Trotter, C.M.G., D.S.O.,
               M.V.O.   .   .   . ,, May 1916
          ,,   S. W. Scrase-Dickins, C.B.   . ,, Oct. 1916
          ,,   F. A. Maxwell, V.C., C.S.I., D.S.O. ,, Sept. 1917
                                       (Passchendaele)
          ,,   W. D. Croft, C.M.G., D.S.O. . ,, to Armistice

28*th Brigade.—*
     Brig.-Gen. S. W. Scrase-Dickins   .   . to May 1916

South African Brigade.—
     Brig.-Gen. H. T. Lukin, C.M.G., D.S.O. Apr. 1916 to Dec. 1916
          ,,   F. S. Dawson, C.M.G., D.S.O. .   . ,, Mar. 1918
          ,,   W. E. C. Tanner, C.M.G., D.S.O.   . ,, Sept. 1918

28*th Brigade.—*
     Brig.-Gen. J. L. Jack, D.S.O. .   . Sept. 1918 to Armistice

9TH DIVISIONAL TRAIN

Lt.-Col. R. P. Crawley, D.S.O., M.V.O.   .   . to Nov. 1917
  „   R. MacLear, D.S.O.   .   .   .   „ Armistice

A.D.M.S.

Col. G. Cree, C.M.G.   .   .   . Apr. 1915 to Nov. 1915
 „ F. A. Symons, C.M.G., D.S.O.   .   . „ Apr. 1917 (Arras)
 „ O. W. A. Elsner, C.B.E., D.S.O.   .   . „ Armistice

(B) BATTALION COMMANDERS

26TH BRIGADE

8th Black Watch—

Lt.-Col. John Lord Sempill   .   . to Sept. 1915 (Loos)
  „   G. B. Duff   .   . Dec. 1915 „ Mar. 1916
  „   C. G. W. E. Gordon, D.S.O.   . „ Sept. 1916
  „   Sir G. Abercromby, D.S.O.   . „ Sept. 1917
  „   R. W. Hadow, D.S.O.   .   . „ Aug. 1918
  „   W. French, D.S.O., M.C.   .   . „ Armistice

7th Seaforth Highlanders—

Lt.-Col. W. T. Gaisford   .   . to Sept. 1915 (Loos) k
  „   F. J. Marshall .   . Dec. 1915 „ Apr. 1916
  „   J. Kennedy, D.S.O.   May 1916 „ Aug. 1916
  „   R. Horn, D.S.O., M.C.   .   . „ Mar. 1918
  „   Hon. D. Bruce   . Apr. 1918 „ Armistice

8th Gordon Highlanders—

Lt.-Col. G. Staunton   .   .   . to Feb. 1915
  „   H. Wright, C.M.G., D.S.O.   . „ Sept. 1915 (Loos)
  „   A. D. Greenhill-Gardyne.   . „ Mar. 1916
  „   H. Pelham Burn, D.S.O., Apr. 1916 to May 1916

5th Cameron Highlanders—

Lt.-Col. D. W. Cameron of Lochiel, C.M.G., to March 1916
  „   G. B. Duff, D.S.O.   .   . to July 1916 (Somme)
  „   H. R. Brown, D.S.O.   .   . „ May 1917
  „   St C. M. G. MacEwen   .   . „ Oct. 1917
  „   A. G. M. M. Crichton, D.S.O., M.C., to March 1918
  „   J. Inglis, C.M.G., D.S.O., March 1918 to Sept. 1918
  „   A. W. Angus, D.S.O.   .   . to Armistice

10*th Argyll and Sutherland Highlanders—*

Lt.-Col. W. J. B. Tweedie, C.M.G., May 1916 to July 1916
        (Somme)

  ,,   J. Kennedy, D.S.O. .   .   . to Dec. 1916
  ,,   H. G. Sotheby, D.S.O., M.V.O. ,, Feb. 1918

27TH BRIGADE

11*th Royal Scots—*

Lt.-Col. H. H. B. Dyson   .   .   . to Oct. 1914
  ,,   R. C. Dundas .   .   .   . ,, Sept. 1915 (Loos) *k.*
  ,,   W. D. Croft, D.S.O.   Dec. 1915 ,, Sept. 1917
  ,,   Sir J. B. S. Campbell, D.S.O. . ,, Oct. 1918
  ,,   E. Boyd, M.C. .   .   .   . ,, Armistice

12*th Royal Scots—*

Lt.-Col. G. G. Loch, C.M.G.   .   . to Feb. 1916
  ,,   H. L. Budge .   .   .   . ,, July 1916 (Somme)
  ,,   N. H. S. Fargus, D.S.O. .   . ,, March 1917
  ,,   H. U. H. Thorne   .   .   . ,, Apr. 1917 (Arras)
  ,,   J. A. S. Ritson, D.S.O., M.C. . ,, June 1918   .
  ,,   J. Murray, D.S.O. .   .   . ,, Armistice

6*th Royal Scots Fusiliers—*

Lt.-Col. H. H. Northey, C.M.G. .   . to Sept. 1915 (Loos)
  ,,   Rt. Hon. Winston Churchill, Jan. 1916 to May 1916

10*th Argyll and Sutherland Highlanders—*

Lt.-Col. A. F. Mackenzie, C.M.G., M.V.O., to Sept. 1915 (Loos)
  ,,   H. Pelham Burn, D S.O., Dec. 1915 to Apr. 1916
  ,,   W. J. B. Tweedie, C.M.G.   . to May 1916

6*th King's Own Scottish Borderers—*

Lt.-Col. J. C. W. Connell, D.S.O., May 1916 to Oct. 1916
  ,,   G. B. F. Smyth, D.S.O. .   . to May 1917
  ,,   H. D. N. Maclean, D.S.O., Aug. 1917 to Oct. 1917
  ,,   G. B. F. Smyth, D.S.O., March 1918 and May 1918 to
          Oct. 1918
  ,,   R. F. Ker, D.S.O., M.C. .   . to Armistice

9*th Scottish Rifles—*

Lt.-Col. H. A. Fulton, D.S.O., May 1916 to July 1917
  ,,   W. Lumsden, D.S.O., M.C. . ,, Feb. 1918

10*th Highland Light Infantry—*
     Lt.-Col. J. C. Grahame, D.S.O. .   .   to Sept. 1915 (Loos)
     ,,   H. C. Stuart, D.S.O.   .   . ,,   Jan. 1916
     ,,   J. C. Grahame, D.S.O.   .   . ,,   May 1916

11*th Highland Light Infantry—*
     Lt.-Col. H. C. Fergusson, C.M.G.   .   to Jan. 1916
     ,,   R. F. Forbes   .   .   . ,,   May 1916

SOUTH AFRICAN BRIGADE

1*st South African Infantry—*
     Lt.-Col. F. S. Dawson, C.M.G., Apr. 1916 to Dec. 1916
     ,,   F. H. Heal, D.S.O. .   .   .   to March 1918

2*nd South African Infantry—*
     Lt.-Col. W. E. C. Tanner, C.M.G., D.S.O., Apr. 1916 to Oct. 1917
     ,,   E. Christian, D.S.O.   .   .   to March 1918

3*rd South African Infantry—*
     Lt.-Col. E. F. Thackeray, C.M.G., D.S.O., Apr. 1916 to Feb. 1918

4*th South African Infantry—*
     Lt.-Col. F. A. Jones, C.M.G., D.S.O., May 1916 to July 1916
                                               (Somme)
     ,,   D. R. Hunt   .   .   .   to Dec. 1916
     ,,   E. Christian, D.S.O..   .   . ,,   Apr. 1917
     ,,   D. M. MacLeod, D.S.O. .   . ,,   March 1918

South African (Composite) Battalion—
     Lt.-Col. H. W. M. Bamford, O.B.E., M.C., Apr. 1918 to Sept. 1918

28TH BRIGADE

2*nd Royal Scots Fusiliers—*
     Lt.-Col. J. Utterson-Kelso, D.S.O., M.C., Apr. 1918 to Oct. 1918
     ,,   R. Campbell, D.S.O.   .   .   to Nov. 1918
     ,,   C. S. Nairne   .   .   .   . ,,   Armistice

9*th Scottish Rifles—*
     Lt.-Col. W. Lumsden, D.S.O., M.C.   .   Apr. 1918 to Armistice

1*st Bn. Royal Newfoundland Regiment—*
     Lt.-Col. T. G. Matthias, D.S.O.   . Sept. 1918 to Armistice

9th Seaforth Highlanders—

Lt.-Col. T. Fetherstonhaugh, D.S.O. . . . to March 1917
" W. Petty, D.S.O. . . . . " Aug. 1918
" S. F. Sharp, M.C. . . . . " Armistice

9th Machine-gun Battalion—

Lt.-Col. F. G. Chalmers, M.C. . March 1918 to June 1918
" H. J. W. Davis, D.S.O. . . . " Armistice

(C) ARTILLERY BRIGADE COMMANDERS

50TH BRIGADE

Lt.-Col. A. C. Bailward . . . . . to Jan. 1915
" C. E. D. Budworth, M.V.O. . . . " March 1915
" C. C. Van Straubenzee . . . " Aug. 1915
" E. W. S. Brooke, D.S.O. . . . " Aug. 1917
" C. W. W. McLean, C.M.G., D.S.O. . . " March 1918
" J. de B. Cowan, D.S.O. . . . " May 1918
" C. W. W. McLean, C.M.G., D.S.O. . . " Armistice

51ST BRIGADE

Lt.-Col. A. H. Carter . . . . . to Aug. 1916
" G. A. S. Cape, D.S.O. . . . " Oct. 1917
" M. Muirhead, D.S.O. . . . . " Armistice

52ND BRIGADE

Lt.-Col. F. W. Boteler . . . . . to March 1915
" A. M. Perreau, C.M.G. . . . " June 1916
" H. M. Ballingall . . . . " June 1916
" H. T. Belcher, D.S.O. . . . . " Jan. 1917

53RD BRIGADE

Lt.-Col. C. N. Simpson . . . . . to Feb. 1915
" K. K. Knapp, C.M.G. . . . . " Nov. 1915
" H. T. Belcher, D.S.O. . . . . " Sept. 1916

(D) FIELD COMPANY COMMANDERS

63RD COMPANY

Capt. C. Doucet . . . . to Nov. 1914
Major L. W. S. Oldham . . . . . . ,, July 1915
,, A. W. Reid, M.C. . . . . . . ,, Apr. 1917
,, R. E. Bruce Fielding, D.S.O. . . . ,, Armistice

64TH COMPANY

Capt. W. E. Francis . . . . . . to Nov. 1914
Major G. R. Hearn, D.S.O. . . . . . ,, Aug. 1916
,, C. G. Woolner, M.C. . . . . . ,, Oct. 1917
,, N. Clavering, M.C. . . . . . ,, July 1918
Capt. T. F. Young, D.S.O., M.C. . . . . ,, Oct. 1918

90TH COMPANY

Major C. S. Montefiore . . . . . to May 1915
,, C. D. Munro . . . . . ,, Sept. 1915 (Loos)
,, G. B. F. Smyth, D.S.O. . . . ,, Oct. 1916
,, S. W. S. Hamilton, D.S.O. . . . ,, Sept. 1917
,, T. G. Bird, D.S.O. . . . . ,, Armistice

(E) FIELD AMBULANCE COMMANDERS

27TH FIELD AMBULANCE

Lt.-Col. O. W. A. Elsner, D.S.O. . . . . to Apr. 1917
,, J. M. A. Costello, M.C. . . . . ,, Armistice

28TH FIELD AMBULANCE

Lt.-Col. W. E. Hardy . . . . . . to June 1915
,, H. C. R. Hine . . . . . . ,, Aug. 1915
Capt. G. P. Taylor . . . . . . ,, Jan. 1916
,, Darling, M.C. . . . . . ,, Aug. 1916
Lt.-Col. T. E. Harty, D.S.O. . . . . . ,, Armistice

29TH FIELD AMBULANCE

Lt.-Col. F. R. Buswell . . . . . to Oct. 1915
Major R. P. Lewis . . . . . . ,, May 1916

S. A. FIELD AMBULANCE

Lt.-Col. G. H. Usmar . . . . May 1916 to Aug. 1916
,, R. N. Pringle, D.S.O., M.C. . . . ,, Sept. 1918

2ND/1ST (EAST LANCS.) FIELD AMBULANCE

Lt.-Col. J. Bruce . . . . . Sept. 1918 to Armistice

APPENDIX IV

CASUALTIES OF THE NINTH DIVISION

(A). *Approximate Number of Casualties suffered by the Division in Battle.*

	Officers.			Other Ranks.			Total.	
	K.	W.	M.	K.	W.	M.	Officers.	Other Ranks.
Loos— 25th to 28th Sept. 1915	63	100	27	798	3,037	2,032	190	5,867
Somme— Longueval and Delville Wood, 1st to 20th July 1916 .	82	214	18	1,148	5,091	964	314	7,203
Butte de Warlencourt— 12th to 24th Oct. 1916	28	74	16	460	2,131	546	118	3,137
Arras— 9th April 1917 . .	26	91	...	382	1,481	68	117	1,931
12th April ,, . .	7	55	3	122	987	189	65	1,298
3rd May ,, . .	13	52	23	161	1,150	459	88	1,770
5th June ,, . .	4	8	1	36	141	19	13	196
Passchendaele – 20th Sept. 1917 . .	22	64	...	411	1,754	124	86	2,289
12th to 25th Oct. 1917	28	69	5	387	1,932	225	102	2,544
Somme Retreat— 21st to 28th Mar. 1918	26	113	105	304	1,799	2,760	244	4,863
The Lys— 9th to 26th April 1918	35	95	39	401	1,832	1,646	169	3,879
Meteren— 19th July 1918 . .	13	20	2	186	537	45	35	768
Hoegenacker— 18th August 1918 .	4	16	1	65	324	23	21	412
Final Advance— 28th Sept. to 27th Oct. 1918	44	139	5	470	2,858	276	188	3,604
	395	1,110	245	5,331	25,054	9,376	1,750	39,761

(B). *Approximate Number of Casualties from May* 1915 *to November* 1918.

	K.	W.	M.	K.	W.	M.	Officers.	Other Ranks.
	474	1744	275	7,425	34,559	10,138	2,493	52,122

APPENDIX V

VICTORIA CROSSES Won by Officers and Men of the Ninth Division during the War

CORPORAL JAMES DALGLEISH POLLOCK, 5th Bn. The Cameron Highlanders

For most conspicuous bravery near the Hohenzollern Redoubt on the 27th September 1915.

At about 12 noon when the enemy's bombers in superior numbers were working up "Little Willie" towards the Redoubt, Corporal Pollock, after obtaining permission from his company officer, got out of the trench alone, walked along the top edge with the utmost coolness and disregard of danger and compelled the enemy's bombers to retire by bombing them from above. He was under heavy machine-gun fire the whole time, but continued to hold up the progress of the Germans for an hour, when he was at length wounded.

PRIVATE WILLIAM FREDERICK FAULDS, 1st Regiment, South African Infantry

At Delville Wood, on 18th July 1916. For most conspicuous bravery and devotion to duty. A bombing party under Lieutenant Craig attempted to rush across forty yards of ground which lay between the British and enemy trenches. Coming under very heavy rifle and machine-gun fire, the officer and the majority of the party were killed or wounded. Unable to move, Lieutenant Craig lay midway between the two lines of trenches, the ground being quite open. In full daylight Private Faulds, accompanied by two other men, climbed the parapet, ran out, picked up the officer and carried him back, one man being severely wounded in so doing.

Two days later Private Faulds again showed most conspicuous bravery in going out alone to bring in a wounded man, and carrying him nearly half a mile to a dressing-station, subsequently rejoining his platoon. The artillery fire was at the time so intense that stretcher-bearers and others considered that any attempt to bring in the wounded men meant certain death. This risk Private Faulds faced unflinchingly, and his bravery was crowned with success.

CAPTAIN HENRY REYNOLDS, M.C., 12th Bn. The Royal Scots

For most conspicuous bravery. When his company, in attack and approaching their final objective, suffered heavy casualties from enemy machine-guns and from an enemy " Pill-box," which had been passed by the first wave, Captain Reynolds reorganised his men, who were scattered, and then proceeded alone by rushes from shell-hole to shell-hole, all the time being under heavy machine-gun fire. When near the "Pill-box" he threw a grenade, intending that it should go inside, but the enemy had blocked the entrance. He then crawled to the entrance and forced a phosphorous grenade inside. This set the place on fire and caused the death of three of the enemy, while the remaining seven or eight surrendered with two machine-guns.

Afterwards, though wounded, he continued to lead his company against another objective and captured it, taking seventy prisoners and two more machine-guns.

During the whole attack the company was under heavy machine-gun fire from the flanks, but despite this Captain Reynolds kept complete control of his men.

LANCE-CORPORAL WILLIAM HENRY HEWITT, 2nd Regiment, South African Infantry

At east of Ypres on 20th September 1917, for most conspicuous bravery during operations. Lance-Corporal Hewitt attacked a "Pill-box" with his section, and tried to rush the doorway. The garrison however proved very stubborn, and in the attempt this N.C.O. received a severe wound. Nevertheless, he proceeded to the loophole of the "Pill-box" where, in his attempts to put a bomb into it, he was again wounded in the arm. Undeterred, however, he eventually managed to get a bomb inside which caused the occupants to dislodge, and they were successfully and speedily dealt with by the remainder of the section.

LIEUTENANT ROBERT VAUGHAN GORLE, "A" Battery, 5th Brigade R.F.A.

For most conspicuous bravery, initiative, and devotion to duty during the attack at Ledeghem on 1st October 1918, when in command of an 18-pounder gun working in close conjunction with the infantry. He brought his gun into action in the most exposed positions on four separate occasions, and disposed of enemy machine-guns by firing over open sights under direct machine-gun fire at 500 to 600 yards' range.

Later, seeing that the infantry were being driven back by intense hostile fire, he without hesitation galloped his gun in front of the leading infantry, and on two occasions knocked out enemy machine-guns which were causing the trouble. His dash and disregard of personal safety were a magnificent example to the wavering line, which rallied and retook the northern end of the village.

PRIVATE THOMAS RICKETTS, The Royal Newfoundland Regiment

For most conspicuous bravery and devotion to duty on the 14th October 1918. During the advance from Ledeghem, when the attack was temporarily held up by heavy hostile fire, and the platoon to which he belonged suffered severe casualties from the fire of a battery at point-blank range, Private Ricketts at once volunteered to go forward with his section commander and a Lewis Gun to attempt to outflank the battery. Advancing by short rushes under heavy fire from machine-guns with the hostile battery, their ammunition was exhausted when they were still 300 yards from the battery. The enemy, seeing an opportunity to get their field-guns away, began to bring up their gun teams. Private Ricketts, at once realising the situation, doubled back 100 yards under the heaviest machine-gun fire, procured further ammunition, and dashed back again to the Lewis Gun, and by very accurate fire drove the enemy and the gun teams into a farm. His platoon then advanced without casualties and captured four field-guns, four machine-guns, and eight prisoners. A fifth field-gun was subsequently intercepted by fire and captured. By his presence of mind in anticipating the enemy intention and his utter disregard of personal safety, Private Ricketts secured the further supply of ammunition which directly resulted in these important captures and undoubtedly saved many lives.

CORPORAL ROLAND EDWARD ELCOCK, M.M., 11th Bn. The Royal Scots

For most conspicuous bravery and initiative south-east of Cappelle St Catherine on 15th October 1918, when in charge of a Lewis Gun team. Entirely on his own initiative, Corporal Elcock rushed his gun up to within ten yards of enemy guns, which were causing heavy casualties and holding up the advance. He put both guns out of action, captured five prisoners and undoubtedly saved the whole attack from being held up. Later, near the river Lys, this N.C.O. again attacked an enemy machine-gun and captured the crew. His behaviour throughout the day was absolutely fearless.

APPENDIX VI

SUMMARY OF WORK done by Sappers and Pioneers in Preparation for the Battle of Arras, 9th April 1917

1. 3500 yards of new communication trenches.
2. New artillery trench (1600 yards) dug for advanced positions of three brigades.
3. 4300 yards of old communications cleared at least once; trench boards raised in part on " A " frames, and berms cleared back.
4. 2800 yards of tramway cleared and track raised 18 feet in places; a very successful job, enabling large quantities of ammunition for trench mortars, etc., to be run up. 1000 yards of new tramway laid, including tramways to gun positions.
5. 10 heavy trench mortar emplacements with at least 10 feet overhead cover, and mined magazines holding 200 rounds; these proved very successful and saved many casualties.
6. 38 medium emplacements proof against 4·2 H.E. shells.
7. 7 artillery observation posts in Arras and 7 trench observation posts with mined dug-outs; also telephone exchange at sewer exit in Arras.
8. 1500 yards of roads cleared and repaired, and 3 subways made for passage under roads.
9. 4500 yards of infantry tracks made, with a small amount of assistance from infantry of the Fourth Division. 3000 artillery tracks made, including 35 bridges. Overland tracks made along 4500 yards of communication trenches. Pontoon bridge over the Scarpe repaired for pack transport.
10. Additional water storage for 1500 gallons, and about 2000 yards of piped supply to battery positions.
11. 74 cellars and a cave in St Nicholas strutted, and 15 dug-outs extended or improved. 3 brigade H.Q. made, one of which was made sufficiently large for advanced D.H.Q.

12.　4013 bunks erected in Etrun, Laresset, and Haute Avesnes. 518 bunks repaired, 8 Nissen huts and 13 cookhouse shelters erected.　A billet for 44 officers made in a French Adrian hut.　Brigade H.Q. made in St Catherine for the Thirty-fourth Division, also dug-outs for the 50th Brigade R.F.A. and signals in St Nicholas.

13.　The large quantity of articles turned out by divisional workshops included :—

> 70 camouflaged targets for marking of objectives when captured.
>
> 143 water-carriers for pack transport.
>
> 350 infantry track posts.
>
> 138 trench bridges.
>
> 260 printed notice boards.
>
> 30 direction posts.
>
> 100 artillery track posts.
>
> 20 stretchers.

In addition, the Sappers made entrances for the 27th Brigade to the craters in its front line, and exploded craters (for assembly purposes) in front of the South African sector.

All this work took about two months.

APPENDIX VII

LIST showing Material Issued and Salved by the Ordnance Department in 1918

	Original Issues on Mobilisation.	Actually issued 1918.	Actually salved 1918.
Boots, ankle, pairs . . .	32,000	24,160	23,520
Greatcoats	16,000	7,440	8,160
Trousers	13,000	21,840	18,160
Jackets	16,000	23,520	22,960
Pantaloons, cord . . .	3,000	8,701	9,183
Puttees, pairs	16,000	24,120	23,200
Ground sheets . . .	16,000	7,248	7,248
Socks, pairs . . .	48,000	41,232	42,000
Shoes, horse and mule . .	...	64,743	*140
Bottles, water . . .	16,000	5,782	5,000
Haversacks	16,000	1,184	1,100
Vests	16,000	25,056	25,056
Caps	16,000	14,560	14,000
Drawers, woollen or cotton .	32,000	37,264	37,000
Shirts	32,000	10,800	10,800
Tins, mess	16,000	11,520	11,000
Flannelette, yards . . .	8,500	111,672	...
Bags, nose	4,000	29,244	29,000
Ropeshead	4,000	3,200	3,000
Chains, collar	2,000	5,892	...
Ropes, heel	4,000	1,992	1,500
Ropes, picketing . . .	70	1,800	...
Dubbin, lbs. . . .	500	9,600	...
Soap, soft, lbs. . . .	500	21,120	...
Soap, yellow, bars . . .	4,004	40,320	...
Grease, lubricating, lbs. .	500	10,188	...
Buckets, water . . .	5,000	7,332	...
Oil, lubricating, G. S., galls.	100	3,216	...
Brushes, dandy . . .	2,000	9,096	...
Brushes, horse . . .	3,000	4,812	...
Blankets, saddle . . .	3,750	1,800	1,800
Blankets, G. S. . . .	32,000	48,000	48,000
Soda, crystals, lbs. . . .	336	34,560	...
Pullthroughs . . .	16,000	19,200	...
Machine-guns . . .	454	700	750
Rifles	16,000	35,000	50,000
Vehicles (various) . . .	963	400	400
Bicycles	441	300	300

* Weight in tons.

2 E

APPENDIX VIII

DIVISIONAL INSTITUTES AND CANTEENS

CANTEENS were instituted in the Ninth Division during September 1915 because of the exorbitant prices charged to soldiers by the private owners of cafés and estaminets. The difficult work of organisation was carried out by Captain, now Major J. R. King, D.S.O., and he was ably assisted by Padre J. Johnston, Presbyterian Chaplain. Two caravans, kindly sent out by some friends at home, and named "Rob Roy" and "Wee Macgregor," were well known to all who served with the Ninth; they traversed the front line many times from the sea to the Somme, and "Jock" was always delighted to see them, for they meant hot coffee and a packet of biscuits or cigarettes. When at the beginning of 1918 Major King was transferred to the 46th Reserve Park, the control of the Canteen arrangements devolved principally upon Captain Carmichael. The duties of the O.C. Canteens were by no means light, as the annual overturn amounted to more than a million francs.

Another venture taken up by the Canteen department was the establishment of a Soda-Water Factory. This factory not only swelled the divisional funds but was an inestimable boon to the men, who were provided with an excellent beverage at very small cost.

Some of the profits were devoted to the purchase of a divisional cinema at the beginning of 1916, and all kinds of places behind the lines—a pantechnicon waggon, barns, wall of houses in the open air, sheets under trees by the roadside—were used for performances; it is needless to mention that the film most in request from one end of the line to the other was "Charlie Chaplin."

During the German offensive in 1918 some of the divisional treasures were lost. The cinema and "Wee Macgregor" had to be abandoned. The soda-water plant was saved by Major King who, moving back with his transport, remembered his old division in its trouble, seized the plant at Péronne, and in spite of all obstacles got it safely away.

The Canteens carried on to the end, and after the Armistice were the only places where the troops could procure supplies.

With the development of the Canteens there arose demands for all sorts of specialists, such as cinema operators, grocers, law assistants, etc., and " Q " often asked brigades to furnish them. On one occasion a brigade which as a rule took no notice of these requests, sent in the following reply : " We regret we have no grocer specialist, soda-water specialist, or law specialist in our ranks, but we have a contortionist, if his services could be made use of." But " Q " scored (whether consciously or not is a matter of doubt) by wiring, " Please tell contortionist to report at H.Q. at once for duty with the Concert Party." This unexpected demand nonplussed the brigade, which after deliberation concocted the following reply : " Regret contortionist became a casualty last evening and is being evacuated."

INDEX

PRINTED BY OLIVER AND BOYD, EDINBURGH, SCOTLAND

MAPS

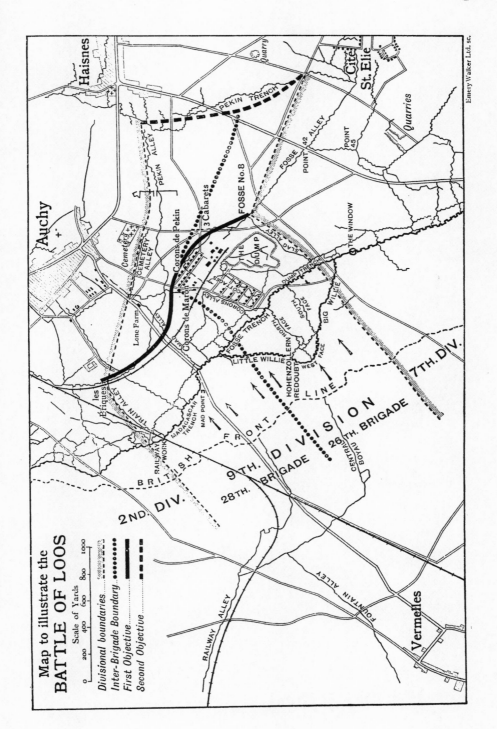

Map to illustrate the
BATTLE OF LOOS

Scale of Yards

Divisional boundaries
Inter-Brigade Boundary
First Objective
Second Objective

Emery Walker Ltd. sc.

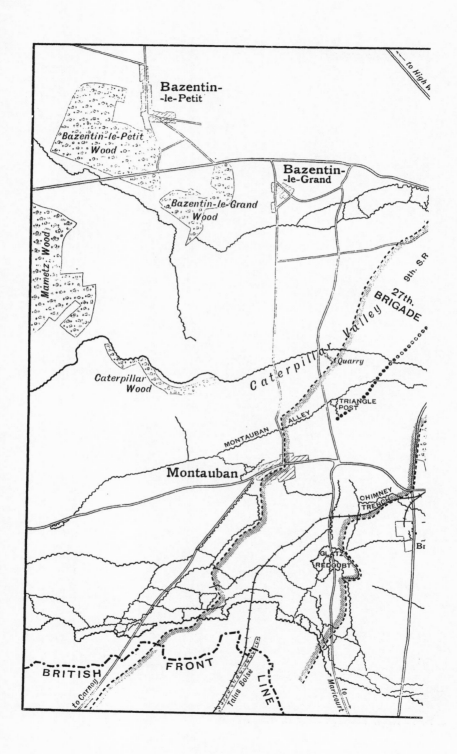

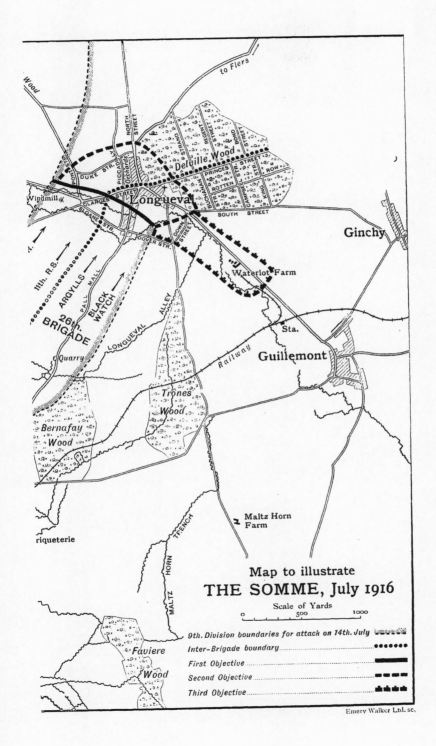

Map to illustrate
THE SOMME, July 1916

Scale of Yards

0	500	1000

9th. Division boundaries for attack on 14th. July

Inter-Brigade boundary

First Objective

Second Objective

Third Objective

Emery Walker Ltd. sc.

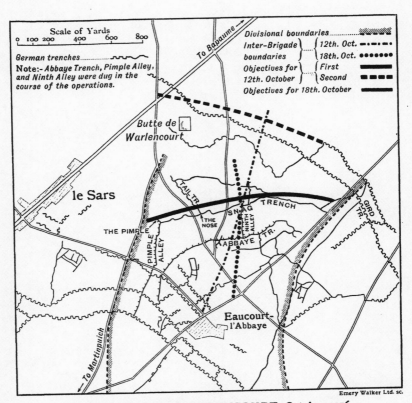

THE BUTTE DE WARLENCOURT, October 1916

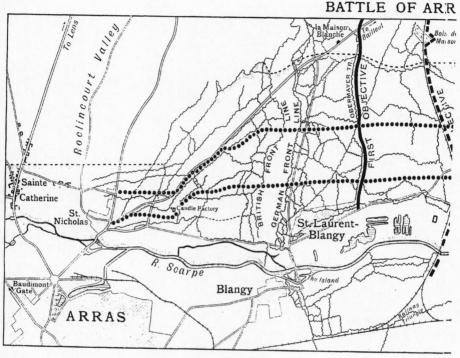

Scale of

0 200 400 600 800 1000   2000

Divisional boundaries......

Inter-Brigade boundaries.

9th. Division ⎰ First Objective.....

⎱ Second Objective......

⎱ Third Objective......

4th. Division Fourth Objective......

RAS. 9th. April 1917

le la
on Blanche

le Point
du Jour

FOURTH OBJECTIVE

SECOND OBJE...

THIRD OBJECTIVE

Athies

Fampoux

To Douai

To Douai

R. Scarpe

Feuchy

Emery Walker Ltd. sc.

Yards

3000   4000

.... ▨▨▨▨▨

s............... ●●●●●●●

_____ (Black line)

▬ ▬ ▬ ▬ (Blue line)

♦♦♦♦ (Brown line)

xxxxxxx (Green line)

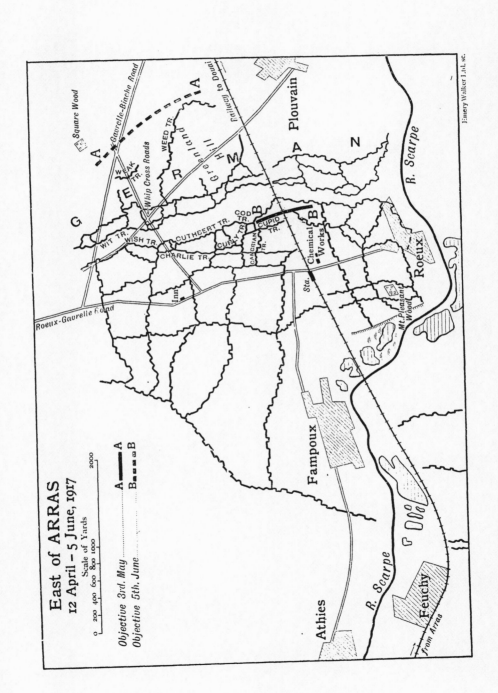

East of ARRAS
12 April – 5 June, 1917

Scale of Yards

0   200 400 600 800 1000   2000

Objective 3rd. May .... A
Objective 5th. June .... B

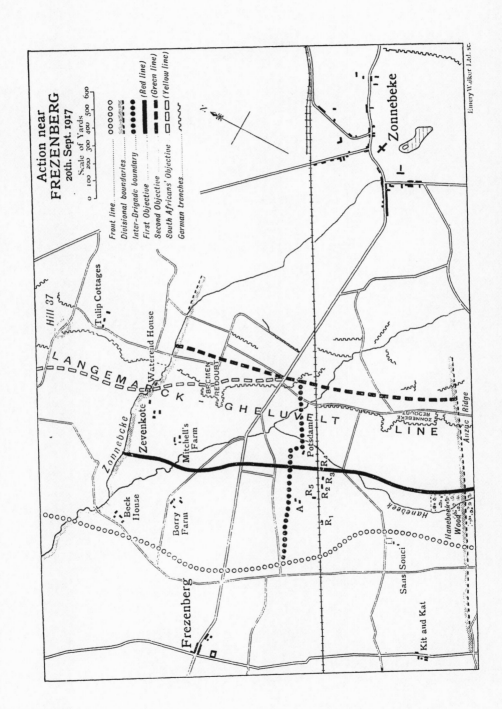

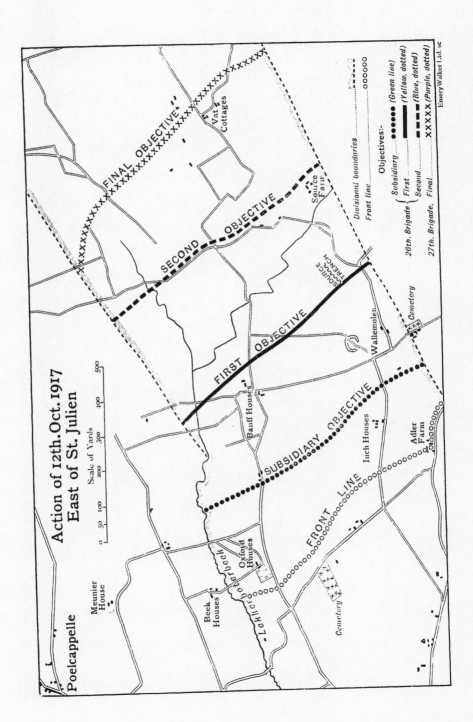

Action of 12th. Oct. 1917
East of St. Julien

Scale of Yards

0 50 100 200 300 400 500

Poelcappelle

Meunier House

Beek Houses

Oxford Houses

Lekkerboterbeek

Banff House

Source Farm

Vat Cottages

Source Trench

Wallemolen

Cemetery

Inch Houses

Adler Farm

Cemetery

FINAL OBJECTIVE

SECOND OBJECTIVE

FIRST OBJECTIVE

SUBSIDIARY OBJECTIVE

FRONT LINE

Divisional boundaries
Front line

Objectives:-
Subsidiary .... (Green line)
First .... (Yellow, dotted)
Second .... (Blue, dotted)
Final .... (Purple, dotted)

26th. Brigade
27th. Brigade

Emery Walker Ltd. sc

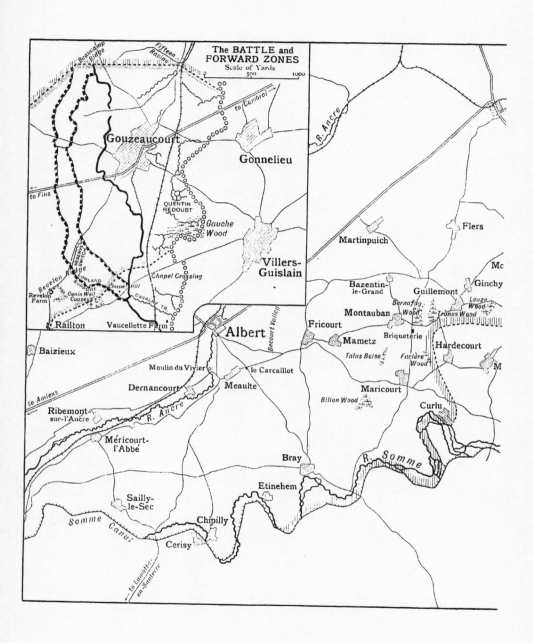

The BATTLE and
FORWARD ZONES
Scale of Yards
500   1000

Beaucamp Ridge

Fifteen Ravine

to Cambrai

Gouzeaucourt

Gonnelieu

to Fins

QUENTIN
REDOUBT

Gauche
Wood

Villers-
Guislain

Chapel Crossing

Revelon Ridge
Revelon
Farm

RESERVE
SUPPORT
LOWLAND
SWITCH

Chapel Hill

Genin Well
Copses

CAVALRY TR.

Railton   Vaucellette Farm

Albert

Bréaucourt Valley

Fricourt

R. Ancre

Flers

Martinpuich

Bazentin-
le-Grand

Guillemont   Ginchy

Bernafay
Wood

Leuze
Wood

Montauban   Trônes Wood   Mc

Mametz   Briqueterie   Hardecourt

Talus Boise   Favière
Wood   M

Baizieux

Moulin du Vivier   le Carcaillot

to Amiens

Dernancourt   Meaulte

Maricourt

Billon Wood   Curlu

Ribemont-
sur-l'Ancre   R. Ancre

Méricourt-
l'Abbé

Bray   R. Somme

Etinehem

Sailly-
le-Sec

Somme Canal

Chipilly

Cerisy

to Lamotte-
en-Santerre

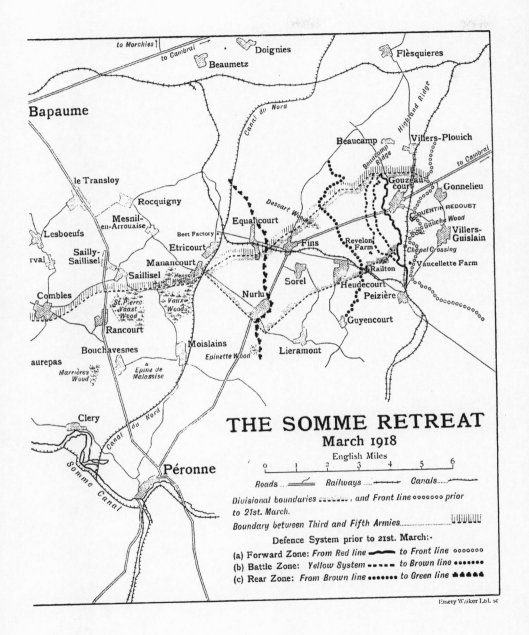

THE SOMME RETREAT
March 1918

English Miles

Roads ⎯⎯⎯ Railways ⎯⎯⎯ Canals ⎯⎯⎯

Divisional boundaries ⋯⋯⋯, and Front line ∘∘∘∘∘∘ prior to 21st. March.

Boundary between Third and Fifth Armies ⎯⎯⎯

Defence System prior to 21st. March:-

(a) Forward Zone: From Red line ⎯⎯ to Front line ∘∘∘∘∘∘
(b) Battle Zone: Yellow System ----- to Brown line •••••••
(c) Rear Zone: From Brown line ••••••• to Green line ▲▲▲▲▲

Emery Walker Ltd. sc

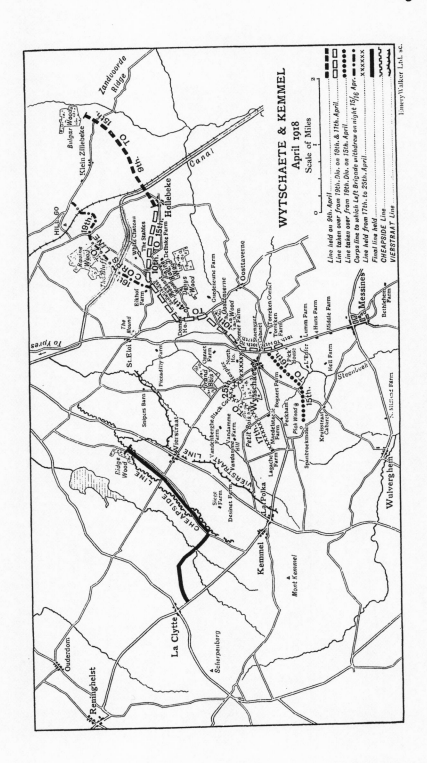

WYTSCHAETE & KEMMEL
April 1918
Scale of Miles

Line held on 9th April
Line taken over from 19th. Div. on 10th. & 11th.April
Line taken over from 19th. Div. on 15th.April
Corps line to which Left Brigade withdrew on night 15/16 Apr.
Line held from 17th. to 25th.April.
Final line held
CHEAPSIDE Line
VIERSTRAAT Line

Emery Walker Ltd. sc.

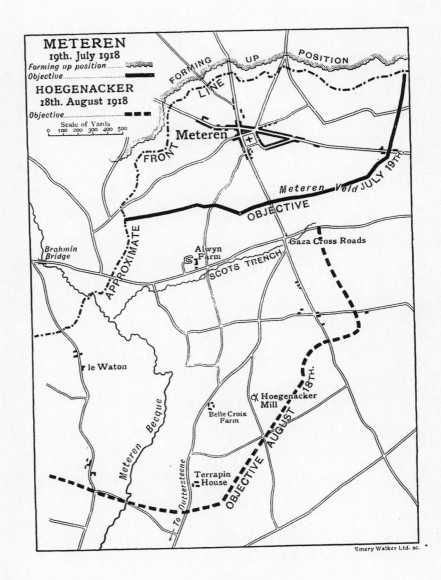

METEREN
19th. July 1918
Forming up position
Objective

HOEGENACKER
18th. August 1918
Objective

Scale of Yards
0 100 200 300 400 500

FORMING   UP   POSITION

LINE

FRONT

Meteren

Meteren Veld JULY 19TH.

OBJECTIVE

APPROXIMATE

Brahmin Bridge

Alwyn Farm

Gaza Cross Roads

SCOTS TRENCH

le Waton

Meteren Becque

Hoegenacker Mill

Belle Croix Farm

To Outtersteene

Terrapin House

OBJECTIVE AUGUST 18TH.

Emery Walker Ltd. sc.

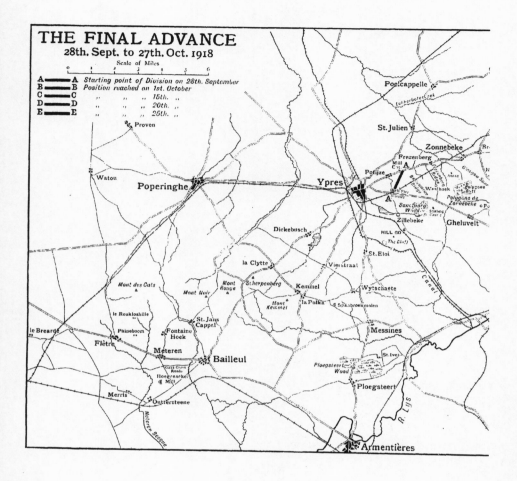

THE FINAL ADVANCE
28th. Sept. to 27th. Oct. 1918

Scale of Miles

A ▬▬ A *Starting point of Division on 28th. September*
B ▬▬ B *Position reached on 1st. October*
C ▬▬ C ,, ,, ,, *15th.* ,,
D ▬▬ D ,, ,, ,, *20th.* ,,
E ▬▬ E ,, ,, ,, *25th.* ,,

Proven

Poelcappelle

St. Julien

Zonnebeke

Watou

Poperinghe

Ypres

Potijze

Frezenberg
Mill
Cot

Westhoek

Polygone
Land

Polygone de
Zonnebeke

Sanctuary
Wood

Zillebeke

Gheluvelt

Dickebusch

HILL 60

The Bluff

St. Eloi

la Clytte

Vierstraat

Mont des Cats

Mont
Rouge

Scherpenberg

Kemmel

Wytschaete

Mont Noir

Mont
Kemmel

la Polka

Spanbroekmolen

le Roukloshille

St. Jans
Cappel

Messines

le Breard

Phineboom

Fontaine
Hoek

Flêtre

Meteren

Bailleul

St. Ives

Ploegsteert
Wood

Merris

Gas Gun
Roads

Hoegenacker
of Mill

Outtersteene

Ploegsteert

R. LYS

Meteren Becque

Armentières

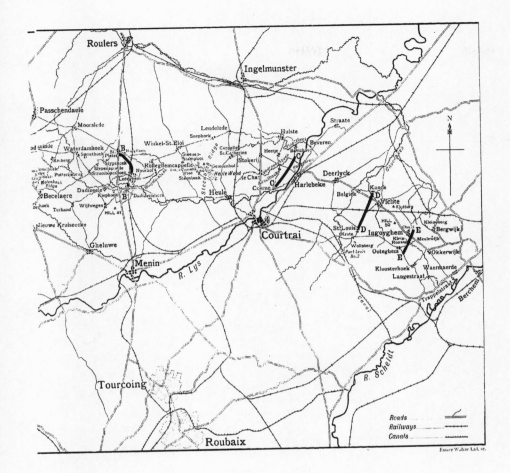

15188085R00312

Printed in Great Britain
by Amazon.co.uk, Ltd.,
Marston Gate.